AGRA

HISTORICAL & DESCRIPTIVE

WITH AN ACCOUNT OF

AKBAR AND HIS COURT

AND OF THE

MODERN CITY OF AGRA

AGRA

HISTORICAL & DESCRIPTIVE

WITH AN ACCOUNT OF

AKBAR AND HIS COURT

AND OF THE

MODERN CITY OF AGRA

ILLUSTRATED WITH PORTRAITS OF THE MOGHUL EMPERORS AND DRAWINGS OF THE PRINCIPAL ARCHITECTURAL MONUMENTS OF THAT CITY AND ITS SUBURBS, AND

A

MAP OF AGRA

BY

SYAD MUHAMMAD LATIF

GYAN

Published by

Gyan Publishing House
5, Ansari Road
Daryaganj, New Delhi-110002
Phone: 011-47034999, 9811692060
E-mail: books@gyanbooks.com

Distribution Network
gyanbooks.com
India, USA, Canada, UK, Australia, France

ISBN : 9788121231015 (PB)
First Published, Calcutta, 1896

2nd Impression 2020

Printed at: Gyan Press, Delhi.

Agra
Historical & Descriptive
with An Account of
Akbar and His Court
And of the
Modern City of Agra
Author: Syad Muhammad Latif

AGRA
HISTORICAL & DESCRIPTIVE,

WITH AN ACCOUNT OF

AKBAR AND HIS COURT

AND OF THE

MODERN CITY OF AGRA.

Illustrated with Portraits of the Moghul Emperors and Drawings of the Principal Architectural Monuments of that City and its Suburbs, and

A

MAP OF AGRA;

BY

SYAD MUHAMMAD LATIF, KHAN BAHADUR,
F.R.A.S., F.R.G.S.,

MEMBRE DE LA SOCIETE ASIATIQUE, PARIS; FELLOW, PUNJAB UNIVERSITY; MEMBER, ASIATIC SOCIETY OF BENGAL; AUTHOR OF THE "HISTORY OF THE PUNJAB," "HISTORY OF LAHORE," &c., &c.

Calcutta:
PRINTED AT THE CALCUTTA CENTRAL PRESS COMPANY, LIMITED,
40, CANNING STREET.

1896.

PREFACE.

"TRULY these Franks are a great nation, and I purpose sending my blessings to my son, the King of Spain," so said the great Tartar conqueror, Timur Beg, or Tamerlane, when, in 1403, he was visited at his far-famed metropolis, the then mistress of Asia, Samarkand, by the good Christian knight, Don Ruy Gonzalez de Clavijo, the plenipotentiary of his sovereign, the King of Castille, who has left an account of the great Chaughattai's court in that city, and of his feasts and displays there held, far more glowing than that painted by Sharf-ud-din, the eminent biographer of Timur. The possessor of twenty-eight crowns, the Lord of the Eastern World was quite unconscious at the time that, fully three hundred years after he had paid this public compliment to the great Franks in his grand hall of audience, where had assembled the nobles and dignitaries of his vast empire and the ambassadors from the greatest potentates of the known world, a hero of the same great nation was, on the distant soil of India, the land of the Mahabharata, to shake hands with one of his lineal descendants and be hailed by him as a deliverer from his oppressors and persecutors. It was the British General, Lord Lake, the conqueror of Delhi, the Indra Prastha of the Hindus, and of Agra of ancient fame, who, in 1803, taking out of his captivity the helpless Shah Alam, *magni hominis umbra*, blinded by the cruel dagger of one of his own co-religionists, and disgraced by the Marathas, gave him his liberty, honour, and throne. "The people," says the author of the *Tárikh-i-Muzaffari*, "were filled with admiring joy and the Emperor with grateful delight:" so much so that "the joyful tears shed by him restored his sight, that had been destroyed by the steel of the hardy Rohilla fifteen year before!"

But it was not the great Timur alone who spoke so warmly of th greatness of the Franks as a nation. Akbar, the seventh in descent from that conqueror, and by far the most enlightened of the race of sovereigns that ruled over the destinies of India for two hundred and fifty years, invariably styled them the *Danayan-i-Farang*, or the Wise Men of the Franks, as we find evidenced by the eloquent pages of

Abul Fazl. A greater sovereign, a greater pacificator, a more beloved ruler, or a more generous and sympathetic friend, India had never seen during the most palmy days of her rule. And true, it is, if India has her just pride in Akbar and his munificent rule, Akbarabad, or Agra, the city founded by him and known after his name, has its chief glory in its associations with that monarch—associations so intimate as to render his great name inseparable from it so long as the bright beams of the sun shine over the castellated battlements of the palace he built there, and the calm, serene light of the moon enhances the immaculate grace of the Taj, the brightest architectural jewel that embellishes the ancient city. It is the history of this city, of its great founder, of his court there held, that I have attempted to relate in the following pages.

And if I am called upon by the critic to reconcile the introduction, at the outest of these lines, of the name of the nation spoken of as 'great' by Timur and by Akbar centuries ago, with Akbar's city at the present time, I shall bring forward 'standing testimony' to plead my cause. Much as you may admire the matchless beauty of the Taj as you stand in wonder to gaze at it; deeply as you may feel the excellence of the Pearl Mosque in the famous citadel, described in the enthusiastic words of Mr. Taylor as "a sanctuary so pure and stainless, as to reveal an exalted spirit of worship," when you see it; great as may be your sense of praise when you behold the mausoleum of the great Emperor himself at Sakandra,—what heart can there be which, while it melts at the sight of past greatness and the thought of the instability of human glory, is not equally impressed with a deep sense of admiration and gratitude for the Power whose generosity, toleration, and goodwill to all has preserved what we to-day see and admire? If, as India had been accustomed to witness, the conqueror of Agra had drawn his sword in retribution; if fire and destruction had followed the war, as they had done for countless ages, neither had the poet been able to pourtray, nor the minstrel to sing, nor the painter to paint, the beauties of the Taj, nor its hereditary custodians to pride themselves on the charge of it. But the British conquerors were lovers of art and literature, and, as scientific men, admirers of human skill and excellence; hence they not only preserved these monuments of ancient fame, but took measures to maintain them at enormous cost. They garnished, cleaned, and, as far as can be, restored them. If Shah Jahan could come back to earth, it is not too much to say he would thank the British rulers for the labour of love bestowed in the preservation and restoration of the great monument of his beloved consort, and for preserving it from the spoiler's hand. May it not, then, be justly said that the character attributed to the Franks by the Chaughattai conqueror at the grand banquet of Samarkand three hundred years before, was fully confirmed on the victory of the British, who brought for the citizens of Agra and Delhi, and the countless millions of the people of India, the reign of peace, of law, and of good order? Thus, the history of Agra, faithfully narrated, is inseparable from the history of British greatness, as admitted by its founder and his great primogenitor, and as evidenced by the victory of the illustrious commander, Lord Lake.

The condition of the country since its conquest by the British cannot escape the attention of the lover of History. The blazing fire that reduced to ashes the palace of the Navab, and burnt in its turn the cottage of the peasant; the hot blasts that scorched the tree of hope; the sharp steel that shed the blood of the innocent, sparing neither sex nor age, have, happily for the country, all disappeared, never more to devastate the land or disturb the public peace. Where the sword was the sole arbiter of fate and the dreaded instrument of destruction, there is now the mild hand of the law to shelter and protect. In dreary jungles and desolate deserts, where not a blade of grass ever grew, or a brook of water was to be seen to quench the thirst of the antelope, may now be seen fields of verdant cultivation, or trees bending beneath their load of fruit, and, by their cool shade, affording shelter to the weary traveller. In village and hamlet, mirth and gladness are the order of the day, and, instead of wailing and lamentation, the traveller hears from afar the songs of village maidens, the sound of trumpets, and the noise of musical instruments, to announce a coming marriage, a pending festivity, or some other joyful ceremony or religious rite. The city environs, once infested by robbers and murderers, and haunted by the jackal and the wolf, have grown into rich and prosperous suburbs, where friends meet in pleasure-gardens for refreshment and amusement.

And to turn to Agra itself. For centuries it was a prey to anarchy and confusion. The Muhammadans, on the invasion of Nadir Shah; the Jats, during the ascendancy of Suraj Mal; the Maratha, in the time of Shah Alam,—each in his turn did their work of destruction and spoliation, and rendered life, property, and honour unsafe. The mighty change that has taken place is the work of Providence, through the agency of a mighty nation. It is this nation, sent in His all-wise wisdom to govern us, that Timur, and later on his illustrious descendant, called 'Great,' and truly great it is in the strictest sense of the term.

Much has, no doubt, been written about Agra by historians and travellers, but beyond Mr. Keene's *Handbook to Agra*, a meritorious little work, intended chiefly as a guidebook for travellers, there is no book that gives a connected account of this historical city, dealing with its past and present history and its archæological remains and antiquities in a way which might commend itself to the attention of the student and the traveller, the antiquarian, and the general reader. The inscriptions, too, which form the chief value of the several more important monuments, and help to furnish correct data on which to base the accounts, are entirely omitted, and what is most important seems not to have received adequate attention, namely, the association of past events with the interesting architectural objects which meet the view.

Again, though to the superficial observer the glory of Agra consists in the far-famed Taj and some other of its chaste monuments, its real pride to lovers of History lies in the circumstance of its having, for half a century, been the capital of by far the most illustrious and the most enlightened sovereign Asia has ever seen, the great Jalal-ud-din, surnamed Akbar. Current histories of India are full of accounts of his wars, carried on in distant provinces, which, though useful, are very tedious. There was no work which dealt with the great Emperor's life in his capacity of reconciler of conflicting religious and enunciator of those measures of amelioration and reconcilement which bound Hindu and Muhammadan alike with one tie of affection, or which pourtrayed his character in the various phases of his life as he passed it in the halls of Fatehpur Sikri, or in the exquisite marble chambers of private and public audience constructed by him in the capital of Agra.

The accounts scattered over various books are confined to general descriptions of monuments, which for the most part repeat one another. There was little in the works extant which could be of special value to the antiquarian, or of interest to the scholar. I have, therefore, consulted the original Persian and Arabic texts, some of them rare, and have supplied much information on subjects connected with Agra which has not hitherto been published in English.*

Such, then, is the scope of the present work, which, be it premised, makes no pretentious to completeness, despite the time and care bestowed upon it. But if, notwithstanding its shortcomings, the courteous public receive it as kindly as former attempts of a similar nature,† I shall regard the time devoted to this undertaking as not spent wholly in vain.

I would now ask the reader's permission to address a few words to my young countrymen, in the hope that they will prove beneficial to them.

My dear young countrymen,—I herewith present you with the history of one of the chief cities of India, one of the most beautiful and splendid cities of Asia, if not of the world. Poets of the East and West have been sanguine in its praise; and travellers from the remotest parts of the earth come to see its beauties. You are welcome to read the pages of this book, and, having read them, to bestow the praise justly due to the memory of the founder of the Taj, or the architect of Sakandra, true triumphs of Saracenic architecture and monuments of past greatness. But remember that the real greatness of a sovereign does not consist in the beauty of the palaces he has built, in their rich decorations and marble pavements, or in the excellence and gorgeousness of a unique and imposing monument raised to the memory of a loving relation, or in the splendour of his throne, or in the brilliancy of his crown. What is it to the world if a king slept in a hall of a thousand mirrors, guarded in his seraglio by Circassian, Georgian, and Calmuck female guards, or watched at the royal gates by brave Rajputs; or if he sat pompously on a sumptuous *musnad*, reclining against a pillow that cost a lakh of rupees, under a *shamiáná* of gold-embroidered work that took several months to produce, and with the lords of great fortune and wealth and the ambassadors of foreign kingdoms standing in his presence with downcast eyes and folded hands. The world is not concerned with his big establishments of birds and beasts of

* In the transliteration of Indian names, the Hunterian system of orthography has been adopted in the following pages, except in the case of familiar names of persons and places, the spelling of which has become stereotyped by popular usage.

† *History of the Panjab* (1891), *History of Lahore* (1892), and the *Early History of Multán* (1891).

prey, or curious domesticated animals, or with the numbers of the Burmese elephants and Arabian and Turkistání horses in the royal stable. These are not the things which make a sovereign great. The real greatness of a sovereign lies in the measures he adopts to protect God's people consigned to his care; in the peace of the country over which he rules; in the prosperity of the nations committed to his charge; in the administration of even-handed justice to all his subjects; in giving them freedom of conscience;—in short, in acting on the principles of justice and toleration, and in introducing measures calculated to make his people contented and prosperous and help to raise them higher in the scale of nations. Nor does the greatness of a sovereign consist in the battles he wins, in the number of prisoners he makes in war, or in the countless millions of treasure he hoards up; but in the triumphs achieved under his sway in science and learning, in the advancement of trade and agriculture, in the development of the resources of the country by the extension of railway communications, in the construction of roads and the guarding of high-ways, in the breaking down of insuperable barriers to human skill and energy, in the cultivation of industrial arts, in the bridging of large and impetuous rivers and streams, in the embellishment of the country with public edifices, in the founding of charitable institutions for the alleviation of the distress of mankind, and in works calculated to promote the public good. These triumphs of peace, these victories of science, are far more brilliant and splendid, far more solid and enduring, than the victories of war, however great. It is these lasting victories that have made the English nation glorious and great, and their greatness the envy of the nations of the world; and it is our good fortune, we are proud to say, to be the subjects of a nation so glorious and great. If rightly read, the history of Agra will, I hope, teach you, my dear countrymen, what the greatness of a sovereign really means—whether that greatness lies in the raising of a memorial to the memory of a beloved wife that cost the public treasury crores of rupees; or, on the other hand, in the inauguration of measures of public utility and good, of which we see abundant evidence around us,—and it will teach you what real greatness in a nation means.

After you have read this history, you will, I hope, no longer labour under any mistake as to the part assigned to you in the great spectacle which this age of progress and enlightenment lays open before you. My friendly advice to you is this: Shun pleasure; give up idle talk (*Vir sapit qui pauco loquitur*); eschew the society of those who fill your brain with an air to inhale which must prove poisonous; imagine that the doorway to the grand palace that leads to the summit of human glory has, by the bounty of the British, been open to you; but, scrambling child as you still are, do not run out precipitately to reach the desired place, for, in a rash attempt to do so, you are likely to fall headlong and break your neck; gain the esteem of your own countrymen (*Virtute et fide et labore*) and the regard of your rulers (*Virtute, non astutiâ, non verbis*); walk in the path of righteous men; obey your rulers, who are the custodians of your life and property, and to whom you owe all you possess of education, wealth, and position; prove the nobility of your race, and the beneficial effect of the education given to you, by acts of loyalty and devotion to them; respect your parents and elders; and pass your life with honour and credit, which can only be done by honourable deeds. And if you do this, I shall feel that a study of this book, read in the way I have enjoined, has given you a wholesome lesson, and great will then be my joy.

The sources of information have, as far as possible, been acknowledged in footnotes and in the context. For the historical portion of the book my acknowledgments are due to the celebrated work, the Ferishta by Mahomed Quasam, the Memoirs of Baber by Abdúl Rahim Khan-i-Khanan, the Tuzk Jahangiri by Motamid-id-Khan, the Ain-i-Akbari and Akbarnama by *Allami* Abul Fazl, the Muntakhibul-Tawarikh of Mulla Abdul Quadar, *Badaoni*, the Tabakat-i-Akbari of Mirza Nizamuddin Ahmed, the Shah Jahan Nama of Mulla Abdul Hamíd, Lahori, the Alamgir Nama of Mahomed Kazim, the Moasiri Alamgiri of Mahomed Sáki, the Syrul Mutaakhirin of Moulvi Gholam Husian Khan, the Muntakhibul Lubab of Khafí Khan, the histories of India in English by the Honorable Monstuart Elphinstone, Wheeler, Keene, Sir William Hunter, Murray, etc. The descriptive portion has been written chiefly from my own notes taken on the sport, but I have also derived much help from the able works of Mr. Keene, the Revd. C. J. French, Mr. James Fergusson, Mr. Rayard Taylor and other writers. The account of the Taj has been chiefly drawn up from an old manuscript history of the Taj in possession of the hereditary custodians of the Mansoleum. The materials for the Chapter on the life of Akbar and his court have been drawn from the works of Abúl Fazl and the historians of Akbar before referred to, but I have also, in writing the chapter, been assisted by the excellent translation of the Ain by that talented Oriental Scholar, the late Professor Blockmann. In writing the last Chapter on modern Agra, I have consulted the Gazetteer of India by Sir William Hunter, the official reports kindly furnished by H. T. Hoare, Esq., Collector, Agra, and the Municipal Reports very courteously furnished by Rai Bahadur Munshi Shiv Narain, the able Secretary, Agra Municipal Committee.

JALLANDHAR :
27th September, 1896. M. L.

LIST OF CONTENTS.

LIST OF ILLUSTRATIONS.

AGRA,

HISTORICAL AND DESCRIPTIVE.

CHAPTER I.

HISTORICAL.

AKBARABAD,* or the city of Akbar, as Agra † is called among the Muhammadans, is situated on the west or right bank of the Jumna about the centre of the district of the same name, 300 miles above its confluence with the river Ganges, 139 miles south-east from Delhi, and 841 miles by rail from Calcutta.

Legendary history. The regions of the Jumna, the Yamuna of the ancient *Puránas*, are the classic spot of the birth of Vyása (from the Sanskrit *vi* and *ás*, literally 'throw in different directions,' hence 'distribute'), the reputed arranger of the Vedas, and the reputed author of the *Mahábhárata*, the *Purânas*, the *Bráhma Sútras* and the *Dharma Sútras*, the son of the celebrated sage Parasárá. Agra was then itself unknown, and Indraprasthá and Hastinápur had not been founded. Yet the regions are interesting, being, according to the Hindu scriptures, associated with the birth and early years of a personage of no less celebrity than Vasáya, who, being a Bráhman in a former life and attaining final beatitude, resumed, by special command of the deity, a corporeal form and human shape at the period intervening between the third and fourth ages of the present world. The hunting excursions of Santanú prove the country to have been dreary and desolate, inhabited by a numerous and powerful tribe of fishermen who had a king of their own and subsisted on the chase.

* According to the *Bádshâh Náma* of Mulla Abdul Hamíd *Lahori*, the name Akbarábád was given to Agra by Sháh Jahán, who ordered that in all public correspondence the city should be called Akbarábád, after the name of the founder, his grandfather.

† Agra is believed to derive its name from the Hindi word *agar*, meaning 'salt-pan,' as, the soil being brackish, it once used to be a place for making salt by evaporation. Some ascribe the name Agra to Agarwál *banias*, whose number so much predominates in the United Provinces.

It is remarkable that the descendants of those men, now living along the banks of the sacred river, should be abstemious.

The place is also held in great reverence by the Hindus, as the scene of the incarnation of Vishnu under the name of Párasu Ráma.

Hindu origin of Agra.

Of the Hindu origin of Agra there can be no doubt. The very root of its name, *Agu*, is Sanskrit, meaning prior, or first, which has led some to conjecture that it was the first of the many groves where Krishna, the sporting shepherd-god of the Hindus, by blowing his famous pipe, captivated alike the dairy-maids of Brindraban and the princesses of the Gangetic regions. It is identified with the Aggrames mentioned by Quintus Curtius, the Greek writer, as a prince of the Pársí inhabiting the country of the Gangarides.

Its antiquity.

The antiquity of Agra is also evidenced by certain ancient towns comprised in the district. Conspicuous among these is Batesar, otherwise known as Surajpur, founded, according to tradition, by Rájá Surásená, identified by General Cunningham as the nephew of the great King Rámá of Ayudhia. Ancient images and sculptures have been found amidst its ruined temples, and the remains of Buddhist structures and figures, the remnants of ancient monasteries, have been discovered in Itimád-pur and the tracts bordering the Chambal. There is no doubt that all these ancient towns were once dependent on the mighty Hindu monarchy which had Mathrá for its capital.

Early Muhammadan period.

Passing from legend to history, the first mention we find of Agra is in a Persian work by Abdullá, known as *Tárikh-i-Dáudi*, being a chronicle of the Afghán Lodí kings from the reign of Behlól-i-Lodí, the first king of the Afghán dynasty, to that of Muhammad Adil-i-Sur and Dáud Sháh, the last ruler of the race. The author writes of the origin of Agra :—"The Hindus assert that Agra was a strong place in the days of Rájá Káns, the ruler of Mathrá, who confined everyone who incurred his displeasure in the fort of that place, hence, in the course of time, it became the established State prison."

Muhammadan historians on early Hindu period.

Invasion of Mahmúd, 1022 A.D.

According to the same author, when the Ghiznivide conqueror, Sultán Mahmúd, invaded India, his armies so devastated Agra that it was reduced to the status of an insignificant village. This was about 1022 A.D.

After the departure of Mahmúd from the country, Agra seems to have regained its importance and become once more a Hindu principality, for, in the poems of Salmán, written in praise of the Ghiznivide Sultáns, Mahmúd,* Ibrahim and Bairámsháh, we find mention of the capture of the city by the Muhammadan army under Mahmúd. Occupied by the Ghiznivide kings.

"The fort of Agra," writes the author, "is built amidst the sand, like a hill, and its battlements are like hillocks. No calamity had ever befallen its fortifications, nor had deceitful time treacherously dealt with it." The city was besieged. In the night the chiefs of Jeypál the Rájá had a dream. The following morning, the Rájá, coming out of the fort, made obeisance to Sef-ud-doula, who introduced him to the King. But the King was determined to bring destruction on the fort, and hated the idea of allegiance with the 'unbelievers.' "I have come," said he, "to this country to prosecute a religious war. I have reduced countless forts, and was in search of a large virgin fortress, such as this one, and I must reduce it and bring it under the sway of Islám." The King, with a drawn scimitar, plunged into the midst of the fight, 'like a lion.' "The falchions of the holy warriors made the ground of Agra flow like a river with the blood of the enemy." The soldiers of Islám, according to the author, surrounded the fort and made the day appear like night. "The stones discharged from the mangonels ascended to the vault of heaven like the prayers of saints." At last there arose, from the warriors of Islám within the fort, the shout, "Victory to our sovereign, Lord Mahmúd." The fort was reduced, and the neighbouring chiefs sent in their presents, in loads of gold and files of elephants, to the conqueror.

Prince Mahmúd, to whom the ode is addressed, returned to Ghiznì after conquering Málwá and Ujjain, having crossed the Indus at the point of Attock. Salmán regards the act as meritorious, and compares his expeditions with that of Moses, who had crossed the Nile in Egypt.

---

* Mahmúd, noticed by the poet Salmán, was a great grandson of Mahmúnd Ghiznewí. The author has been also quoted by Jahángír in his auto-biography, as will be found further on. There can therefore be no doubt that Agra was an important city before it became the capital of the Lodí Afghán kings of Delhi.

Agra under the Ghori, Khiljí, Tughlak and Sayyid dynasties.

Under the Ghori, Khiljí, Tughlak and Sayyid dynasties, Agra seems to have been an insignificant place, comprised in the *sarkár*, or dependency, of Biáná. On the return of Muhammad Ghori, to Hindustán, in 1195 A.D., he proceeded to Biáná, took it, and conferred the government on his general, Baha-ud-din Toghral.* The power of the Chohán chief of Chandáwar, who then occupied the country about Agra, was effectually crushed; but the Hindu chiefs, who had been compelled to pay tribute to the Muhammadan sovereigns, soon returned to a state of semi-independence. On the invasion of Tamerlane, in 1398, the Rájput chiefs enjoyed a brief interval of independence. During the Sayyid dynasty, the Muhammadan emperors of Delhi re-established their authority in the district of Agra, but during the latter period of the dynasty the Hindus asserted their independence.

Under the Lodí dynasty.

On the accession of Sultán Sakandar Lodí to the throne of Delhi, Sultán Sharaf, Governor of Biáná, on behalf of Azim Humáyún, grandson of Behlól-i-Lodí, having closed the gates of the fort of Biáná, prepared to defend himself against the troops of Umar Khán Sherwání, who had been directed by the new King to take charge of the fort. The King, however, choosing to overlook the circumstance, proceeded to Agra, where Haibat Khán Jahroni, who held the fort under Sultán Sharaf, also shut the gates. This insult incensed Sakandar Lodí, who made war on Sultán Sharaf, and the forts of both Biáná and Agra fell; * Sultán Sharaf, after his defeat, being banished to Gwalior.

Re-peopled by Sultán Sakandar Lodí, 1505.

Sultán Sakandar now directed his attention to re-peopling the town of Agra. The city of the Lodí kings, however, lay on the eastern bank of the Jumna. Niamatullá, the author of the *Táríkh-i Khán Jahán Lodí*, a contemporary with Ferishta, who compiled his work in 1612 A.D., or the eighth year of the accession of Jahángír, furnishes the following account of the foundation of Muhammadan Agra by Sultán Sakandar:—The Government officers and the peasantry in general in the *sarkár* of Biáná having complained to the Sultán of the excesses committed by the refractory population of that division of the empire, His Majesty resolved on founding a town on the banks of the Jumna which should be utilized as the

* *Ferishta.*

head-quarters of his army and government, and serve as a point from which an effectual check could be exercised on the rebel tribes. With this view, the Sultán, in the year 1505, deputed a number of deserving and intelligent officials of State to explore the banks of the river and report on the best locality which could be used for the purpose. The exploring party left Delhi by boats, and, as they proceeded along the banks, examined them carefully until they arrived at the place where the city now stands. Having approved of the site, they communicated their selection to the Emperor, who marched in person to inspect it. As His Majesty approached the site indicated, he observed two spots on an eminence which appeared suitable for building purposes, and asked Mehtar Mullá Khán, styled the *Náyak* who commanded the royal barge, which of the two mounds would best suit. He replied : "That which is *Age-ráh*," namely, that which is in advance on the way. The King smiled and said : "Then let the name of the town be also called *Age-ráh*" (or Agra). The Sultán then lifted up his hands to read the *fatíha*, or prayers, and so did all the amírs who surrounded him. At an auspicious hour, orders were issued for founding a city, and portions of the villages Páshi and Poyá, Parganá Duli, *sarkár* of Biáná, were occupied for the purpose. Agra was constituted a separate parganá and added to the fifty-two parganás which comprised the *sarkár* of Biáná.

The city continued to grow in importance, and became the seat of the government. The Sultán, having given orders for the construction of a fort, proceeded to Dhôlpur. The Lodi kings of Delhi had their residence on the east bank of the Jumna, which was occupied by Sultán Bábar, after his victory of Pánipat, in 1526. Its foundations are still to be traced opposite modern Agra.

Becomes the capital of the Indian Empire, under Sultán Sakandar Lodí.

The author of the *Tárikh-i-Daudi* admits the antiquity of Agra and says that, although it became a town in the time of Sultán Sakandar Lodí, it was a place of old standing before his time.

In the history of Khán Jahán Lodí, already mentioned, it is noted, with reference to the events of 1510 A.D., that Muhammad Khán, the ruler of Nagore, having tendered his submission to Sultán Sakandar, ordered the *Khutba* to be read and coin to be struck at Nagore in the Sultan's name. The report of this submission delighted the King, who sent him a horse and honorary dress. His Majesty then left Dhôlpur, and, visiting Agra, spent some time there in a round of pleasure and festivities, in visiting gardens and in hunting expeditions. "It was about this time," continues the author, "that Agra, formerly a dependency of Biáná, was fixed upon as the residence of the Sovereigns."

Who fixes his residence there.

Agra, a grand resort of the people of all nations.

In the time of the Sultán, Agra became a grand resort of the people of all nations, and learned men from Arabia, Persia, Bokhara, and other countries of Asia, flocked to his court, and were honourably received and handsomely provided for. It was from this place that the Sultán issued the many edicts having for their object the welfare of his people, the prosperity of his country, and the suppression of crime and abominable usages in his dominions, which have obtained for him a foremost place among the Muhammadan sovereigns of Hindustán. Among his other edicts, may be mentioned the abolition of the annual procession for the display of the spear of Sálár Masúd,* which had become a standing nuisance; the prohibition of visits by females to tombs or pilgrimage, and the establishment of factories where the young nobles' and soldiers' sons were taught useful handicrafts. The King led a most simple life, and was averse to pomp and show.

Munificent measures of Sultán Sakandar.

Curious way of receiving the Sultán's mandate.

A strange custom prevailed at this time, to express the awe and reverence in which the King was held. It was the practice for every chief who heard of the coming of a royal mandate to travel two or three *kos* to meet the bearer. A high platform was then constructed, and cushions of the richest workmanship were spread upon it. The messenger seated himself on this platform, while the noble who was to receive the mandate, standing beneath, raised both his hands with the utmost humility and respect, and instantly the *farmán* was placed in them, and he kissed it and placed it on his head and touched his eyes with it. If it was a private communication, he read it silently; if it was on public business, it was read out from the pulpit of a mosque. This was in imitation of a Tartar custom, which still obtains in China, but Sakandar had it discontinued.

* The *Charión-ká-melá* is still held in honour of this saint throughout Hindustán. At this fair a display is made of long bamboos or canes, which are held erect and balanced on the head or the forehead, or on the teeth of the lower jaw.

On the 3rd of Safar, 911 (5th July 1505 A.D.), Agra was visited by a violent earthquake. It was so severe that "lofty buildings were levelled with the ground, and several thousands of the inhabitants were buried under the ruins."* Such a severe earthquake had never been experienced in India before.

Great earthquake, 1505.

In the year 923 (1517 A.D.), the Emperor Sakandar Lodí summoned all the distant nobles to Agra with a view to reducing Gwalior, and was in the midst of his preparations for war when he was taken ill with quinsy, and died in his palace in Agra, on Sunday, the 14th December, 1517. He founded Sakandra, the famous burial-place of one of the most illustrious sovereigns India ever had, and built the fine red-stone summer house which subsequently became the last resting-place of Mariam Zamáni, Akbar's Portuguese wife.

Death of Sultán Sakandar 1517.

Sakandra.

On the day on which the celebrated battle of Pánípat was fought (29th April 1526), and the Emperor Ibrahim Lodí, the son and successor of Sultán Sakandar, slain in the battlefield, Bábar pushed forward two detachments, the one to Delhi and the other to Agra, to secure the public treasure in those cities. He himself reached Delhi on the third day after the battle, and on the Friday following, the *Khutba* having been read in his name in the grand mosque, he sealed up the different treasures there and hastened on to Agra, where he had sent Prince Humáyún in advance. Agra was taken from the house of Lodí on 10th May, 1526.

Agra conquered by Sultán Bábar, 1526.

Agra was occupied, without any severe resistance, by Prince Humáyún. At this time there lived in Agra the family of Bakráma Jít, the Rajá of Gwalior, whose country had been conquered by Azím Humáyún Sirwání, a General of the Emperor Ibrahím. Bakráma Jít was called to service in the battle of Pánípat and slain in the battlefield. His wives and children and the heads of his clan, who were in the fort, tried to escape, but were seized and detained there. Humáyún treated this ancient Hindu family with consideration in the hour of their misfortune, and saved them from being plundered. In return for this generous conduct, they, of their own accord, made to Humáyún a present of jewels, among which was a famous diamond which,

Prince (afterwards Emperor) Humáyún.

History of the Koh-i-Núr diamond.

* *Ferishta.*

according to Bábar, had been acquired by Sultán Alá-ud-din of Málwá. "It is so valuable," writes the Emperor in his Memoirs, "that a judge of diamonds valued it at half of the daily expense of the whole world. It is about eight *miskals* (or 320 *ratís*)."

Bábar at Agra.

Bábar, on his arrival at Agra, took up his residence in the old palace of Sultán Ibrahím. Humáyún's first act, on his father's arrival, was to present him with the diamond he had received from the family of Rajá Bakráma Jít. Bábar gave it back to Humáyún as a present. This was the valuable diamond which was shown by Aurangzeb to Tavernier, the jeweller and merchant, and valued by the latter at nearly £880,000 sterling, and is believed to be the famous Koh-i-Núr (or Mountain of Light).*

The Emperor pardoned Malik Dáud *Karaní*, the chief officer of Ibrahím in the fort, showed him favours, and permitted his followers to retain their property. On Ibrahim's mother he bestowed a parganá of seven lakhs of rupees, and she was conducted, with all her effects, to a place which was fixed on for her residence about a *kos* below Agra.

The great battle with the Rajputs at Fatehpur Sikri, 1527.

Bábar often resided at Agra, and it was at Fatehpur Sikri, near Agra, that his great and decisive battle with the Rájputs was fought, in 1527. The Emperor has given a graphic account of this battle in his Memoirs. Rájá Sanga, sixth in descent from Hámir, who had recovered Chittor in the reign of Alá-ud-din Khiljí (A.D. 1316), and re-established the Rájput dominions over Mewát, Eastern Málwá, and Ajmere, was at this time recognised as the leader of all the Rájput princes. He had opened friendly communication with Bábar while that monarch was advancing against Sultán Ibrahím; but, now that the power of the Mughal sovereign had been established in Delhi and Agra, he began to enter into intrigues against him, and was, on this occasion, joined by Mahmúd, a Prince of the house of Lodi, who had in his train a force of 10,000 men. He also found a valuable auxiliary in Hasan Khan, chief of Mewat. The Rájá, with the combined forces of his allies and the picked warriors of the Rájput tribes, advanced to Biáná, within the dependency of Agra, and, defeating the garrison of that place, cut off all communication between them and the capital. Bábar on this

Rájá Sanga.

* For a full history of the Koh-i-Núr diamond, see my *History of Lahore*, pp. 376-383.

The Emperor Babar.

Page 8.

reached Sikri, but his advanced guard was defeated with great loss. These defeats greatly dismayed Bábar's veteran troops, and they began to regard the contest in a very serious light. While the Mughal army was yet in a state of alarm and panic, Mahammad Sharif, an astrologer from Kábul, foretold its defeat, maintaining that at that time Mars was in the West, and that whoever should engage coming from the opposite quarter would be defeated. "Without listening to his foolish predictions," writes the Emperor in his Memoirs, "I proceeded to adopt such steps as the emergency seemed to demand, and used every exertion to put my troops in fit state to engage the enemy." He recognised the difficulty of his position, and became penitent before God. He forswore drinking, to which he had been so much addicted, sent for his gold and silver goblets and cups and other utensils used for drinking parties, broke them in pieces, and gave away the fragments to the *darweshes* and the poor. His *amírs* followed his example. The choice wine of Ghizni, which Bàba Dost, the butler, had a few days before brought from Kábul on three camels, was mixed with salt and converted into vinegar. Other wine which the Emperor had, at the time, was poured on the ground. He made a vow to let his beard grow, and promised to remit the *tamgha*, or stamp tax, on all Musalmáns. Observing that general consternation and alarm prevailed among the ranks of his army, he assembled all his amirs and officers, and addressed them:—"Noblemen and soldiers!—Every man that comes into the world is subject to dissolution. When we are passed away and gone, God only survives, unchangeable. Whoever comes to the feast of Life, must, before it is over, drink from the cup of death. He who arrives at the inn of Mortality, must one day inevitably take his departure from that house of sorrow in the world. How much better is it to die with honour than to live with infamy!

The Kabul astrologer.

Penitence of Bábar.

His address to the *amirs* of the army.

> It is my glory to die a death of fame,
> Rather than to live a life of disgrace and shame.

The most high God has been propitious to us, and has now placed us in such a crisis that, if we fall in the field, we die the death of martyrs; if we survive, we rise victorious, the avengers of the cause of God. Let us, then, with one accord, swear on God's holy word, that none of us will even think of turning his face from the warfare, nor desert from the battle and slaughter that ensues, till his soul is separated from his body."*

The army reassured.

The reply was a fervent shout of devotion. All swore on the *Kurán* to conquer or die. The courage of the army having been revived, Bábar drew up his troops in front of his intrenchments. He then galloped along the lines, cheering the soldiers and giving instructions as to how they were to act. The Rájputs fought bravely and desperately. Bábar has given an account of this great battle in the elaborate despatch of his secretary, who thus describes the action of the Mughal troops in the thickest of the fight :—"The warriors of the faith, who were in the temper of self-devotion, and prepared to submit to martyrdom, heard from a secret voice the glad tidings, '*And be not dejected nor sorry, ye are exalted;*' and from the infallible informer heard the joyful words, '*Assistance is from God, and victory is at hand ; spread the glad tidings among the Faithful.*' They fought with such enthusiasm that praises were showered down on them from the pure above, and the angels, who are near to God, hovered like butterflies around their heads. And between the first and second prayers, the fire of battle blazed so that its flames raised the standard above the firmament." Victory at last declared for Bábar. Hasan Khán and many other chiefs fell in the action, and Rájá Sanga escaped with difficulty. After his victory Bábar assumed the proud title of *Ghází*, or Champion in the cause of the Faith. The battle was fought within view of a small hill near Sikri. He had a tower constructed of the skulls of the enemies slaughtered in the battlefield. The Kábul astrologer came to congratulate the Emperor on his victory. "I poured forth," says the Emperor, "a torrent of abuse upon him, and when I had relieved my soul by it, although he was heathenishly inclined, perverse, extremely self-conceited, and an insufferable ill-speaker, yet, as he had been my old servant I gave him a lakh as a present, and dismissed him, commanding him not to remain within my dominions."

Bravery of the Rajputs.

Victory of the Mughals.

Punishment of the Kabul astrologer.

Bábar's description of Hindustán.

Fresh from a country that abounded in beautiful scenery, green vales, luxuriant lakes, and running waters, and gifted by nature with a lively imagination and poetical genius, Bábar was the first of the Muhammadan sovereigns who created a taste in

* Erskine's *Memoirs of Bábar*, p. 357

India for laying out beautiful gardens and pleasure-grounds, constructing artificial water-courses, and arranging places of public recreation. "We were disgusted," observed His Majesty, "with three things in Hindustán: one was its heat, which was unbearable; another, its strong winds, which carried everything before them; and the third, its dust, which found its way into every nook and corner of a house." To remove these inconveniences, Bábar had baths constructed at Agra. We can do no better than give the talented King's own description of the bath, from his celebrated *Memoirs*:—"The bath-room in which is the tub, or cistern, is constructed entirely of stone. The water-channel is constructed of white stone; all the rest floor and roof, is made of red stone brought from Biáná. The temperature of the air cannot affect the bath; for, when the hot winds blow, the bath can be artificially cooled, so that a man can hardly bear the cold produced."

Bábar's bath at Agra.

Bábar laid out a garden beyond the Jumna and founded a palace. The garden he called *Gulafshán*; in the Persian dialect it was called *Chárbágh.* The following is his description of the laying out of these places and the causes which led him to adopt such a course:—"It occurred to me that one of the chief drawbacks of Hindustán, which proved an obstacle to the development of its agricultural resources, was want of artificial water-courses (*abi-rawán*). To remove this defect, I resolved, wherever I fixed my residence, to excavate artificial streams and water-courses, to cause water-wheels to be constructed, and elegant and well-planned pleasure-grounds to be laid out. Shortly after my arrival at Agra, I made a close inspection of the banks of the Jumna, with this object in view, and to select a suitable spot for a garden. The whole country appeared so ugly and desolate that I passed the river thoroughly disgusted, and gave up for a time all idea of making a garden in this locality. However, as no better situation presented itself in the neighbourhood of Agra, I concluded that I could do no better than make the best use of the same spot that was in my power. I began by sinking the large well which supplied water to the baths; next, I put in order the spot of ground where there are the tamarind trees and the octagonal tank; then I proceeded to make the large tank with its inclosure. This done, I had a hall of audience constructed in front of the stone palace. The hall is open in front, and supported by pillars. Next, I finished the apartments and the baths with a

His garden and palace.

The garden palace of *Gulafshan* or *Charbágh.*

fine garden attached to them. Going on in this way, after the Hindu fashion, without, I must own, much regard to neatness or order, I produced edifices and gardens which, on the whole, looked elegant and afforded an agreeable and pleasing sight."

His love of gardening.

The Emperor's love of gardening and planting led him to lay out gardens after the fashion of Túrkistán. He observes:—"In every corner I planted beautiful gardens; in every garden I sowed roses and narcissus in a regular fashion, and in beds corresponding to each other."

The suburbs of Agra in Bábar's time.

His example was followed by the *amírs* and nobles of his court, who vied with each other in the excellence of their designs and the elegance of their arrangements. The suburbs of Agra looked quite green and fresh. Wheels, after the fashion of Lahore and Depálpur, were constructed for raising water from wells; and among the *amirs* who constructed gardens and tanks on the banks of the Jumna in this way, Bábar mentions the names of Khalifa Sheikh Zen and Yunis Ali. "The men of Hind," writes the Emperor, "who had never before seen places formed after such fashion, or laid out with such elegance, gave the name Kábul to the quarters of the Jumna on which these gardens and places were laid out and constructed."

Underground chambers.

On an empty space within the fort of Agra, between the palace of Sultán Ibrahím and the ramparts, the Emperor had spacious underground chambers constructed, the floor of which was on the same level with the surface of well water. There were three open halls, each hall higher than the other by three steps, and the descent was by means of flights of steps. In connection with the middle story was constructed a dome for the bullocks to move round to work the wheels. The way in which water was raised from the bottom of the reservoirs (that had been constructed by the side of the wells to receive water) to the upper gardens was most ingenious, and several water-wheels were constructed which, lifting the water from one reservoir to the other, raised it to a level with the ramparts and made it run smoothly through the various beds of the gardens that had been laid out.

Bábar's death, 1530.

Bábar died in his palace at the Charbágh on 26th December 1530, while yet only forty-eight years of age. He died honoured for his noble and affectionate heart and endeared by his easy and sociable temper, which, amid the grandeur of a monarchy and the gaieties and splendour of royalty, never blunted the delicacy of his knightly generosity, his faithful companionship, and his genial and jovial disposition, or diminished in any way his sensibility to the enjoyment of Nature. He was, at the time of his death, ruler-in-chief of all the territories of India, from the Hindu Kush to the borders of Bengal, and was master of Kabul. In the eloquent words of Abul Fazl, "he departed from this world of sorrow, in the Charbágh, on the banks of the Jumna, which he had himself laid out and rendered green and verdant by his unrivalled taste." * He had been joined at Agra, a short time before his death, by his son, Humáyún, who had left his government of Badakhshán without leave. He was, nevertheless, affectionately welcomed by his father; possibly he had received the news of his father's indifferent state of health, and wished to be on the spot. His own health, however, seriously broke down, on his coming to Agra, and a strange story is told of how the Prince was able to shake off his own illness and to transfer it to his father, who ultimately succumbed to it. It is said that, when the physicians of Humáyún pronounced his case to be hopeless, the affectionate father, in accordance with a superstitious practice, passed round the sick man's bed three times and prayed. He was shortly after heard to exclaim: "I have borne it away! I have borne it away!" Soon afterwards he began rapidly to sink, and death was the result. Certain, however, it is that the climate of India and immense personal exertions had shattered his constitution and accelerated his death. His remains were temporarily buried in the Charbágh, but were subsequently, in pursuance of a will made by him, carried to Kabul, where they were buried in a beautiful spot marked out by himself. A running and clear stream still irrigates the fragrant flowers of this cemetery, which is the great holiday-resort of the people of Kabul."†

Superstitious story concerning Bábar's death.

Humáyún, the late Emperor's eldest son, then in the twenty-third year of his age, was crowned in the palace at Agra on 29th December, 1530, or three days after the late Emperor's death. It was an occasion of great solemnities. The chief nobility

Humayún crowned Emperor of Hindustan, 1530.

* *Akbarnama*, vol. I., p. 91, Ed. of 1883.

† *Bernier's Travels into Bokhara*, vol. II., pp. 121-123.

presented themselves before the new Emperor and tendered their allegiance, money was scattered among the populace, public prayers were read, and coin was struck in the name of the new Prince.

Agra occupied by Sher Sháh *Sur* Afghàn, 1540.

After the great discomfiture of Humáyún at Kanauj, Sher Sháh Sur Afghan took possession of Agra, in 1540, and, seizing its treasures and arsenals, hastened on to Delhi, whence parties of Afghans pursued Humáyún across the Sutlej.

His strict justice.

Sher Sháh was one of the most enlightened Princes that ever ruled the destinies of this Empire. His justice was proverbial, and the impartiality with which he administered it obtained for him a high place among the sovereigns of India. The author of the *Khulásut ul Tawárikh* has related an instance of his justice which will serve to illustrate the character of this King.

Anecdote.

One day his eldest son, Adil Khán, riding on an elephant, passed through one of the streets of Agra, attended by his cavalcade. As he was making his round, he happened to see a young wife of a citizen who was bathing naked in the upper story of her house, the walls of which were in a dilapidated condition and allowed the objects inside to be seen by a man riding on an elephant. The Prince was charmed with her looks. The moment he saw her, he served her with a *betel*, or *bira pán*, which he threw to her to secure her affections. She was not a woman of easy virtue, and, when her husband came home, narrated the circumstance to him. The husband, feeling his honour wounded, laid his complaint before the Emperor, who was convinced of its truth. He gave it as his verdict that the principle of retaliation enjoined by the Muhammadan Law should be enforced. It was directed that the complainant, seated in his turn, on an elephant, should pass through the street and see the Prince's wife when undressed and bathing. Great was the excitement that prevailed in the court, and the alarm caused in the King's harem at the prospect of a female member of the royal household being thus publicly dishonoured. The King was inflexible in his resolution. In vain did his *amirs* and counsellors exert themselves to mollify him. "Such is," said His Majesty, "the law of our religion, and it must be enforced in its entirety. That the accused happens to be a king's son, is no reason why his guilt should be passed over with impunity. Law is meant to be obeyed, and, in administering justice, there should be no difference between a prince of royal blood and a peasant." The complainant, seeing that his honour had been sufficiently vindicated, withdrew his complaint, declaring that he had gained his right, and was satisfied with the Sultan's justice, and at his earnest solicitation the matter was dropped. Such was the kind of justice administered at Agra during the prosperous days of Sher Shah *Súr*.

Architectural remains of Sher Shah. Sher Shah was a great patron of architecture, and of the public buildings constructed in his time throughout India many exist to this day, the admiration of the world. The only architectural relic of his time in Agra is the interesting mosque of Alawal Bilawal, or Shah Wilayat, in Nai kí Mandí, which has sunk into the ground up to about the middle of the walls.

Salem Shah Sur, second son of Sher Shah. The peace of Agra was disturbed during the reign of the last monarch's son and successor, Sultán Islám, better known as Salem Shah *Sur*, the second son of Sher Shah. Agra was still the *Dár ul Sultanat* of India. **Adil Shah, his elder brother.** The claim of Adil Shah, the eldest son, having been set aside on account of his weakness of character and imbecility, Salem Shah was saluted Emperor of Hindustan. Immediately on his accession, he invited his elder brother, Adil Shah, to Agra, feigning a desire to tender his allegiance to him and telling him that he had been forced by circumstances alone to occupy the throne, his object being to prevent commotion, and that, as soon as he made his appearance in the capital, he would resign in his favour. Adil Shah arrived at Agra, and a meeting between the brothers was arranged. Salem had given strict orders to the guard of the citadel that his brother should be allowed to enter it with only two or three attendants. Adil Shah, suspecting the sincerity of Salem, pushed forward into the hall of public audience with a large number of followers, and thus the plan of Salem to seize the person of his brother was defeated.

Resigns the throne in favour of Salem Shah. Undeterred by the failure of his scheme, Salem tried to gain by his eloquence and by flattery what he had failed to do by stratagem. He renewed his former assertions that he had been constrained to assume the royal titles and prerogatives against his will, merely from political considerations and to keep the turbulent classes of the public in check, and he loaded Adil Shah with marks of distinction and honour. Then, approaching him and holding him by the hands, he placed him on the throne. Adil was not deceived by the apparent sincerity of his brother's professions but, being himself a lover of ease and freedom, and feeling that his situation on the throne would be unsafe, forthwith came down, and, in his turn, seating Salem Shah on it, saluted him as the Emperor, and offered the customary congratulations. The grandees of the court instantly followed his example, and, tendering their homage to Salem, presented him offerings. Adil Shah retired to his *jagirs* at Biáná.

Is prompted to make war on Salem.

This did not, however, satisfy Salem. Hardly two months had elapsed when he despatched Gházi Mahlí, a eunuch of rank, to Biáná, with a pair of golden fetters, and with orders to seize the person of Adil Shah and bring him a prisoner to the court. Khewas Khan, of Mewat, a partizan of Adil, whose exertions had chiefly led to the late amicable settlement between the brothers, having heard of this breach of faith on the part of Salem, set out for Agra at the head of a large army. He was joined by Adil and a number of chiefs who had guaranteed the safety of that Prince.

But is defeated, 1545.

A battle was fought in sight of Agra (A.D. 1545), in which, in spite of the exertions of Khewas Khan, victory declared itself for Salem. Adil Shah fled from the battlefield, escaped to Tabia, and was heard of no more.

The history of Humayun resumed.

After his defeat, in Monghyr, by a detachment sent by Sher Shah, in June, 1539, Humayun continued his flight with a small retinue to Kalpi, with the view of proceeding thence to Agra. His army, including the best part of his father's veterans, had been cut off for the most part, or perished in the inundations. Humayun's Empress, whom it had been the last endeavour of that sovereign to save, had been taken prisoner by the Afghans; but Sher Shah treated her with every mark of courtesy and attention and sent her to Agra in safety. Humayun shortly afterwards joined the Empress at Agra, and, after making preparations there, once more moved from Agra, in April, 1540, to give battle to his adversary, who was now in possession of Bengal. His army was at this time strengthened by a reinforcement

The Emperor Humayún.

Page 16.

of 3,000 men belonging to Kámrán, who had himself retired to Lahore. The final defeat of Humayun at Kanauj has been already noticed.* The defeated monarch turned his thoughts to Sindh; but, his attempts to re-establish his authority in that part of the country having failed, he fled to Persia, where he was magnificently received by Shah Tahmasp, the Safvi King (1544). The Shah sent an army, under his son, to restore Humayun, who recovered Kabul (April 1547), and marched to recover India in January, 1555, after an exile of ten years. He engaged Sakandar Shah *Sur* Afghan at Sirhand, and gained a decisive victory, the Afghans flying to the mountains under the Himalaya. This victory once more decided the fate of the Empire of Hindustan and established a dynasty which proved more prosperous and enduring than any of those which had preceded it. An advance force of the victor immediately took possession of Delhi and Agra (July 1555).

His defeat at Kanauj, 1540.

His flight to Persia, 1544.

Marches to recover India, 1555.

Recovers Agra, 1555.

The death of Humayun in Delhi, and the absence of his successor, the young Akbar, in the Punjab, gave fresh courage to Hemu, the Hindu minister of Muhammad Shah Adili, to recover the capital for his master. Hemu was originally a shop-keeper who, by the force of his talents, had risen to the highest post in the gift of the crown. At this time he set out with a powerful army of 30,000 men and 2,000 elephants against Agra, and his numbers increased as he advanced through a friendly country. The Mughal officer in charge of Agra was hardly prepared to meet this formidable invasion and thought it his best policy to fall back on Delhi. Zamán Khan, another Mughal officer, at the head of 3,000 horse, tried to oppose the advance of Shadi Khan, one of Hemu's Generals, but he was defeated, and almost the whole of his force was cut off. Agra was taken, after a short siege, by Hemu, who, now advancing on Delhi, took possession of it, and, setting aside the pretensions of Sakandar *Súr*, assumed the title of Raja Bakrama Jit, of ancient fame.

Agra occupied by Hemu, 1556.

The Mughal army under Bairam Khan gradually assembled at Nowshera and advanced upon Delhi. Hemu marched out with a considerable army to Panipat, the old battlefield which had so often decided the fate of the Empire since the age of the

The battle of Panipat, 1556.

* See page 14 *supra*.

Mahabharat. Hemu was defeated and captured. The victorious Bairam Khan and the youthful Akbar both displayed prodigies of valour in this battle. After the victory, Sakandar Uzbek, a General of Humayun, was sent forward to occupy Agra, and the place was surrendered without any resistance in 1556.

Agra re-occupied by Humayun, 1556.

Akbar founds modern Agra, 1558.

Modern Agra was founded on the west bank of the river Jumna by Akbar, the son of Humayun, who removed the seat of government to that place. The original idea of the Emperor was to build his entire metropolis at Fatehpur Sikri, south-west of Agra, in honour of the birth there of his eldest son, Salem (afterwards Jahangir), believed to have been born through the blessings and benedictions of Salem Chishti, a *fakír* of great religious sanctity who resided there at the time; and traces of fortifications still exist there. The reason why the idea was abandoned is explained further on. The establishment of the metropolitan capital in its present locality is attributed by some to the superiority of Agra on a navigable river, coupled with its salubrious climate, and by others to the circumstance of the saint, Salem Chishti, having told the Emperor Akbar that the presence of a royal court at the residence of the *fakír* seriously interfered with his devotions, and that His Majesty would do well to remove it to some more convenient locality, and leave Fatehpur for the undisturbed engagement of the *fakír* in his spiritual pursuits.

Account given by Abul Fazl.

Abul Fazl, in the *Akbarnáma*, gives the following account of the foundation of modern Agra by Akbar:—"His Majesty made Agra the capital of the Empire, and, in the third year of the reign (1558 A.D.), took up his residence in the citadel formerly known as Bádalgarh. He assigned different quarters for the accommodation of the grandees of the realm, thus rendering the palace the centre of wealth, happiness and prosperity. Through the auspicious attention of His Majesty, the city, within a short time, became an ornament of the seven climes. It is a city possessing a salubrious climate, the heat and cold being moderate in their respective seasons; the soil is congenial to the growth of the trees and fruit of Khorasán and Iráq; the river Júu (Jumna) the water of which has few rivals for lightness and taste, flows in the midst of the city; on either side of it the nobles and servants

The Emperor Akbar.

Page 18.

of State have constructed edifices of such beauty and elegance that they surpass description. With all its noble buildings and charming suburbs, it has once more become the capital of the Empire. The fortunate event of the royal residence having been fixed at the capital of Agra was signalized by the conquest of Gwalior, which followed immediately after the happy incident." The citadel was henceforward called the *Daulat Khána*, or 'House of Wealth.'

In the events of the fifth year of the reign, mention is again made of the new buildings on the banks of the Jumna and of the measures adopted to improve and embellish the imperial city. Bairám Khán, the tutor and general of Akbar, who raised the standard of revolt, was defeated by the royal troops. All his houses in the city of Agra were confiscated to the State and made over to Munim Khán, the new Khán-i-Khánan.

European influence in India.

The Mughal Empire of Hindustán, founded by the genius of Bábar and re-established by the adventurous Humáyún, reached its completion, though not the zenith of its splendour, during the reign of Akbar. For a century and a half after Akbar's death, or until the Játs occupied Agra, the Empire was maintained chiefly through the principles of justice and toleration enunciated by that great monarch during his long and prosperous reign. The British first appeared in India five years before the Emperor's death, and it was in the year 1600 that the celebrated East India Company obtained their first charter from Queen Elizabeth. He was the first of the Indian sovereigns after Porus who was known to Europeans, and he was the first great Indian potentate who was interviewed by them.

Akbar compared with Asoka.

Akbar was a contemporary of Queen Elizabeth, and his reign was one of the most important in the history of India. The likeness between Akbar and Asoka, who preceded him by eighteen centuries, in matters of religious sentiments and toleration, the suppression of priests, abstinence from flesh and meat, the encouragement of learning, and the peace enjoyed by all subjects, of whatever creed, are most marked. Finally, as Asoká in the end took refuge in Buddha, so Akbar in the end recited the formula of Islám, "There is but one God, and Muhammad is His Prophet."*

---

* Wheeler.

Akbar's mode of administering justice.

Akbar held public audience every day, in the afternoon, in the public hall of assembly, known as *Darbár-i-Am*, which was an open court with a royal throne set up in it. It was not, however, customary with him to sit on the throne: he stood at the foot of it, on a platform, still preserved in the *Díwán-i-Am*, and gave all orders in a standing posture, while all his ministers and *amirs* stood before him with folded hands.

According to the testimony of European travellers, Akbar devoted special attention to the administration of justice. "In the city where he dwelt he heard all causes himself. No malefactor was punished without his knowledge." Mutilation of hands was the punishment for theft and piracy; while murderers, adulterers and highway robbers were impaled or hanged. No sentence of execution was carried out until Akbar had personally pronounced it three times. He poisoned his enemies by administering to them with his own hands *betels*, or so-called digestive pills, which he carried with him in a box, divided into several compartments, and which no one dared to refuse when offered by the Bádsháh. *

The *ghusl khana*.

At evening a private darbár was held in the *ghusl khána*, or imperial drawing-room, at which petitions from the Viceroys of Provinces were read out to His Majesty, who passed orders on them, and other state business was transacted.

During religious discourses, or when hearing histories, Akbar sat on carpets, always accompanied by twelve learned men.

Akbar's marriage with Rajput Princesses.

Alá-ud-dín Khiljí was the first Sultán of India who married a Hindu Princess, Koulà Devi, the Rájput Queen of Rai Karan, the Rájá of Gujrát (1306 A.D.). She had been taken prisoner during the Rájá's lifetime, and so fascinated Alá-ud-dín by her beauty and talents, that she gained a great share of his favour. Her equally beautiful daughter was married to Khizr Khán, the Emperor's eldest son, and their loves form the subject of a celebrated Persian poem, by Amír Khusro, the great poet of India.

Akbar compared with Ala-ud-din Khilji.

Alá-ud-dín, in external qualities, very much resembled Akbar. Like him, he married a Hindu Princess. He was the first to set

* This practice was followed by Akbar's two immediate successors. Sháh Jahán caused the culprits to be bitten by a cobra.

aside the authority of the *Kuran* as propounded by the *Ulamas;* as also did Akbar. He was the first Muhammadan Sultán who founded a new religion and sought to become a prophet; as also did Akbar. In Alá-ud-dín's case it was probably his Hindu wife who upset his religious faith; the same was the case with Akbar. Both were illiterate and of eccentric temper. Akbar married two Rájput Princesses—first, the daughter of Rájá Bihári Mal and sister of Rájá Bhágwán Dás, and then Jodh Bái, a Princess of Jodhpur, the mother of Jahángir, commonly called Mariam Zamáni. There was, however, this distinction between Alá-ud-dín and Akbar, that, while the former secured his alliance with the Rájput Princess as the result of war and oppression, the latter gained his by means of conciliation and friendship. There was the further difference between the two, that, while Alá-ud-din was a tyrannical despot, Akbar, on the contrary, was generous, forbearing, clement and affable. Akbar was no fanatic, and was not carried away by religious frenzy. During the time of both, the wealth of India increased and led to various forms of luxury and improvements.

Akbar's mode of government.

Religious reform was dear to Akbar's heart: but he hated no Hindu or Muhammadan on account of his religion. He raised Hindus to the highest State offices. His land settlement, carried out by his friend and minister, Todar Mal, was based on good judgment and humanity. According to the testimony of contemporary Europeans, he was plain in his habits, frugal, self-controlled and devoted to the useful arts. A sketch of Akbar's career has been separately given, and it is only necessary here to describe briefly how he closed his eventful life.

His private life.

His domestic bereavements.

The murder of Abul Fazl deeply afflicted Akbar. By his death he lost a trusted counsellor and a personal friend.* Other calamities befell him about the same time. His mother, Hamida Bano Begum, commonly known by her title of Mariam Makáni, (dwelling with the Virgin Mary) died. Prince Danial, his own son, died of *delirium tremens*, in 1013 (1604 A.D.), in the Deccan. Salem's jealousy of his son, Khusro, created a dispute between the former and the latter's mother (the sister of Raja Man Singh),

* For the grief felt by Akbar on Abul Fazl's death, see "Life of Abul Fazl," Chapter III.

who was so affected that she swallowed poison, and thus a fresh sting was inflicted on the already distressed mind of Akbar. The Emperor's own end was drawing near. His last days were embittered by the rebellion of the heir-apparent, Salem. A reconciliation was effected between father and son, and Salem repaired to the court at Agra and made submission. The Emperor conferred on him the privilege of using the crown jewels, but placed him under temporary restraint. Domestic troubles had already undermined the old monarch's health, and he grew worse in September, 1605. He lost his appetite, and was for the last ten days confined to his bed. Prince Khurram (afterwards Sháh Jahán), then a mere boy, was constantly by the bedside of his grandfather. Finding his end approaching, the old monarch invited the nobles of his court to his chamber, together with the heir apparent, Salem; and when all had assembled, he earnestly looked on them all round and asked them to forgive him if he had been guilty of any offence towards any of them. Salem now threw himself at his royal father's feet and burst into a torrent of tears. The kind-hearted Akbar, looking on him with feelings of tenderness and affection, pointed to his favourite scimitar, and made a sign to Salem to bind it on him in that assembly. Having recovered from his exhaustion, he addressed a few words of admonition to Salem. He eagerly asked him to look to the comfort of the ladies of the *harem* and not to forsake his old friends and dependents. He then permitted the chief *mullah*, who was a personal friend of Salem, to be brought to him, and in his presence he repeated the confession of faith and died in all the forms of a good Musalmán.

(His death is accelerated; His last moments.)

(His death, 1605.) The event occurred in the Fort of Agra, on 13th October 1605, in the sixty-third year of his age and the fifty-first of his reign.

(His burial.) The burial ceremonies of Akbar were performed in a simple style. He was interred in a splendid mausoleum in Sakandrá, near Agra, built by himself.* The body was placed upon a bier. Salem and his three sons carried it out of the fortress. The young princes, assisted by the officers of the imperial household, carried it to Sakandrá. Seven days were spent in mourning over the

* It was finished by Jahangir.—See Chapter II.

grave. Provisions and sweetmeats were distributed amongst the poor every morning and evening throughout the mourning, and twenty readers were appointed to recite the *kurán* by the grave every night without ceasing.*

The chief buildings of Akbar's period in Agra are his own mausoleum at Sakandrá, the Agra Fort, and the palaces and mausoleum of Sheikh Salem Chishti in Fattehpur Síkri. **buildings in Agra.**

The period of mourning of the late Emperor being over, Salem entered the Fort of Agra by the western gate, and was crowned Emperor of Hindustán, in October 1605, in the thirty-eighth year of his age, under the pompous title of Núr-ud-dín Jahángir (Conqueror of the World). The people filled the air with acclamations of joy. Every demonstration of mirth was made, and festivities and rejoicings were the order of the day. The royal kettle-drum was beaten for forty days, and the palace was illuminated with thousands of lights every night. Largess was profusely distributed. Rájás and Nawábs, grandees and nobles, prostrated themselves before the new King, and, to commemorate the event, an inscription was cut upon the sandstone panel of the guard-room in the Delhi gate of the Fort, where it is still to be seen, ending with the prayer, "May our King Jahangir be the King of the World, 1014." The new Emperor conferred the title of Mahábat Khán on his *ahdi* (or exempt), Zamána Beg, with a *mansab* of fifteen hundred and appointed him Paymaster of the Royal Household. He had been attached to the new Emperor while the latter was still Crown Prince. Another faithful friend of his early days and his school companion, Sharíf, son of Khwája Abdul Samad, was created *Amír-ul-Umra*, or premier noble, with a *mansab* of five thousand. Salem was much attached to him, and when that Prince rebelled against his father in Allahábád, he had been sent to him to effect a reconciliation. Sharíf acted so that he widened the breach between the father and the son, who made a rash promise to him to give him half the kingdom on ascending the throne. When a reconciliation was effected between Akbar and Salem, Sharíf had to fly for his life; but on hearing of Akbar's death, he returned to Agra and was honourably received by the new Emperor, who created him *Amír-ul-Umra*, and put him in **Jahángír ascends the throne, 1605.**

* Wheeler.

charge of the great seal. Nár Singh, the murderer of Abul Fazl, was made a grandee of three thousand.

Jahángír showed himself at the *jharoka* (window) every morning to the multitude who assembled beneath to offer their obeisance to the Emperor, as in the days of Akbar. He attended the *darbár* court and the *ghusl khána.* At noon there were parades, games, sports, and animal fights, at which the King attended. The nights were spent in revelry and merriment with boon companions—a strong contrast with the mode in which the philosophical and good Akbar spent his nights in talking with learned men until early morning.

Agra as described by Jahángír.

Jahángír, in his *Tuzk*, or autobiography, gives the following account of old Agra and the foundation of the new city by his father, Akbar :—"Agra is one of the most ancient and important cities of Hindustán. It had an old fort on the bank of the Jumna ; but my father, before my birth, having levelled it with the ground, built on its site a fort of red sandstone so magnificent that men who have travelled through the world maintain that they have seen the like of it nowhere during their travels. It took fifteen or sixteen years to complete. It consists of four gates and two smaller gateways, and was constructed at an outlay of thirty-five lakhs of rupees, equal to one hundred and fifteen thousand *tamans* of Irán and one crore five lakhs of *khanis* of Turan. The city population extends along either bank of the Jumna. The part to the west, which is very densely populated, is seven *kos* in circuit, two *kos* long, and one *kos* broad; that to the east, two and a half *kos* in circuit, one *kos* long, and half a *kos* broad. The buildings are so numerous, that several cities of the size of those in Iraq, Khorasan, and Mahwaral Nahr could be made of them. Most people have built their houses to the height of three and four storeys, and the city is so overcrowded with population that one cannot pass through a lane or street without trouble."

Jahángír's description of ancient Agra.

The Emperor writes as follows of its history previous to the time of the Afghán Lodí kings:—"Before the time of the Afghán Lodís, Agra was a large city and had a fort. Masúd Sád Salmán, in a poem composed by him in praise of Mahmúd, son of Ibrahím, son of Masúd, son of Mahmúd Ghiznaví, on the occasion of the

The Emperor Jahangir.

Page 24.

capture of the fort of Agra by that Prince, writes as follows of its ancient Hindu fort:—

حصار آگرہ پیدا شد از میانۂ گرد بسان کوہ برو بارہ ہائے چون کہسار

Seen from afar, amid dust-laden clouds,
The citadel loomed forth, severe and grand,
Like mountain overspread with shadowy knolls,
Whose tracery the setting sun scarce limned."

Of the fruits and flowers, foreign as well as indigenous, grown at Agra, Jahángír writes:—"In Agra and its environs the best kinds of melons, mangoes and other fruits can be had. Of all the indigenous fruits, I have much liking for the preserve or confection of mango. During the time of His Majesty Arsh Ashiání * (Akbar), most of the fruits of *Vilayat* (Kábul, Herát, &c.), which were not forthcoming in India, were imported, and various kinds of grapes, such as *sáhibi* (white), *habshi* (black), and *kishmishi* (brown), were grown in various towns. In the bázárs of Lahore, for instance, every kind of grape can be had in any quantity in the grape season. Among other fruits, there is one deserving of special mention; it is called *ananás* (pine-apple), and it has been imported from the ports of Frang (Frank, or Europe). It possesses a sweet flavour and delicious taste, and is produced in thousands each year in the Gulafshán garden of Agra. **Fruit trees.**

Of odoriferous flowers, it may be said that the flowers of Hind are superior in fragrance to those of any country in the world. There are many flowers here of which no name or even trace exists anywhere else. First in order may be mentioned the *champa.*† It is a flower full of sweet odour, and is exquisitely pleasant. In shape it resembles the saffron flower, but in colour it is yellow-white. The plant is large, handsome, laden with leaves, full of branches and shady. In the season of flowers, one tree is sufficient to fill the whole garden with sweet fragrance. **Flowers.**

Next is the flower of *kewra,*‡ in shape a small plant, the scent of which is so strong and effective that it is by no means inferior to that of musk.

---

* Titles were given to the Chaughattai Emperors after death. Thus, Timur was called *Sáhibqirán*; Babar, *Firdous Makani*; Humáyún, *Jannat Ashiáni*; Akbar, *Arsh Ashiáni*; Jahángir, *Jannat Makani*; and Sháh Jahán, *Firdous Ashiani Ala Hazrat.*

† *Michelia champaca.* ‡ *Pandamus odoratissimus.*

Then comes *rai bel*, * which is of a snowy colour and gives out fragrance like that of the jasmine. The leaves grow in several layers, one over the other.

Another is the *moulsri* † flower, the plant of which is also of agreeable size, symmetrical and shady. It possesses a very mild odour.

Seoti ‡ is a species of *kewra*, with this difference, that the latter has thorns in it, while the former is without thorns. It is of a yellowish colour, while *kewra* is of a white colour. From the flowers above-mentioned and the jasmine (the white jasmine of *Vilayat*) they extract perfumed oils."

Captain Hawkins in Agra, 1608.

In 1608 Captain Hawkins waited on the Emperor Jahángír with a letter from James the First, King of England. Mokarrab Khán, Viceroy of Gujrát, met him at Surat, and he was conducted to Agra in safety. The Emperor took a great fancy to Hawkins, who settled at Agra to promote the interest of the English Company. Jahángír spent the earlier years of his reign in Agra. According to Father Catron, all Franks (or Europeans) had free access to the palace during the reign of Jahángír. The Emperor drank with them all night, even in the month of the Musalmán fast.

Jahángír's daily life.

According to Hawkins, who was in Agra in 1608-11, Jahángír was a stout man of forty-five. Coryat, who was in Agra about 1615, says he was fifty-three. Hawkins has furnished an interesting account of Jahángír's daily life.

In the morning at daybreak, with his face turned towards Mecca, he repeated the different names of God on a string of beads of pearls, diamonds, rubies, emeralds, lignum aloes and coral. He then appeared at the *jharoka* (window) to receive the salutations of the multitude who resorted to the plains opposite every morning. This done, he went to sleep for two hours more. He then took his meals with the ladies of the seraglio. At noon he again showed himself to the people at the balcony of the palace

The *jharoka* (window).

jharoka (window), and sat there until three o'clock to witness pastimes by men and beast. "At three o'clock the nobles in

* *Jasminum Zambac.* † *Baulsiri.* ‡ China rose. *Rosa glandulifera.*

Agra, whom sickness detaineth not, resort to the court, and the King comes forth in open audience, sitting in his seat royal, every man standing in his degree before him: the chief within a red rail, the rest without. The red rail is three steps higher than the place where the rest stand. Men are placed by officers; there are others to keep men in order. In the midst, right before the King, standeth an officer with his master hangman, accompanied by forty others of the same profession, with badges on their shoulders, and others with whips. Here the King heareth causes some hours every day; he then departs to his house of prayer." At evening the Emperor was in the *ghusl khána*, or private room, where ministers and selected officers and *amirs* waited on His Majesty, and State business was transacted. The State writers were in constant attendance until the King slept, and they wrote all that the King did. A rope with ringing bells, plated with gold, was fastened to two pillars in the King's chamber, with an end hanging over the ground opposite the palace. Any poor man who demanded justice, shook the rope, and the King hearing the bells ring called him forthwith, heard him and did justice to his cause.

Public audience.

The *ghusl khána.*

Chain of justice.

Hawkins drank with Jahángír in the *ghusl khána.* He had his enemy, Mokarrab Khán, summoned to Agra on a charge of extorting money and seizing a Hindu girl under the pretence of sending her to the King. All his property was confiscated; but Mokarrab heavily bribed the officials and was restored to favour. He revenged himself on Hawkins. Jahángír was led to believe that, if the English once got a footing in India, they would soon become masters of the country. Jahángír was alarmed; and forbade them from trading in India. Hawkins, with his Armenian wife, whom he had married in Agra, left that city for England in 1611.

Hostile proceedings of Mokarrab Khán.

Hawkins leaves Agra, 1611.

Jahángír was not at Agra when Sir Thomas Roe landed at Surat, in 1615, as Lord Ambassador from King James I. Journeying from Burhanpur, he visited Mándú, and then Chittor, the ancient capital of Rájputána, and waited on the Emperor at Ajmere, which His Majesty had made his head-quarters about that Roe never visited Agra or Delhi, but he has left a graphic thful account of Jahángír's court. The presents from the

The embassy of Sir Thoma Roe, 1615-18

King of England consisted of virginals, knives, an embroidered scarf, a rich sword, and an English coach. The ambassador had a musician in his train, and he was ordered to play on the virginals. Jahángír gave the coach to Núr Mahal, his beloved queen. The English lining was taken off and the coach covered with gold velvet and decorations. Jahángír asked Roe if the English would give him jewels, to which the ambassador replied that jewels came from India where Jahángír was King ; how then could the English bring back his own jewels? Roe accompanied Jahángír to Mándú and Gujrat, and left him in the end of 1618.

Núr Mahal.

Núr Mahal's influence over Jahángír was unlimited. For twenty years she ruled the King and the kingdom. No important office in the State was filled without her consent, nor any treaty with a foreign State concluded without her approval. Money was coined in her name, with the inscription, "Gold has gained a new value since it bore the name of Núr Mahal." Her father became the *wazír*, and her brother, Asaf Khán, was raised to the first rank of the nobility.

The Seraglio.

The seraglio of Jahángír consisted of six thousand women, including female slaves, attendants, women soldiers and guards. There were Chinese, Circassians, Georgians, Turks, Persians Abyssinians and Hindus. In Jahángír's palace, in the Agra fort, are to this day to be seen numerous labyrinth of courts, of apartments and of passages, in which these female servants and guards were posted to watch the stately suites of chambers, most exquisitely carved and painted, that were once the lovely home of some lady of rank or the wife of some chief.

The Jasmine Bower.

The part of the palace where Núr Mahal spent the greater portion of her life still stands in the fort of Agra. It is known as the Jasmine Bower (*Samman Burj*). It has lately been repaired, under the orders of Lord Mayo, late Viceroy of India. It still bears the stamp of Núr Mahal's artistic instincts, skill, and refined judgment. Her private rooms and balcony may

Núr Mahal's apartments.

also be seen on the high castle walls. It was in these r
that Núr Mahal passed the gloomy days of her widowhood,
the murder of her brave husband, Sher Afgan, and before her marriage with Jahángír, who had neglected her for four years and even refused to see her. Here she lived quite forgotten

Núr Mahal.

Page 28.

her royal lover, who had once passionately loved her; but she was kindly received by her former patroness, the good-hearted old lady, Mariam Zamàni (Princess of Jodhpur), mother of Jaháng'ír. Núr Mahal had adorned these chambers with extraordinary splendour and magnificence. All the designs were her own, and the workmanship was by the hands of her own female slaves, under her personal direction. All the ladies of the harem consulted her in matters of jewellery and the painting of silk, and she introduced quite novel styles and fashions into the court. The seraglio resounded with her charms and talents. It was in these apartments that, Jaháugír happening to see her one morning in her plain dress of white muslin, his passion for her was renewed. Instantly he threw round her neck a necklace of forty pearls which he wore, each pearl being valued at £4,000, and Núr Mahal was removed to the imperial quarters and became his favourite queen.

Jahángír reigned in peace, but that peace was disturbed in Agra by the rebellion of his son, Sháh Jahan, in 1623. The Prince marched from Mándú with his army towards Agra. Jahángir sent Asaf Khán to Agra to remove the imperial treasures before Sháh Jahán should arrive there. Sháh Jahan occupied the city of Agra and sacked it, but he was unsuccessful in capturing the fort, which contained the imperial treasures. According to the particulars furnished by Della Valle, a noble Italian from Rome,* who has written them on the authority of letters received by him at Surat from Agra, Sháh Jahán and his soldiers committed fearful barbarities at Agra on this occasion. The citizens of Agra were subjected to torture to compel them to give up their hoarded treasures, and many ladies of quality were outraged and mangled.†

Sack and outrage at Agra by Shán Jahan, 1623.

All the European travellers who visited Agra during the time of Jahángír have written of its wealth and splendour in glowing terms. Calbauke, writing about it to Sir Thomas Smith, in the beginning of the seventeenth century, speaks of it as "a

Agra during the time of Jahángír.

* He was a Roman Catholic, and had visited India, in 1623, "out of an intelligent curiosity, begotten of the learning of the time, to discover any affinity that might exist between the religion of Egypt and that of India."—*Wheeler*.

† Wheeler.

Testimony of European travellers.

great and populous city entirely built of stone, with a great deal of merchandise, the whole city being even more imposing than London of that age." Finch, noticing the splendour of its grandees and nobles, remarks that they never allowed the garments of their concubines once worn to be put on again, but that they were buried in the ground as unfit for further use. There were many nobles in Agra so rich that each had a thousand *Mashalchis* or torch-bearers in his service. Edward Terry and Thomas Coryat each describe Agra as a magnificent city, worthy of the capital of the great Mughal.

Edward Terry, who accompanied the mission of Sir Thomas Roe, as Chaplain, mentions Agra as one of thirty-seven large Provinces under the Mughal, which the traveller has described in Chapter II of his work. He writes of Agra thus:—"Agra, a principal and very rich province, the chief city so-called, this great Emperor's metropolis in north latitude about 28 degrees and a half. It is very well watered by the river Jumna. This and Lahore are two principal and choice cities of this Empire, betwixt which is that long walk (which I have mentioned before) of four hundred miles in length, shaded by great trees on both sides. This is looked upon by the travellers, who have found the comfort of that cool shade, as one of the rarest and most beneficial works in the whole world." *

Thomas Herbert, who visited Agra during the reign of Jahángír, describes it as semilunary in shape, like London, with streets long and narrow. Akbar is mentioned as having commenced the building of the fort, after his victorious return from Ahamadábád, in place of the old castle, which was pulled down. He describes Agra as a populous and flourishing city.

On his return from Gujrat, Jahángir visited Ujjain, and thence he came to Agra, where he became reconciled to his eldest son, Khusro, through the intervention of Parwez, his second son. After some wanderings he proceeded to Lahore, and thence went to Kashmir, in the hot months of 1627. He was compelled by asthma to return, but death overtook him on the way at Rajouri, on 12th October, 1627. His remains were brought to Lahore, and, according to his will, interred in the garden of Núr Mahal, on the banks of the Ravi.

Death of Jahangir, 1627.

* *A Voyage to East India*, by Edward Terry, p. 81.

There were about sixty Christians in Agra during the reign of Jahángír. According to Roe, the Emperor knew a little Italian, for he had been heard calling out to Khurram (Sháhjahan) in full darbar, "Mio figlio, mio figlio"! when there was some misunderstanding between the Prince and the Christians. At the Protestant cemetery of Agra there are still a dozen tombs of Europeans who must have visited India about this time. Christian influence in Agra in Jahangir's time.

The principal buildings of Jahángír's period are a portion of the mausoleum at Sakandrá, the Jahángíri Mahal in the Agra palace, the mausoleum of Itmad-ud-daula, all showing signs of Hindu influence, the Bath of Alí Verdi Khán, in the Chipitola quarter of the city, the mosque of Motamid Khán, in the Kashmirí Bazar, and the tower and garden known after the name of Boland Khan, the chief eunuch of Jahángír's palace. Principal buildings of Jahangir's period.

The power of Nur Jahán vanished with the last breath of Jahángir. The court was at this time divided into two factions. Nur Jahán favoured the succession of her own son-in-law, Shaharyar, the fourth son of the late Emperor. Her brother, Asaf Khán, wished for the succession of his son-in-law, Sháh Jahán. Khusro, the eldest son of Jahángír, having rebelled against his father, was blinded, as a punishment; but Jahángír, out of affection for his son, always kept him near his person. Sháh Jahán, who had deep designs of his own regarding the Empire, persuaded Jahángír to allow the blind Prince to accompany him to the Deccan, on the plea that it was distressing to keep a son who had been deprived of sight before his eyes. As soon as the poor Prince was in his power, Sháh Jahán found means to remove him by secretly procuring his death. The succession of Shah Jehan, 1628.

On the news of Jahángír's death being reported at court, Asaf Khán took immediate steps to enthrone at Delhi Prince Dáwar Baksh, otherwise known as Boláki, the eldest son of Khusro and the legitimate heir to the throne, who was still a youth. This was, however, done as a matter of policy to appease the *umeras* and nobles, who had been sorely afflicted by the murder of the unhappy Khusro, and wished to see the eldest son of the deceased, as the rightful heir, on the throne; and also to give time to Sháh Jahán, who was then in the Deccan. Meanwhile Shaharyar had assumed the regalia of the empire at Lahore. Asaf Khán carried A sham king.

Boláki in triumph to Lahore, where Shaharyar was taken prisoner and deprived of his sight. The youthful king was then brought to Agra, where he assumed royal functions, with Asaf Khán as *wazir.* Asaf Khán was now all-powerful both in the army and in the empire. He had by this time succeeded in furthering the interests of Sháh Jahán by gaining over a great number of officers and nobility to his side. In order, however, better to conceal his game and to lull the suspicion of the young King, who was wanting in experience, if not in intelligence, it was given out at Agra that Sháh Jahán was dangerously ill; next, that he

A stratagem. was dead. The young Badsháh was, according to a desire expressed by Sháh Jahán, solicited to allow his burial in the precincts of Akbar's tomb at Sakandrá. Overjoyed at the intelligence of the death of his rival, Boláki gave his sanction to the *wazir's* proposal. An empty bier, followed by a funeral *cortege*, proceeded in solemn grief from Agra to Akbar's mausoleum. The living dead (Sháh Jahán) himself followed it in disguise! Asaf Khán impressed on the young king that the rules of etiquette required that His Majesty should come out of Agra to do honour to the body of the deceased Prince, who was no other than the brother of his own father, when it should come within a league or two of the city; and, following this advice, he came out to meet the body, with a small escort. Squadrons of Rájputs followed the bier, and Sháh Jahán, having gradually approached it, secretly got into it, an aperture sufficient to enable him to breathe having been left in it. The bier was then carried into a tent, where all the principal chiefs, who were acting in concert with Asaf Khán, assembled as if to do honour to the dead Prince. It was, says Tavernier, at this juncture that Asaf Khán saw "that the time had come for the execution of his design; he had the bier opened before the eyes of all the army; Sháh Jahán was saluted as king by all the generals and other officers." The young king, who was still on the way, finding himself deserted by almost all the *amirs*, withdrew and fled to Lahore.

Shah Jahan enters Agra.

Immediately the trumpets sounded; and Sháh Jahán was proclaimed Emperor amidst the acclamations of an enthusiastic multitude. He entered the fort of Agra in great state, and the same moment began his auspicious reign. Thomas Herbert has thus noticed the event in his *Travels*:—"With great pomp he

The Emperor Sháh Jahán.

Page 32.

made his intrude into Agra, and forthwith gave orders for his coronation, which accordingly, by a general assembly of the *umras* and nobles of his empire, was performed. Then by a proclamation he assumed the name of Sultán Shahab-ud-dín Muhammad."

Coronation of Shah Jahán at Agra.

Sháh Jahán, on ascending the throne, avenged himself on the Portuguese, who had refused to render him assistance when he was in rebellion against his father, and who had joined the army of Parwez and fought against him. Five or six hundred of them were taken prisoners and sent to Agra. Some were compelled to embrace Muhammadanism ; others suffered death.

Persecution of the Portuguese.

Khán Jahán Lodí, who had been placed in the chief command in the Deccan by the Emperor Jahángír, asserted his independence in Malwa. He returned to obedience after Sháh Jahán's accession to the throne, and was invited to the court, where he was treated with the utmost consideration. His distrust, however, having been excited by some circumstance, he assembled all his troops one night soon after dark, and, placing his women in the centre on elephants, suddenly quitted Agra, accompanied by twelve of his sons, with his kettle-drums beating and escorted by 2,000 of his veteran Afgháns. He proceeded to the Deccan, whither the Emperor marched in person. After many conflicts, Khán Jahán was compelled to fly from the Deccan, but was cut off in Bundelkhand by a Rájput, who struck him through with a pike, 1630 A.D. It was in this expedition that the Emperor lost his favourite wife Arjumand Bano, a niece of Núrjahán, who died in Burhanpur at the end of 1629. The war in the Deccan continued, and the Emperor returned to Agra in 1632, leaving Mahábat Khán in supreme command in the Deccan. Great improvements went on in the palace for some time, and Sháh Jahán now commenced the construction of the mausoleum of his deceased wife on the bank of the Jumná, which was to become the wonder of the Eastern World. In 1639 Sháh Jahán founded new Delhi, to which he gave the name Sháhjahánabad, and the capital was removed there.

Flight of Khan Jahán from Agra, 1628.

Death of Arjumand Bano Begum 1629.

Shah Jahán's return to Agra, 1632.

The capital removed to new Delhi, 1639.

In 1657 the Emperor was seized with a dangerous illness, and, as a temporary measure, Dara Shekoh, his eldest son, was entrusted

The Emperor's illness.

with the administration of the Government. Dara Shekoh was a high-spirited, generous prince, whose religious views were as broad and liberal as those of Akbar. Aurangzeb, having been informed of his father's illness through his sister, Roushan Ara, marched from the Deccan, after concluding a hasty treaty with the King Adíl Sháh of Bíjapur, and left Sultán Moazzam, his second son, in charge of affairs in the Deccan. The Emperor's two sons, Shuja, Viceroy of Bengal, and Murad, Viceroy of Gujrát, asserted their independence in their respective provinces and marched their armies to the capital. Aurangzeb marched to join Murad. Dara marched from Agra to oppose his brothers, and the two armies having met at Samagarh, one march from Agra, in the beginning of June 1658, Dara was totally defeated and fled to Delhi.

Wars among his sons.

The battle of Samagarh, 1658.

Aurangzeb marches to Agra, 1658.

Three days after the battle, Aurangzeb marched to Agra, and encamping before the walls, at once took possession of the city. He interfered in no way with the interior of the palace, his object being to find a favourable opportunity for seizing the person of the old Emperor. Meanwhile a report was assiduously spread by him that Sháh Jahán was dead, and he pretended to believe it in order to have an excuse for entering the citadel. Sháh Jahán, on the other hand, spared no pains to make it known that he was alive. Exasperated at the conduct of his son, the old King sent for Fázil Khán, the grand chamberlain, and asked him to assure Aurangzeb that his father was alive, and that he had no longer any pretence for prolonging his stay at the capital, but should retire forthwith to his kingdom of the Deccan, in which case all that had happened would be forgotten. Aurangzeb, who had his own designs to serve, affected to disbelieve the statement of Fázil Khán, and replied that he was quite convinced that he had become fatherless, and that it was upon that ground that he had fought for the throne, thinking that he had as good a right to it as any of his brothers. If, urged he, the King was alive, well and good; he was his dutiful son, ever ready to obey his commands as an humble suppliant. But in order that he might be convinced that he was alive, he desired to see him and to kiss his feet, after which he would retrace his steps to his kingdom of the Deccan, and implicitly carry out the royal commands,

Strategy of Aurangzeb.

The reply having been conveyed by Fázil Khán to the King, His Majesty at once expressed his approval of his proposed interview; but Aurangzeb, more astute and cunning than his father, assured Fázil Khán that he would not venture into the citadel until the garrison located in it was entirely withdrawn. Sháh Jahán, seeing the reasonableness of the demand, ordered the garrison to withdraw. The garrison accordingly vacated the Fort.

The action of Roushan Ara Begam.

Roushan Ara Begam sent a message from the *harem* to Aurangzeb, warning him of the presence of armed Tartar women, who would seize and murder him if he entered the Fort without a strong guard. Aurangzeb met device by device. He postponed his visit to his father from day to day, on various pretences, pleading at one time that he awaited an auspicious hour for an interview, and at another that he had important State business to transact. Meantime, Aurangzeb won over *amírs* and grandees to his side. His eldest son, Sultán Mahmud, acting under the orders of his father, subjected the palace to a blockade. Sháh Jahán saw this from the towers of his palace. He planted cannon on the ramparts, but these had little effect on the besiegers. Aurangzeb now tried another artifice. He sent his confidential eunuch to Sháh Jahán with a message that the troops had attacked the citadel without his orders, and a request to be allowed to send his son, Mahmúd, to tender his submission and beg forgiveness, adding that he would himself pay his respects to his parent as soon as his health showed some signs of improvement.

Sháh Jahán consented to receive his grandson. Mahmúd gained over the soldiers of the guard, and, entering the fortress, made himself master of the palace without difficulty. Slaughtering everyone who came in his way—soldiers, slaves, eunuchs, women,—he forced his way into the interior of the palace with a strong contingent of troops. He entered the royal chamber of Sháh Jahán. The Tartar women, who surrounded the old king, remained motionless, like statues. Mahmúd then personally announced to Sháh Jahán :—"Your great age, my lord, has rendered you incapable of reigning. Retire with your wives into the palace gardens; pass the remainder of your days in tranquillity. We do not grudge you the right of the day, but you dishonour the throne: you must resign it to your children." *

* Wheeler.

Sháh Jahán a prisoner.

At this demand the Tartar female-guards roused a great shout; but Mahmúd was equal to them, and Sháh Jahán, yielding to circumstances, retired to the inner pavilions with his wives and became a prisoner. Inviting Mahmúd to a second visit, Sháh Jahán offered him the crown and the possession of Agra, provided he cast off his adherence to his father, who, having dethroned his own father, was not likely to spare the son. Mahmúd for a time considered the matter, but resisted the temptation and secured the palace keys from the Emperor. Henceforth Aurangzeb became master of Agra and the citadel. The peace of Agra was not disturbed on the change of sovereigns. Shayasta Khán was appointed new Governor of the place.

His helpless condition.

Sháh Jahán, incensed at the conduct of his son, made some efforts to effect his escape, and slew some of the guards who opposed him. This induced Aurangzeb to subject him to a closer confinement. The gates and entrances were walled up and the ex-king's chamber was placed under strict guard. "It is most surprising," writes the traveller, Tavernier, "that not one of the servants of the grand King offered to assist him; that all his subjects abandoned him, and that they turned their eyes to the rising sun, recognising no one as king but Aurangzeb—Sháh Jahán, although still living, having passed from their memories. If perchance there were any who felt touched by his misfortunes, fear made them silent, and made them basely abandon a king who had governed them like a father and with a mildness which is not common with sovereigns. For although he was severe enough to the nobles when they failed to perform their duties, he arranged all things for the comfort of the people, by whom he was much beloved, but who gave no signs of it at this crisis."

Testimony of Bernier.

The traveller, Bernier, who was at the time (1658 A.D.) in Agra, expresses the same surprise. He writes:—"I can indeed scarcely express my indignation when I reflect that there was not a single movement, nor even a voice heard in behalf of the aged and injured monarch; although the Omeras who bowed the knee to his oppressors were indebted to him for their rank and riches, having been, according to the custom of the court, raised by Sháh Jahán from a state of the lowest indigence, and many of them even redeemed from absolute slavery."

Sháh Jahán, before his death, expressed a wish to see new Delhi, which had not yet reached completion. Aurangzeb, fearing lest the appearance of the aged king on an elephant might cause excitement among the people and raise a party in his favour, consented to the proposal, provided the monarch made his journey to Delhi by boat and returned in the same way to Agra. Sháh Jahán, perceiving the severity of his son, abandoned all idea of a journey to his new city, but was greatly mortified at the insult inflicted on him.

Sháh Jahán's desire to visit new Delhi not fulfilled.

With the exception of the rigour of his confinement, Aurangzeb treated Sháh Jahán with respect in his prison. He even treated with indifference the slights he deliberately showed his son at times. Thus, some days previous to his ascending the throne, Aurangzeb sent word to Sháh Jahán to have the goodness to send him the crown jewels, that he might wear them on the ceremony of his accession. The old king was exasperated at this message and repeatedly called for a pestle and mortar and threatened to grind up all his precious stones and pearls, so that his son might never possess them. Aurangzeb acted with forbearance, and softened the rigour of his father's captivity, by sending him presents from Delhi. According to Bernier, Sháh Jahán subsequently relented, and, of his own accord, sent to Aurangzeb some of the jewels which, he had before told him, hammers were ready to reduce to powder.

Sháh Jahán treated with respect in his prison.

The old King maintained his high tone throughout his imprisonment until death overtook him. Once the Governor of Agra insulted the imperial captive; Sháh Jahán, in return, struck the Governor in the face with a pair of slippers. The Governor ordered the guards to arrest the King; but not a man dared to lay his hands on a sovereign who had been respected like a deity.

Sháh Jahán continued to live in regal state in Agra for seven years, and died in the Fort of Agra, December 1666.

Mullá Muhammad Kázim, author of the *Alamgir Nama*, has given particulars relating to the death of Sháh Jahán. They are interesting, as furnishing information regarding scenes with

Particulars of his death.

which the citadel of Agra is associated. The following are extracts from this work:—

His illness.

"In consequence of protracted illness, the Emperor became very weak. His bodily strength failed, and on this account he was attacked with various complaints, so that the treatment of one proved directly injurious to the other. The best physicians thought his case had become very complicated. His hands and feet trembled through extreme weakness, and medicines were of no avail. At length, in an early hour of the night of Monday, the 28th of Rajab (1666 A.D.), his case having become quite hopeless, the signs of death became visible. His Majesty kept his courage at this time of trial, and struggled bravely with the last enemy. He turned his mind to God, and, in an audible voice, offered thanks to the Almighty for the thousand gifts He had conferred on him. With all sincerity and humility he then prayed forgiveness for the sins he had committed in the world; then, in full possession of his consciousness, he repeated the confession of faith. While he was repeating this, his affectionate daughter, the Málika Jahán Begum (Jahan Ara), and other female members of the family, began to weep. His Majesty admonished them to be content with God's will and resign themselves to His pleasure. He spoke a few consoling words to them, and, immediately after, his soul departed from the body.

His last moments.

His death, 1666.

The funeral ceremonies.

"By command of Málika Jahán Begum, Raad Andáz Khán, the commander of the fort, and Khawja Phúl presented themselves in the *ghuslkhana*. The windows of the gates of the fort were opened, and men were sent to call the most revered Syad Muhammad Kanauji and Kázi Kurbán, the chief Kázi of Akbarábád, to perform the funeral ceremonies. They came two watches before sunrise. Although His Majesty, since he had attained the age of discretion, had never missed a single prayer of the prescribed five times daily prayer, or a single fast of the month of Rámzán, atonement for them was given in a large sum of money, which was set apart for the purpose. The two religious men above named were, by order of Málika Jahán, called to the Samman Burj, where the Emperor had breathed his last. From this place his body was removed to the hall (*ewan*) close by, where it was washed according to the form prescribed by the Muhammadan law. The body having then been enclosed in a coffin, holy passages were read over it. Finally, the body was placed in a chest or receptacle of sandal-wood, and the coffin, followed by a procession of mourners, was conveyed out of the fort through the low gate *(darwázá nasheb)* of the said tower, which used to remain closed, but was opened for the occasion. The procession then passing through Sher Hájí gate opposite the low gate, the coffin was brought out of the fort enclosure. Hoshdar Khán, Viceroy of Agra, accompanied by officers of state, reached the bank of the river at day-break, and the coffin, having been conveyed across the river, was interred with due formalities, by the side of the tomb of Mumtaz Zamáni, in the mausoleum built in her honor by the deceased Emperor, who was now following her to the grave. The prayers over the coffin before its interment were read by his holiness Syad Muhammad, Kázi Kurbán, and other learned and pious men."

The funeral procession.

The burial.

Sháh Jahán had lived seventy-six years and reigned for thirty-one.

His age.

At the time of the Emperor's death, Prince Muhammad Moazzam (afterwards the Emperor Sháh Alam, Bahadur Sháh), the eldest son of Aurangzeb, and the heir-apparent, was encamped at a distance of seven *kos* from Agra. The intelligence of the Emperor's demise having reached him the same night, he arrived in the city the next day, and on the third day went to the fort and offered condolence to the Begum Sahib, his aunt, and the other female members of the royal family. "On that day, under orders of the Prince, the whole *Kurán* was read by the pious and learned men, and holy passages were recited. A meeting to celebrate the birth-day of the Prophet was held on a truly royal scale, and large sums of money were distributed among the poor and needy as alms."*

Arrival of Prince Moazzam at Agra.

Aurangzeb was at Delhi when his father died. On hearing of his death, he could not refrain from shedding tears. Mullá Muhammad Kázim writes:—"Although His Majesty possesses a strong mind and a resolute and inflexible temper, he wept so bitterly on hearing the intelligence of his royal father's death, that the courtiers and nobles, who were present, were shocked."

---

* *Alamgirnámá.*

The mourning.

His Majesty and the Princes Royal and the ladies of the *harem* put on white clothes, and the whole court went into mourning. The Emperor-elect said to his nobles:—"It was my desire to be present at the last moments of my father, to have a last look at his face, take part in his burial ceremonies, and thus to obtain his benedictions; but, unfortunately, none of these desires have been fulfilled. I shall now proceed to Akbarábád at once, and pay respects to the tomb of my father, and offer condolence to my sister and other members of the royal family in that capital city."

Aurangzeb proceeds to Agra.

The royal camp accordingly moved to *Mustakirul Khiláfat** (Agra). The new Emperor, marching by stages, reached Agra on the sixth day. It was decided that, before entering the fort, the Emperor, on this occasion of mourning, should put up temporarily in the house of Dara Shekoh (styled throughout by the historians of Alamgír as Dara '*Be Shekoh*,' meaning Dara, 'without dignity,' in contradistinction to '*Shekoh*' meaning 'dignity').† A few miles from the city, His Majesty was received by Hoshdar Khán, Viceroy of Agra, and other notables and officers of the metropolitan city. From the village of Bahádarpur, His Majesty, with the royal party, came by boats to Agra, and, as previously arranged, put up in the house of Dara Shekoh. The following day he paid his respects to the tombs of his parents and read the *fateha*, or prayers for the benefit of their souls. He shed again tears of grief at the sight of the tombs of his parents. Having then distributed twelve thousand rupees as alms among the servants and attendants of the mausoleum, he read the afternoon prayers in the mosque of the mausoleum. The following day he entered the fort and offered his condolence to the Begum Sahib and other members of the *harem*, and spoke to them words of consolation and kindness. The Begum Sahib on this occasion presented her brother with a large golden basin full of jewels. He then caused the female members of the family to put aside their mourning and bestowed on them rich dresses, in accordance

Visits the tombs of his parents.

* In the Persian histories of the time of Sháh Jahán and Aurangzeb, Agra is called *Mustakirul Khilafát*; Delhi, *Darul Khilafat*; Lahore, *Darul Saltanat*; and Multan, *Darul Aman*.

† Aurangzeb generally disregarded good or bad omens, and was very scrupulous, but it seems that he was led away by superstition in regard to his first entry as a monarch into the fort of Agra.

The Emperor Aurangzeb

Page 40.

with their position and dignity. Two watches after sunrise, he returned to the city. Two days afterwards His Majesty went again to the fort, on a visit to the Begum Sahib, and, at his instance, all the nobles of the Empire and officers of state offered their salutations to her and presented *nazars*, or offerings, in money. The Princess was pleased to confer on them *khilats*, or dresses of honor, according to the rank and dignity of each. A few days after the new King again paid her a visit, and the Princess performed the ceremonies of *nissár*, namely, she offered money by way of sacrifice for His Majesty's welfare. His Majesty went daily to the mausoleum, and read the *fateha*. Twice he held there the meetings of *maulúd*, or the celebration of the birth of Muhammad, when thousands of rupees were distributed to religious people and the poor.

Visit to the Begum Sahib' who is treated with every mark of considera- tion.

It being considered advisable that His Majesty should prolong his stay in Mustakirul Khiláfat (Agra), he sent for the members of his family from the Darul Khiláfat (Sháh Jahánábád), and accordingly Abdul Nabi Khán, Mukhalis Khán, and Khizmat Khán, the head eunuchs, were sent to the latter place, with a large party, to conduct the *Begums* and ladies of the *zanána* to Agra on elephants. As the *Id* festival of Rámzán was approaching, it was further ordered that the Peacock Throne be brought to Agra, together with all the articles of decoration and embellishment used on festival occasions.

The *Id* festi- val at Agra.

On the *Id* festival His Majesty proceeded on an elephant, surmounted by a golden *howda*, to offer prayers at the grand mosque. Returning before noon, he held a grand reception in the hall of public audience and made his appearance with all the pomp and magnificence of an Emperor, taking his seat for the first time on the celebrated Peacock Throne of Sháh Jahán, which he had won with such disrepute. Muhammad Kazim, the historian of Alamgir, is here profuse in his panegyric of the King, who bestowed honours and rewards on the grandees and nobles with the true generosity of a King. A meeting was then convened in the *ghuslkhana* and the business of state transacted in the presence of the officers and nobles assembled there. The rejoicings in honour of the first *Id* festival continued for three days. His Majesty was on this

Grand durbar held at Agra.

Presents to the members of the royal household.

occasion, pleased to bestow one lakh of gold mohurs on the Begum Sahib, and made an addition of five lakhs of rupees to her annual allowance of twelve lakhs. One lakh of rupees was bestowed on each of her two younger sisters, Parhez Bano Begum and Gowher Ara Begum. Prince Muhammad Moazzam received two lakhs of rupees and a special dress of honour, with armlet and bracelets set with precious jewels, and an addition of 2,000 horse to his rank of 15,000 foot and 12,000 horse; and Prince Muhammad Azim, a dress, an aigrette and a dagger set with diamonds, with an addition of 2,000 horse to his rank of 12,000 foot and 7,000 horse. Then follows a long list of grandees (Muhammadans and Hindus), Rájás, and Nawábs who were presented with dresses and an increase of *Mansab*, or rank. In the fifth year of the reign, the State treasures had been removed from Agra to Delhi, but at this period—namely, the ninth year of the reign—it was ordered that the treasure be again conveyed to Agra. Námdár Khán, having been presented with a horse and jewelled trappings, was entrusted with this duty, and the treasure was brought from Delhi to Agra on 1,400 *irabas*, or carriages drawn by bullocks, and safely deposited in the fort.

Agra visited by Wandelslo, 1638-40.

Agra was visited in 1638 by Wandelslo, a page to the Duke of Holstein, who had travelled in Persia in the retinue of an embassy which the Duke had sent to the Sháh. He describes it as a beautiful city, at least twice as large as Ispahán (then in its greatest glory). It was the favourite residence of Sháh Jahán; all the nations of the East carried on trade in Agra; and the streets were broad and lined with fine shops. There were eighty *caravanserais* for travellers, each being in charge of a superintendent. The traveller has left graphic accounts of the bázár, the darbár court, the *ghuslkhána*, the *mahal* (or *harem*) and the *jharoka*. Wandelslo left India in 1840, and, after he left Agra, Sháh Jahán fixed his capital at New Delhi.

And by Francis Bernier, 1655-67.

Francis Bernier, with more political insight, was in India for twelve years (1655-67), and he has given a description of Agra in his travels very similar to that given by Wandelslo.

The chief buildings of Sháh Jahán in Agra are the *Shish Mahál*, or Palace of Mirrors, in the palace; the *Motí Masjid*, or Pearl Mosque; and the famous *Taj Mahál.* Chief buildings of Sháh Jahán.

Elphinstone has written in high terms of the great prosperity of India under Sháh Jahán, who in point of munificence has been compared with the Roman Emperor Severus, whose magnificence is immortalized in the pages of Gibbon. Notwithstanding his pre-occupation with foreign wars, his love of ease and pleasure, his magnificence, his construction of celebrated edifices and works which cost crores of rupees, his finances suffered no embarrassments, and he left large accumulations of coin, bullion and jewels. According to Tavernier, Sháh Jahán "reigned not so much as a King over his subjects, but rather as father over his family and children." The foundation of so splendid a capital as New Delhi affords evidence of great private as well as public wealth. High prosperity of India under Sháh Jahán.

With the dethronement and imprisonment of Sháh Jahán ended the palmy days of Agra. Aurangzeb resided for some little time there; but it soon became a second-class city, the residence of a provincial Governor, who proved too weak to keep in check the neighbouring turbulent Ját tribes. The Emperor grew old in the distant province of the Deccan, and, although his spirit of perseverance, indefatigable industry, and attention to the minutest details, kept together the component parts of the Empire, the spirit of intolerance which he displayed throughout his life, the inequality of his treatment of the various classes of his subjects, and the offence he gave to a great section of the community in India, helped to undermine the throne of Timúr and ended in the final dissolution of the Mughal sovereignty of India. Aurangzeb. 1658-1707.

The Sisters Jahán Ara and Roushan Ara.

Not the least significant personages who figured prominently in the Mughal history of the time of Sháh Jahán were his two daughters, Jahán Ara Begum and Roushan Ara Begum. Jahán Ara, or the Begum Sahib, as she was called, was the second child of Sháh Jahán by his most affectionate consort, Mumtaz-uz-zamáni, commonly known as the Taj Mahal. Her Jahan Ara. Her unbounded influence over Sháh Jahán.

unbounded influence over the Emperor and her ascendancy in the court have already been referred to. According to Bernier, she was very handsome, of lively parts, and passionately beloved by her father. He reposed the most implicit confidence in his favourite child; she watched carefully over the safety of her royal father and was so scrupulous about it that no dish was allowed to appear on the royal table that had not been prepared under her eyes. She regulated the humours of her father, and the most weighty concerns of State were settled through her. She drew large allowances from the Imperial treasury and received the most valuable gifts from the amírs, whose affairs were confided to her charge, and was thus enabled to amass a great fortune.

Espouses the cause of Dara.

She espoused the cause of her brother, Dara, and promoted his interests in court, while his younger sister, Roushan Ara, supported the party of Aurangzeb. Dara, finding in Jahán Ara a valuable coadjutor, had, according to Bernier, promised her that, on his accession to the throne, he would grant her permission to marry.

"This pledge," says the traveller, "was a remarkable one, the marriage of a Princess being of rare occurrence in Hindustán, no man being considered worthy of royal alliance; and an apprehension being entertained that the husband might thereby be rendered powerful, and induced, perhaps, to aspire to the crown."

Roushan Ara.

Roushan Ara was less beautiful than her elder sister, and less remarkable for wit and intelligence; nevertheless, she possessed sprightliness of temper, was not deficient in cunning, and she conveyed, by means of spies, intelligence of the doings at court to Aurangzeb, which was of such importance and value that it enabled the crafty Prince not only to escape the snare which his father is reported to have spread for him in Agra, but tended materially to pave his way to the throne.

Supports the party of Aurangzeb.

The battle of Samagarh. Aurangzeb dupes Murád.

The battle of Samagarh, nine miles east of Agra, resulted in the discomfiture of Dara Shekoh by the combined forces of Aurangzeb and Murád Bakhsh. Aurangzeb duped Murád by concealing his own ambitious designs of sovereignty in the garb of disinterestedness, saying;—"I am a *fakír* of the threshhold of

God. I live as a *fakír*, and my highest ambition is to die as a *fakír*. The kingdom and country is Murád's." Turning to Khalilulla Khán, he said that Murád Baksh alone was fitted to wear the crown, and that it was due to his skill and valour that the victory over Dara was gained, he having only acted as his lieutenant. Three or four days after the victory, Aurangzeb and Murád presented themselves before the gate of Agra and put up in a garden about a league distant from the palace. A confidential eunuch of Aurangzeb was then despatched to the old King, who was saluted in the name of his master and assured of the royal son's undiminished respect and affection for his august parents, deep regret being expressed at recent events, which were attributed to the sinister designs of Dara, and an assurance given that the Princes had come to Agra to receive and execute the King's commands.

Sháh Jahán affected to express his unqualified approval of his son's conduct, and sent a trustworthy eunuch, who, in behalf of his master, explained to Aurangzeb how sensible the King was of Dara's improper conduct and incapacity, and reminded the Prince with what affection and tenderness he regarded him. He was therefore invited to visit his loving parent in order that arrangements for the future conduct of affairs might be concluded. Sháh Jahán was trying by artifice and dissimulation to entrap Aurangzeb, little thinking that his dutiful son surpassed all men in both. Aurangzeb had been apprised by his sister, Roushan Ara, of the presence in the fort of a large number of strong and robust Tartar women who acted as female guards in the seraglio; and who would fall on him with arms as soon as he entered the palace.

Sháh Jahán and Aurangzeb try to ensnare each other.

The conduct of Roushan Ara.

He knew full well that the Begum Sahib would not quit the King, day or night, and that he was entirely under her influence. He knew, from the information supplied by Roushan Ara, how strongly Sháh Jahán was attached to Dara. She had informed him that, after the discomfiture of Dara, the King had sent him two elephants laden with gold mohurs, and this furnished him with the means to collect new armies and prolong the war. He doubted very much the sincerity of the old King's professions, though he considered it impolitic to disclose his mind to him. The Prince thanked his father for all the favours he had been pleased to shower on him, but would not venture within the walls of the citadel, and, though he fixed the day for obeying the monarch's summons, he, day by day, deferred his visit. Matters went on in this fashion for several days, when at last the resolution and skill of Sultán Mahmud, son of Aurangzeb, drove the old lion into a cage. This intrepid young man, having previously posted a number of armed men in the vicinity of the palace, entered it on the pretence of taking a message to the King. The armed retainers immediately followed, and, falling suddenly on the guards, who were unprepared for an encounter, expelled them. Thus in a few minutes the Prince made himself master of the fort. "If ever man was astonished," says Bernier, "that man was Sháh Jahán when he perceived that he had fallen into the trap he had prepared for others, and that he himself was a prisoner." In vain did the old King send a messenger to his grandson, entreating him to liberate him, and swearing on his crown and the *Kurán* to acknowledge him as King if he served him loyally. The young Prince, actuated by a sense of duty to his father, disregarded these offers, and even refused to enter the King's apartments. He asked the King for the key of every gate in the fort, in order that Aurangzeb might come with a perfectly settled mind "to kiss the King's feet." The old King, seeing that his own men were deserting him, delivered up the keys with much hesitation after two days. Aurangzeb appointed his trustworthy eunuch, Itibár Khán, Governor of the fort, and placed Sháh Jahán and the Begum Sahib in close confinement. Many of the gates of the fort were walled up and communication between the King and his friends was effectually stopped. His confinement was so rigid that the King was not permitted to leave his apartment without the permission of the Governor.

The resolution of Sultán Mahmúd, son of Aurangzeb.

He makes himself master of the fort.

Sháh Jahán a prisoner.

Roushan Ara wreaks her vengeance on Dara.

The deep-rooted animosity which Roushan Ara bore towards her brother, Dara Shekoh, rankled in her heart when the latter had been reduced to the condition of a helpless prisoner in the hands of his hypocritical brother Aurangzeb. When a second council of the *ulemas* was convened in Delhi, to discuss the question whether

Dara should be sent to Gwalior to be confined in the fortress there, agreeably to the original plan, or executed without further delay, Roushan Ara betrayed her enmity towards him by joining Dánishmand Khán, Khalilulla Khán, and Shaesta Khan in proposing the extreme penalty of the law, which was ultimately carried out. He is executed.

After Aurangzeb had firmly established himself on the throne of India, his sister Roushan Ara Begum exercised privileges and powers very much the same as had been exercised by her elder sister, Jahán Ara, during the reign of Sháh Jahán. She had laboured hard for Aurangzeb during his father's reign, and it was in fact mainly due to her help that he ascended the throne. She became now the sole mistress of the seraglio. She was allowed an extensive establishment, and like her elder sister in the days of Sháh Jahán's reign, drew enormous allowances from the State. Her retinue and equipage were immense, and she enjoyed all the privileges of a queen of the first rank. Her power quite cast into the shade the influence of the first Sultáná, a Rajput Princess, the mother of the heir-apparent, Sháh Alam. The traveller Bernier has furnished a graphic description of Roushan Ara's state procession. She came out in state in a litter gilt and covered with magnificent silk nets of diversified colours, encircled with embroidery, fringes and rich tassels. This elegant litter, which was open, was suspended between two beautiful camels, or between two small elephants. In front of the litter walked a young, well-dressed female slave, with a *chauri* of peacock feathers in her hand, with which she kept off the flies from the Princess. Of the Princess's journey on elephants, Bernier observes:—" Stretch imagination to its utmost limits, and you can conceive no exhibition more grand and imposing than when Roushan Ara Begum, mounted on a stupendous Pegu elephant, and seated in a *howdah* blazing with gold and azure, is followed by five or six other elephants with *howdahs* nearly as resplendent as her own, and filled with ladies attached to her household." The elephant of the Princess was surrounded by a troop of female armed retainers, Tartars and Kashmirians, fantastically attired and riding handsome pad-horses. Between these and the Princess, rode the chief eunuchs richly dressed. Then came footmen and lackeys, with large canes, bearing ensigns

The ascendancy of Roushan Ara.

Her equipage and state.

of royalty in their hands. These travelled a long way before the Empress, right and left of the road. The principal lady of the court, mounted and attended in very much the same style as the Princess, immediately followed the equipage of Roushan Ara. This was followed by the elephant of the third lady, and that by a fourth, and so on until fifteen or sixteen elephants, with ladies of rank, passed, each having a retinue proportionate to her rank and office. Sixty or more elephants passed in state and royalty with brilliant and numerous followers, and the spectacle was so grand and imposing that, according to Bernier, if he "had not regarded this display of magnificence with a sort of philosophical indifference, he would have been apt to be carried away by such flights of imagination as inspire most Indian poets when they represent the elephants as conveying so many goddesses concealed from the vulgar gaze."

Serious illness of Aurangzeb, 1664.

In the year 1664, the health of Aurangzeb seriously broke down. He sank into a state of debility, which made him unconscious for hours of all that was going on. Roushan Ara was in sole charge of his chamber, which was guarded by Tartar women, armed with swords and bows. The strictest secrecy was observed as to the state of the Emperor's health, and not even the ladies of the seraglio knew whether His Majesty was alive or dead. At this moment, when the King's life was in peril, Roushan Ara thought of plans of self-aggrandisement, in the event of His Majesty's death. She resolved to set aside the King's eldest son, Sháh Alam, by his first wife, a Rajput Princess, then in his nineteenth year, and to place on the throne his younger brother, Azum Sháh, then a boy of six, by a Mahomedan Sultáná. She contrived to withdraw the Emperor's signet ring from his hand and issued letters under this seal to various Rájás, Viceroys and Governors in favour of Azum Sháh. Her policy was to act as regent during the long minority of her ward, and thus to secure the throne for herself, to the exclusion of the rightful heir.

Roushan Ara's plans of self-aggrandisement.

Action of the Rájput Sultáná.

The ladies of the seraglio feeling suspicious of what was going on, the first Sultáná heavily bribed the female guards over the doors, and they allowed her admittance into the sick man's room. The Rájput Princess saw her royal husband lying unconscious, and unable to recognise her. Meanwhile Roushan Ara, having observed the intruder, gave her a beating so severe that her face was torn and she was forced to quit the room.* This was a great insult to a Rájputáni Princess, the wife of the youth of Aurangzeb, who, as the first lady in the *harem*, possessed enormous influence. She was so much dreaded that she burnt incense before her idols in the palace, and her husband, who was known to be a strict Muhammadan, never interfered with her religious observances. She informed Sháh Alam of the treatment she had received at the hands of her aunt, and he adopted measures for defeating the latter's plans. Sanguine hopes were entertained at Agra that Aurangzeb might die, and Sháh Jahán, still in captivity, be restored to the throne of his ancestors; but such was the dread of Aurangzeb that there was no attempt even at an outbreak.

Recovery of Aurangzeb.

Aurangzeb recovered and gave public audience at Delhi. Admittance was given to the meanest of his subjects in the public hall, and the joy and gratification of the people at seeing their King seated on the throne passed all bounds. He asked his sister about his missing signet ring, and was not satisfied with he explanation. She had become very unpopular with the seraglio, and the ears of Aurangzeb were filled by the ladies and the eunuchs with all sorts of stories about her intrigues and ambitious designs. The emperor was greatly incensed at the slight put by Roushan Ara on his first Queen. To console the Sultáná, he conferred on her new titles and honours and eulogised her patience under adverse circumstances. Roushan Ara, feeling herself mortified, intimated her desire to leave the palace and live in the town; but her request was refused, on the ground that she supervised the tuition of the King's younger daughters.

The fall of Roushan Ara.

Meanwhile the Emperor's own daughters had grown up, and a spirit of rivalry was created between them and their aunt Roushan Ara. According to Catron, Zebulnissa, the eldest daughter, was a more ambitious Princess. She had once proved a valuable auxiliary to her aunt, sharing in her gallantries, but she now quarrelled with, and sought to supplant, her. She

Zebulnissa Begum, the daughter of Aurangzeb.

* Wheeler, through Manouchi.

supplied her father with information about her aunt's irregularities, and Roushan Ara soon disappeared for ever from the scene. It was said she was removed by poison. This was before the Emperor left for Kashmir.

Roushan Ara removed by poison.

ZEBULNISSA BEGUM.

Birth of Zebulnissa, 1639.

Zebulnissa Begum, better known by her poetical name *Mukhfi* (Concealed), now took her aunt's place in the *harem*. She was born of a Muhammadan Princess on 5th February 1639. The Emperor devoted personal attention to her studies, and she soon became a learned and accomplished lady. At an early age she committed the *Kuran* to memory, and for this meritorious act was rewarded by His Majesty with 30,000 gold mohurs. She was well versed in Arabic and Persian, and was skilled in various modes of writing, such as *Nastalik*,* *Naskh*† and *Shikasta*,‡ and composed excellent prose and poetry. She was also the author of some books. Her library was most extensive, containing several thousands of volumes on religious and literary subjects. She had in her employ a large staff of learned men, poets, authors, pious men, and men versed in caligraphy. Mullá Safi-ud-din Arzbegi stayed under her orders in Kashmir, and wrote the translation of *Tafsír-i-Kabir*, which was, after her name, called *Zebul Tafasir*. Numerous other compilations and original works were dedicated to her. Zebulnissa exercised an ascendancy in the court and over her imperial father, that was felt and known. She was thoroughly proficient in Arabic and Persian, and, by her sagacity and wisdom, made herself complete master of the court politics. According to Manouchi, "she was worshipped as the dominant star of the Mughals." She was now (1664 A.D.) twenty-five years of age. The Emperor was still far from well. Zebulnissa advised him to travel to Kashmir for the benefit of his health; his physicians also recommended a change to that place. The Princess urged the matter from considerations of self-aggrandisement. She was anxious to show the world her superior position in the court and was envious to appear, in her turn, amid a pompous and magnificent equipage, as her aunt had done before her. Aurangzeb was most reluctant to move to Kashmir as long as his

Her literary accomplishments.

Her vast influence at court.

---

* A fine round hand.
† The Arabic character.
‡ A running hand.

father was alive in Agra. On the other hand, it was feared that the approaching heat of summer would be injurious to his health, and a relapse of his disease was apprehended. Thus, to stay at Delhi was to risk his life; to march to Kashmir was to risk his empire. A parricide was contemplated. The Emperor consulted his daughter on the subject. Zebulnissa allayed her father's fears, and dissuaded him from committing the crime he had contemplated. The old monarch was now in his seventy-fifth year, and she begged her father to let him pass the few remaining days of his life in peace.

Notwithstanding the admonition of Zebulnissa, grave suspicion rests upon Aurangzeb of having carried out the contemplated parricide. A European physician, whose name is not known, was sent for to treat the aged monarch, and his death was announced soon afterwards. Zebulnissa congratulated her father on the event.

Aurangzeb suspected of committing parricide.

Aurangzeb, with his mind now at rest, consulted his astrologers as to the propitious hour for his departure from Delhi to Kashmir, and, the time having been fixed, the king left the city on 6th December, at three o'clock in the afternoon. He was this time, according to Bernier, attended by 35,000 cavalry 'which at all times accompanied his bodyguard,' and by more than 10,000 infantry, besides 70 pieces of heavy artillery, mostly of brass. His daughter, Zebulnissa, accompanied him in state. Her death occurred in the year 1113 Hijri (1701 A.D.) or six years before that of her father.

Trip to Kashmir.

Death of Zebulnissa, 1701.

According to Elphinstone, the Játs inhabiting the neighbourhood of Agra and Mathura caused much embarrassment during the latter part of Aurangzeb's reign. A well-organised force, commanded by a prince of the blood, was sent against them and the disturbance quelled.

Insurrection of the Játs.

Aurangzeb died in 1707. The principal buildings of his reign are the hall of public audience in the fort, of which the date given is 1684, and the beautiful marble screen enclosing the tombs of Mumtaz Mahal and Shah Jahan, contributed by him to the Taj Mahal, which is evidence of the last respect paid by him to his parents.

Death of Aurangzeb, 1707.

Principal buildings of Aurangzeb's time.

Shah Alam Bahadur Shah, 1707-12.

On the death of Aurangzeb, when a struggle for the sovereignty arose between his eldest son, Prince Moazzam, and his brother Prince Azím, Agra occupied a prominent place in the conflict. The brothers assembled large armies in its neighbourhood to assert their pretensions. The forces of Moazzam concentrated near Agra. He was joined by the Ját chief, Churaman. Azím Shah advanced from the Deccan at the head of a large army. A bloody battle was fought not far to the south of Agra, in which Azím Shah, with his two grown-up sons, was killed, and the youngest son, a minor, was taken prisoner. Mukhtiar Khan, Governor of Agra, who had taken the side of his father-in-law, Azím Shah, was taken prisoner. Moazzam proclaimed himself Emperor under the name of Shah Alam Bahadur Shah. The victory was commemorated by the construction of a mosque and hostel in Jajan.*

Battle of Jajan, 1712.

Accession of Jahandar Shah, 1712.

On the death of Bahadur Shah, the usual struggle for empire ensued among his sons. Azímushán, the second son of the deceased Emperor, was defeated and put to death by the eldest son, Jahandar Shah, who, succeeding to the throne, appointed Zulfikár Khan, who had been mainly instrumental in securing the victory, to be his *wazír*.

Battle of Kuchbehari, near Agra, 1712.

Fírokhsere, son of Azímushán, who was in Bengal at the time of Bahádur Shah's death, assembled an army at Allahabad to give battle to his uncle. He was aided in his project by Syed Husein Ali, Governor of Behar, an old adherent of his father, and his brother, Syed Abdullah, Governor of Allahábád. The neighbourhood of Agra was again the scene of a great struggle for sovereignty. Fírokhsere advanced at the head of a large army, and was met near the city by Jahandar Sháh and his *wazír*, Zulfikár Khán, with an army of 70,000 men. The battle was fiercely contested, and Jahandar Shah was defeated and put to flight. The vanquished King fled in disguise to Delhi, but, with his *wazír*, was put to death. The site of the battle was Kuchbehári, identified with Bichpuri, near Agra, on the high road to Delhi.†

---

* The place of battle, according to *Serul Muta-akhirin*, is "Ajaju, close to Akbarabad."

† *Serul Muta-akhirin*, Chap. I.

Fírokhsere was still on the field of battle, when he resolved at once to assume the crown. Accordingly, on 1st January, 1713, he ascended the throne at daybreak and gave public audience.* Fírokhsere succeeds, 1713.

Churaman Jat, a powerful *zamindar* in the neighbourhood of Agra, belonged to a family which had risen to importance during the time of the previous emperors. The family had attained so much ascendancy that it had been necessary to despatch royal troops to punish the conduct of Churaman's ancestors. Churaman becoming troublesome again, the Emperor, in September, 1717, appointed Rájá Jai Singh *Sewai* of Jeypur, to punish him. The Rájá was on this occasion presented by the Emperor with an elephant, a suit of jewels and several lakhs of rupees, and promoted to a higher military rank. Syed Khán Jahán, brother of the *wazír* Syad Abdulla, was also despatched to the Rájá's assistance with a large body of troops. The fort of the Játs was laid under siege for a whole year. At length the refractory chieftain made his submission through the *wazír* Abdulla, and repaired to Delhi to offer his personal submission to the Emperor. Churaman Ját, 1717.

Fírokhsere occasionally resided in the palace of Agra. He was dethroned and put to death in 1719, and was succeeded by Rafí-ud-dara-jat and Rafi-ud-daula, nominal Kings, set up by the Syad brothers, who each reigned a few months and died. During the reign of the latter, Nikosere, son of Prince Akbar, youngest son of Aurangzeb, whose sister had been married to Rafi-úl-kadr (or Rafí-ud-daula), having been taken out of his prison in the citadel of Agra, was proclaimed Emperor by the Governor and officers of that place, as well as by the militia of the villages subordinate to the fortress. His accession was announced by salvoes of artillery, and coins of gold and silver were struck in his name.† The Prince was also supported by the inhabitants of the city of Agra, who, on seeing the convulsions that shook the empire, gladly embraced his cause. The Syad brothers, who had caused the downfall of Fírokhsere, and who were now acknowledged as the king-makers, were much alarmed when the news of the accession Fírokhsere deposed and put to death, 1719. Nikosere proclaimed Emperor at Agra, 1720.

* *Serul Muta-akhirin*, Chap. 1.

† Muntakhibul Tárikh of Kháfi Khán.

The Syad brothers with the young Emperor march to Agra.

of Nikosere reached the court at Delhi. *Amír-ul-Umra* Syad Husein Alí Khán sent Haidar Kulí Khán, with a force in advance, against Agra, and on the 7th *Shaban* he himself marched to that city, with an army of about 25,000 men. Nikosere was at this time joined by Rájá Dhiráj Jai Singh, with a contingent of 10,000 horse, and Rájá Chabila Ram. Towards the end of *Shaban*, Kutbul Mulk Syad Abdulla, taking with him the young Emperor Rafí-ud-daula, marched from Delhi to Agra with Maharaja Ajit Singh and other *amirs* and an army of upwards of 30,000 horse. The fort of Agra was besieged, lines of approach were formed, and batteries were raised. A heavy cannonade was opened, and many houses, both inside and outside the fort, were destroyed. The siege lasted three months. At length, the provisions in the fort falling short, the defenders were put to great straits. A proposal to surrender was accepted and an assurance of safety to life and honour was given. The keys were given up and possession of the fort was secured. Nikosere and his principal adherents were made prisoners. Mitr Sen, the author of the revolt, killed himself with a dagger.

Siege of the fort.

Nikosere taken prisoner.

Treasures and rarities found in the fort of Agra.

After the fall of the fortress, *Amir-ul-Umra* Husein Ali Khan, having entered it, took possession of all the treasures, jewels, and valuables which had been deposited there for three centuries, and which successive Emperors, from the time of Sakandar Lodi, had accumulated. "There were the effects of Nur Jahan Begum and Mumtaz Mahal, amounting in value, according to various reports, to two or three *crores* of rupees. There was, in particular, the sheet of pearls which Sháh Jahan had caused to be made for the tomb of Mumtaz Mahal, of the value of several *lakhs* of rupees, which was spread over it on the anniversary and on Friday nights. There was the ewer of Nur Jahán and her cushion of woven gold and rich pearls with a border of valuable garnets and emeralds." * The elder brother, Abdulla Khan, got nothing of this spoil, till after four months, when twenty-one *lakhs* of rupees were grudgingly given to him. The quarrel between the brothers about the treasures of the Agra fort was settled through the intervention of Ratan Chand, Dewan of Husein Ali Khan.†

Sheet of pearls for covering the tomb of the Táj.

Ewer of Nur Jahán.

Her cushion of woven gold.

---

* Kháfi Khán. † Elliot.

On the death of Rafi-ud-daula, the Syad brothers raised Roushan Akhtar, son of Khujista Akhtar, commonly called Jahán Shah, one of the sons of Bahádur Shah, to the throne. The young Prince was then in his eighteenth year, and from the time of the accession of his uncle Jahandar Shah he had lived in obscurity in the castle of Salemgarh, Delhi. The ceremony of installation took place at Fatehpur. The new Emperor assumed the title of Abul Fath Násir-ud-din Muhammad Sháh. The seat of Government was removed to Agra, where the Emperor remained for two years. Distrust between the Emperor and the Syad brothers soon arose. Chin Kilich Khan, surnamed Asaf Jah (whose descendants are known as the Nizams of the Deccan), who had been brought up at the austere Court of Aurangzeb, defied the authority of the Syads, and assumed independence in the Deccan. He was now advancing in the direction of Burhanpur. After much hesitation, the brothers quitted Agra, but their troops under Diláwar Ali Khán, who commanded the Wazir's army, were defeated. The report of this defeat, having reached Agra, afforded secret but sincere satisfaction to the Emperor and to all those who professed attachment to him, but it caused no small degree of consternation to the two brothers.* Husein Alí Khán was, about this time (October, 1720), assassinated by a hired ruffian. The surviving brother, Abdullá, despatched two noblemen of consequence to Delhi to raise one of the princes of the house of Timur to the throne. Accordingly, Prince Ibrahim, son of Rafi-ul-Kadr, grandson of Bahádur Sháh, was placed on the throne, under the title of Abul Fath Zahír-ud-din Muhammad Ibrahim. Abdullá Khán, arriving two days after, paid his homage to the new King. He conferred new dignities and offices in his name, and began to assemble an army to support him. He was joined by Churaman, Rájá of the Játs, and by many of his deceased brother Husèin Alí Khán's soldiers, who deserted the Emperor. Muhammad Sháh was, on the other hand, reinforced by 4,000 horse from Rájá Jai Singh Sewaí and by contingents furnished by some Rohillá Chiefs. An army for the defence of the Empire was organized at Agra. The two armies met between Agra and Delhi. Abdullá Khán

Muhammad Sháh ascends the throne, 1719.

Seat of government removed to Agra.

Distrust between the Emperor and the Syad brothers.

Assassination of Husein Ali Khan, 1720.

A new Emperor set up.

Abdulla Khan assembles an army.

* *Sairul Muta-akharin.*

Is defeated, December, 1720.

was defeated and taken prisoner. His life was spared, probably out of respect for his sacred lineage. Muhammad Sháh, after this victory, proceeded to Delhi, and the seat of government was removed there.

Asaf Jah becomes Prime Minister.

After the above victory, Asaf Jah was appointed *Wazir;* but a breach soon afterwards occurred between him and the Emperor, and the Mughal monarchy exhibited signs of rapid decay.

Saadat Khan appointed first Governor of Agra, 1722.

Sáadat Khán, surnamed *Barhan-ul Mulk* (whose descendants subsequently became the Nawábs of Oudh), was appointed the first Viceroy of Agra, in addition to his government of Oudh. Desirous of visiting his former government, he left for Lucknow in 1722, leaving as his deputy at Agra one Rai Nilkanth Nagar, a man of ability. This deputy had some difference with a neighbouring Ját zamíndár. One day, followed by a gorgeous retinue, he had gone out on an elephant for the sake of recreation when a Ját, who had taken his seat on a lofty tree and was watching his opportunity, levelled his piece leisurely at Rai Nilkanth in the midst of his numerous retinue and killed him at the first shot. The culprit, having accomplished his end, found means to effect his escape. The news of the outrage having reached the court, Raja Jai Singh Sewaí, of Jeypur, the old enemy of the Játs, having been appointed Governor of Agra, was sent thither with instructions to revenge the murder of the Deputy Governor.

Murder of the Deputy Governor of Agra, 1722.

Raja Jai Singh succeeds Saadat Khan as Governor of Agra

Punishment of the Jats.

Rájá Jai Singh marched against Churaman, the leader of the Játs, and laid sieze to his fortress of Tún. By a dexterous arrangement, he caused a dissension among the Chief's relations of the blood, and secured the co-operation of Badar Singh, his nephew, who joined him in the attack on the fortress. Mohkam Singh, son of Churaman, had a quarrel with his father and rebuked him in open darbár. This mortified the old Chief to such a degree that he swallowed poison and died. Mohkam Singh gave way to the superior power and talents of Rájá Jai Singh, who appointed Badar Singh to the zemindari of the late Chief and got the appointment confirmed by the court.*

Death of Churaman, Jat.

* Sairul Muta-akharin.

In 1736 the Maratha horse, under Mulhar Rao Holkar, penetrated as far as Agra. Bájí Rao, son of Balájí Wiswa Náth, the ablest of the Peshwás, except Sivají, carried on his incursions and ravages in the country beyond the Jumna. Khán-i-Douián and Kamar-ud-dín Khán, two of the ablest Imperial generals, marched against Bájí Rao, while Mulhar Rao was sharply attacked by Sáadat Khán, the Viceroy of Oudh, who forced him to retreat. The Viceroy then moved on to Agra, writing a magniloquent despatch to the Emperor, in which the check was magnified into a great victory.

Rise of the Marathas, 1736.

After the sack of Delhi by Nádir Sháh, that conqueror levied contributions on the Governors of Provinces, and Agra contributed its quota. The power of the Játs continued to increase after the death of the Emperor Muhammad Sháh, which occurred in 1748, and during the reign of his son and successor Ahmad Sháh, Suraj Mal, nephew of the famous Churamun, attained such power that he materially assisted Safdar Jung, the son of Sáadat Khán, Viceroy of Oudh, who had been appointed *wazir*, against the Rohillas, who were defeated in a pitched battle and driven to the lower ranges of the Himaláyas.

Invasion of Nádir Sháh, 1739.

Death of the Emperor Muhammad Sháh, 1748.

Ahmad Sháh succeeds.

Suraj Mal Ját, 1751.

A breach soon after occurred between Safdar Jung, the *wazir*, and the Emperor, who promoted Ghází-ud-dín, grandson of Asaf Jah, to the high office of Commander-in-Chief. The result of the measure was a civil war, but the *wazir* consented to make peace. The Emperor now, disgusted with the arrogance of Ghází-ud-din, plotted against him, but was deposed, taken prisoner and deprived of his sight.

Emperor Ahmad Shah deposed, 1745.

Az-ud-dín, son of Jáhandar Sháh, and grandson of Bahadur Sháh (Sháh Alam I.), was proclaimed Emperor, under the title of Alamgir II, with Ghazi-ud-dín, as *wazir*. Safdar Jung died soon after this revolution, and was succeeded in the Viceroyalty of Oudh by Shuja-ud-daula.

Alamgir II succeeds, 1745.

During the third invasion of Ahmad Sháh *Durani*, that conqueror, after marching to Delhi, sent an expedition to Agra and Mathrá under his *wazir* Sháh Wali Khán, who laid siege to Agra. Sardar Jahán Khán, one of the principal lieutenants

Third invasion of Ahmad Sháh Abdali, 1757.

of the Duráni sovereign, was at the same time sent to levy contributions from the Játs, and he laid siege to one of the Ját forts. Fázil Khan, the Mughal Governor of Agra, defended the city with great valour; but the summer season was far advanced and, mortality breaking out among the *Duraní* troops, Sháh Wali Khán was compelled to retire.

The invaders indemnified themselves by suddenly falling on the neighbouring city of Mathra, which they plundered at a religious festival, putting the helpless votaries to the sword without distinction of age or sex. After these transactions, the *Abdali* directed his steps to his own native dominions.*

The Marathas take possession of Agra fort, 1758.

Ahmad Shah Abdali, on retiring from the country, had appointed Najib-ud-daula, a Rohilla nobleman of ability and character, to be Commander-in-Chief of the imperial forces. This excited the jealousy of Ghazi-ud-din, who called the Marathas under Mulhar Rao Holkar to his aid against the Emperor. Najib-ud-daula retired to his own country about Saharanpur. The royal fort of Delhi was taken after a month's siege; the Emperor opened the gates and received Ghazi-ud-din as his *wazír*. It was at this time that a Maratha Governor took charge of the Agra fort.

Murder of Alamgir II by Ghazi-ud-din. 1759.

Ghazi-ud-dín, the *wazír*, now plotted against the Emperor, and had him assassinated by a savage Uzbek, as he alighted from his palanquin to pay his respects to a hermit of peculiar sanctity, who, it was given out, had taken up his abode in the ruined fort of Ferozabad, near Delhi, and to consult whom the harmless devotee had repaired thither.

Shah Alam II succeeds, 1759.

Ali Gohar, son of the deceased Emperor, was raised to the throne, by the title of Sháh Alam II. The power of the Marathas had now reached its zenith, their frontier extending on the north to the Indus and Himalayas, and on the south nearly to the extremity of the Peninsula.† But a fatal blow was inflicted on them by the Abdali Ahmad Sháh in the famous battle of Panipat, fought in January 1761. Najib-ud-daula,

---

* The Memoirs of Abdul Karim.

† Elphinstone. Vol. II., p. 637

who had been appointed to the chief military command by the Abdali monarch, governed the affairs of the dwindled Empire with vigour and success. The Maratha collectors were expelled from the districts of the Doab, and Agra admitted a Jat garrison.* Suraj Mal, who had reinforced the Maratha Peshwá with a contingent of 30,000 Játs, availing himself of the Maratha disaster at Panipat, took an early opportunity of displacing the Maratha Governor of the important fort of Agra, which was garrisoned by the Ját troops. The Chief was at this time joined by the notorious Walter Reinhardt (Samru), who had left his late protector, the Nawab Wazir of Oudh, at the head of a battalion of troops and some artillery. It was during the capture of the city by the Játs that the minarets on the gates of Sakandra are stated to have been blown away; the armour and books of Akbar, said to have been deposited in that mausoleum as a sacred curiosity, removed, and the massive silver doors of the celebrated Táj, said to have cost over a lakh of rupees, taken away.

Agra garrisoned by the Jats, 1764.

Silver gates of the Taj.

Hostilities soon after commenced between Suraj Mal and the Mughals. Suráj Mal was killed in a battle near Sháhdara, six miles from Delhi. His head was borne on a horseman's lance as the standard of the Mughal army. He was succeeded by his son, Jawáhir Singh, who took up his abode at Agra, where, not long afterwards, he was murdered, it is said, at the instigation of the Rájá of Jeypur.

Suraj Mal Jat killed, 1765.

While at Agra, Jawáhir Singh had once the arrogance to take his seat on the black marble throne of Jahangir on which, so the story goes, a long fissure was caused in the middle of the stone.

Fissure in the throne of Jahangir.

The power of the Ját was at this time at its height. Their capital was at Bhartpur, and their territory extended from Alwar on north-west to Agra on south-west. The whole of this country was governed by Ranjit Singh, the surviving son of Suraj Mal.

The Jat Power at its zenith.

---

* The Mughal Empire, by Keene, Ed. of 1866, pp. 76 and 78.

The Marathas re-occupy Agra, 1770.

The Marathas re-appeared and occupied the whole Doáb in 1770. In 1772 they sent a force from Agra, which, joining with the Bhartpur Játs, forced the imperialists to retreat towards Delhi.

But are expelled by the Delhi Minister, Najaf Khan, 1773.

The Maratha forces having retired southwards in 1773, in consequence of the death of Mádho Ráo Peshwá, Mirza Najaf Khán resumed his office as Minister at Delhi, and, assisted by Shuja-ud-daula, the Wazír of Oudh, expelled their garrison from Agra and the provinces still possessed by the Emperor.*

Muhammed Beg Hamadán, Governor of Agra.

The Játs recovered Agra, but only to be finally expelled by the minister in 1774. The imperial minister wrested from them the fort of Agra and occupied it with a garrison of his own, under a Mughal officer, Muhammad Beg of Hamadán, who held the post of Governor of Agra for the next ten years. Najaf Khán continued to live in Agra in viceregal state, surrounded by his faithful Mughals and Persians. His chief subordinates were Samru, Najaf Kuli, his adopted son, a Hindu convert, Muhammad Beg of Hamadán, and Mirza Shafi, the minister's nephew.

Death of Mirza Najaf Khan, 1782.

Samru died at Agra on 4th May 1778, and Mirza Najaf Khán at Delhi, where he had been called by the facile monarch, Sháh Alam, on 20th April 1782. The Mirza had held the direct civil administration, with the receipt of surplus revenues of the Province of Agra and the Ját territories, for a considerable period.

A tragedy.

On the death of the minister, Afrasyab Khán, a near relation of the deceased, was elected minister, with the title of *Amír-ul-Umera*, or the Premier noble.

A contest now arose among the survivors of the deceased minister and resulted in a tragedy as shocking as it was barbarous. On 23rd September 1783, Mirza Shafi, nephew of the deceased minister, who was then at Agra, was refused admittance into the palace as he returned after an excursion. Suspecting Afrasyab Khán as the author of the affront, the Mirza assumed a hostile attitude towards him. A meeting was subsequently arranged between the Mirza and Muhammad Beg of Hamadán in the open air in front of the Delhi Gate of the fort, with the avowed object of settling the dispute amicably. As the elephants on which the

---

* *Taylor's History of India*, p. 508, ed. of 1863.

two noblemen were seated drew near to each other, the Mirza stretched forth his hand for greeting, whereupon Muhammad Beg, at once seizing his pistol, fired at him below the arm and shot him dead. Some say, according to an account furnished by Prince Jawán Bakht, eldest son of the Emperor, that the perpetrator of the crime was an attendant who occupied the back seat of the *howdah*, probably Ismail Beg, nephew of the Hamadán.

The assassination of Mirza Shafi at Agra, 1883.

In 1784 the confederate armies of the Mughals and Mádhoji Sindhia marched to Agra to punish the refractory governor Muhammad Beg.

Muhammed Beg rebels at Agra, 1784.

The Emperor signified his wish to proceed to Agra in person, but he was dissuaded from carrying out his purpose by Najíb-ud-daula, the Finance Minister. In November 1784, the Premier Afrasyab Khán was assassinated by Zenul-abi-din, the brother of Mirza Shafi, who thus avenged his brother's death.

His death facilitated affairs and the party he had created lost spirit. Muhammad Beg, being deserted by his troops, threw himself on the mercy of Sindhia. The fort of Agra surrendered on 27th March 1785, and property of Afrasyab Khán to the value of a crore of rupees fell into the conqueror's hands. The power of Sindhia now reigned supreme in Hindustán.

The fort surrendered to Sindhia, 1785.

In 1787 a battle was fought between the Marathas under Sindhia and the Rájputs under the confederates Rájá Partap Singh of Jeypur, Rájáe Singh of Jodhpur, the Ráná of Odeypur and other minor Chiefs of Mewár. On the side of the Marathas were Ambáji Ingia, Appá Khandi and General M. de Boigne. Muhammad Beg, with his nephew, Ismail Beg, a desperate leader, was at the head of the Mughal horse on the side of the confederate Chiefs. The battle took place at Lál Soti, in Jeypur territory. Muhammad Beg was killed, but the Marathas were worsted and fell back upon Alwar. Ismail Beg proceeded to Agra with 1,000 horse, four battalions and six guns. On this Sindhia made terms with Ranjit Singh, the Rájá of the Játs, and strongly reinforced the fort of Agra, the garrison of which was placed under the command of Lakwa Dádá, one of his best generals.*

War between Maráthas and Rajputs, 1787.

Muhammad Beg killed in the action.

His nephew Ismail Beg.

* Keene, p. 149.

Ghulam Kádir, the Rohilla Chief.

Towards the end of the rainy season of 1787, another personage appeared on the scene. This was Gholám Kádir, son of Zábitá Khán, a Rohilla Chief, who aspired to the dignity of Premier Noble at the Court of Delhi. Under the guise of religion, he made a violent attempt to revive the Musalmán cause, and he was aided in his attempt by Ismail Beg. The Emperor, who had hitherto supported the cause of the Marathas, was, about this time, known to be in private correspondence with the Rájput Chiefs, who shortly after inflicted another heavy defeat on the Marathas. On this Sindhia was compelled to fall back on Gwalior, leaving his army, under Lakwa Dádá, shut up in the fort of Agra, which was closely besieged by Ismail Beg. Following these transactions, Gholám Kádir was, through his principal adherents, introduced to Sháh Alam, who invested him with the dignity of the Premier Noble, *Amír-ul-Umera,* His Majesty himself binding the jewelled fillet on his head.

Ismail Beg besieges Agra Fort, 1787

Is joined by Ghulám Kàdir.

Gholám Kádir then proceeded to effect a junction between his forces and those of Ismail before Agra, and the siege continued for some months. While these operations were going on, news reached Agra, at the end of the cold season of 1787-88, of Sindhia having crossed the Chambal with large reinforcements from the Deccan. Ismail Beg and Gholám Kádir forthwith raised the siege of Agra and marched to meet the advancing Maratha army. A fierce battle took place near Fatehpur Sikri on the Bhartpur road, on the 24th April, 1788, in which the Marathas under Ráná Khán were defeated and withdrew to Bhartpur under cover of night. Gholám Kádir then moved northward, while Ismail Beg renewed the siege of Agra.

The battle of Fatehpur Sikri, 1788.

Mirza Jawán Bakht the titular Governor of Agrá.

Enticed by a handsome *nazar* and the presentation of the golden key of the fort of Ajmere by an embassy of the Rájput Rájás from Jodhpur, the imbecile Sháh Alam took active steps against Sindhia and his own minister. He appointed Mirza Jawán Bakht titular Governor of Agra. That Prince, with the aid of Ismail Beg, made strenuous efforts to take possession of the fort and the province. His attempts failed, and, narrowly escaping an attack made on his life by Gholám Kádir, he fled to Benares, in British territory, where he died of a broken heart, in 1788.

His death, 1788.

Lakwa Dádá, the Maráthá General, still held out in the fort of Agra. Ráná Khán having joined Sindhia on the Chambal with a fresh contingent from the Deccan, Sindhia, thus reinforced, once more moved to the relief of his General. The charge on this occasion was made from the eastward, and was met by Ismail Beg with a furious cavalry charge. Before, however, Gholám Kadír could cross the Jumna and effect a junction with the Mughal, the Maratha infantry and cavalry under General de Boigne had repulsed the Muhammadan troops. Ismail Beg was severely wounded in the action and fled, fording the swollen stream (June 1788).

The siege of the fort finally raised, 1788.

The confederates, Ghulám Kádir and Ismail Beg, now collected their scattered troops at Shahdara, near Delhi—the scene, it may be recollected, of Súraj Mal's fall.

Transactions in Delhi.

Ghulam Kadir negotiated with Sháh Alam to throw off Sindhia's yoke, and, the Emperor hesitating to act on his advice, the desperate man, dropping all disguise opened fire on the palace of Delhi. Mádhoji Sindhia sent small reinforcements which were of no avail, and the confederates took possession of Delhi. The Emperor was deposed and blinded (10th August, 1888). In March following the Maratha put Ghulám Kádir to death, and in 1792 Ismail Beg was sent into confinement at Agra, where he remained till his death, which occurred the same year.

Sháh Alam blinded, 1788.

Death of Ismail Beg, 1792.

The Maratha Governor having rebelled in 1799, the fort was captured by General Perron, in the employ of Sindhia, after a siege of nearly two months. John Hessing, a Dutch Officer, was commandant of Agra for some years; he died in the fort in 1803.*

The Maratha Governors of Agra.

By the decisive victory of 11th September 1803, gained by General (afterwards Lord) Lake, the British became Masters of Delhi On the memorable 14th September, the British Army under that hero crossed the Jumna and entered Delhi. The unhappy blind old King, Sháh Alam, was liberated from confinement and his freedom and dignity were restored. On 24th September, General Lake, with his army, left Delhi for Agra.

Sháh Alam restored by the British, 1803.

Conquest of Agra by the British, 1803.

* For an account of his tomb see Chapter II.

Arriving at Agra on 4th October, he encamped within long cannon shot of the fort. The Agra garrison at this time consisted of 4,500 fighting men under the nominal command of the Dutch Officer, John Hessing, and other French and European adventurers, about six in number; but the troops, distrusting them, had mutinied and put them in confinement. In addition to this force, there were stationed under the walls of the fort three battalions of the troops that had been defeated at Delhi, and four battalions of Perron's, fifth brigade, just arrived from the Deccan, under the command of Major Brownrigg, with 26 pieces of cannon. The garrison had refused them admittance, because there was a treasure of 25 lakhs of rupees within the fort, the result of spoliation of the country, and it was feared that, if they were admitted, the spoil would have to be divided with them. The troops therefore occupied the city and the glacis. Besides these, twelve battalions of regular troops took up position in the rear of the besieging army, on the Delhi road, with the view, in the event of the siege being protracted, of saving the imperial city.

The enemy's strength in the fort and city.

Operations against the city.

The consummate British General, observing the state of affairs, resolved, with his usual energy and determination, to move against the troops located outside the fort; before commencing the siege, so as to dislodge them from the city and the glacis. Accordingly, on the morning of 10th October, he detached two battalions of Native Infantry, under Brigadier-General Clarke, to attack the city: one battalion, under Colonel M'Collough, to attack the enemy to the west of the fort; and another battalion, under Captain Worsley, to attack them on the southern side. The enemy made a sharp and obstinate resistance which lasted for some days, but they were at length defeated and dislodged from their position. The loss on the side of the British was 213 men killed and wounded; the enemy lost 600. All their guns, 26 in number, were captured. The defeat so much dispirited the enemy that, two days after, 2,500 of them surrendered to the British General, on condition that they should be taken in the service of the British Government on the same salaries as in Sindhia's service.

Siege of the fort.

The city being occupied, the British General commenced in earnest the siege operations against the fort. A promiscuous fire was opened from the batteries on 16th April; but the next day the garrison sued for terms of capitulation. After some discussion, the terms were agreed to, and the fort was occupied by the British on the 18th. By this victory 25 lakhs of rupees that were hoarded in the fort, and 162 pieces of cannon, fell into the hands of the conquerors. Among the latter was a great brass gun, which was celebrated in history as the great gun of Agra. The Governor-General intended to send it to England, as a trophy, to be presented to King George III. and the gun was embarked on a country boat, but it sank into the deep torrent of the Jumna and never afterwards emerged.

Settlement of the District, 1805.

The newly-conquered District of Agra was placed under a Collector in 1805. The head-quarters of Government for the ceded and conquered provinces were fixed at Firokhábad under a Board of Commissioners, to which the Collectorate of Agra was made subordinate. Under the renewed Charter of the East India Company, in 1833, the first Lieutenant-Governorship in India for the North-Western Provinces was constituted at Agra, in 1835. The first Lieutenant-Governor of Agra was Sir Charles Metcalfe, and Agra continued to be the capital of the North-Western Provinces for a period of twenty-two years.

Constitution of a Lieutenant-Governorship, 1835.

In 1838 a great famine raged in the North-Western Provinces and the Punjab, and it was in that year that the Christian missionaries established the charitable institution known as the Sakandrá Orphanage.

The Sakandrá Orphanage, 1838.

Under the strong and prosperous rule of Great Britain, the annals of Agra call for no special notice until the Sepoy War of 1857. The Agra Presidency, as then constituted, comprised the District of Delhi, and the news of the Mutiny was flashed to Agra from Meerut, which was one of its subordinate Collectorates. From Agra, as the seat of Government, intelligence of the great crisis was communicated to Lord Canning, the Governor-General, who received it with the utmost composure and proceeded to concert measures to restore order in the country. The ruling Lieutenant-Governor was Mr. John Russell, one of the ablest and most conscientious Civilians in the country, who stood high in public estimation.

The Sepoy War, 1857.

Alarming accounts of mutiny having been received from Cawnpur and Firokhábád, a council of the principal Civil and Military officers of the station was held at Agra, and it was resolved to remove all the Christian families into the fort. On the morning of the 31st May, the native regiments of the place were disarmed. Early in July, the mutineers who had revolted in Nimach and Nasirábád advanced towards Agra. Their strength consisted of 4,000 infantry, 1,500 cavalry and 11 guns. Brigadier Polwhele, at the head of a small force, moved to meet them, and a brisk engagement took place at Sucheta in the suburbs of the city, in which the British troops were compelled to retreat. The mob of the city, taking advantage of the tumult that followed, rose at once, plundered the city and killed a number of Europeans. Bungalows were fired and public offices burnt and destroyed; and, on the 6th July, the chief native police officer proclaimed the Government of the Delhi Emperor. The mutineers, however, did not enter the city, but proceeded towards Delhi, to join their comrades there. The Lieutenant-Governor succumbed to the complaint of which he had been long ailing, and his remains were interred in front of the Dewán-i-Am. The British Officers remained shut up in the fort for three months, though occasional assaults were made against the mutineers from various points.

On the fall of Delhi, in September, the fugitives from that city, together with the rebels from Central India, advanced towards Agra. About the same time Colonel Greathead's column arrived from Delhi in time to engage the mutineers, who, after a short contest, were utterly routed, and broke up and fled precipitately. Order was restored in the city and the suburbs. In October following, the troops under Major Cotton inflicted a heavy defeat on the remnants of the rebel fugitives from Fatehpur Sikri, and peace was completely restored throughout the District.

Since the days of the Mutiny, Agra has developed into a great Indian city and has become the centre of the Railway system in Upper India. In 1861 a great famine raged in the Agra District. In 1867, the first Industrial Exhibition was held in Agra in which the manufactured industries and natural products of the District were largely displayed.

The head-quarters of the N.-W.P. government were removed from Agra to Allahábád (whence they had been removed in 1835) in 1868, and the High Court, in turn, changed its seat from Agra to Allahábád in May 1869. Since that time Agra has dwindled down to the position of a provincial town, being the head-quarters of a Division and a District; nevertheless, it retains its fame as one of the finest cities of the East. Seat of Government moved to Allahabad, 1869.

During the cold weather of 1860, Lord Canning made his Viceregal tour through the Northern Provinces, and at Agra he received the homage of the loyal Chiefs of Rajputana and Central India, to whom His Excellency announced the rewards they were to receive for their conspicuous services during the Mutiny. Visit of Lord Canning, 1860.

Lord Elgin,* Her Majesty's Plenipotentiary in China, who had brought the transactions there to a successful close, succeeded Lord Canning as Governor-General of India in March 1862. In the winter of 1863, His Lordship held a public reception of the Chiefs of Rajputana and Central India at Agra, as had been done before him by his prodecessor. It was a most magnificent spectacle in which the nobility and gentry of Agra and the surrounding country assembled to do homage to the representative of their sovereign. It was from Agra that he set out on his journey to the Himalayas, where, to the great grief of the country, he died. And of Lord Elgin, 1863.

Sir (afterwards Lord) John Lawrence, as Governor-General, held his great darbar at Agra in November 1866. It was, in certain of its aspects, more imposing than the darbar he had shortly before held at Lahore and of equally historic significance. Eighty-four of the Chiefs of Rajputana and Bundelkhand responded to his summons. There were altogether 350 Chiefs and native gentlemen, and fully 1,00,000 people assembled in and around Agra to witness the scene. At the head of the assembled Princes was the Chief of one of the two great Maratha houses, Mahárájá Sindhia. Next to him were Jodhpur and Jeypur, two of the oldest Rajput families, and the famous Begum of Bhopál. The darbar of Sir John Lawrence, 1866.

* By a fortunate circumstance, his son, at the present moment, holds the exalted office of Viceroy of India.

At the investiture Darbar the Mahárájás of Jodhpur and Karauli became Knights Grand Cross of the Star of India. The Mahárájá of Karauli had stood conspicuously loyal during the Mutiny and fought the mutineers. The Mahárájá of Balrampur had saved the lives of Sir Charles Wingfield and others in Oudh, and the Rájá of Morár Mow had done the same for the fugitives from Cawnpur. They received their respective orders from Sir John Lawrence, who in a short speech warmly recorded the services of each.

The speech of Sir John Lawrence. For the first time in the annals of British Administration in India, did a British Viceroy address the chiefs and gentry present in the language of the people. His Excellency's Urdu speech was a model of its kind. Simple in its character, frank and paternal, philanthrophic and earnest, it produced a profound impression on his hearers and was listened to with an absorbed attention. After bidding all who had assembled a hearty welcome to the famous city, "renowned for its splendid Táj, and above all as having been, in former days, the seat of the government of the great Emperor, from whom it derived its name Akbarábád," Sir John Lawrence said:—

"Great men, when living, often receive praise from their friends and adherents for virtues which they do not possess, and it is only after this life is ended that the real truth is told. Of all fame that such men can acquire, that alone is worth having which is accorded to a just and beneficient ruler." The speech of Sir John is full of sympathetic advice and admonition. "The names of conquerors and heroes," he said, "are forgotten; but those of virtuous and wise Chiefs live for ever." The days of war and rapine had passed away from Hindustán never to return. The time must have been within the recollection of some of the Chiefs present, and all must have heard of it, when neither the palace of the ruler, nor the cottage of the peasant, nor the most sacred edifices of Hindu or Muhammadan were safe from the hands of the plunderer and destroyer. In those days whole provinces were one scene of devastation and misery; and in vast tracts of country scarcely the light of a lamp was to be seen in a single village. English rule in India has put an end to all this. No longer is the country a waste and a wilderness. It is now, to a great extent, covered with populous villages and rich with cultivation, while the inhabitants live in comparative safety under the shade of the English power. Sir John advised the Chiefs to refrain from wasting their time in disputes with their neighbours, in quarrels with their feudatories, and in still less satisfactory ways. If a Chief neglected his own proper duty, the care of his estate, how could he expect that a deputy would perform it for him? Good laws and well-selected officials, carefully supervised, were necessary to ensure good government. An efficient police and a well-managed revenue were equally desirable, so that people might live in safety and enjoy the fruits of their industry. Schools for the education of the young and hospitals for the cure of the sick should also be established. The British Government, said the Viceroy, would honour that Chief most who excelled in the good management of his country.

The speech of Sir John Lawrence laid down, in short, the theory of government, and will ever stand high in the estimation of the people as a specimen of imperial eloquence.

Visit of the Duke of Edinburgh, 1870.

In 1870, Agra was honoured with a visit by His Royal Highness Prince Alfred, Duke of Edinburgh, second son of Her Imperial Majesty Queen Victoria Empress of India, and was received with every demonstration of loyal welcome and rejoicing.

Visit of the Prince of Wales, 1876.

In January 1876, His Royal Highness the Prince of Wales graced Akbar's capital with a visit, and a most cordial and splendid reception was accorded to him. On 26th January, he received the respects of fourteen Chiefs. First came the Maharao Rajá of Bundi, a noted hunter, a fine specimen of a Rájput. The Prince won his heart by remarking that "he heard the Maharao had attended a Darbár held by Lord William Bentinck, and had witched him by noble deeds of horsemanship." After him came the Rájá of Bikaneer, lord of the desert; then the Mahárajá of Kishengarh, whose Chief, the Prince was glad to hear, had devoted himself to works of irrigation and had executed tanks and other public works of great utility. Then came the Mahárájá of Bhartpur. After Bhartpur, the chief of Alwar paid his respects. Then came in succession the Nawab of

Tonk; the Rana of Dholpur; the Maharaja of Orcha, a hunter and a sportsman; the Nawab of Rampur, a poet and literary man, whom the Prince invested with the insignia of G.C.S.I.; the Rao Maharaja of Datia; the Maharaja of Chikari; the Raja of Tehri; the Maharaja of Shalpura; and the Jagirdar of Alipura. The Prince the next day honoured these Chiefs with return visits. A Civil Service Ball was organized by Sir John Strachey, the ruling Lieutenant-Governor, and, after brilliant festivities and excursions to Sakandrá and Fatehpur Sikri, His Royal Highness proceeded to Dholpur.

Agra Water Works, 1890.

The Agra Water Works were opened with great ceremony by Lord Lansdowne in December, 1890.

Lord Elgin's visit to Agra, 1895.

In October 1895, His Excellency Lord Elgin, Viceroy and Governor-General of India, paid a visit to Agra. The Municipal Corporation presented His Excellency with an address of welcome, in which they dwelt on the happy coincidence that this was not the first time Agra had been visited by a member of the illustrious Elgin family, for some of the Municipality could remember when Lord Elgin's father, with an imposing military escort, rode across the pontoon bridge in February 1863 to preside at a Darbar. Great changes had occurred since then. Agra was then the terminus of the E. I. Railway, and the late Lord Elgin, when he left for the hills, continued his journey on horseback. Now three lines of railway were united under the roof of the railway station, and a survey for a fourth line from Mathra had lately been completed by the Bombay, Baroda and Central India Railway. Since 1863 population had immensely increased, new hospitals opened, and vast progress made in education and sanitation. Referring to the relations between the religious sections of the native community which had been strained and formed the subject of a speech by Lord Lansdowne when a Viceroy last visited Agra, the Corporation remarked that, thanks to the energy and decision of those responsible for the public safety, aided by the good sense of the bulk of the inhabitants, no overt acts of hostility had taken place, and the feeling on both sides was more pacific than before.

The Municipal Address.

His Excellency replied as follows:—

Lord Elgin's Speech.

"Gentlemen of the Municipal Committee of Agra,—I have to thank you for the address which you have presented to me, and for the terms in which you have been pleased to express your welcome. They are well calculated to rouse anew memories which, though 32 years ago I was far away a boy at school in England, I trust I may almost claim to share with you, and gentlemen, I may also say that if the changes which 30 years have brought about and to which you have drawn my attention are such that you could scarcely have foreseen them, still less could I imagine then that I should ever come here as my father did to study questions that are of interest to this great city, and to enjoy those unrivalled sights which have given it a worldwide renown. Gentlemen, I rejoice to observe that the record, which you are able to submit, is one of progress. It may be that taken by itself an increase of 20 per cent., in the population might not ,perhaps, necessarily denote prosperity. It is no light matter to find food for 20,000 or 30,000 more mouths, or employment for so many extra hands, but the other facts of this case give a sufficient and a satisfactory explanation. It was one of the chief objects of my father's journey, in 1863, to examine the progress of the railway which was then about to complete communication between this city and Calcutta. Nothing has in the last 30 years, nothing in my opinion will have in the next 30 years, so materially affected and improved the condition of the people of the Indian Empire as the extension of its railways, and in respect of railways you are able to boast of great if not exceptional good fortune. Already 30 years ago you had tasted the first fruits of railway communication. Now I suppose there are few cities in India that in this respect could compete with you. I am well aware that there is another side to this picture, and you have not omitted it from your retrospect. Increasing population and increasing prosperity must always bring increasing responsibilities to those who, like you, gentlemen, are charged with the duty of providing for the health of the community. I know also well the anxieties that arise when we see clearly the importance of taking certain steps and carrying out special works, and the means and expenses are not so obvious. I am glad to see that you frankly admit what I believe to be the case, that the Government of India has dealt with municipal bodies in this matter in a liberal spirit, and also that you recognise that the extent to which assistance can fairly be claimed must be determined by the state of the imperial exchequer. I need not remind you as men of business that, when we speak of the state of the imperial exchequer, that does not imply merely counting the cash which may at any moment be in the treasury, but that we have to look to other considerations and particularly to weigh carefully the demands that have been made upon the general tax-payer. Unfortunately during the last two years the Government of India has had to make increased demands upon the general tax-payer, and we have just seen in the last few hours how that sensitive instrument, the money market, upon which the commercial transactions of men depend, may suddenly upset the best calculations. Therefore, although I do not differ from the opinion expressed elsewhere that the financial prospects of the Government are brightening, I should be holding out false hopes if I led you to expect at present any material alteration in the conditions, fair and honourable as they have been, of the assistance we can offer you. But, gentlemen, if I am obliged to say that, I hope you will not take it as sarcasm if I ask you to persevere in your patriotic efforts. I trust from what you have said in your address that you will be able to successfully appeal to that generous and patriotic spirit which you tell me has secured you the support of your leading citizens in the great causes of education and hospital accommodation, and, perhaps, I may be allowed to say, speaking on behalf of the President of the Lady Dufferin Fund, Lady Elgin, that she sincerely recognises the great efforts made here for the benefit of Indian women and their medical treatment. Gentlemen, I feel deeply thankful that it is not necessary for me to-day to repeat the solemn warning of my predecessor, to which you have alluded in the concluding paragraph of your address. You have given just credit to the energy of the local authorities in fearlessly carrying out the policy of impartiality, both in the tolerance of opinion and the repression of the executive, which Lord Lansdowne proclaimed, and to which the Government of India unreservedly adhere. But I have equal pleasure in joining with you in placing beside the action of the executive as instrumental in the cause of peace the good sense of the people, and I would add the efforts made in various parts of the country by leading members of various phases of religious thought, by whom I gratefully acknowledge that much has been done to promote good will and remove the causes of strife. I trust they will never forget, but rather increasingly appreciate how much of the responsibility lies with them. If, as you are kind enough to wish, I should be in a position again to visit Agra, I can hope for nothing better than to be able to refer to the growth and development of this spirit of conciliation which it is the constant desire of many who love India best to foster."

At noon the same day (25th October) His Excellency received formal visits from the Maharaja of Karauli, the Maharaja Rana of Dhoulpur and the Nawab of Rampur. With the exception of the Maharaja of Karauli, who spoke in Hindustani, conversation was carried on in English. The Viceroy visited Fattehpur Sikri and Akbar's tomb at Sikandra. On the 28th His Excellency gave audience to the Maharaja of Bhadawar, the Raja of Mainpuri, the Raja of Awa, the Raja of Pirwa and Seth Lachman Das, the celebrated millionaire banker of Mathra. The Rajas are the descendants of ancient Rajput families, those of Bhadawar and Awa having rendered good service to the Government during the Mahratta war and the Mutiny. **Visit of ruling chiefs.**

The Bikaneer Camel Corps, the only corps of the kind in India, paraded before His Excellency on the morning of 28th October. It was 440 strong under the command of Thakur Dip Singh, and its organization was admitted in every detail to be perfect. As it was drawn up in line 420 yards long, its appearance struck all spectators with surprise. An eye witness writes of it in the *Civil and Military Gazette*, Lahore:—"It looked most imposing, while the smartness of the men's turn-out in their neat *Khaki* coloured uniforms, with red facings and the gold *turrea* of Rajputana in their turbans, the excellent condition of the camels, and the remarkable steadiness of their movements, commanded universal admiration." His Excellency was pleased to see this manœuvring power of corps and complimented Thakur Dip Singh on its general appearance and smartness. **Manœuvring of Bikaneer camel corps.**

His Excellency visited the principal architectural monuments at Agra and left it for Gwalior on the 30th, carrying with him very pleasant impressions of his first visit to Akbar's city.

CHAPTER II.

DESCRIPTIVE.

THE FORT.

The ancient fort.

THE old fort mentioned by Jahángír, on the site of which Akbar built his fort, was constructed by Salem Sháh *Súr*, who gave it the name *Bádalgarh*. The old fort was blown up during the war between Sakandar and Ibrahím, and the date of the incident was found in the words *Atish-i-Bádalgarh* (the fire of Bádalgarh), which, according to the *Abjad* rule, gives 962 A.H, equal to 1556 A.D., as the date.

The modern fort.

The modern fort, a vast and imposing structure on the banks of the river Jumna, built by Akbar in 1571, is one of the greatest architectural works of India. It does not all belong to Akbar, its founder, the greater part of it having been constructed by his successors; but, as a triumph of engineering and as one of the best specimens of the Saracenic style of architecture, the credit of designing the outlines is given to that Emperor.

It is a mile and a half in circuit and is surrounded by a double wall of red sandstone, the outer one being about 40 feet high from the ground and the inner towering 30 feet above the outer, with flanking defences, numerous turrets, and crenellated battlements. The stones are joined together and fastened to each other by iron rings which pass through them. The foundation everywhere reaches water. The outer ditch and rampart that formerly surrounded the fort, have disappeared. The inner moat, 30 feet wide and paved with freestone, still exists. Crossing by a drawbridge over this moat, we enter the principal, or north, gateway, known as the Delhi Gate, a massive and imposing structure, built of solid masonry ten feet thick and flanked by two enormous octagonal towers, of red sandstone, inlaid with ornamental designs of white marble

The Delhi Gate of the fort.

THE FORT

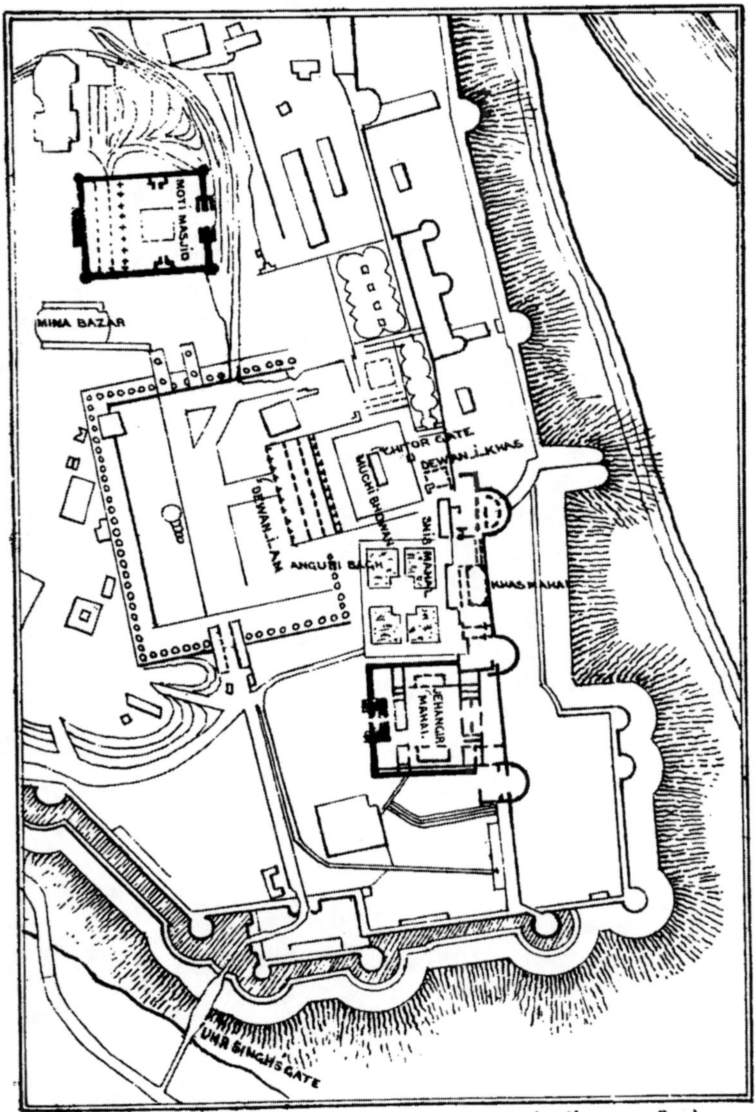

ENLA: BY HUSSAIN B. 16-7-96

"MUFID-I-'AM" PRESS. Lahore:

The Fort (from the river side).

Page 74.

and assuming a castellated appearance. The upper and lower apartments are used as guard-rooms, while from the summit a fine and extensive view of the surrounding country is obtained. An old unoccupied guard-house, close to the Delhi Gate of the fort, has the following inscription of the time of Akbar over the archway

Inscription on the gate.

عصر شہنشاه خلافت پناه ظل الله جلال الدین محمد اکبر باد شاه
فی سن ۱۰۰۸

In the time of the King of Kings, the Protection of the Realm, the Shadow of God, Jalál-ud-dín Muhammad Akbar Bádsháh, in the year 1008 A.H. (1599 A.D.)

The remainder of the inscription is unintelligible, being very much defaced, owing to the gradual scaling off in blisters of the stone, which bears the inscription in raised letters. As the inscription shows, the building was constructed in the time of Akbar, in 1008 A.H., or A.D. 1599.

On the same archway, below the former inscription, are inscribed the following poems of the time of Jahángír :—

شاه جهان چون گرفت جای بتخت شرف
تخت ز رفعت نهاد بر سر چرخ پا
دست دعا برگشاد پیر فلک از نشاط
گفت که بادا مدام حکم تو فرمان روا
خواست نهانی کند سال جلوسش رقم
بود در آندم لبش پر ز دعا و ثنا
میل دو چشم عدو کرده ز آتش بگفت
باد جهان باد شاه شاه جهانگیر ما

قایله و راقمه محمد معصوم البکري

When the king of the world took his seat on the magnificent throne,
The throne, feeling itself exalted, put its feet on the Sky.
Old heaven through excessive joy stretched forth its hands in prayer,
And exclaimed, 'May thy authority last for ever'!
As Nihani wished to write the date of His Majesty's accession,
His lips were at that time filled with praise and prayer.
Having blinded the two eyes of the enemy with red-hot bodkins, he said:
'May our King Jahángir be the king of the world!'
The writer and composer of this is Mahomed Masum-al-Bukra.

Between the colossal towers is a passage covered by two domes, which, rising majestically from accretions of prismatic stalactites, give succession to a beautiful range of buildings comprising alternate niches and small arched openings, adorned with carvings and mosaics. Surrounding these edifices is the

The Nakkar Khánà.

Nakkar Khana, or Royal kettle-drum, which announced to the populace the functional hours of the Court. The elegant portal opens on a noble courtyard, and the centre of the palace, 500 feet by 370, surrounded by spacious arcades, which formerly served as a tilt yard.

The Háthi Pol gate.

The inner gateway, on the side of the open space between the quay and the fort, is known as the *Háthi Pol*, or Elephant gate. Here were placed, in the time of Akbar, two stone elephants of exquisite workmanship, with their riders Jaimal and Patto in statues of stone representing two Rajput heroes of Chittore, whose memory was thus honoured by the politic Emperor.*

The Darshan Darwaza.

The gateway is the *Darshan Darwaza*, or the Gate of Sights of William Finch, who visited Agra in the time of Jahángir. Here the King showed himself every morning at sunrise to his nobles and *Umras*, who stood on a kind of scaffold, and to the multitude who assembled beneath the window. The same was done each morning by Akbar, who worshipped the sun at this window, the crowd who thronged the plain below worshipping Akbar. Here, later in the morning, he appeared again, to witness

Combat of elephants and other sports and amusements.

the combats of animals in the plain below. He took much delight in fights between trained elephants, camels, buffaloes, rams and harts, and was entertained with the combats of cocks, the performances of gladiators, wrestlers, actors of comedies, dancers and fencers. Singers, male and female, remained in waiting, while

* The storming party failed in its first attempt to carry the bastions, and another was in progress when the Emperor chanced to see Jaimal, the Governor of the Fort, directing the repair of one of the breaches by torchlight. His Majesty, having seized a match-lock from a soldier who stood by, shot Jaimal in the forehead. The Rajputs, seeing their leader dead, became desperate; and resolving to die the death of heroes, performed the ceremony of *jowhar*, putting their women and children to death and burning them with their commander's body; they then retired to their temples and awaited the approach of the Muhammadans. The Emperor, seeing the walls deserted, entered the place at daylight. The statues of Jaimal and Patto were fine specimens of art, but were broken to pieces by Aurangzeb. The fragments of one of them having been subsequently collected, the statue of the elephant was restored. This statue is still to be seen in the Empress Garden, Delhi.

Fort (from the Jamá Masjid).

Page 76.

clever jugglers and tumblers displayed their dexterity and agility.*

South of the fort is the Amar Singh Gate, known after the name of Amar Singh, Rajput. **Amar Singh Gate.**

On one side of the great court-yard is the Diwan-i-Am, or Hall of public audience, the judgment-seat of Akbar, where the court receptions were held and business was transacted. Here the monarch daily sat on his throne raised, on an estrade, as we still see it, and surrounded with inlaid work of marble. Here he gave audience to his splendid court, received the tributary ruling chiefs of Hindustan and the ambassadors and envoys from foreign countries, administered justice and issued orders. At the foot of the alcove, on which the throne was placed, is an immense slate, of white marble, raised some three feet above the ground, on which the ministers took their stand to present and hand up petitions to the Emperor and to receive and convey his commands. It was formerly fenced with silver rails, but they have now disappeared. The hall is 192 feet in length by 64 in breadth It is an open portico, or *loggia*, the roof being supported by three rows of high pillars placed at regular intervals and connected by Saracenic arches of white marble, which give it a majestic appearance. Towards the eastern side is the elevated oblong niche, or gallery, before mentioned, in which the King took his seat on a throne. The throne described by Edward Terry, chaplain of Sir Thomas Roe, was "ascended by steps plated with silver and ornamented with 4 silver lions, spangled with jewels, which supported a canopy of pure gold." The pavilion is of pure marble, with beautifully carved recesses, and inlaid with mosaics. The court hall in Akbar's time was profusely scented with sweet perfumes and fragrant odours. On this subject *Allami Abul Fazl* writes in the *Ain*:—"The court hall is continually scented with ambergris, ale wood, and compositions according to ancient recipes, or mixtures invented by His Majesty; and incense is daily burnt in gold and silver censers of various shapes, while sweet smelling flowers are used in large quantities." The seat royal was separated by successive railings, the innermost of which, raised from the ground and enclosed by a red rail, was occupied

Diwan-i-Am.

The seat royal.

The order of precedence in the Darbar.

* *Ain-i-Akbari.*

by Princes Royal, ambassadors, high officers of State and nobles and grandees of the first rank. The space within the outer railing was filled with chiefs of secondary dignity, while a large open area outside the second railing was assigned to the multitude. All stood in respectful silence and enjoyed a full view of His Majesty's person.* In this vast court the *Ahdis,* or exempts of the guard, paraded in full armour, while horses and elephants, richly caparisoned, were arrayed further on, adding greatly to the brilliancy of the spectacle, which was truly royal.

The ceremony of prostration. The ceremony of prostration, after the fashion of the Tartar Mughals, was revived by Akbar, and was performed during the reign of his successors.† As a man entered the first rail which separated the commonalty from the nobility, he was conducted to the seat royal by two heralds, one on each side, carrying gold maces set with rubies and emeralds, who repeated the king's titles in a loud, monotonous voice. Here he made his first reverence. He then passed through the nobility to the red rail, where he made his second reverence; then, led to the platform, he made his third reverence, and at once found himself among Princes, Rajas, Mahárájás, Nawabs, Grandees, Nobles and Lords of great fortune and wealth. The passage intervening between the *Naubatkhana,* or the music gallery, and the royal throne comprised one hundred and twenty yards; and people were required to bow down lower and lower as they approached the monarch. Nothing upon earth surpassed the grandeur and solemnity of the scene. The presence of the King, the presiding figure of the whole assembly, so glowing with emeralds, diamonds, precious metal, pearls and rubies as to represent one solid mass of gold and gems, and the concourse of ruling Chiefs, Foreign ambassadors and the picked nobility of the Empire—all brilliantly clad and displaying in their sumptuous attire the

* "When His Majesty seats himself on the throne, all who are present perform the *Kornish* (salutation) and there remain standing in their places, according to their respective ranks, with their arms crossed."—*Ain-i-Akbari.*

† Akbar was convinced by Sheikh Tajuddin of Delhi, son of Sheikh Zakaria of Ajhuddan, (Pak Pattan). and other *Ulmás* of his court who followed the *Sufia* sect, or pantheism, that, according to the Koran and the Traditions of the Prophet, the phrase *Insan-i-Kamil* (perfect man) referred to the ruler of the age, from which it was inferred that the nature of the King was holy. It was argued that the *Sijda* (prostration), which was nothing else than *Zaminbos* (kissing the ground), was due to *Insan-i-Kamil.* Hence respect due to the King was looked upon as a religious command. The face of the King was *Kabah-i Muradat,* the sanctum of desires, and *Qiblá-i-Hájat,* the cynosure of necessities. See *Badauni.*

The Dewan-i-A

best and choicest riches of the country—inspired deep awe. One unbroken silence prevailed. All stood in solemn silence, motionless like statues, not a soul daring to cast his eyes on the King, no one venturing to raise his voice except the masters of ceremonies, and that only to announce to the assembled multitude the King's high sounding attributes and epithets. The Emperor was prepared to hear the meanest of his subjects who desired to make any representation to His Majesty. If any petition was raised from afar in the assembled multitude, it was instantly brought to the Emperor and the contents read to him.

The Diwán-i-Am was formerly used as an arsenal; but it was most considerately and tastefully restored by Sir John Strachey, Lieutenant-Governor of N.-W. P., in 1876. In the spacious Hall of this edifice, His Royal Highness the Prince of Wales was entertained, on his visit to the capital of the Mughals, in January, 1876. A marble slab inserted in a wall bears the following inscription :—

"In grateful commemoration of the services rendered to posterity by the Honorable Sir John Strachey, G.C.S.I., to whom, not forgetting the enlightened sympathy and timely care of others, India is mainly indebted for the rescue and preserved beauty of the Taj Mahal and other famous monuments of the ancient art and history of these provinces formerly administered by him, this tablet is placed by order of his friend the Earl of Lytton, Viceroy and Governor-General of India, A.D. 1880."

Inscription in memory of Sir John Strachey.

In the court opposite the Diwan-i-Am, is a simple tombstone to the memory of Mr. John Colvin, the Lieutenant-Governor, N.-W. P., who died in the fort during its siege by the mutineers of the Bengal Army in 1858.

The tomb of Mr. John Colvin.

Close to the above tomb lies the *Cistern of Jahángir.* This curious *hauz*, or circular cistern, is an enormous bowl, hewn out of a single stone, and from its size and construction is an object of artistic value. It is nearly 5 feet in height, 4 feet in depth, 8 feet in diameter and 25 feet in circumference. The exterior portion has several inscriptions in the Persian character; but the letters are so much defaced that the inscriptions cannot be deciphered. The unbroken portions of the inscriptions show that

The cistern of Jahangir.

the *hauz* was constructed for Jahángir Sháh, the son of Akbar Sháh, in 1019 A.H. (1016 A.D.), the year in which the Emperor was married to Nurjahán. I had to devote some time before I could decipher the following two couplets on this remarkable cistern, which can still be read :—

پناه ملک و دین شاه جهانگیر ابن اکبر شاه
شهنشاهی که از تدبیر او شد کار تقدیر
طلب کردند چون از خضر سال او خرد گفتا
نهان شد از خجالت زمزم از حوض جهانگیری

Asylum of State and religion, King Jahángir, son of the King Akbar,
An Emperor to whose wisdom fate owes its success.
Khizr* having been asked the date of its construction, Wisdom replied :
'The Zamzam†, on seeing the cistern of Jahángir, concealed its face out of shame.'‡

To the right and left of the hall are galleries of lattice-work through which the ladies of the Harem peeped to see the proceedings of the Court. A door at the back of the throne admitted the Emperor and his confidential servants to the interior of the *Zenana*, or seraglio.

Machi Bhawan. The same door leads to the Machi Bhawan. In the court-yard of the palace, the water of the Jumna was conveyed by artificial channels and used to be accumulated here to form a store-house for fishes which afforded spoitive amusement to the Emperor and his favorite *Harems* and courtiers, who took delight in ensnaring them. The place consists of an oblong room of white marble, most elaborately carved, and communicates with an open marble loggia of beautifully carved arches in the Saracenic style. The chambers on two sides served as office rooms. Between the Machi Bháwan and the small mosque (known as *Mina*

---

* God of wood and water. A saint skilled in divination, who is said to have discovered the water of life. Mahomedans offer oblations to him, of lamps, flowers, &c., placed on little rafts launched on the river. Travellers by boat always invoke him on starting.

† The name of a sacred well at Mecca, called also Hagar's well.

‡ The numerical value of the words, Hauz Jahangiri, is 1113. When from this the numerical value of Zamzam (94) is taken away, the date of foundation (1019 A. H.) is found.

The author of the *Travels of a Hindu* has in his work alluded to the favourite drinking cup of Jahángir. It had been scooped hollow out of an uncommonly large sized ruby, more than three inches long by as many broad, in the fashion of a goblet with the name of Jahángir inscribed on it in golden letters. Side by side was placed a similar but smaller cup with a leg to stand on, which had belonged to the great Tamerlane. Both were the property of the ex-King of Oudh and were placed for sale in one of the English jewellery shops in Calcutta a few years before 1860. Their ultimate fate is not known.

The Dewan-i-Am (interior).

Page 80

The Dewan-i-Kha's.

Page 81.

The Dewan-i-Khas (interior).

Page 81

15

The Dewan-i-Khas, the Throne and the Samman Burj.

Page 81.

Masjid), formerly used by the inmates of the palace, are the bronze gates of Chittore, brought here by the Emperor Akbar after his celebrated siege of that fortress in 1567.* The marble tanks and reservoirs of the Machi Bháwan were all excavated by Suraj MalJát, who carried them to Dig, near Bhartpur, where he built garden-houses, summer houses and bathing *ghâts*, which to this day are the admiration of travellers. A large quantity of inlaid marble in the Diwán-i-Am and neighbouring buildings was also sold by auction in the time of Lord William Bentinck, Governor-General of India; but the buildings were repaired at considerable outlay by the late Lord Mayo and the late Viceroy Lord Northbrook.

The Diwan-i-Khas.

To the north of the above, overlooking the river from an elevated terrace, is the *Diwan-i-Khas*, or the Hall of special private audience. It is an oblong room of white marble, 64 feet 9 inches long, 34 feet broad, and 22 feet high, with two splendid halls, most beautifully sculptured, which, by an arched colonnade, join an open marble gallery of equal extent. The halls are models of perfection. The columns and arches, elegantly constructed in Saracenic style, are exquisitely carved and inlaid, while the walls are ornamented with vases and flowers in relief.

Tavernier's account of the Diwan-i-Khas.

Tavernier, the French merchant and jeweller, who visited Agra in 1640,† while Sháh Jahán was still on the throne, thus describes the *Diwan-i-Khas*, or Hall of private audience :—

"At the end of the Court (*viz.*, the *Diwan-i-Am*, or Public Hall of audience) there is, on the left hand, a second gateway

* Ferishta has given a minute and spirited account of this siege. Rana Ude Singh, Chief of Chittor, was the head of the Rajput clans, and the place was the stronghold of Hindu independence. The Rajputs offered a desperate resistance, and the brave garrison, declining the Emperor's offer of quarter, perished to a man. The conquest of Chittor conduced greatly to the pacification of Rajputana.

† Keene, in his Handbook to Agra, erroneously gives the date as 1666. Tavernier seems to have paid a visit to Agra in November 1665, but Sháh Jahán was alive then. and in close confinement in the palace. He died in 1666. The traveller could not have been shown over all the buildings of the palace described in Book I. Chapter VII, while the old King was in confinement there. Tavernier commences this Chapter with an interesting note describing how he had a full view of the palace. He says:—" Before the King (namely Sháh Jahán) had given up his residence at Agra for that at Jahanabad, whenever he went to the country on a visit, he entrusted the custody of the palace, where his treasure was, to one of the principal and most trustworthy of his Omerahs, who, until the return of the King, never moved, neither day nor night, from this gate where his lodging was. It was during such an absence that I was permitted to see the palace at Agra. The King having left for Jahanabad, where all the Court followed and even the women too, the government of the palace was conferred on a noble who was a great friend of the Dutch, and, in general, of all the Franks.

which gives entrance to another great court, which is also surrounded by galleries, under which there are also small rooms for some officers of the palace. From this second Court you pass into a third where the King's apartments are situated. Sháh Jahán had intended to cover the arch of a great gallery which is to the right hand with silver, and a Frenchman, named Augustin De Bordeaux, was to have done the work. But the great Mughal, seeing there was no one in his kingdom who was capable to send to Goa to negotiate an affair with the Portuguese, the work was not done, for, as the ability of Augustin was feared, he was poisoned on his return from Cochin. This gallery is painted with foliage of gold and azure, and the floor is covered over with a carpet. There are doors under the gallery giving entrance into very small square chambers. I saw two or three of them which were opened for us, and we were told that the others were similar. The three other sides of the Court are altogether open, and there is but a simple wall to the height of the support. On one side overlooking the river there is a projecting *Díwán*, or belvedere, where the King comes to sit when he wishes to enjoy the pleasure of seeing his brigantines and making his elephants fight. In front of the Díwán there is a gallery which serves as a vestibule, and the design of Sháh Jahán was to cover it throughout by a trellis of rubies and emeralds which would represent, after nature, green grapes and those commencing to become red; * * * but this design, proving too expensive, had to be abandoned."

The Khas Mahal. Next to the Díwán-i-Khás, overhanging the river, is the Zenana, or Harem, before alluded to, called the Khás Mahal, or the private apartments of the ladies of the Royal Harem. The substructures of the palace are of red sandstone, the Jumna washing the walls seventy feet below; but the whole of its chambers, corridors, and pavilions are of pure white marble, most elaborately carved, and exquisitely ornamented with flowers

M. Velant, Chief of the Dutch factory at Agra, as soon as the King had left, went to salute this noble and to make him a present according to the custom. * * * Compliments having passed on both sides, the Governor asked Mr. Velant what he desired him to do to serve him, and, he having prayed him to have the goodness, as the Court was absent, to permit him to see the interior of the palace, it was granted him and six men were given to accompany us." *Travels in India by Tavernier*, Vol. I., page 106. The account has clear reference to the traveller's second voyage when he visited Agra from a journey to Surat in 1640, when Sháh Jahán was enjoying a peaceable reign. See Introduction, page xiv, *ibid.*

The Kha's Mahal.

Page 82

Interior of the Palace.

Page 83

and festoons. This lovely mansion was built by Sháh Jahán before new Delhi; and its luxurious pavilions, with gilded roofs and domes, are all of the rich style of Florentine mosaic, and of singular elegance and beauty. They glitter all over with jasper, cornelian, lapis-lazuli, agate and bloodstone, and the balconies and terraces are wrought in open patterns of such rich designs that, according to an American traveller, "they resemble the fringes of lace when seen from below." The adaptation of one part to another, the perfect harmony prevailing in the various sections of the building, the richness of style, and above all its elegance, are proof of the taste of the authors, and fill the curious observer with a sense of admiration and awe. No chamber, no pavilion, no terrace or window is wanting, and it seems as if the imperial halls had just been vacated by their occupiers, and were ready to be repeopled with the household of the great Emperor. They bring vividly before the eye a living picture of the daily routine of his public duties and his private pursuits and domestic life.

In a balcony overlooking the river are marks of blank spaces. The balcony.
In these spaces were pictures of the Mughal Emperors from Timúr, mounted on glass placed against the walls. Suráj Mal, the *Ját*, Rájá of Bhartpur, took away these pictures, and the spaces are left blank as signs of spoliation of the Játs.

The injurious effects of time and spoliation are visible here and there. A cannon ball burst through the marble trellis-work in a small courtyard in front of the Diwán-í-Khas, causing a rent in the screen of the royal pavilion. This was the result of the cannonade by General Perron, Commandant of Sindhia's troops, who besieged the fort in 1803, and selected that side as the most assailable. Many flowers and blossoms of cornelian, with leaves of bloodstone and gems, inlaid in the marble, have been wantonly dug out, and the polished fountains and tanks are dry.

The following Persian poems are beautifully inscribed on the walls of the Khás Mahal.

ازين دلکشا قصر عالي بنا   هر اکبر آبان شد عرش سا (عثمان)
بود کنگرش از جبين سپهر   نما يان چو دندان مين سپهر

سجود در این سرای سرور　　کند سرنوشت بد از جبهه دور
شرافت یکی آیه در شان او　　سعادت در آغوش ایوان او　(ابوبکر)
ره جور از بیش و کم بسته است　　بزنجیر عدلش ستم بسته است
بنازم بزنجیر کز عدل شاه　　همه چشم شد در ره داد خواه
بر احوال مردم چنان در حساب　　که داند چه بینند شبها به خواب　(الله محمد)
در ایوان شاهی بصد احتشام　　چو خورشید برچرخ بادا مدام
چو ایوان او عالم آرائی شد　　سر خاک ز و آسمان سای شد
شهنشاه آفاق شاه جهان　　که نازد باو روح صاحبقران　(عمر)
باین رونق و زیب و زینت مکان　　ندیده بروی زمین آسمان
بود صحن بامش چو سیمای مهر　　بزیرش فتاده چو سایه سپهر
بتاریخش اندیشه آورد رو　　در فیض شد باز از چار سو
چنین گفت طبع حقایق شناس　　سعادت سرای وهمایون اساس

By the construction of this delightful palace of spacious foundation,
Akbarabad has raised its head to the ninth heaven.*
Its parapet walls touch the forehead of sky
And are visible like the teeth of the letter *Sin*†.
Bowing ‡ in adoration before the gateway of this mansion of delight,
Removes the dictates of misfortune from off the forehead.
Nobility is but one word in its praise ;
Prosperity is the inseparable companion of its galleries.
The path of oppression under any phase is closed,
By the chain § of its justice the hands of tyranny are bound.
Proud am I of the king's chain of justice,
For it is ever ready to do justice to those who seek it.
It has such an intimate knowledge of the condition of the people
That it knows even what they see in their dreams.
May it, in the King's palace, with a thousand splendours,
Remain like the sun in the sky.
When the King's castle adorned the world,
The head of the earth touched the sky through pride.
Emperor of the World, Sháh Jahán,
Who is the pride of the soul of Shahib Qiran,||

---

* *Arsh* (عرش) Ninth heaven, where the Throne of God is.

† That is, the parapets of this palace are as clearly visible as the sharp points or projections in the Persian letter *Sin* س, which resemble teeth.

‡ The word used is *Sajud*, from *Sijda* سجده, bowing so as to touch the ground with the forehead in adoration, especially to God.

§ The famous chain of justice was tied in this hall with the other end on the ground opposite the Jumna. Any man aggrieved pulled it, and the bells and rings attached to it informed the King of the petitioner's presence, and the petitioner was heard and redress given direct from the Royalty.

|| Namely, Tymur, who is called Sahib-i-Qiran, or the Lord of constellation.

The Shish Mahal or Palace of Mirrors.

Page 85.

Founded a mansion with such beauty, splendour and grace
That the like of it the sky has never seen on the earth's surface.
The courtyard of its upper storey shines like the forehead of the moon ;
Below it lies the sky like a shadow.
When I consulted Reason for its date,
The gates of bounty opened on me in all directions.
So said the mind which ever stands on the side of truth :
'This is a mansion of prosperity of fortunate foundation'.– *

In front of the *Khas Mahal*, is the Angurí Bágh, still overrun with green shrubs, roses, jasmine and vines and studded with elegant fountains and parterres. It is an immense court, 235 by 170 feet, surrounded by three sets of chambers on three sides, all built by Akbar, and intended for the use of the King's Harem. It is surrounded by a colonnade, and on the fourth side is a spacious marble pavilion. The Court communicates with the *Shish Mahal* and the Royal Baths. It was to these chambers that the British officers and their families flocked for protection during the troublesome days of 1857. A small passage to the north of the Angurí Bágh leads to the most remarkable of the female apartments, the *Shish Mahal*, or Palace of Mirrors so called from the walls being lined with talc, or small bits of glass, disposed of so as to represent clusters of mirrors in miniature. This glazed mansion consists of two compartments. In the centre is a beautiful *jet d'eau*, discharging its contents into marble basins so curiously carved that the moving water over it produced the appearance of fish. The walls over which the mimic cascades tumbled are so constructed at the northern end as to be lighted from within, and the light, reflected by thousands of transparent glasses all round, and the sheet of water below and the rays caused by the descending showers, afforded a most dazzling and enchanting scene. The spectacle must have once realized all the splendours of Arabian story. It is a pity that the marble flags with which the floors of these luminous chambers were paved have been dug out.

The Anguri Bagh.

The Shish Mahal.

The Hammam, or Bagnio close to the female apartments, consists of several rooms for bathing. The water, rising from a hundred springs, spread a delicious coolness throughout the

The Hammam.

* The numerical value of the letters in the last sentence is, according to *Abjad* rules, 1046, which represents the Hijri year corresponding to 1636 A. D. This was the year when Sháh Jahán concluded peace with Adil Shah, king of Bijapur. In the space after each couplet are written the words God, Muhammad, Abu Bakr, Umar, Usmán, and Ali.

room, while the carving in bold relief and the superior polish of the marble used contributed to the perfection of the work. Two passages from the Hammam, both of red sandstone, lead to the Jumna, which washes the walls. One of these was a passage for the Royal ladies and their fair concubines, and the other for Jodh Bai, the Hindu Queen of Jahangír. From the balconies of the Palace Royal, a beautiful view of the gardens and palm-groves on the opposite bank is obtained, while about a mile down the stream is to be seen that wonder of India, the Taj, shining like a palace of ivory and crystal.

The Pachisi.

The next Court is paved with squares of white and black marble so as to represent a *Pachisi* board. The game is a kind of Eastern backgammon, or trictrac. Each square in this spacious board is wide enough to allow a man to sit within it. In ordinary games ivory pieces or figures are used. But it is said Akbar and his wives played on this board with gaily clad girls, distinguished by badges to specify their position in the game, who trotted from square to square, according to the movements of a wand used by the players.

The *Samman Burj.*

On one side of the court of the *Pachisi* board is the *Samman Burj*, or octagonal tower, the boudoir of the chief Princess. It is the work of Sháh Jahán, and it was here that that Emperor breathed his last with his eyes turned towards the glittering mausoleum of the wife of his youth and his affectionate daughter, Jahán Ara, sitting by his side.* The mansion is of pure marble and most elaborately carved and inlaid. In the midst is a small but neat reservoir of marble in the shape of a rose. This was the reservoir used by Arjumand Báno Bagum, the King's favourite wife, and the lady of the Táj, for washing her face, hands, and feet. It was decorated with precious stones, all of which were carried away by the *Játs.* Two small windows higher up the wall are pointed out as having been used by the chief Sultana as a repository for her jewels and ornaments, access to which was obtained by a golden staircase. It was from this tower that the Royal ladies witnessed the animal fights in the open space below. The King sat on the marble throne opposite.

* *Badshah Nama*, p. 933.

The Samman Burj.
Page 86.

The Marble

The open terrace facing the river, where the marble throne now is, was originally roofed, and formed part of the *Diwan-i-Khas.* But, the hall having been dismantled by the Raja of Bhartpur, the materials were removed by him. Five marble blocks of the material were sent to London as a curiosity, while seven are lying on the spot at the moment of writing.* To the north of the white marble palace, called the Diwán-i-Khas of Sháh Jahán, is to be seen a rarity of the sculptor's art, *viz.*, a black marble throne, hewn out entire, with its four legs, from one block. It is 10 feet 7½ inches long, 9 feet 10 inches broad, and 6 inches thick. The stone is 1 foot 4 inches in height and is supported by octagonal pedestals, or feet. It is completely penetrated by a long fissure, which is ascribed to its having been profaned by the feet of the Ját usurper, Jawáhar Singh, Rajah of Bhartpur, son of Suraj Mal Ját, who was in temporary possession of Agra in 1765. The credulous maintain that, having been profaned by the Ját chieftain, not only did it crack from side to side, but blood rushed out of it in two places. The usurper was shortly afterwards assassinated in the palace, while his father was slain in the battle with Najibuddaulá. The presence of red marks on the throne is, however, due to a mineral substance. The throne was used by the Emperor Jahángir in private audiences with his ministers. An inscription in large Persian letters runs round all the four sides of the thickness of stone and is as follows:— **The black marble throne.**

چون شاه سلیم وارث تاج و نگین   بر تخت نشست و بست گیتی آئین
شد اسم مبارکش جهانگیر چو ذات   وز نور عدالت لقبش نورالدین
بادشاهی که تیغ او سازد   چون دو پیکر سر عدو بدو نیم
باشد این تختگاه فرخنده   تکیه گاه خدایگان کریم
محک خسروان پاک ملک   مهر و مه را عیار بر زر و سیم
مسند با صفا ز نور و ضیا   گوهر بی بها چو در یتیم
پئے تاریخ او بفکر شدم   مدد ے جستم از خدائے حکیم
تا فلک تختگاه خورشید است   گفت ماند سریر شاه سلیم

When Shah Salim, the heir to the crown and seal,
Sat on the throne and administered the world,

* September 1892.

His name became Jáhángir, or Conqueror of the World, as was his nature,
And from the light of his justice he received the title of Nuruddin, the splendour of the Faith,
A King whose sword,
Cuts the enemy's head into two halves like the Gemini star.
May this fortunate throne
Be the asylum of many future Kings!
It is the test for such Kings as are on an equality with angels,
A touchstone for the gold of the sun and the silver of the moon.
This elegant throne, through brilliancy and splendour,
Is like unto an invaluable and precious pearl.
In thinking of its date,
I sought help from Almighty God;
The voice came at last,
'As long as the heaven is the throne for the sun, may the Throne of the King Sálim last !' 1011 H.

North face (centre).	South face (centre).
همیشه باد مزین بنور مهر الله	سریر حضرت سلطان سلیم اکبر شاه

May the Throne of Sultan Salim, son of Akbar Sháh,
Ever receive its splendour by the light of God's mercy.

Below the inscription on the eastern side is the following inscription:—

اسم سامي پیش از جلوس شاه سلیم وبعد ازان نورالدین محمد جهان گیر یاد شاه غازي

"His exalted name, before accession, was Sháh Salím, and afterwards, Nuruddin Mohamed Jahángir Badsháh Ghází."

بلند مرتبه باد ازفلک زحکم اله سریر شاه جهانگیر ابن اکبر شاه

May the dignity of the Throne of Jahangir Sháh, son of Akbar Sháh by God's command, excel that of heaven.

The following table illustrates the actual position of the inscriptions as they appear on the Throne:—

معنی خسرو ان پای مای	مهرو مه راعیار بر زر و سیم	مسند باصفا زنور وضیا	گوهر بے بہا چون در یتیم

مدد ت جستم از خداے حکیم		با شد این تختگاه فرخنده
•		یا حافظ
سر پر حضرت سلطان سلیم اکبر شاه		همیشه باد مرز عن قبور مهر اله
•		یا حفیظ
بنگی تا دلیخ او بفکر شدم		تکیه گاه خدا ایگان کرم

چون دو پیکر سر عدو بدو نیم	باد شاهي كه تيغ او ما زن	گفت ما نه سرير شاه سليم	تافلک تختگاه خورشید ست

The Moti Musjid.

The prettiest structure in the fort is the *Moti Musjid*, or Pearl Mosque, as it is poetically and justly called. It stands north of the Diwan-i-Am, on a lofty plateau, to which access is obtained by a long flight of steps. Entering a simple gateway by steps of free-stone roughly hewn, and expecting nothing very grand, one is surprised by coming suddenly in sight of a structure at once grand, fascinating and sublime, which, with majestic and colossal form, combines exquisite simplicity refined taste and elegance. It is, as a writer says, "an agreeable surprise," filling the curious observer with a fervour of admiration. You see before you a sanctuary of white marble rising gracefully over the silvery surface formed by its lovely court. The mosque measures 187 feet by 234 feet. The square court is paved with large white flags, and is surrounded by a chaste gallery and colonnade of the same material. "The beauty of the mosque," says Fergusson, "resides in its courtyard, which is wholly of white marble from the pavement to the summit of the domes." At the extremity of this spacious court, and removed about 100 feet from the gateway, is the noble mosque, comprising a single room, 150 feet by 60, supported by a triple row of pillars, joined to one another by the most exquisitely proportioned Saracenic arches. The three lovely domes of white marble, with their gilded spires springing gracefully from the pavilions, rise considerably above the ramparts, giving it a truly grand appearance. In the enthusiastic language of Mr. Taylor, "in all distant views of the Fort these domes are seen like silvery bubbles which have rested a moment on its walls, and which the next breeze may sweep away."

European artists and travellers have pronounced the architecture to be absolutely perfect, and, while its style is the purest Saracenic, it possesses the simplicity of Doric art. The whole design is instinct with life, and, whether judged from the exact proportions of its dimensions, or the admirable skill of its design, the mosque is justly the admiration alike of the student of art, the traveller and the spectator. "It is truly the gem of mosques." One eminent authority writes of its surpassing beauty: "Any woodcut cannot do it justice; it must be seen to be appreciated." Another writer, comparing it with the grand mosque of Sháh Jahán at Delhi, expresses his

The Moti Masjid or Pearl Mosque (exterior view).
Page 90.

opinion, that "while the colossal Juma Musjid of Delhi, from its magnitude and its bold outline, may be likened to the masculine of its kind, the one under discussion, from its *tout ensemble*, may, so to speak, be styled the feminine, in appearance at least." The graphic pen of Mr. Taylor thus paints its beauty: "It is a sanctuary so pure and stainless, revealing so exalted a spirit of worship, that I felt humbled, as a Christian, to think that our noble religion has never inspired its architects to surpass this temple of God and Mohammad." A recent writer (Sir Richard Temple) remarks: "No place is more fitted to inspire men with deeper religious culture than this spotless mosque." Another writer says: "It is the purest object yet dedicated by the vanity of man to the worship of the Almighty Being alone." That much of this enthusiasm is well deserved, there can be no room for doubt.

In the midst of the courtyard is a beautiful fountain for the ablutions of the faithful. On a platform of stone there is also a sun-dial, and the Musjid is joined to the private apartments of the palace by staircases on both sides. There are also side-rooms, separated by lattice work of marble for the worship of the ladies of the Harem. The mosque affords accommodation for 600 worshippers. An inscription in black marble letters inscribed on the entablature over the front arch shows that it was built by Sháh Jahán in 1063 A. H. (1654).

Cost of building. The building of the mosque, which was commenced in 1056-57 H. (1648 A. D.), occupied seven years and was completed in 1063 H. (1652 A. D.), being the 26th year of Sháh Jahán's reign. The cost was three hundred thousand rupees.

Inscription. The following inscription runs along the entablature over the front row of supporting pillars, towards the western end of the interior of the Musjid:—

این کعبه نورانی و بیت المعمور ثانی که صبح در جنب صفائی آن
شامیست تیره و خورشید از فرط ضیائی آن چشمه‌ایست خیره - گرمی پایدارش
با طارق عرش همدوش و گنبد فیض بارش با اوراق فردوس هم آغوش
بنیان عالی شانش تبیان لمسجد اسس علی التقوی - و ذروه سپهر
اقرانش ترجمان فاستوی وهو بالافق الاعلی - هر گلدسته اش دسته
نورے بانوار کواکب بسته - یا فواره فیضی چشمهٔ آفتاب جسته - هر کلس
زرینش شمع فروغ بخش قنادیل آسمانی - هر محراب نور آگینش هلال

نو يدر سان عيد جاوداني- بر اطرافش قلعه لال فام مستقر الخلافة اكبر
آباد كه با زمردين حصار سبع سياره پيوسته-گوي ها له ايست دور بدر
منور كه بر فيضان سحاب رحمت برها نيست متين - باد ايره ايمت گرد
مهرا نور كه بر ترشح امطار كرامت نشا نيست مبين - همانا بهشتي
قصريست والا-از يك لولوے لالا-كه از سرآغاز معمو ره دنيا مسجدے
سرا سر ازسنگ سر مر مصفا عديل آن بر روي كار نيامده - واز بدو ظهور
عا لم معبدے منور ومجلي نظير آن جلوه ظهور نداده-بفرمان خاقان
سليمان احتشام وسلطان خليل احترام چهره افروز مسلماني باني مباني
جهانباني شهنشاه عرش بارگاه-ظل الله-خلا يق پناه-موسس اركان خلافت
مرصص بنيان عدل ورافت-به يمن قدمش زمين رابر آسمان هزاران ناز
وازفور نعمش آسمان را با زمين فراوان نياز- بخت ودو لت راازعشق
خدمتش دوام بيداري-ملك وملت را باجمال طلعتش كمال هواداري-
باد بهشت ازخاك درگاه فلك جاهش در يوزه گرے-آتش دوزخ ازآب
شمشير دشمن كاهش وظيفه خورے——

بناے ملک را زو استوا ري   اساس عدل رازو پا يداري
مدام از چشمه تيغ ظفر خيز   كند پيما نه كفا ر لبر يز
جنا بش را فلک خد مت گذا رے   جبينش را سحر آئينه دارے

قطب آسمان دين پرودي وشر يعت نوا زي-مركز دوران عدل گستري
ومملكت طرا زي-ابوالمظفر شهاب الدين محمد صاحب قران ثاني شاه
جهان باد شاه غازي بنا يافت ودر عرض هفت سال بصرف سه لكه روپيه
اواخر سال بست وششم جلوس اقبال مانوس مطا بق سنة هزار وشصت
وسه ١٠٦٣ هجري ماپيرا يه انجام در برو تاج اختتام بر سرگرفته-ايزد
بيهمال بدوامن نيت حق طو يت اين پاد شاه دين پناه همگنان را توفيق
ادائے طاعات وآقتنا ے حسنات روز افزون كناد راجر دلالت وهدايت آن را
برروزگار فرخنده آثار اين حق گز ين حقيقت آگاه عايد گردا ناد -آمين
يا رب العالمين—

"This bright *Kaába* and second Tabernacles of Bliss is so pre-eminently luminous that, compared to it, the bright dawn of morning looks like the dusk of evening; the effect of its great brilliancy is such that the sun, compared to it, is like an eye that is dazzled by brightness. Its firm foundation is as high as that of the highest heaven. Its bounty-showering towers are as lofty as the porticoes of paradise. Its grand foundations indicate that it is a mosque founded on the basis of piety; and its turrets

The Moti Mosjid (interior).

Page 92.

vie in brilliancy with the meridian sun when passing through the zodiac, while they surpass it in height. Each of its flower-pinnacled shafts is like a bunch of light connected with a cluster of brilliant stars, or like a fountain of beneficent rays emanating from the sun. Each of its gilded pinnacles affords light to the heavenly luminaries ; each of its resplendent arches resembles the new moon, and is ever hailed as the festival of *Id*.

On either side of it is the fort, built of red sandstone, of the metropolis of Akbarabad ; the Masjid is to this fort as the seven planets are to the sky ; one may say it is a halo round the moon, which is sure proof of the advent of clouds of mercy ; or it is a circle round the luminous sun, which is an unmistakeable sign of the coming fall of beneficent rain. Verily, it is a lofty mansion of paradise, made (as it were) of one precious pearl, for from the beginning of the inhabited world the like of a mosque built entirely of pure marble was never produced ; and since the creation the parallel of a temple so brilliant and bright from top to bottom has never appeared.

Built by the command of the potentate of Solomon's magnificence ; the Sultán of Abraham's honour ; the embellisher of the countenance of Islám ; the founder of the Empire ; the king of kings, whose court equals in dignity the highest heaven ; the shadow of God ; the asylum of the people ; the strength of the pillars of State ; the prop of the basis of justice and benignity ; the earth, being blessed with his footsteps, feels more dignified than the heavens in a thousand ways; through the profusion of his gifts the heavens are compelled to acknowledge the earth's superiority; prosperity and wealth, through love of service to him, are ever awake to their duty; State and religion are greatly attracted by the beauty of his countenance; the zephyrs of Paradise crave the dust of his Sanctuary; dignified as the heavens; the destroying fire of hell solicits a stipend from the polish of the steel of his sword, which destroys the enemies;

The foundations of State receive strength from him ;
The basis of justice obtains duration from him ;
His victorious sword
Ever despatches the infidels ;
Heaven is one of his slaves ;
The dawn of day is a mirror-holder for his countenance ;

He is the supporting axis of the heavenly faith and of the laws; the centre of the circle of justice and administration; the father of victory; Shahabuddin Mohammad, the second lord of the fortunate conjunction of the planets, the valiant King Sháh Jahán.

This building was completed in a space of seven years, at a cost of three lakhs of rupees towards the end of the 26th year of the fortunate reign corresponding to the year 1063 Hijri.

May it so please God, the God without compeer, that, through the blessings of the good intentions of this sovereign, the defender of the Faith, all people may have an increased desire for performing devotions and doing virtuous deeds! And may the direction and guidance in the right way have as their result the salvation of this righteous King, the accepted of God! O Lord of the universe! Amen!"

The Nagina Masjid. A passage to the north-west corner of the Machi Bhawan leads to the *Nagina Masjid*, a small but very handsome mosque, 60 feet square. It was founded by Aurangzeb for the ladies of the Zenana, and, being built entirely of white marble after the fashion of the Moti Masjid, may be called its smaller counterpart. Connected with it, on an elevation overlooking the waters of the Jumna, is a set of chambers in which Sháh Jahán was kept in honourable confinement by his ambitious son Aurangzeb, and the room is still pointed out where he used to live, with little to console his heart except the sight before him of the monument raised by his own genius to the memory of the wife of his youth, the renowned Lady of the Táj. In a wall opposite is a cavity where used to be stored warm water for the purpose of ablution before going to prayers.

The gates of Mahmud's tomb. The apartments which were the actual quarters of Sháh Jahán while reigning Emperor of Hindustan are also noticeable for containing the reputed "Somnáth" gates. The avenging army of Lord Ellenborough, under the command of General Pollock, brought these gates from Ghazni, as a trophy of British success in Afghanistan. The gates are 12 feet high by 9 in breadth, and are elaborately carved and inlaid. They were the subject of a proclamation from the Governor-General announcing to the native rulers and people of India that the victorious British army had borne the gates of Somnáth in triumph from Afghanistan, and that "the insult of 800 years was avenged." The proclamation was correct enough so far as it announced that the gates were brought from Mahmúd's tomb at Ghazni. But it was a mistake to suppose that they were the gates of Somnáth, believed to have been carried away by Mahmúd and put on his tomb after his death as evidence of Mohammedan conquest. The original gates were of sandal-wood and of great celebrity, from their elaborate design. The conclusion arrived at by the best judges was that they were destroyed by fire, and that, when the tomb was repaired and renewed, a new set of gates made of deodár were set up. A microscopic examination revealed the further fact that, while the framework contains *Cufi* inscriptions, there is not a single figure of the 33 millions of Hindu gods, nor any other Hindu symbol, on it. Nevertheless, the gates are interesting, as bearing evident marks of great age, and as the relics of the last resting-place of the greatest Asiatic conqueror, whose ambition could only find rest in his grave. The ornamentation in the framework consists of panelling in small compartments, each containing a star of six points, in the shape of two interlaced triangles, and is wrought in well-relieved fret-work of the most chaste and florid arabesque, surrounded by borders of running patterned arabesques, which all plainly point to their Mohammedan origin.

The Mina Bazar.

A door, close to the chambers of the Mína Masjid, opens on a beautiful balcony with a courtyard lined with apartments of red sandstone. This was the place where the ladies of the Zenana brought and sold their fancy and artistic wares, the King and his wives taking the part of purchasers. Here it was that Jahángír conceived a violent passion for Núr Jahán. As she, in her youth, accompanied her mother, the wife of the Lord High Treasurer of Akbar, to attend the fancy fair, the eyes of the two met, and a walk free and independent, a face smiling, handsome, childish, and happy, a figure tall and graceful, and a waist Cypress-like, fascinated the future Emperor of Hindustan, himself possessed of a handsome exterior, a tall figure, with broad chest and long arms, and eyes ominously keen and piercing. The passion was mutual. The court is now used for lawn-tennis.

The Jahangiri Mahal.

To the south of the Khás Mahal, and close to the Amar Singh Gate, is a massive building in redstone, called the Jahángíri Mahal, or the Palace of Jahángír, a singularly elegant and beautiful structure. It is a two-storeyed building, most exquisitely carved and inlaid with relieving lines of white marble, and two courts paved in red sandstone, the largest of which is seventy feet square. The peculiarity of the structure lies in the general avoidance of arches, the roofs resting on flanks of free redstone, supported by massive but singularly handsome and richly carved pillars of the same material. The structure is most perfect, and, as Fergusson remarks, "is singularly elegant in detail; and having escaped the fate of so many palaces of India, time has only softened, without destroying, the beauty of its features." The stones on the interior and ceiling were once covered with lovely paintings in gold; but these have all been obliterated through lapse of time. The Hindu brackets, exquisitely carved, the moulding of conventionalised lotus-flowers, supported by a pair of birds on either side, the carvings of elephants on the roof of the building in red sandstone, facing the river, are all unique decorations in the Saracenic style, and exhibit Hindu proclivities. This was the palace, the residence of Jodh Bái, the wife of Jahángir, and daughter of Moth, the Rájá of Jodhpur, called by Mohammedan historians Mariam Zamáni. In a niche in one of the walls was placed the image of *Hanumanji*, one of the principal gods of Hindu mythology, which was destroyed by Aurangzeb. Behind the ladies' chambers is a covered passage, separated from the rest of the building by lattice work. This was the place for the female guards who performed watch and guard duty to the royal personages when they retired to rest. There are chambers of peculiar construction in which the game of hide-and-seek was played by the royal inmates.

The *ankh michouli*.

The upper storey consists of two pavilions, of massive style, elaborately carved and exquisitely ornamented. One of these has been modernized, and has been converted into a residence for a warrant officer, and the other is still perfect. On the roof there

Jahangírí Mahal (exterior view)

Page 96.

24

Jahangir's Palace.

Page 96

Palace of Jodh Bai, Fort, Agra (exterior view).

are also a number of cisterns, in which the water of the Jumna used to be accumulated and distributed to the various parts of the palace, by means of copper pipes, still extant, the name of the palace to which they belonged being engraved on the medallions which surmount each pipe.

Among the wonders of the palace are the curious underground chambers, descent to which is obtained by broad stairs to the south of the Khas Mahal. The windows of these labyrinths, overlooking the Jumna, may be observed from the base of Jahángir's palace. The buildings extend over a considerable area and terminate in a Baoli, or well-house. In these vaulted chambers the Emperor and his delicate Harem found shelter from the burning heat of the sun and scorching winds in the summer. Fountains of water played and made the atmosphere cool and delicious. Here the Emperor, in his pleasant retreat, dashed through the pure and cold waters, the royal party was entertained with dancing and music, the chambers resounded with festive merriment. The avenues in the *Baoli* that surrounded the waters of the wall were carpeted with cushions of soft velvet, on which sat the royal ladies, chattering and making merry, 'while the apathic boatmen, gliding down the river, gazed up at the lofty walls, wondering what the laughter meant.' A dark and dreary chamber at the extremity of the well was designed for the incarceration of women found guilty of misdemeanour. It is said one of these under-ground passages communicated with the Taj and the Sekandara; but no outlet has yet been discovered. The underground chambers.

Abul Fazl notices the fact of the foundation of the Fort of Agra by Akbar in the records of the 9th year of His Majesty's reign (1564 A. D.) thus :—

"The buildings of the old fort on the bank of the river (Jumna) having become dilapidated * through lapse of time, a new fort of red sandstone was built on its site, under orders of His Majesty. The plan was designed by skilful engineers and accomplished artisans. The width of the wall was fixed at 30 yards *Badshahi*, and the height at 60 yards of the same. It Cost of building the fort

* The old fort called Badalgarh suffered much during the earthquake of 911 A. H. (1505 A. D.), and was nearly destroyed during the explosion which took place in 962 A. H. (1556 A. D.)– see page 74 *ante*.

comprises four gateways, which open the door of wealth and prosperity on the four quarters of the world. A number of 3,000 to 4,000 masons and artisans was employed daily on the work, and it took eight years to build the fort.

The superintendent of the architecture was Qasim Khán, * the Lord of the Admiralty. The cost was 7 krore Tankas, or 35 lacs of rupees."

BURIED TOMBS DISCOVERED IN THE FORT.

According to Mr. Beal, the author of *Miftahul Tawarikh*, when, in 1218 A. H. (1803 A. D.), the Fort of Akbarabad (Agra) came into the possession of the East India Company, the Judge's Court was built in it. Forty-two years afterwards, or in 1845 A. D., orders were received for the demolition of the old . court-house, and a new one was built in its stead on the same spot. On digging the foundations of the old walls, four tombs were found, at a distance of one hundred paces from the tower called *Jhan Jhan Katora.* Two of these were without inscription ; but the other two contained marble sarcophagi with Persian inscriptions. One of these inscriptions shows that the tomb belonged to some grandee who died in the 46th year of the *Ilahi* year of Akbar, or 1010 A. H. (1601 A. D.). This was the time when Akbar was occupied in military operations in Khandesh, and Salem, the Crown Prince, had rebelled against him. Both tombs, from their locality in the fort, seem to have belonged to some beloved members of the Royal family who died a premature death, thus causing intense grief to their relations.

One of these inscriptions was thus :—

آه وا ویلا که آن جا نات من   رفت و مارا ساخت در غم مبتلا
سال فوتش چون بجستم از خرد   گفت با من کای غریب بی ریا
یکهزار و ده ز هجرت بود کان   رفت سوی خلد ازین دار فنا
گوش کن تاریخ شمسی را دگر   از الهی گشت نازل این ندا
روح پاکش را همین گویم بصدق   در بهشت عدن یارب باد جا

---

* In the 23rd year of the reign Qasim Khan was made Governor of Agra. He conquered Kashmir for Akbar, and was appointed Governor of Kabul in the 34th year. He was assassinated at Kabul in 1593 A. D.

Ah! Alas! my beloved
Has departed subjecting me to grief.
When I asked Reason the year of his death,
He replied, 'O poor unpretending man!
It was 1010 of the Hijra
That he proceeded to the paradise from this mortal world.'
Listen another year of *Shamsi*:
He died in 46th of *Ilahi*.
With perfect sincerity I pray for his sacred soul.
O God! may it find place in the paradise of Aden!

The sarcophagus containing the above inscription was in the fort at the time when Mr. Beal wrote his work in 1264 A. H. (1847 A. D.). The other tomb has the following inscription on it:—

واحسرتا که جان جهان از جهان برفت   بے او بماند قالب بے جان و جان برفت
لازم بود که زار بگریم به هائے هائے   خود بود ماه چون ز جهان نوجوان برفت
فرزند آنکه بود مرا روح وهم روان   بر ما نکرد مهر و بسویش روان برفت
تاریخ فوت او ز خرد جستم و بگفت   برگ گلے و شاخ گل از بوستان برفت
جیب حیات چاک بکن کا تبان گر   کان طوطی شکر لب شیرین زبان برفت

Alas! the life of the world has departed from the world;
Without him the body is without soul and life extinct.
It behoves that I should weep bitterly and cry out, *Hai! hai!*
For he was like the moon and has died young.
My son, who was as dear to me as life,
Has had no mercy on me, and proceeded towards Him.
When I asked reason the date of his death, he replied
'Both the branch of the rose and its leaf have left the rose-garden.'
Put an end, it behoves, to thy life, O writer!
For the sweet-tongued and sweet-beaked parrot has gone.

The above poems seem to have been written by a loving father to commemorate the mournful death of a youthful son who pre-deceased him. How short and unstable human life is, and how changeable and uncertain are its affairs, when it is seen that the affectionate mourner, to whom life must have become a misery, as his poetic effusions show, is no more, too, nor the dwellers in those high palaces and gorgeous edifices, lifting their heads to the sky, which are left on the spot forsaken and forlorn, as a mark of world's evanescent and transient nature; and further, what trace had been discovered of a dearly beloved during life, was by mere accident, centuries after he had shrivelled into dust and clay! *Tempora mutantur et nos mutamur in illis.*

THE TÁJ.

ABOUT a mile distant from the Fort is that wonder of the East, the jewel and glory of Indian architecture, the far-famed Táj. Being situated on a bend of the river Jumna, it looks much nearer the direction of the city than it really is. The road is by the river strand and was constructed by the labour of the destitute poor in the famine of 1838. The strand, eighty feet wide, is excellent, and the beauty of the town is enhanced by the commodious bathing *Gháts* along the river bank. The numerous temples, towers, summer-houses, and other elegant buildings on the river side render the sight of the city exceedingly charming and picturesque. The space between the Fort and the Táj was once studded with the villas of the nobility, the stately edifices and superb palaces and garden houses of the Omerahs of the Moghal Empire; but nothing now remains of them except huge mounds and shapeless masses of earth. Bernier, who saw these buildings, describes them as a "row of new houses with arcades resembling those of the principal streets in Delhi."* They have been also noticed by contemporary historians, Mulla Abdul Hamíd, author of *Bádsháh Náma,* and Mohammad, Sáleh, author of *Amal-i-Sáleh.* There were extensive Bazars in which commodities of all descriptions were sold by merchants from various parts of India and distant countries and the merchant classes had built edifices of solid masonry work and shops in which they exhibited the articles for sale. In making the strand, old masonry works and foundations, sometimes ten feet thick, were found, and they were so solid that they had to be blasted by powder.

The strand. The bathing ghats. Ruins of old villas.

History of Arjumand Bano. Begam.

Arjumand Bano Begam, surnamed Mumtaz-uz-Zamaní, or Mumtáz Mahal, was the daughter of Mirzá Abul Hasan Asif Khan, or Asif Jáh, the son of Mirza Ghías Beg Itimáduddaula, whose daughter, Núr Jahán, was the wife of Jahangir. She was thus niece to Nurjahan, the step-mother of Shah Jahán. As the aunt was famous for her surpassing beauty and accomplishments, so was the niece; as Núr Jahán had fascinated the libertine Jahángir with her charms, so Mumtaz subdued the stern Sháh Jahán with her loveliness. Both,

* Bernier's Travels in the Moghal Empire, p. 293.

Arjumand Bano Begam *alias* Taj Mahal.

Page 100.

in their turns, exercised great influence over their lords and husbands.

Jahángír betrothed Mumtáz-uz-Zamání to Sháh Jahán when the latter was fifteen years and 8 months old. After the expiry of five years and three months while Sháh Jahán was twenty years and eleven months old, he was married to Mumtáz. The bride, at the time of marriage, was 19 years eight months and 9 days old. The marriage took place on the night of Friday, the 9th of Rabí-ul-Awál, 1021 A. H. (1612 A. D.). The affectionate royal father, at a propitious moment, bound the wreath of pearls to the turban of the bride-groom with his own hands. The nuptials took place in the palace of Itimad-ud-daulá, the Emperor Jahángir gracing the occasion with his presence. The dowry was fixed at five lakhs of rupees. The couple remained on terms of deep affection throughout their lives. **Her marriage with Sháh Jahán.**

It must be noted that Sháh Jahán was already the husband of a wife when he married Mumtáz-uz-Zamani. One year and eight months before that marriage, he had been affianced to the daughter of Muzaffar Hussain Mirzá, son of Sultán Hussain Mirzá, son of Behram Mirzá, son of Sháh Ismaíl Safvi, King of Persia. The marriage took place in Rajab, 1019 A. H., when Sháh Jahan was above 19 years of age. The result of the union was Purhunar Bano Begam, born 12th Jamadiul-Ákhir, 1020 A. H. Five and a half years after his marriage with Mumtaz-uz-Zamani, he was married to the daughter of Sháh Nawáz Khan, son of Abdul Rahim *Khan-i-Khanán*, "out of," according to Abdul Hamíd, "motives of policy." The marriage took place in Agra, and the result of the union was a son named Prince Jahán Afroz, who died in Burhanpur at the age of one year and nine months. **Sháh Jahán's other wives.**

Notwithstanding these two marriages, His Majesty was so much attached to Mumtaz-uz-Zamani, that she was his inseparable companion, and he could not part with her even when engaged in military expeditions in remote parts of India such as the Deccan. What she wanted was never refused. She, in particular, acquired great fame for obtaining the free pardon of persons sentenced to undergo the extreme penalty of the law, and many whom she, out of **His attachment to Mumtaz-uz Zamani.**

compassion, recommended for the exercise of the King's prerogative, owed their life to her.

Issue from her.

Sháh Jahán had fourteen children by Mumtaz-uz-Zamani, of whom eight were sons and six daughters; of these seven were alive at the time of the Empress's death.

The following are the names of the children :—

1. Hurul-Nisa (daughter) born in Agra on 8th Safar 1022 A.H.; died in 1025 A.H, aged three years and one month.

2. Jahan-Ara-Begam (daughter), commonly known as the Begam Sahib, born on Saturday, the 21st Safar, 1023 A.H., when Shah Jahan was engaged in an expedition against the Rana of Mewar.

3. Mohammad Dara Shekoh (son), born in Ajmir after the return of the Emperor from Mewar, on the night of Saturday, the 29th of Safar 1024 A.H.

4. Mohammad Sháh Shuja (son), born in Ajmir on the night of Sunday, the 18th of Jamadiul-Akhir, 1025 A.H.

5. Roshanara Begam (daughter), born in Burhanpur on the 2nd of Ramazan 1026 A.H.

6. Mohammad Aurangzeb (son), born on the night of Saturday, the 15th of Zikad 1027 A.H.

7. Ummed Baksh (son), born in the neighbourhood of Sarhand on 11th Muharram 1029 A.H.; died in Burhanpur 1031 A.H.

8. Suria Bano Begam (daughter), born 20th Rajab 1030; died 1037 at the age of seven years.

9. Another son, born 1031 A.H., but died a few days after. No name had been given to him.

10. Murad Baksh (son), born in the fort of Rohtas on Wednesday, the 25th of Zilhij, 1033 A.H.

11. Lutfullah (son), born in Safar 1036; died in Ramazan 1037, aged one year and 7 months.

12. Daulat Afza (son), born in 1037; died the following year.

13. A daughter, born in 1039 A. H.; died the same year.

14. Gauhar Ara Begam (daughter), the last issue, born on the night of Wednesday, the 17th of Zika-ad, 1040 A. H. (1630 A. D.) in Burhanpur.

It was in giving birth to her last child that the Empress died. **Her death, 1630 A D.**

The authors of the *Bádsháhnáma* and *Amali Saleh,* both contemporary historians, have furnished touching particulars of the last moments of Mumtaz-uz Zamani.

Her last moments. Her Majesty being pregnant and the usual time of delivery being near, she became suddenly ill and suffered from anguish of travail in child-birth, from the morning of Tuesday to the midnight of Wednesday following, it being the 17th of the month of Zikad 1040 A.H. (1630 A.D.) After midnight she gave birth to a daughter; but, on account of some internal derangement, her troubles increased and she had fainting fits. At length seeing that her end was near, she asked the Princess Jahan Ara Begam, who sat by her side, to call the Emperor, her Royal consort, from a room in the *Zenana* where His Majesty then was. The Emperor hastened to the queen's apartment and took his seat at the head of his dying beloved wife's bed. Mumtaz-uz-Zamani looked on the king with despair and tears in her eyes, and admonished him to take good care of her children and her own aged father and mother when she was herself no more. Then fixing her eyes on the companion of her life and casting a deep look on him, she breathed her last at three watches before sunrise.

The mourning. The entire court went into mourning. His Majesty put on white robes, and the Princes Royal, the grandees of the realm and officials and servants of state dressed themselves in mourning costume.

Her age. Mumtaz-uz-Zamani, at the time of her death, was 39 years 4 months and 4 days old. The poet Bebadal Khan found the date of her death in the hemistich :—

جا ئے ممتاز محل جنت باد

"May paradise be the abode of Mumtaz Mahal."

The above gives the date 1040 A.H. (1630 A.D.)

Temporary burial at Burhanpur. The remains of the Empress were, according to the Eastern fashion of temporary burial, called *amanat* (trust), deposited in the garden of Zenabad across the Tapti river, in Burhanpur, where the king was then encamped, prosecuting the war against Khani-Jahan Lodi in the Deccan. The body was interred in a plot of ground in the midst of which was a beautiful fountain which adorned the garden palace of Zenabad.

On the afternoon of Thursday, the 25th of the month before mentioned, His Majesty, having crossed the Tapti, visited the garden of Zenabad to recite the Fatiha, or prayer, on the temporary tomb of the Empress. He made it his rule, as long as the camp was in Burhanpur, to visit the tomb every Friday. Grief so overwhelmed him that for a week he refused to see any Amir of the Empire and did not appear at the *Jharoka* window of the *Khás Am*, or transact any business of State. He was more than once heard to say that, if the burden of an Empire had not lain on his shoulders, and if the precepts of Mohammedan law (Shara) had not strictly forbidden demonstrations of sorrow on the death of any one which in any way infringed the rules of resignation and full reliance on the will of the Creator, so overpowered was he with grief, that he would have at once resigned the Empire and diadem and made a partition of the country among his sons. For two years he abandoned all sorts of pleasurable pursuits, especially the hearing of music and musical instruments, the wearing of jewels, the use of perfumes, the partaking of rich food and the wearing of precious costumes. On the *Id* festivals and other festivities when the ladies of the royal household assembled, according to custom, about his person, the Emperor, missing his beloved wife among them, could not help shedding tears. Whenever he went to the apartments in which the deceased had lived, not finding the object of his heart there, he invariably for a long time afterwards could not help bursting into tears. Mulla Abdul Hamíd, who has furnished these accounts, says that, at the time of the death of Mumtaz-uz-Zamani, there were not more than twenty white hairs in the king's beard, but in a short time after the Queen's death the number of such hairs greatly increased.

Grief of the Emperor.

According to Mulla Mohammad Sáleh, for a long time after the death of Mumtaz, mourning was observed in Court for the whole month of Zika-ad each year, when the Emperor put on white garments and all the Omerahs dressed themselves in mourning costume.

The Emperor was much attached to his eldest daughter, Jahan Ara Begam. Of the jewels, ornaments, and gold and silver coin, all valued at more than a karor of rupees, the Emperor gave one half to the Begam Sahib and the other half to the other children. All the household establishments previously in charge of the deceased Empress were put under the control of the Begam Sahib. The annual allowance of six lacs, allowed to the deceased, was, on her death, transferred to the Begam, with an addition of four lacs, half of which was cash and half represented by a jágir, or royal grant of land. Mirza Ishaq Beg *Yezdi*, the Mir Sámán of the deceased, was appointed Diwan to the Begam Sáhib, and Basti-ul-Nisa Khanam was, as in the time of her mother, appointed to the charge of her seal and the household affairs. **The Begam Sahib.**

Six months after the melancholy event, or on Friday, the 17th of Jamadiulawal, 1041 A. H. (1631 A. D.), the mortal remains of the deceased Empress were sent to Akbarabad (Agra), the *Darul-khilafat* under charge of Prince Mohammed Shah Shuja Bahadur, Bastiul-Nisa Khanam, the head of the Royal household in the time of the late Empress who enjoyed her fullest confidence, and in the words of Abdul Hamíd, 'understood her temper,' and who now was the head of the Royal household affairs under the Begam Sáhib, and Wazir Khán,* the Physician Royal. Under orders of the Emperor, food and cash in silver coin were distributed to the poor and needy all the way from Burhanpur to Agra, the last resting place of the Empress. The site selected for the mausoleum was to the south of the city. It was originally a palace of Rájá Mán Singh; but it was now the property of his grandson, Raja Jey Singh. His Majesty gave the Rája a lofty edifice from the Khalsa estate in exchange for this building, and the spot was used for the mausoleum of the deceased Empress. The interment at this spot took place on 15th Jamdi-ul-Sáni, 1041 A. H. At first a temporary dome was built over the tomb, so that it might **Remains of the deceased Empress removed to Agra, where they are interred in the ground of Raja Mán Singh.**

* His name was Ilmuddin, a native of Chiniot in Punjab. He founded the celebrated mosque bearing his name in Lahore.

The famous mausoleum built.

remain concealed from the public view; but, under orders of the Emperor, an edifice was built over and around it which to this day remains the wonder of the world. The expenditure on this building was estimated at fifty lakhs of rupees.

Description of the Taj.

The Caravan Serae.

A large outer gateway opens on to a spacious quadrangle, surrounded by arcaded rooms of solid masonry and adorned by four gateways. This is the *Caravan Serae* where the travellers and the poor were accommodated and entertained at State expense. It has been aptly remarked by the best of judges that 'beautiful as it is in itself, the Táj would lose half of its charm if it stood alone.' It is the combination of the most chaste structures and of diverse beauties and plans each subordinated to the other in the most exact and perfect proportions that have rendered the Táj, as a whole, what it is and such as the 'world cannot match.' As you attempt to see it, on entering the *caravan sarae*, it does not burst upon your view all at once, but, like a coy maid, conceals its face, the grand portal opposite serving as a veil to cover its transcendent form. Passing over a broad pavement of stone, you enter a great gateway of red freestone, a noble structure most elaborately carved and inscribed with sentences from the Koran. It is surmounted by 26 white marble cupolas, which rise over an octagonal room of about 45 feet square, with a roof like the inverted curve of a dome and galleries disposed in the most appropriate manner. Right and left of the inner passage are platforms, raised about eight feet from the ground, on which merchants exhibit articles for sale.

The great gateway.

The gateway opens on to a spacious quadrangle, 1,860 feet from east to west, and 1,000 feet from north to south. It is surrounded by lofty red sandstone walls, with turrets at the angles and a gateway on three sides, and the fourth facing the river Jumna. Slowly, as the demi-vault whose arch hangs high above is passed, a descent by a flight of steps reveals before your eyes the lovely Táj with its thousand charms. You see before you a sanctuary, pure and spotless as the sanctuary of heaven, displaying at once in the grace and symmetry of its form, the chasteness of its appearance and the majesty and effulgence of its style, the lofty spirit of its founder. A long and wide pathway,

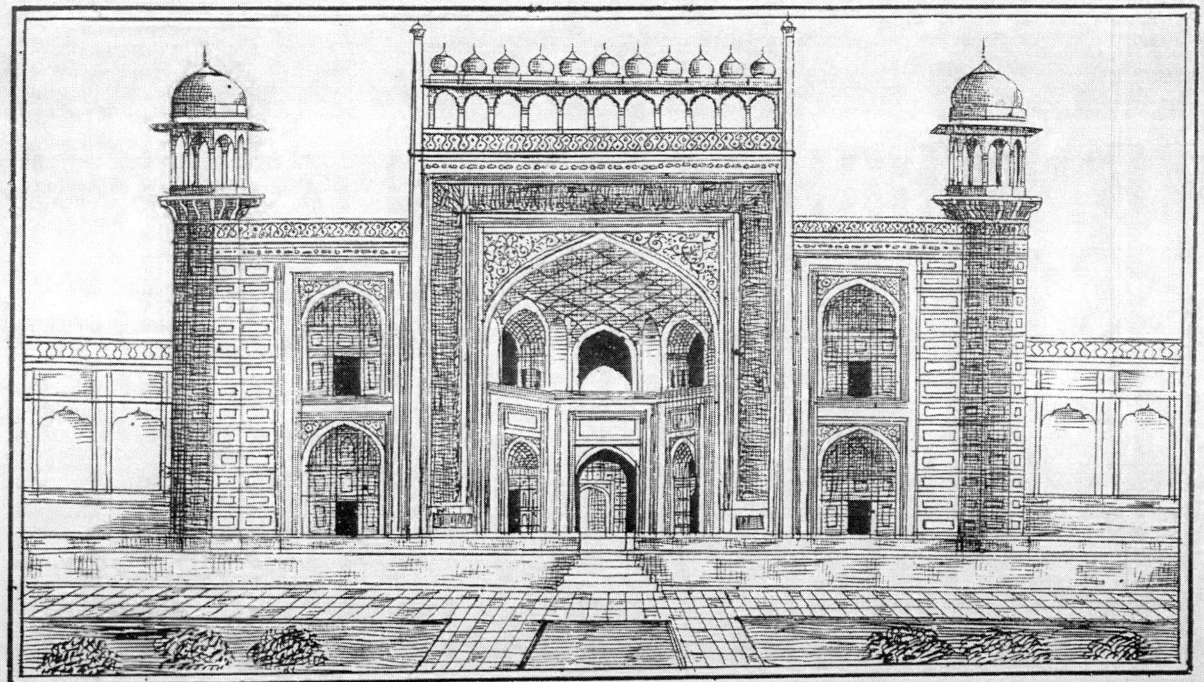

Gateway of the Taj.
Page 106.

paved with square stones and dividing the whole of the garden into two equal parts, now lies before you. It is shaded by a delightful avenue of tall, dark cyprus trees, all in exquisite harmony with the solemnity of the scene.

Galleries for distribution of alms to the poor. After advancing a few paces towards the garden, the visitor would do well to turn round and view the back portions of the architecture, which he will find as splendid and magnificent as the front in all its details, from the columns to the architraves and the cornices. On either side of the pavilion along the garden wall, are a series of wide galleries, supported by low columns. According to Bernier, the poor were admitted into these galleries three times a week during the rainy season to receive the alms founded in perpetuity by Shah Jahan. The traveller was an eye-witness of the distribution of these charities, and thousands were the needy fed here and to whom cash money and clothes were also given by the State officers.

The Taj garden. Between the gateway and the Táj itself is a spacious marble platform, in the centre of which sparkles a lovely little fountain of the same material and a long row of *jets dèau* placed some feet from each other and carried from end to end. The beautiful walks on either side of this row of fountains, each of which sends up a single slender jet, branch off in different directions and are shaded by trees of various kinds. The stately palm, the feathery bamboo, the handsome green banian and the shady orange tree mingle their luxuriant foliage, while the odoriferous lemon flowers, roses, jasmine and other fragrant shrubs and plants sweeten the air. The garden is most tastefully kept up at Government expense. The eye thus cooled and refreshed, the mind thus cheered and enlivened, a gentle walk of a quarter of a mile through the principal avenue, brings you in contact with a dead wall of white marble, to the right and left of which are a double flight of marble steps of great smoothness and elegance. These marble steps lead to a platform, 18 feet high and 313ft. square, in the midst of which stands the mausoleum itself.

The platform. Arrived at the terrace or platform and pausing here, one is lost in admiration at the beauty and magnificence of the structure. At every step he discovers new beauties. As one examines each part, he is left in astonishment at the grandeur of the soul that planned and the genius that executed so marvellous a task. The tesselated pavement of black and white marble, forming a mosaic of great neatness and elegance, is surrounded on all sides by a low parapet about two feet high. At each angle

The minarets. of the terrace stands a minaret, 133 feet in height, of most exquisite proportions, built of white marble, surmounted by a light, graceful cupola supported on eight elegant pillars and reached by a spiral staircase. In the centre of the platform

The Mausoleum. stands the mausoleum, a square of 186 feet, encircled by a number of turrets, all of the purest marble, descending one below the other in regular succession. From the centre springs the principal dome, 38 feet in diameter and 80 feet in height, surmounted by a gilt crescent, about 260 feet from the ground level. The upper terrace round the spring of the dome is protected by a higher parapet of about 6 feet, each angle being surmounted by cupolas supported on slender pillars of marble. These structures, viewed from the garden below, give the *tout ensemble* a light and aerial appearance, affording, on comparison with the bulky dome near it, a relief to the sight; for without them the vast swelling would wear a heavy look.

The sides of the central octagonal room, about 60 feet in diameter, face the four cardinal points and contain entrances, each about 130 feet long. There are suites of octagonal rooms all round, to the number of eight, having direct communication with the centre apartment. In these rooms the Koran was constantly read by the Mullahs for the benefit of the soul of the royal couple whose ashes lie buried here. Bernier, in his travels, has referred to the reciting of the Koran by these Mullahs. Tavernier, noticing the same subject, writes:—"From time to time, they change the carpets, chandeliers and other ornaments of that kind, and there are always there some Mullahs to pray." The elliptic arches forming the doors are each 18 feet high, and above each is an elliptic window. The grand entrance is formed of a single pointed arch rising nearly to the cornice. The entrances and arches from the top to the basement, the dome and the upper galleries of the minarets, are decorated with flowers in relief, cut out of marble in various patterns and inlaid with ornamental designs in marble of different colours, especially

The Taj.
Page 108

pale brown and a bluish violet variety. From the pavement to the top of the arches and along the walls are inserted passages from the Koran in letters of black marble let into the white marble ground with so much exactness that, if you pass a needle point over the stone, it will not be interrupted anywhere, so smooth and soft has the surface been made, although the work is purely inlay. Each letter so inserted is about a foot in length. According to one writer, 'they are cut out so regularly, with such precision and so elegantly, that the best calligraphist could not produce, with the pen on paper, better *Tughra* or *cufi* characters, if he took ever such great care in the attempt.'

Concerning the arrangement of light in the central octagonal room and the cool temperature maintained here, Fergusson writes: "The light in the central apartment is admitted only through double screens of white marble trellis-work of the most exquisite design, one on the outer and one on the inner face of the walls. In our climate this would produce nearly complete darkness; but in India, and in a building wholly composed of white marble, this was required to temper the glare that otherwise would have been intolerable. As it is, no words can express the charmed beauty of that central chamber, seen in the soft gloom of the subdued light that reaches it through the distant and half-closed openings that surround it. When used as a Bara Dari, or pleasure palace, it must always have been the coolest and loveliest of garden retreats, and now that it is sacred to the dead, it is the most graceful and the most impressive of sepulchres in the world." The screens referred to, which are of marble and jasper, are decorated with a wainscotting of sculptured tablets, representing flowers of various patterns.

The tombs of Mumtaz Mahal and Sháh Jahán.

In the grand octagonal hall, and under the principal dome previously described, stand the tomb of Mumtaz Mahal in the centre, and that of Sháh Jahán, raised somewhat above hers, on one side. The tombs are sarcophagi of the purest marble, exquisitely carved and elaborately inlaid with agate, bloodstone, lapis lazuli, cornelian and other polycoloured and precious stones and gems which have been imbedded in the white marble ground-work with extreme elegance and exactness. According to some of the best judges, a few of the flowers on the cenotaphs are carved with such exactness and accuracy that they comprise fifty or sixty varieties of stones of different colours within a space of less than an inch each, and with such finish and delicacy of execution are they blended together that, seen with the naked eye, they produce the appearance of natural flowers truly imitated. It is only with the aid of a microscope that they can be distinguished. The cenotaphs are surrounded with an octagonal screen eight feet high, carved out of solid blocks of white marble, highly polished, the doorway to the enclosure, in the shape of an arc, being a couple of feet higher. The carving is open tracery in excellent devices, the lilies, irisis and other flowers being inter-wrought in the most intricate ornamented designs. The surface of the walls internally is highly polished and furnishes evidence of sculptural art in its greatest intricacy, minuteness and elegance. All the spandrels and angles are embellished with white marble of the purest description, inlaid with precious stones such as bloodstone, jaspers, agates and the like, representing wreaths of flowers, scrolls and frets, and set in a hundred ways, forming, according to the best judges, "the most beautiful and precious style of ornament ever adopted in architecture."

The screens surrounding the cenotaphs.

"The judgment, indeed," says Fergusson, "with which this style of ornament is apportioned to the various parts is almost as remarkable as the ornament itself, and conveys a high idea of the taste and skill of the Indian architects of that age."

Inscriptions on the tombs.

The following is the inscription on the tomb of Sháh Jahán :—

مرقد منور و مضجع مطهر بادشاه رضوان دستگاه خلد آرامگاه اعلیحضرت علیین
مکانی فردوس آشیانی صاحبقران ثانی شاه جهان بادشاه غازی طاب ثراه
وجعل الجنة مثواه در شب هشت و ششم شهر رجب سنه هزار و هفتاد
وشش هجری از جهان فانی به بزمگاه جاودانی انتقال کردند

The illuminated sepulchre and sacred resting place of His most exalted Majesty, dignified as Razwan,* having his abode in paradise and his dwelling in the starry heaven,† dweller in the regions of bliss, the second lord of constellation, Shah Jahan, the King valiant, may his mausoleum

---

* Razwan is the name given by the Mohammadans to the guardian of paradise.

† The word is *Illiyin*, some region above the starry heavens, where, according to the belief of the Mohammadans, all souls of the pious assemble after death. These are the regions where only the angels have access.

The Taj (from the river side).

Page 110.

ever flourish, and may his abode be in the heavens. He travelled from this transitory world to the world of eternity on the night of 28th of the month of Rajab 1076 A.H. (1665 A.D).

The following is the inscription on the tomb of Mumtaz Mahal:—

مرقد منور ارجمند بانو بیگم مخاطب بممتاز محل توفیت فیه سنه ۱۰۴۰

The illuminated sepulchre of Arjumand Bano Begam, entitled Mumtaz Mahal. Died in 1040 A.H. (1630 A.D. or 36 years before the King's death).

Above the sarcophagus are inscribed the 99 names of God.

On the head of the sarcophagus is the inscription:—

القیوم الکافونا

He is the everlasting. He is sufficient.

On one side is inscribed the following:—

المقربون الذین قالوربنا الله

Nearer unto God are those who say 'our Lord is God.'

On the head of the sarcophagus is inscribed the following passage from the Koran:—

هوالله الذی لااله الاهوعالم الغیب والشهادة هوالرحمن الرحیم

God is He beside whom there is no God. He knoweth what is concealed and what is manifest. He is merciful and compassionate.

The real tombs are in a low vault placed exactly underneath those in the hall above. As in the upper hall, the tomb of Sháh Jahán is higher than that of his queen, the latter being in the centre of the vaulted underground chamber, while the former is at its side, to the left. The real tombs.

The spacious vaulted chamber is reached by a sloping passage, so highly polished that particular care has to be exercised in stepping on it to avoid slipping. The light from the door falls directly on the tombs, which are of much plainer workmanship. Beneath these lie the ashes of the beautiful Mumtaz Mahal, in whose memory the mausoleum was built by her consort, Sháh Jahán, who was himself buried by her side by his son Aurangzeb.

The vault is ever filled with perfumes, and flowers are found sprinkled in profusion on the tombs and around them.

The following is inscribed on the Emperor's sarcophagus in the real tomb :--

مرقد مطهرا علیحضرت فردوس آشیانی صاحب قران ثانی شاه جهان
بادشاه طاب ثراه سنه ۱۰۷۶

The sacred sepulchre of His most exalted Majesty, dweller of paradise, the second lord of constellation, the King Sháh Jahán, may his mausoleum ever flourish, 1076 A. H (1665 A. D.).

The inscriptions on the tomb of the Empress are the same as on the upper sarcophagus.

The vaulted chamber was, during the lifetime of Sháh Jahán, opened once a year, namely, on the anniversary of the death of the queen Mumtaz Mahal, with great ceremony, and professors of other religions were not admitted into it. Bernier, in his travels, has thus referred to this prohibition of admission:—"As no Christian is admitted within, lest its sanctity should be profaned, I have not seen the interior, but I understand that nothing can be conceived more rich and magnificent."

The Echo. The stately dome of the Taj produces an echo at once pure, sweet and prolonged. A single tone floats and soars in the vault overhead in a delicious vibration; reverberated echoes augment into a volume of harmonious voices, fading away gradually until they are swallowed up in the blue vault of heaven. Writers are most enthusiastic in describing the effects produced by the undulation. "I pictured to myself," says one, "the effect of an Arabic or Persian lament for the lovely Mumtaz sung over her tomb. The responses that would come from above in the pauses of the song must resemble the harmonies of angels in paradise." Another, referring to the vibrations caused by a low sweet song of praise and peace, says, "It is as though some congregation of the skies were chanting their earnest hymns above our heads." The masterly pen of Raynor thus paints the majesty, the awe, and the profound and dignified stillness of the vaulted chamber:—

"The hall, notwithstanding the precious materials of which it is built, and the elaborate finish of its ornaments, has a grave and solemn effect, infusing a peaceful serenity of mind, such as we feel when contemplating a happy death. Stern, unimaginative persons have been known to burst suddenly into tears on

The Tomb of Sháh Jahan.

Page 112.

The Mosque of the Taj.

Page 113.

entering it, and whoever can behold the Taj without feeling a thrill that sends the moisture to his eye, has no sense of beauty in his soul."

On either side of the Taj, and removed from it by a distance of about a hundred yards, are two large mosques of red sandstone, with three domes inlaid with white marble. That to the west only was intended for prayers, and has recesses pointing to the *Káaba.* The floor is marked off into small partitions, each sufficient for one man to stand, bend his knees and sit to go through the genuflections and prostrations prescribed by the faith of Islam. The one to the east, which is precisely similar, but has no recesses towards the *káaba*, or seats for prayers, was intended as a counterpart to the other, so as to preserve the symmetry of the group and the uniformity of appearance externally. The false mosque is known as the *Jamáat Khána*, or place for the congregation to assemble before prayers, or on the anniversaries of the death of the Emperor Sháh Jahán, or his consort, Taj Mahal.* In an enclosure beneath the true mosque is pointed out the place where the body of the Empress was deposited embalmed, while the mausoleum was in course of construction. **The Masjid** **The Jamáat Khana.**

The *Masjid* and *Jamáat Khána* are connected by a low parapet, while there are stairs from them leading to the river. In the latter a suite of upper apartments has been added for the accommodation of visitors to the Taj wishing to make a temporary stay for the benefit of their health, or for the purpose of pleasure.

From the summit of this structure and of the minarets a beautiful view of the surrounding country is obtained.

Exactly opposite the Taj, on the opposite bank of the river, are ruins of old foundations. Sháh Jahán had intended these foundations for a monument for himself corresponding with the Taj, and to connect the two tombs by a magnificent marble bridge, to show the bond of affection between himself and his beloved consort **The intended tomb of Sháh Jahán.**

* Mr. Taylor writes of this building:—
"On the opposite side there is a building precisely similar, but of no use whatever, except as a proof of the sense of balance and symmetry which actuated the whole design." But as its very name implies, it was built for an object, namely, the assemblage of the people before the time of prayers and before the ceremonies observed on the anniversaries of the death of the Emperor and his consort.

even after death. But his subsequent captivity prevented the execution of his design, and, when he died, his austere son, Aurangzeb, as has been already noted, buried him by the side of his wife, observing "My father entertained a great affection for my mother; so let his last resting place be close to hers." Thus, in the words of Mr. Taylor, "Fate conceded to Love what was denied to vanity."

The Taj by moonlight.

The sight of the Taj by moonlight is most entrancing. The whole structure appears to sparkle like a diamond in the bright slanting rays; and the pure white dome, raised on a marble pavement, viewed from a distance, looks like a brilliant pearl on a silvery plate. The decorations on the marble wall seem like so many gems set on an ornament, while the calm stream flowing by its side, coupled with the soft shadow cast around by the trees, adds to the loveliness of the scene. Nothing but a whispering breeze breaks the surrounding calm.

The design of the Taj.

Recent writers differ as to the origin and conception of the design of the Taj. Some suppose that it was planned by an Italian artist, and others that a French artist was the author of the exquisite inlaid work on marble which is to be seen here in the highest perfection. The court of Sháh Jahán was visited by the French travellers, Bernier and Tavernier, and they have given a full account of the building in their respective Travels. Tavernier saw the commencement and completion of the Taj, and Bernier came to India only five years after it had been finished. If any of their countrymen, or if any European artist, had been the author of the design, it is not at all likely that they would have omitted mention of it in their chronicles, and would not have been the first to give them the credit which might have been justly due to them. But not even an allusion to it has been made by them in the accounts they have furnished to posterity of the results of their inspection of this wonderful building. Moreover, the Taj itself affords the best evidence that it owes its existence to no foreign design. "One look at it," writes an English author, "ought to assure any intelligent man, that this is false, nay, impossible from the very nature of the thing. The Taj is the purest Saracenic in form, proportions and ornamental designs. If that were not sufficient, we have stil

It is purely Oriental.

the name of the Moslem architect sculptured upon the building." Another English writer observes: "The idea stamped upon the building is entirely Mohammedan and Oriental." The idea is in perfect accord with the love of symmetry characteristic of the Moslem nations, and the Taj is most assuredly the highest work of art of Saracenic style, the very marvel of mausoleums.

The building of the Taj was commenced in 1630, or one year after the death of Mumtaz Mahal. The date of the completion of the building, inscribed on the front gateway, is 1057 (1648). It thus took eighteen* years to complete. The cost was three millions sterling. **Date of building and cost.**

The silver gates of the Mausoleum, which were removed and melted down by the Jats, alone cost Rs. 1,27,000. **Silver gates.**

We are told in the *Badshah Namah* that, in 1042 A.H. (1632 A.D.), a fence or enclosure of solid gold studded with gems was placed around the Empress's sarcophagus. It was made under the directions of Bebadal Khan, the Superintendent of the Royal Kitchen (*Khásá Shàrifá*), and was a perfect specimen of the art of Indian jewelry. It weighed forty thousand tolahs of pure gold and was valued at six lakhs of rupees. The interior of the Mausoleum was decorated with a variety of chandeliers, candles, and ornamental lamps, lanterns of various sizes, shades and colors, which had cost lakhs of rupees, and which, coupled with the highly-finished carpets of Tehran and Constantinople that were spread on the floor, made the place resemble a fairy scene, or a paradise on earth. **Solid gold fence.**

In the year 1052 A.H. (1642 A.D.) the golden palisade above-mentioned was removed, as it was feared that gold in such mass would be exposed to the danger of theft by ill-disposed people, and in its stead the present net work of marble, previously referred to, was put up.† This structure, which in elegance and beauty is a master-piece of sculpture, was, according to the *Badshah Nama*, prepared in a period of ten years, at a cost of fifty thousand rupees. In 1720 a sheet of pearls, made by Sháh Jahán for

* According to Tavernier, 22 years, which, no doubt, includes the period of the construction of the buildings attached to the Taj, the Caravan Serae, &c.

† See page 110 *ante*.

covering the tomb of Mumtaz Mahal, at a cost of lakhs of rupees was removed.*

Tavernier's account of the building.

"I witnessed," says Tavernier, "the commencement and accomplishment of this great work, on which they have expended twenty-two years, during which twenty thousand men worked incessantly; this is sufficient to enable one to realise that the cost of it has been enormous. It is said that the scaffoldings alone cost more than the entire work, because, from want of wood, they had all to be made of brick, as well as the supports of the arches; this has entailed much labour and a heavy expenditure. Sháh Jahán began to build his own tomb on the other side of the river, but the war which he had with his sons, interrupted his plans, and Aurangzeb, who reigns at present, is not disposed to complete it. An eunuch in command of 2,000 men guards both the tombs of Begam and the Tasemacan, to which it is near at hand."

The artists.

The Persian historians of Sháh Jahán have given full lists of the workmen from diverse countries who assisted in the building of the Táj, and of the materials used, as well as their dimensions and price. We give only a summary of these here, from a manuscript Persian work called the *Turikh-i-Táj Mahal*, in possession of the *Khádims*, or hereditary custodians of the mausoleum.

The chief architect.

The chief architect was *Ustad* Isá, called the *Naksha Nawis*, or the plan-drawer; his salary was Rs. 1,000 a month. His son, Mohamed Sharíf, was employed as an architect on Rs. 500 a month. The passages from the Koran in the *Tughra* characters, inscribed on different parts of the building, were executed by the Illuminator, Amanat Khan of Shiráz, who received a salary of Rs. 1,000 a month. His name is found inscribed in bold Tughra characters on the right hand side as the tomb is entered. It is thus given after the date, A. H. 1048. "The humble *fakir* Amanat Khan of Shiráz." The master mason was one Mohamed Haníf, from Baghdád, also on Rs. 1,000 a month. There were also Ismail Khan, the architect of the dome, a resident of *Rúm* (Asiatic Turkey), on Rs. 200 a month; Mohamed Khan, writing

* See page 54 *ante*.

master of Baghdád, on Rs. 200; Mannu Beg *Pachikar*, or worker in Mosaic, of *Rúm*, on Rs. 780; Manohar Singh, of Balkh, on Rs. 200; Mannu Lal, of Candhar, on Rs. 200; Din Mohamed, of Peshawar, on Rs. 80; Mohamed Usuf, of Akbarabád, on Rs. 100; Káyam Khan, pinnacle maker, of Lahore, on Rs. 695; and a great many others from Turkey, Persia, Delhi, Catack and the Punjab, who received salaries ranging from Rs. 100 to Rs. 500 a month.

Superintendents of the building.

According to the *Badshah Nama*, the buildings of the Taj were constructed under the superintendence of Makramat Khan and Mir Abdul Karím, at a cost of 50 lakhs of rupees. The suburbs developed into a large town which was called Mumtazabád. The income of thirty villages in Pargana Haveli, a subdivision of Agra, with a revenue of forty lakhs *dams* or one lakh per annum, was set apart for the maintenance of the mausoleum. In addition to this, the income of all the shops, streets and *seraes* attached to the mausoleum, and amounting to two lakhs of rupees per annum, was assigned for its maintenance, the savings from this expense being applied towards defraying the salaries and allowances of servants of the institution and officials attached to it.

The suburbs are called Mumtazabad.

Grant for the maintenance of the mausoleum and its establishments.

The materials and cost of each kind of material.

The white marble came from Jeypur in Rajputana; the yellow from the banks of the Narbada; a square yard of this cost Rs. 40. The black marble came from a place called *Charkoh* (four hills); a square yard of this cost Rs. 90. Crystal from China, one square yard Rs. 570; jasper from the Punjab; cornelian from Baghdád; turquoises from Thibet; agate from Yaman; lapis lazuli from Ceylon; the square yard cost Rs. 1,156; coral from Arabia and the Red Sea; garnets from Bundelkhand; Diamonds from Panna in Bundelkhand. The plum-pudding stone from Jesselmer; rock spar from Narbada; the loadstone from Gwalior; the onyx from Persia; the chalcedony from *Vilayat*; the amethyst from Persia; sapphires from Lanka (Ceylon,) and the red sandstone, of which 1,14,000 cart loads were used, came from Fatehpur Sikri. Many other stones were also used in the work of inlay which have no English name. Many of the precious stones have been picked out by the *Játs*. Most of the stones were received as tribute from the tributary ruling Chiefs of India, while many were received as presents.

The Taj described by eminent scholars.

No building in the civilized world has been the subject of so much enthusiastic admiration on the part of writers and travellers of diverse countries and nationalities as the Táj at Agra. Human taste and human ideas always differ. Yet historians of the East and poets of the West have united in eulogizing it ssplendour as the most magnificent architectural monument ever raised by the vanity of man. Travellers from the remotest parts of the globe have been equally enthusiastic in its praise.

Sháh Jahán's own description of the Taj.

It may be interesting to know, first of all, what the opinion of the founder himself was of this edifice, which he left in the world as a glory and monument of his genius, thus leaving an everlasting stamp of his passionate love for his departed wife on the earth's surface, and also of his pride and vanity.

The following eloquent poems of Sháh Jahán's own composition in praise of the Taj are reproduced from the pages of the *Badshah Nama* of Mulla Abdul Hamíd of Lahore:—

ابيات مصنفه شاهجهان

زهي مرقد پاك بلقيس عهد   كه با نوي آفاق زاگشت مهد
منور مقامي چو باغ بهشت   معطر چو فردوس عنبر سرشت
بصحنش زخال معنبر بخور   بجاروب مژگان درش رفته حور
جواهر نگارست ديوار و در   هوا تازه وتر چو آب گهر
عمارت گر اين مقدس جناب   زسر چشمه فيض آورده آب
برين بقعه پاك والا مقام   ترشح كنان ابر رحمت مدام
اگر مجرم آرد برين در پناه   شود همچو مغفور پاك از گناه
اگر عاصي آرد برين روضه روي   كند نامه خويش را شست وشوي
زوقت بنظاره اين مراد   شود چشم خورشيد ومه اشكبار
نمود اين عمارت بنا روزگار   كه ظاهر شود قدرت كردگار

How excellent the sepulchre of the lady of Bilqis's * fame
That a cradle for the body of the Princess of the world became.

---

* Bilqis was a queen of the city of Saba in Yaman in the time of Solomon the Prophet. She was famous for her beauty and was a fire-worshipper. Solomon, according to the Mussalman writers, sent her a letter inviting her to renounce the faith of her ancestors and embrace that of his own. He sent this letter through a hoopoo bird which acted as a messenger. The Queen presented herself to the Prophet and became a convert to his faith. She became the concubine of the Prophet. Hafiz, the celebrated poet of Shiraz, has said with reference to the message of hoopoo to the city of Saba:—

مژده ایدل که دگر باد صبا مي آيد   هد هد خوش خبراز شهر سبا مي آيد

Hail mind! for once more has blown the morning breeze;
The hoopoo from the city of Saba has brought the happy tidings.

Like the garden of heaven a brilliant spot,
Full of fragrance like paradise fraught with ambergris.
In the breadth of its court perfumes from the nose-gay of sweetheart rise,
The nymphs of paradise use their eye-lids for cleaning its threshold.
Its walls and gates glitter with gems,
The air is there fresh and delightful like the brilliancy of pearl.
The architect of this sacred edifice
Brought water for it from the fountain of grace.
On this sacred edifice of high renown
Showers of mercy are ever pouring.
Should guilty seek asylum here,
Like one pardoned, he becomes free from sin.
Should a sinner make his way to this mansion,
All his past sins are sure to be washed away.
The sight of this mansion creates sorrowing sighs
And makes sun and moon shed tears from their eyes.
In this world this edifice has been made
To display thereby the Creator's glory.

As was to be expected, Sháh Jahán, in praising the edifice, his own creation, has written in hyperbolic style, and, according to the fashion of the time, composed his poems in figurative language; nevertheless, they show the warmth of his heart, and that he fully realized the idea of the greatness of the mausoleum which he has left to posterity, a wonder of the world, and a gorgeous and glorious gift to this splendid Empire.

Sir William Hunter takes the beautiful domes of the Taj for "a dream of marble." "The Taj," says he, "represents the most highly elaborated stage of ornamentation reached by the Indo-Mohammedan builders, the stage in which the architect ends and the jeweller begins." Bayard Taylor describes it as "a thing of perfect beauty and of absolute finish; in every detail it might pass for the work of genii who knew naught of the weakness and ills with which mankind are beset."

"It is too pure," says a writer, "too holy to be the work of human hands. Angels must have brought it from heaven, and a glass case should be thrown over it to preserve it from every breath of air."

A Russian artist describes it as "a lovely woman, abuse her as you please, but the moment you come into her presence, you submit to its fascination." Mr. Keene on this remarks: "Admitting that there is something slight and effeminate in the general design which cannot be altogether obliterated or atoned for by the beauty of decoration, the simile seems just and calls to mind the familiar couplet in the *Rape of the Lock.*

'If to her share some female errors fall,
'Look in her face and you'll forget them all.'"

In the words of Bishop Heber, "though everything is finished like an ornament for a drawing room chimney-piece, the general effect produced is rather solemn and impressive than gaudy."

Mr. James Fergusson writes of it, "With its purity of material and grace of form, the Taj may challenge comparison with any creation of the same sort in the world. Its beauty may not be of the highest class, but in its class it is unsurpassed." As observed by a writer, "while the sepulchral works adorning the valley of the Nile will be regarded as wonders of art for their solidity of construction and sublimity of conception, the Taj at Agra shall always call forth the admiration of mankind for its being the most exquisite specimen of human architecture and the most gorgeous romance of wedded love." "I asked my wife," says Sleeman, "when she had gone over it, what she thought of the building? 'I cannot,' said she, 'tell you what I think, for I know not how to criticise such a building, but I can tell you what I feel; I would die to-morrow to have such another over me.'"

It has been truly said of the Taj that "it is in architecture what the Venus de Medici is in sculpture, or Shakespeare in poetry."

"No description, however vivid or precise," observes the Reverend French, "no colouring, however brilliant or varied, even if supplemented with paintings or drawings, can give one a correct idea of the Taj for its nobleness, an edifice unparalleled in the annals of Eastern architecture."

The parting scene.

Having once come in contact with this marvel of monuments, it is not without some reluctance that one severs himself from a spot made so lovely by art and so rich and attractive by memories.

A visitor thus paints his impressions of a parting sight: "One returns and returns to it with undiminished pleasure, and though at every return one's attention to the smaller parts becomes less and less, the pleasure which he derives from the contemplation of the greater of the whole collectively seems to increase, and he leaves it with a feeling of regret that he could not have it all his life within his reach and with the assurance that the image of what he has seen can never be obliterated from his mind *while memory holds her seat.*"

We close our imperfect description and feeble outline of this gem of Eastern architecture with the following poetical productions of lady authors in praise of the mausoleum :—

O thou! whose great imperial mind could raise
This splendid trophy to a woman's praise!
If love or grief inspired the bold design,
No mortal joy or sorrow equalled thine!
Sleep on secure! this monument shall stand,
When desolation's wing sweeps over the land,
By time and death in one wide ruin hurl'd,
The last triumphant wonder of the world.*

Pure as Mumtaza's spotless fame,
The unsullied marble shines;
Rich as her lord's unrivalled love,
The wreathes that deck their shrines.

On fanes more glorious I have gazed,
Witness St. Peter's dome;
And costlier gems shine bright around
The Medician tomb.

But this Love's temple—beauteous pile,
The pride of Eastern art!
This boasts the present deity,
That seizes on the heart.

All ruling Power! to thee we bend,
Thy potent charm we own,
This structure, simple, graceful, pure,
Oh! this is Love's alone! †

---

* By Lady Nugent, wife of Sir George Nugent, late Commander-in-Chief.

† By Mrs. C. Fagan, the wife of Col. C. Fagan, Adjutant-General under Lord Combermere.

16

No Eastern prince for wealth or wisdom famed,
No mortal hands this beauteous fabric framed.
In death's cold arms the fair Muntaza slept,
And sighs over Jumna's winding water crept,
Tears such as angels weep, with fragrance filled,
Around her grave in pearly drops distilled.
There fixed for ever firm, congealed they stand,
A fairy fabric, pride of India's land.*

The 1st anniversary after death.

The first anniversary of the death of Mumtáz Mahal took place in the month of Zikad, 1041 A. H. (1631 A.D.). According to the *Badshah Nama*, grand preparations were made on the occasion in the Taj Mahal. The officials of the Royal household *(Mutasaddian-i-Bayutat)*, acting under the king's order, adorned the courtyard of the mausoleum with superb tents and costly *Shamianas*. All the princes of blood royal and the *Amírs* and grandees at the metropolitan city assembled to do honour to the occasion. So did all the learned men of the faith, the *Sheikhs*, the *Ulamas* and the *Hafizes* (those who recollect the *Koran* by heart). The grandees took their seats according to rank under the *Shamiana*, and the Emperor graced the assembly with his presence. At His Majesty's command, Yaminuddoula Asif Khan, the father of the lamented Empress, took his seat along with Mohamed Ali Beg, the Persian envoy. A table-cloth having been then spread, the most magnificent dinner, consisting of a variety of delicious foods, sweetmeats, and fruits, was served to the guests assembled, and verses from the Korán were read and prayers offered for the benefit of the soul of the deceased. Out of one lakh of rupees set apart for distribution as alms to the poor assembled on the occasion, fifty thousand were distributed the same day, while the remaining fifty thousand were distributed on the following day. It was also ordered that, on the anniversary of each successive year, fifty thousand rupees be spent in alms when His Majesty should be in the metropolis, but when he should be out in camp, then a sum of rupees twelve thousand should be spent for the purpose.

Sháh Jahán's visits to the mausoleum.

Whenever the King was in the metropolis, he attended the anniversary of his queen in the company of his affectionate daughter, the Begam Sahib, and the ladies of the *harem*. The

* Anonymous.

ladies occupied the central platform, being concealed from the public gaze by *Kanats*, or screens of red cloth and velvet, while the *Amirs* assembled under *Shamianas* which were pitched for the occasion. The fixed sum of rupees fifty thousand was on each occasion distributed in alms, half on the day of the anniversary and half on the following day.

People assembled on the occasion of the anniversary from all parts of India.

FATTEHPUR SIKRI.

About 23 miles south-west of Agra and 14 miles from the Bhartpur fort lie the magnificent ruins of Fattehpur Sikri, the Windsor of Agra, the imperial residence of Akbar. It is situated on the same line as the old Moghul road, and crosses, on the way, some ancient irrigation works and bridges now no longer in use. Fattehpur Sikri, now a municipal town of the Karowli Tehsil, or Sub-Division of Agra, derives its name from two villages that lie close to each other. Sikri, once a lonely hamlet, is adorned with substantial buildings, prominent among which is that belonging to the descendants of the chief architect who superintended the construction of the palaces for which Fattehpur is justly famous. Fattehpur was the name given to it by the Emperor Akbar, in honour of the birth there of his son Salem, afterwards Jahangir. In the Ain-i-Akbari, Fatehpur, alias Sikri, is mentioned as one of the 42 Parganas, or Sub-Divisions, of the Suba (Province) of Agra called the Darul Khilafat. **Origin of Fattehpur Sikri.**

It was a dependency of the Sirkar of Biana, comprising 33 *máhals*. Abul Fazl thus notices it in the Ain-i-Akbari:— **Account in the Ain-i-Akbari.**

" Fattehpur Sikri, a village of Biana, is situated at a distance of twelve kos from the Darul-Khilafat. Through the auspices of His Majesty it has become one of the most magnificent cities of the world. A fort of sandstone has been founded here, and on one of its gates have been placed two elephant statues. It has been embellished with lofty edifices. On the summits of hills have been constructed the Royal palace and the houses of the grandees of the Empire, while the plains overlooked by the hills are adorned with numerous summer houses and sumptuous gardens. By the command of His Majesty a mosque, school and mausoleum have been built on the hills, and they are of such beauty and elegance that, according to persons who have travelled through the world, there are few edifices on earth which can equal them in magnificence. Close to the city are extensive hunting grounds on which His Majesty has laid out a cricket ground and built a tower from which he witnesses the combats of elephants. Here is a mine of red sandstone out of which stones for pillars and flanks can be cut in such quantity as may be wished. Through the auspices of the Asylum of the Universe, cloth and silk textures of excellent quality can be manufactured here, and the artizans of all classes are thriving."

Foundation of the city. In the record of the 16th year of the reign (1571 A.D.) Abul Fazl gives an account of the buildings at Fattehpur Sikri. He writes :—Sikri, a dependency of Biana, became the chief city (*Misri jama*). The Emperor of the world, who has the good of his subjects at heart, directed his attention towards the embellishment of this place. Sikri being the fortunate place of the birth of Royal Princes and being the residence of Sheik Salem the chosen of God, His Majesty resolved on fixing his royal residence here, as well as making it the abode of the grandees of the Empire. Accordingly under orders of His Majesty, royal palaces of great beauty and magnificence were built here, and the nobles of all rank constructed elegant edifices for their residence. Order was also given to lay the foundations of a fort of red sandstone. In a short time, Sikri became a great city with mausoleums, college and public baths ; a bazar was built of stone, and the grounds in the environs were laid out with fine gardens, canals and aqueducts. The city became the envy of the great cities of the world. His Majesty gave it the name Fattehabad, but the place came in time to be called Fattehpur by the people, and the Emperor accorded his sanction to that name.

Date of foundation, 1569 A.D. The fort of Agra was commenced in the 10th year of Akbar's reign, or in 1566 A.D., and it was not until the commencement of the 14th year of the reign, or three years later, that Fattehpur Sikri was selected as a royal residence. Traces of fortifications that had been begun are still to be seen at the last-mentioned place, and it was the intention of the Emperor to build his entire metropolis there. For the next 17 years, or until the 31st year of

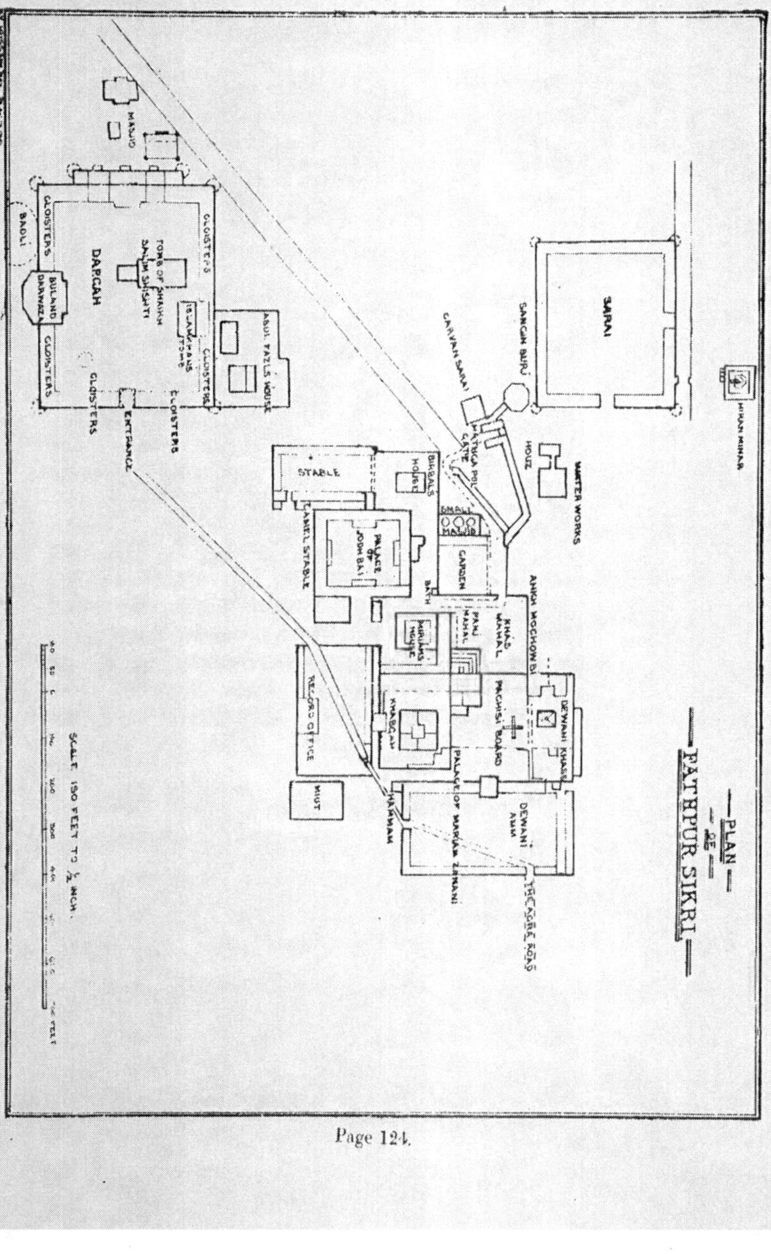
PLAN
OF
FATEHPUR SIKRI
MIRAN MINAR
SARAI
SANGIN BURJ
CARVAN SARAI
HATHIA POL GATE
HOUZ
WATER WORKS
ANKH MICHOWLI
KHAS MAHAL
PANJ MAHAL
GARDEN
SMALL MASJID
BIRBALS HOUSE
STABLE
CAMEL STABLE
PALACE OF JODH BAI
BATH
MIRIAMS HOUSE
DEWANI KHAS
PACHISI BOARD
KHABGAH
RECORD OFFICE
MINT
HAMMAM
PALACE OF MARIAM ZAMANI
DEWANI AAM
THE AGRA ROAD
ABUL FAZLS HOUSE
CLOISTERS
ENTRANCE
DARGAH
TOMB OF SHAIKH SALIM CHISHTI
ISLAM KHANS TOMB
BULAND DARWAZA
BAOLI
MASJID
SCALE 150 FEET TO ½ INCH.

Page 124.

the reign (1586 A.D.), he held his court at Fattehpur Sikri, which came to be styled in public correspondence the Darul Khilafat, and Agra was the nominal capital. Whenever the Emperor set out on expeditions, he left his wives and family at Fattehpur Sikri, his favourite place of residence. Abul Fazl in the *Akbarnamah* gives a graphic account of the arrivals of His Majesty at Fattehpur after long journeys and the way in which he was greeted by the members of his household, the royal princes and the nobles on such occasions. When, after quelling the disturbance at Gujrat, raised by Mirza Hussain (when he performed the marvellous journey of more than 450 miles with such celerity that, in spite of the season, he collected an army and reached the seat of war on the ninth day from leaving Agra), he returned to Agra, after an absence of only 43 days (on Monday, the 6th of October 1573), the return of the royal camp was made an occasion of great rejoicings. As the Emperor approached his favourite residence, Sikri, he mounted his war-horse, a grey charger with henna-stained mane and tail, gracefully holding his spear in his hand. Before him marched his body-guard and his royal comrades with lances adorned with golden balls on the top. The entire royal household and the *Amirs*, who had been left behind, came out to the foot of the hills to greet him. Intense was the joy and enthusiasm that prevailed. The uproar of the acclamations and the strains of music from the portals of the grand mosque filled the air and announced the news of victory far and wide. It may be interesting to describe the event in the author's own beautiful language. Abul Fazl says:—

Is called and becomes the Darul Khilafat, 1569 to 1586 A.D.

آنحضرت پاس از روز مزکور ما نده چون عافیت درجان وروح دربدن
بدار الاقبال فتحپور آمدند آب تازه بجوي آمد و عالم گلستان شد
حضرات بیگمات و شهزاده هائے رفعت پیوند و پرده گیان سرا پرده عصمت
بدید ار سعادت بخش کامیاب صورت ومعني گشتند وسرا سم نياقي
بخو بترين وجه بظهور آمده دیده هاے مشتاقان نور افزا گشتند

"At one watch before sunset His Majesty came to Fattehpur, the seat of the Empire, like health in life and soul in body. Fresh waters came into the brook, and the world became like a garden. Their Highnesses the Begams, the princes of high dignity and the secluded inmates of the chaste household, gained honour and prosperity by beholding His Majesty's countenance. The ceremonies of offering were performed in the best style, and the eyes of those who had longed for an interview acquired increased brightness."

An arrival after an absence of ten months in the Punjab is thus celebrated in the poems of Mulla Fyzi quoted by his brother Abul Fazl in the same work :

نسیم خوشدلی از فتحپور می آید   که بادشاه من از راه دور می آید
چه دولتست قدومش که هر دم از دل خلق   هزار گونه طرب در ظهور می آید
خجسته باد بعالم قدوم او فیضی   که عالمے بمقام حضور می آید

The breeze of joy is scented from Fattehpur,
For my King is coming from a long journey.
How prosperous His Majesty's arrival, for every moment from the heart of the people
A thousand joys are displayed.
May his arrival be fortunate to the world, O Fazi,
For the whole people are coming to greet him.

His Majesty entered Fattehpur through a *via triumphalis* of nobles and elephants, and was greeted by troops, dancers and performers and moved to the sound of the martial drum.

Becomes Akbar's favourite residence. The rebellion of his half brother, Mohammad Hakím Mirza, to whom Akbar had given the kingdom of Kabul, and his incursions into the Panjab, compelled Akbar to move from Fattehpur to Lahore, which for fourteen years enjoyed the distinction of being the capital of the Empire. It was not until the 43rd year of the reign, or 1598 A.D., when the Emperor returned to Hindustan, that Agra became the real capital. The reasons which led His Majesty ultimately to choose Agra for his metropolis have been described elsewhere.* From 1598 to 1605, when Akbar died, he held his court at Agra, though Fattehpur continued to be his favourite residence. Fattehpur was, properly speaking, Akbar's Windsor, Agra his London. **The Gates.** The gateways are called respectively Delhi, Lal Agra, Ajmere, Tahira, Surajpol and Chandanpol.

Birth of Salem afterwards Jahangir. Allamí Sheikh Abul Fazl, in giving an account of the 14th year of Akbar's reign, informs us in the *Akbarnamah*

* See the closing portion of these accounts.

that about this time His Majesty, having, through Sheikh Mohammad Bokhari, Hakim-ul-mulk and other grandees who had access to the royal throne, heard of the religious fame and piety of Sheikh Salem of Sikri, resolved to lodge the members of the royal seraglio close to the residence of the venerable Sheikh at that village, expecting that the spiritual power of the holy man, combined with the sanctity of the place, would result in his being blessed with a son. 'Before that time,' writes the talented historian, 'the Emperor had several children born to him, but in the mysterious wisdom of the creator, they had all travelled to the world of eternity; unthinking people attributed this to the unluckiness of the locality; and the King, wishing to shut the mouth of triflers with the seal of silence, determined on a change of place. The choice falling on Fattehpur, the Dar-ul-khilafat, a son was born to the Emperor at an auspicious hour, by the Hindu princess, Mariam-uz-Zamani,* daughter of Raja Behari Mal of Amber in the Soobah of Ajmer, sister to Raja Bhagwan Das and aunt of Kour Man Singh.'

Great rejoicings.

Fattehpur was in those days connected with Agra by a long Bazar. Akbar, having heard the happy tidings at Agra, forthwith repaired to Fattehpur, where great rejoicings took place in honour of the event. All the life convicts and prisoners throughout the Empire were set at liberty and merriment and gaiety was the order of the day. The newly born prince was named Salem, after the holy man whose prayers were supposed to have had the effect of bringing about the happy event.

Jahangir's account.

Jahangir, in his autobiography, relates the incidents connected with his birth and the foundation of Fattehpur thus:—

"Up to the age of 28 no children born to my father remained alive. He therefore always had recourse to the Darweshes and hermits, who are ever near to the Almighty, and implored them for the gift of a child who should live. The venerable Khwaja Moinuddin, surnamed Chishti, being the head of most of the

* Akbar married her at Sambhar. She died in Rajab 1032 A. H. (1622 A. D.). She must not be confounded with Jodh Bai, the Hindu wife of Jahangir, the daughter of Moth Raja of Jodhpur.

saints of India, His Majesty, in order to gain the desired end, conceived the idea of having recourse to his blessed threshold. He therefore made a vow to himself that, should God the Most High endow him with a son, he would travel on foot from Agra to the mausoleum of his holiness, a distance of 140 kos, to pay his homage to it. It so pleased God that I was born on Wednesday, the 17th of Rabi ul Awal 977 A. H. During the time when my father was desirous of being endowed with a child, there lived on a hill near Sikri, a village of Agra, a Darwesh, Shekh Salem, a perfect devotee and a man of very advanced years. People living in the vicinity of the hill had great respect for his spiritual powers. My father, who had much confidence in the Darweshes, made the acquaintance of the Shekh. One day, as the Shekh was in a state of excessive enthusiasm and rapture, he asked him how many sons he would have. The Fakir answered :—'The bestower who maketh his gift unsolicited will endow thee with three sons.' My father rejoined :—'I make a vow to place my first born son in your lap and consign him to your care, so that you may become his protector and guardian.' The Shekh consented to this and exclaimed: 'Hail! I, on my part, give him my own name.' When my mother was about to be confined, she was sent to the Shekh's house in order that my birth should take place there. When I was born, I was named Sultan Salem. But I never heard my father call me, either in a state of consciousness or unconsciousness, by the name Mohammad Salem, or Sultan Salem. While speaking to me, he always called me Shekhu Baba.

My revered father, regarding the village of Sikri, my birthplace, as fortunate for himself, made it his capital, and in the course of fourteen or fifteen years the hills and deserts which abounded in beasts of prey, became converted into a magnificent city comprising numerous gardens, elegant edifices and pavilions and other places of great attraction and beauty. After the conquest of Gujrat, the village was named Fattehpur."

Akbar fulfilled his vow by performing a pilgrimage on foot from Agra to Ajmere, where the shrine of the saint Moinuddin Chishti is.

Grand sight of ruins.

In modern times Fattehpur Sikri is famous as the seat of one of the grandest groups of ancient architectural remains in Upper India. Nowhere in the whole of India is to be found collected in one spot such a collection of ancient buildings and monuments of all shapes and sizes and of such solidity, massiveness and excellence, still, for the most part, in a state of perfect preservation, as is to be seen at this place. Their stability is accounted for by the circumstance that they are built of the most substantial materials and durable cement. According to one authority, 'the adhesive qualities of the latter have surprised engineers and puzzled even chemists in their endeavours to analyze the various ingredients of which it is composed.' The deserted palaces and court rooms are specimens of the most elaborate carving. As remarked by an acute observer :—'It is a wilderness of sculpture, where invention seems to have been taxed to the utmost to produce new combinations of ornaments. Everything is carved in a sandstone so fine that, except where injured by man, it appears nearly as sharp as when first chiselled.'

The buildings still in a state of perfect preservation.

It is a dead city; an unburied Pompeii. Although the buildings have stood deserted for nearly three hundred years, they are still in a state of perfect preservation, and produce the most vivid impression on the mind of the visitor. The graceful originality of the design and the splendour and beauty of the architecture create an exalted idea of the founder and bring before the eye a lively image of the splendour of the great Mughal. The animated picture of ancient grandeur thus brought before the observer requires no great force of imagination to picture Akbar, his *harem* and his court in occupation of these lovely courts and palaces.

Their extent.

The architectural remains of Fattehpur Sikri, about six or seven miles in circuit and surrounded by a battlemented lofty wall of red sandstone, are situated on the extremity of a low range of hills. Approaching the ruins from the Eastern, or Agra, direction over a fair road which is easily traversed by dawk-ghary, the first object which greets the traveller's eye is a spacious gateway, on either side of which are dwellings in a state of dilapidation and long since deserted. Musing on the sad solemnity of the scene, you toil up a deep ascent, with long

The gateway.

ranges of ruins and the remains of palaces and habitations; some in tolerably good condition, others shapeless masses of hewn stone. The mint. On one side are a series of vaulted chambers, known as the mint, The Hall of Account. and on the other a hall, said to be the Hall of Accounts. To the left of the mint is a spacious quadrangle, 360 feet by 180, with a series of cloisters on its four sides, supported by columns of free sandstone. This forms the court of the Dewan-i-Am, or The Dewan-i-Am. the Hall of Public Audience, a small hall with a wide verandah overlooking the court. The colonnade afforded accommodation to the vast multitude who assembled here to pay their homage to the Emperor, or to present petitions before him, or represent their grievances, or witness the administration of justice by one of the greatest monarchs who ever wielded the sceptre of this great Empire. Akbar took his royal seat in the small oblong balcony on one side of the court or stood, as he was accustomed to do, in the vestibule, to receive the salutations of the crowds who assembled there, thus gaining the confidence of all his subjects. Here were also held parades of men at arms and of animals.

The Record Office. Passing through a narrow passage, we come across another wide court, to the left of which is a spacious building of red granite, now used as a rest-house for travellers, but formerly the Emperor's Record Office (Daftarkhana).

The Khas Mahal. A little further on is a paved courtyard, 210 feet by 120, with a corridor, or suite of chambers, supporting all round an upper tier, or range of rooms, having cupolas at the four angles. This is the Emperor's Palace, or Khas Mahal.

The outer walls of trellis work of white marble and red granite that concealed the royal inmates from the public view, have all disappeared; but the remains of the screens are still to be traced due east to the opposite angle. On the south of the courtyard is the khwabgah, or King's sleeping chamber, a square The Khawb gáh. of less than fifteen feet, where the Emperor and his wives took their siesta after a dinner time.

It is surmounted by the royal bed-room, a small chamber of 15 feet square, but of singular beauty and simplicity. It has four doors, one on each side, over each of which is inscribed a

33

The Khawbgáh or Royal bed-room.

Page 130.

hemistich in Persian, the whole forming a stanza complimentary to the Royal occupant. It is as follows :—

فرش ایوان ترا آئینه سازد رضوان

خاک در گاه ترا سرمه کنند نور العین

قصر شاهست بهر رنگ به از خلد برین

سخنی نیست درین باب چه خلد ست برین

> The janitor of Paradise may see his face in thy chamber floor,
> The dust of thy court is collyrium for the light of the eyes.
> The palace of the King is in every respect better than sublime paradise—
> It is beyond question, what is heaven compared to it ?

The Ladies' Chapel.

North-west of the Khas Mahal is a small mosque intended as a chapel for the royal ladies, and a suite of chambers which were used as a hospital. On the east are the apartments known as those of Istamboli Begam, the Emperor's Turkish wife. The palace last named comprises specimens of the most elaborate carving and workmanship, representing highly imaginative scenes from nature and art. There are to be seen the forest scenery, the Himalayas, the lovely birds of the hill regions, the wild beasts of the jungle, alternate with the sprawling dragons of China, the palm trees of Africa, the vine and other fruit trees of India, wreaths of flowers and bunches of grapes hanging over the doors in festoons. The pillars outside are decorated with representations of trees and flowers of various kinds in bold relief.

Palace of Istamboli Begam.

The Sonehri Manzil.

To the right of the Emperor's palace, or Khas Mahal, and adjoining it, is the building known as the Sonehri Manzil, or the golden palace, an upper roomed square pavilion, now no lenger embellished with golden ornaments or gilt decorations. The interior walls are covered with paintings in fresco. There are the scenes of the adventures of the hero Rustam, as described in the Sháhnámá; the history of the Persian kings in poetry, by Firdousi, the celebrated poet of Mahmud the Ghiznivide Sultan, a work of which Akbar was particularly fond. The niches and arches over the doors and windows contain scenes and pictures of various character, but chiefly of religious significance. The house was once decorated throughout with gildings and paintings, within and without, the arches of the verandahs being inscribed with eloquent couplets by Fazi, brother of Abul Fazl, but all these have been obliterated. The zeal of the modern Moslems has destroyed many carved figures and images, but traces of them are still visible.

Akbar's views of the art of painting.

The art of painting is not encouraged by Mohamadanism, on the ground that man, however skilled in art, is imperfect, and his knowledge of the nature and beauties of God's vast creation, however advanced in comparison with particular sections of the human community, is defective, and that it is idle to imitate the works of God and attempt making likenesses of them. Akbar, who was a man of broad principles, did not share such conservative views. From his early youth His Majesty showed a great predilection for the art of painting and gave it every encouragement, for he looked upon it as a means of both culture and amusement. Abul Fazl, in the Ain, has written interesting notes regarding Akbar's views on the art. One day, at a private party, when the subject of Musalman views on the subject was being discussed, His Majesty observed that painters, in his opinion, had peculiar means of recognising God and appreciating his perfections. "A painter," continued he, "in sketching anything that has life and in designing parts of a living subject, must come to feel that he is incapable of real creation, and thus his mind is turned to God, the Bestower of life, and the knowledge of his heart is enlarged." His Majesty himself sat for his likeness and the likenesses of all the grandees of the realm were taken. He had more than one hundred painters in his employ.

The palace is identical with Bibi Mariam's house.

The chief feature in the ornamentation and architecture of the Sonehri Manzil is a Greek Cross, and the remains, on one of the doors of an Annunciation, the figure of the Virgin and an angel, parts of which only can be now traced. Tradition ascribes this palace as the abode of Akbar's Christian wife, one Bibi Mariam; and the guides assert she was a Portuguese lady. Certain writers seem to entertain doubts, whether Akbar married a Christian lady at all. It is not likely, they urge, that a fact so significant would have been omitted in contemporary histories like the Akbarnama and the Tabakat-i-Akbari. It must, however, be borne in mind that the works above referred to, notwithstanding the elaborate manner in which they have treated their subject, cannot be assumed to contain full information of all that Akbar did. The tendency in the historians of the Mohamadan period to omit from their works mention of all incidents which in their estimation reflected unfavourably on the doings of their sovereigns, or which were otherwise considered to be distasteful according to the tendency of the age, requires no explanation. Wheeler on the authority of the Revd. John Robson, seems to admit that Akbar married a Christian wife, known as Mariam, or Mary. 'The palace of Mariam', writes the author, 'is still shown at Fattehpur Sikri.'* Abul Fazl, in the Akbarnama (Vol. III), notices the garden of 'Mariam Makani, wife of Akbar,' as being situated at a distance of four kos from Fattehpur, styled the Darul Khilafat (or Capital). The Emperor used to go there for the sake of pleasure, and remained for days in the company of the ladies of the household.

Portuguese Jesuits at the court of Fattehpur Sikri, 1568 A. D.

It was at Fattehpur Sikri that the gravitations of Akbar towards Christianity assumed singular interest. He invited Christian Fathers from the Portuguese Settlement at Goa to his court at Fattehpur to instruct him in the holy books. Accordingly three—Aquaviva, Monselrate, Enriques—having taken their departure from Surat in December 1568, were escorted to Fattehpur. The Fathers describe Akbar as a man of about fifty, of European complexion and bearing in his face strong marks of intelligence. His Majesty received them with every mark of favour and distinction. Being presented with a polyglot Bible in four languages and images of Jesus and the Virgin Mary, he placed the Bible on his head and kissed the images. When asked by the Jesuits for the Emperor's protection, he replied :—" What would you have? I have more crosses in my palace than you in your Churches." Saturday evenings were set apart for controversies between the Fathers and Mullahs. After the disputations, in which each party claimed to have gained the victory, were over, a great Mohamadan doctor undertook to leap into a furnace with the Koran in his hand, asserting that he would undergo the horrible trial without injury to himself, provided one of the friars did the same with his Bible, and that this would prove the superiority of his religion. The friars declined to have resort to such a questionable criterion of religious faith, and the matter was dropped. Akbar was so impressed with the doctrines of the Christian faith

Controversies with the Mullahs.

* Wheeler's History of India, Vol. I, page 163, Edition of 1875.

The Mohamadan formula changed.

that he instructed Abul Fazl to prepare a translation of the gospel and ordered prince Morad* to take lessons in Christianity.† The usual Mohamadan formula, *Bisimullah irrahman irrahim* (I commence in the name of God the Merciful), was changed into *Ai nami tu Jesus wa Kristu* (O thou whose names are Jesus and Christ) which means 'O thou whose name is gracious and blessed.' To the above, Sheikh Fazi added the following, to complete the verse. *Subhanaka la Siwaka ya hu* (We praise thee, there is no one besides thee, O God !)‡

A chapel built for the Christians.

The Fathers built a small chapel for their own use, and that of the Portuguese traders and residents in Agra and its neighbourhood. The detailed narrative of Du Jerrie, one of the missionaries, has been fortunately preserved, and it gives a clear idea of the doings at the Court of the Great Emperor at Fattehpur. Thither, we are informed, came Akbar, alone, without attendants, removed his turban and offered prayers, after he had first knelt in the fashion of Christians, then in his own, that is, according to the mode used by Persian Saracens (for he clung to the externals of this faith) and finally after the fashion of the heathen. He compelled his nobles to treat the missionaries, their pictures, books and services with reverence. A Portuguese Christian died about the same time, in Fattehpur. With the permission of the Emperor, his funeral procession, after the Catholic fashion, was conducted through the streets of Fattehpur with great pomp. The inhabitants, both Hindus and Mohamadans, were gratified by the pageantry and participated in the ceremonies. The Fathers were also allowed to build a Hospital.

Akbar's respect for Christianity.

The Jesuits, judging the Emperor from his Christian tendencies, urged upon him the advisability of winning for himself the glory of a new hero in religion by formally embracing Christianity; but Akbar was inflexible. He assured the Fathers of the great respect he held for their religion, and that he

* He was born three months after Jahangir (Salem). Having been born in the hills of Fattehpur Sikri, he got the nickname Pahari (hill man). He was then only eight years old.

† Budaoni II 256.

‡ Akbar allowed the Fathers to preach Christianity in any part of his Empire, but he did not embrace Christianity himself, saying he waited for the divine illumination. It awakened interest in other men besides Akbar, and Abul Fazl and his elder brother Abul Faiz seemed to have been greatly influenced by it. Both were of Sufi persuasion.

honoured their church and its many doctrines, still he could not understand the mystery of the Trinity, and asked with much concern how it could be that God could have a son who was a man.

"The heathen," argued he, "believed their creed to be true, the Moslem the same, and so, too, the Christians:—which religion are we to believe and which reject?" The explanations offered by the holy Fathers failed to make any impression on the sharp witted Akbar. Du Jerrie laments His Majesty's stiff-neckedness and complains that he was never content with one answer, but drove him over to further enquiries.

He is inquisitive.

"This," he observes, "is the peccadillo of this prince, as of many another atheist; they will not shackle reason by obedience to faith, because they think nothing true which does not enter into the circle of their powers of comprehension; with the measure of their intellect they would mete out The Infinite, which transcends all human understanding." When Aquaviva asked the Emperor's permission for the three missionaries who were then at Fattehpur to preach Christianity in all the provinces of Hindustan, Akbar answered evasively that this matter was entirely in the hands of God, who alone had it in his power to fulfil their wishes, and that he on his part desired nothing more ardently. Meanwhile the attraction of novelty having faded away, less attention was paid to the Fathers, who, having been privately told by one of the courtiers that they had been kept more for the sake of amusement and novelty than anything else, and that His Majesty had not the slightest idea of adopting their tenets, returned to Goa in 1582, with the exception of Aquaviva, whom Akbar detained, on account of his great accomplishments. He was honoured alike by Hindus and Mohamadans, and he learnt the Persian language, to facilitate his discussions with the Mohamadans, his object being to win over Akbar; but, perceiving that it was lost labor to scatter seed on a land so barren, he too, after some time, followed his brethren to Goa.

The Fathers return to Goa, 1582.

Mirza Nizamuddin Ahmad, author of the *Tabakat*, has given a description of the ceremonies observed at the Court of Fatteh-pur Sikri. The occasion was the arrival of Mirza Suleman, ruler

Ceremonies in Akbar's Court at Fattehpur Sikri.

of Badakhshan, grandson of Abu Said Mirza and sixth in descent from Timur, in Rajab 983 (1575 A D). The author writes, "on his reaching Mathra, twenty kos from Fattehpur, the Emperor sent several nobles to meet him. When the Mirza was at a distance of five kos from Fattehpur, all the nobles and officers were sent out to receive him. And when the intelligence of his having left his stage was brought, His Majesty himself went out on horseback to meet him. Five thousand elephants, with housings of velvet and brocade, with gold and silver chains and with white and black fringes on their neck and trunks, were drawn up in lines on each side of the road to a distance of five kos from Fattehpur. Between each two elephants there was a cart with leopards in it which had collars studded with gold and housings of fine cloth; also two bullock carts drawn by animals that wore gold embroidered headstalls. When all the arrangements were made, the Emperor went out with great pomp and splendour. Upon his approaching, the Mirza hastened to dismount, and ran forward towards His Majesty; but the Emperor, observing the venerable age of the Mirza, also alighted from his horse and would not allow the Mirza to go through the usual observances and ceremonies. He fondly embraced him; and then mounted and made the Mirza ride on his right hand. All the five kos, he enquired about his circumstances, and, on reaching the palace, he seated him by his side on the throne. The young princes were also present and were introduced to the Mirza, and, after a great entertainment, he gave the Mirza a house near the royal palace.

Orders were in the meanwhile issued to Khan Jahan, Governor of the Panjab, to accompany the Mirza, on his return from Fattehpur, to Badakhshan, with 5,000 horse, to recover the country and restore it to him, and then to return to Lahore.

The Dewan-i-Khas. One of the most unique of the buildings is the Dewan-i-Khas, or Privy Council chamber. It is situated due north of Mariam's house and west of the Dewan-i-Am. Externally it appears to have two storeys surmounted by a cupola at each corner. Entering, however, we find that it is in reality of but one storey, open from the floor to the dome. In the centre there is

The Dewan-i-Khas, Fattehpur Sikri.

Page 136.

a singular massive column, richly carved, rising to the height of the upper windows and supporting a palisaded octagonal seat, an immense capital of the richest sculpture, three times its diameter, with four stone causeways, each about ten feet long, leading to four side-entrances or corners of the pavilion, where they meet a quadrant which communicates with the ground floor by a flight of sixteen steps. In times of yore, the seat in the middle, being covered with silk textures and made comfortable with satin and velvet cushions, was occupied by the Emperor Akbar, the four ministers (Khan-i-Khanan, Bir-Bal, Fyzi and Abul Fazl) standing at the four corners to receive orders for their respective Departments.

Dialogue between Abul Fazl and Badaoni.

The place is associated with many historical scenes. It was here that the grandees of the Empire met in Akbar's time and talked on religious, social and political subjects. Mulla Abdul Qadar Badaoni, in his *Muntakhibul Tawarikh*, has recorded an interesting dialogue which took place between him and Sheikh Abul Fazl in the hall of the Dewan-i-Khas. The Mulla was a Mussulman of orthodox type, while Abul Fazl was an atheist. The Mulla writes:—

"I remember that, in the early days of these discussions, I happened one night to meet Sheik Abul Fazl in the Privy Audience Chamber of Fattehpur. He said: 'I have a fair objection to make to all writers on two grounds: first, why should they have not written as detailed a history of the older Prophets as they have done in the annals of their own Prophet? (God bless him and his descendants and peace be on him).'* I replied, 'In the Kasasul Aulia ample accounts are given,' to which he rejoined, 'No, that book is too compendious; they ought to have written in detail.' I answered, 'owing to the lapse of time, that much only might have stood the test of enquiry by the critics and historians, and the rest remained unauthenticated.' He said: 'This is no answer.' He continued, '*Secondly*, there is no kind of handycraftsman who is not mentioned in the *Tazkiratul-aulia* and the *Nafahatul Uns*, &c.' 'What harm had the members of the Prophet's own family done that no mention is therein made of them. This is

* Note that the para. in bracket is by the author, Badaoni.

a matter of great surprise.' * On this topic whatever the time allowed was said; but who would listen? Afterwards I asked: 'Of the known religions which are you the most inclined to accept?' He answered: 'I wish to wander a few days in the vale of unbelief and apostasy.' I rejoined ironically, 'It would not be a bad thing if you removed entirely the restriction of the marriage tie, for they have said':—

بر داشت غل شرع بتا ئید ایزدی از گردن زمانهٔ علي ذکرہ السلام

By the help of God the chain of law has removed he
From off the neck of the world, peace to his memory be!

He smiled and went away."

Badaoni then goes on to describe how Abul Fazl was emboldened to offend the Ulmas, countenanced by the Emperor, and would listen to neither arguments nor reason in contradiction of what he himself urged. 'True is the saying' says the author:

یکعنا یت قاضي بهازهزار گواه

'One favour of the Judge is better than a thousand witnesses.'

The Ibadat Khana.

In the Dewan-i-Khas there is a beautiful side gallery identified as the *Ibadat Khana*, or house of worship, as no other edifice answers the description given by *Badaoni* and the Tabakat in noticing the *Ibadat Khana* at Fattehpur Sikri.

The *Ibadat Khana* was built in 1574. It was a place for the reception of men of learning, genius and accomplishment.

Abul Fazl thus describes it in the Akbarnama, Vol. III, in connection with the events of the 19th year of the reign (1574 A.D.):—

"It consists of four *Ewans*, or upper storey chambers, in the courtyard of which thousands of people from all quarters of the world assemble and wait for the arrival of His Majesty, who talks to them with cheerful countenance, hears them patiently and answers their enquiries. He is accessible to all and free in

* The book mentioned by Abul Fazl contains the biographies of saints. Many of these saints were handicraftsmen. The objection of Abul Fazl was that, while all handicraftsmen should have been mentioned in these works, the members of the Prophet's own family had been omitted. Badaoni does not say what his reply to this objection of Abul Fazl was; but the reply is clear. The *ahel-i-bet* or members of the Prophet's family are treated by Mohammadans as far superior to *Walis* or religious saints, and they were not counted in that category. They are next to the Prophet himself to all true believers.

conversation. From the lowest man, covered with dust and rags, to the highest, clothed in shawl and velvet, gain the object of his heart in this assembly of the wise. His Majesty, sitting at a distance, sees all men, and calls any one to whom he wishes to speak." Four assemblies used to be held. In the eastern hall assembled the *Amirs*, or grandees of the Empire; in the western the *Ulemas*, or the learned and men of religious sanctity; in the northern the *Sufis*, or followers of theism; and in the southern the philosophers. Different topics were discussed and difficult problems solved. Sometimes whole nights were spent in discussion. People did nothing here but enquire and investigate; profound points of science, the subtleties of revelation, the curiosities of history and the wonders of nature were discussed. What Akbar maintained was, if true knowledge was to be found everywhere, why should truth be confined to one religion and creed; why should one sect assert what another denies and why should one claim a preference without having superiority conferred on itself?*

Assemblies held here.

Subjects of discussion.

The meetings were conducted by Abul Fazl. The fashion after which they were conducted has been described by Badaoni. He writes: 'He (Abul Fazl) fell boldly into disputation on religious matters with such imbecile old men as the Suddur, the Qazi, the Hakim-ul-mulk and Mukhdumui Mulk, and had not the slightest hesitation in putting them to disgrace, at which the Emperor was pleased.' These men sent private messages to Abul Fazl by Asif Khan Mir Bukshi, asking him why he always fell foul of them. He returned answer,—

مانوکرمردی ایم نوکر بادانجان نیستیم

'I am a servant of a man and not of an egg plant.' 'By the dint of his own genius,' continues the author, the 'assistance of his father, the countenance of the Khalif of the Age, and by the favour of his own fortune, he cast them all in a short space of time down to the ground of scorn and contempt, and not one of the people of Islam, except Hakim Abul Fath and Mulla Mohamad Yezdi, were a match for him in the discussions.'

At one of these meetings the Emperor asked those who were present to mention each the name of a man whom he considered

---

* Badaoni.

the wisest man of the age, pointing out that they should not count kings, who formed an exception.

On this Hakim Hamam mentioned his own name and Abul Fazl that of his father, Sheikh Mobarik.

The Emperor's visits to these meetings were invariably made occasions for the distribution of largesses and gifts, and scarcely any one of the guests departed with empty hands. The meetings were usually held on Friday night, and on the nights of holy days.*

Places of worship built.

According to Badaoni, many places of worship were built by command of His Majesty during the year 983 (1575 A.D.). His Majesty passed whole nights in contemplation and prayer. He occupied himself in repeating the names *Ya Hu* (O He—God) and *Ya Hadi* (O Guide). He would sit many a morning alone in prayer and melancholic meditation on a large flat stone of an old building which lay near the palace in a lonely spot, 'with his head bent over his chest, and gathering the bliss of early morn.'

Akbar's place of worship.

The Byragi's pavilion.

In the same court, there is a pavilion of singular structure, where the tolerant Akbar accommodated a Byragi Fakir. It is a cupola forming a pyramidal canopy, with traceries and carvings in the Buddhist fashion, supported on four granite pillars, connected at the angles by serpentine brackets. The pavilion, although of Hindu design, is no departure from the general style of architecture of the place, which is a massive kind of Saracenic. As Akbar tolerated all religions, and was more particularly inclined towards the Hindus, a Hindu friar, or priest, in the midst of the Royal Court was not out of place.

The *Ankh Micholi* or hide-and-seek playing house.

Close by the side of the Privy Council Chamber is a labyrinthine edifice, of curious design and construction, where it is represented the Emperor played hide-and-seek with the ladies of the Royal household. The place consists of a central strong room, with two more on the south and north, a precipice, surmounted by a gallery, and quarters for sentinels all round. Here are marks of hinge holes, showing that the doorways were of stone, closed by heavy padlocks. This, coupled with the fact that it is situated

* Religious assemblies presided over by the Emperor used also to be held in the grand mosque of Fattehpur Sikri.

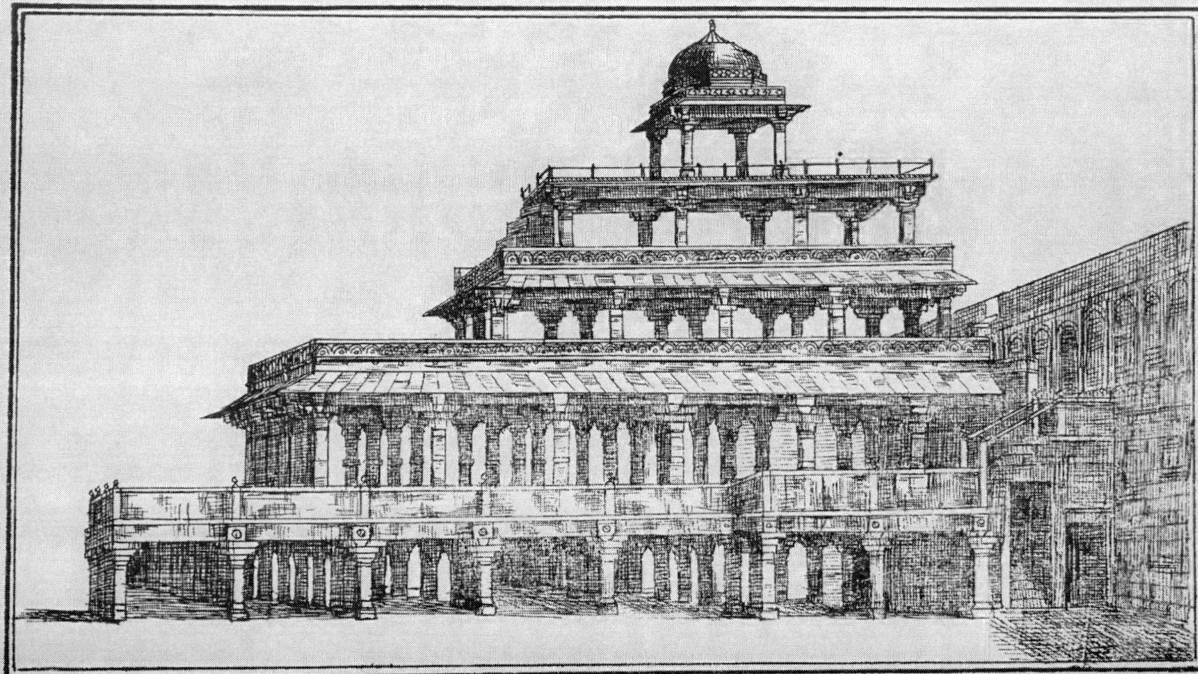

The Panj Mahal.

Page 141.

beyond the female apartments and quite close to the Privy Council Chamber, has led modern enquirers to conclude that it was really the Royal Treasure House where were also probably kept for safe custody the valuables and regalia of the Empire.

Near the palace reputed to have belonged to the Christian Queen is a most curious structure, of pyramidal shape, open on all sides. It is a five storeyed colonnade, with a succession of open galleries in the shape of square flat forms rising one above another and resting on rows of richly carved pillars, each storey successively lessening in dimensions till the uppermost, comprising a large cupola supported on columns, is reached. The pillars in the lowermost storey, numbering fifty-six, are of singular style and beauty. The capitals represent a variety of interesting objects in sculpture. On one of them are a couple of carved elephants, standing opposite each other, with interlaced trunks; on another is the image of a man plucking fruit from a tree. The first floor has thirty-five pillars; the next fifteen; the next eight; while the uppermost pavilion rests on four only. The carving on these pillars is so highly finished and of such delicate execution as to afford evident proof of superior taste and skill; consequently they have been often drawn and photographed as curiosities of sculptural art. The Panj Mahal.

Opinions differ as to the origin and object of this curious building. Some maintain that it was designed as a place for the *muazzan* to call for prayers at the appointed hours; others that it was intended as a place for hanging a large bell at the highest point, to announce to the citizens the functional hours of the Court, and others that it was a place for Akbar to survey the surrounding country from. Certain it is that it was intended as a place of recreation and pastime, where the Emperor, sitting in the uppermost kiosque, took fresh air and enjoyed the moonlight during summer nights, the ladies of the royal household occupying seats lower down, with probably curtains of net work hung over the arches to admit of free air and a full view of the country and the adjacent female apartments. The Panj Mahal, from its exquisite beauty and excellence of design, has properly attracted the attention of the Archæological Department of the Government of India, and during the Viceroyalty of Lord Mayo Object of the building.

was put under repairs at a great cost, and the ornamentations were restored as far as possible.

The Pachisi Board. North-east of the Panj Mahal, over an extensive pavement of stone, is a colossal chess board on which the game known as *Pachisi* was played. The board, carved out upon stone pavement, consists of squares of unusual dimensions, each being wide enough for a man to sit in. The guides say that women, attired in beautiful costumes of diverse colours, denoted the positions in game. The board is similar to that in the Agra fort with this difference, that, while the one in Agra is of marble, this is of red sandstone. Quite near to the *Pachisi* board there is a small throne of red sandstone on which the dice for the game were thrown.

The tomb of Sheikh Salem Chisti. But the chief ornament of the whole group of buildings, and indeed the paragon of the place, is the mausoleum of Sheikh Salem Chishti, the holy saint, confidence in whose spiritual powers led Akbar to found here a mighty city and embellish it with royal palaces, gardens and other public edifices. It is situated to the south-west of the royal palaces already mentioned, and forms the nucleus for the other buildings which gradually sprung up here under the auspices of the Emperor.

An account of the Sheikh. Sheikh Salem, the son of Sheikh Baha-ud-din, was a descendant of Sheikh Farid Shakurgunj, the famous saint of Pak Pattan, in the Montgomery District of the Panjab. He always kept fast and went to Mecca three times to perform the holy pilgrimage. After travelling all over India in the garb of a Fakir, he came to the vicinity of Sikri, at that time an inconsiderable hamlet, and ensconced himself in the forest surrounding the hillocks, which, removed from human habitations, was frequented by beasts of prey. The spot, from its lonely and retired situation, attracted his attention. He lived here the life of a recluse, and from the reeds of the forest and such leaves and branches as he could gather, built a hut on the summit of a hillock under a shady tree. In this rude and solitary cell, he passed his days in devotion, making

"Prayer all his business, all his pleasure praise,"

his pallet being of stalks and straw, and his pillow of bushes and pebbles. Akbar's former children had died in infancy and he had been long without a son. Conscious that the Empire founded by

Mausoleum of Sheikh Salem Chishti (exterior view).

Page 142.

The Mausoleum of Sheikh Salem Chishti.
Page 142.

the enterprise and energy of his father and grandfather, which he had himself taken considerable pains to consolidate, would lapse to strangers, and his dynasty become extinct if he were not blessed with a son, he stood in need of the prayers of the Fakir and the pious, who, he was convinced, were nearer to God, and whose prayers in his behalf would, he was assured, gain for him the object of his life, namely, an heir to the throne. He acquainted his councillors with the distress of his mind, and, as before stated, they advised him to seek the spiritual aid of Sheikh Salem, which they thought would secure for him the desire of his heart. The Emperor acted on their advice and the result was the birth of Salem. Ever afterwards Akbar entertained the highest esteem for the Sheikh, whose sons and other near relations were raised to high honours of State. When the Sheikh died, Akbar built over his tomb a mausoleum, which, in elegance and beauty, is surpassed by few edifices of the kind in India.

A magnificent portal to the east leads to a spacious quadrangle of paved red stone, 433 feet by 366, the four sides of which are taken up each by a lofty and majestic colonnade, forming a verandah of arcaded chambers 50 feet high, all of the same material as the pavement. Inclining towards the northern angle is the tomb of the saint, an elegant structure made entirely of the purest marble with the finest polish, and elaborately carved. The tomb rises on a square base and ends in a graceful, melon-shaped dome of exquisite beauty. It is surrounded by a vestibule, or verandah, of deep clipstone, supported by serpentine brackets of variegated shape and design, and projecting out of substantial columns of white marble terminating at the base in a tulip shaped aperture. The marble trellis work that surrounds the sarcophagus containing the body of the Saint is of such surpassing beauty and delicate execution that, looked at from a distance, it resembles lace work on the finest silk. His Royal Highness the Prince of Wales was particularly struck with its chaste beauty when he visited the mausoleum in 1876. The verandah encloses an inside chamber, the walls of which are of marble up to 4 feet from the floor and are inlaid with cornelian, onyx and jasper. Above that point, the walls are embellished with a highly polished stucco and wainscoted with red

Account of building.

sand-stone. The floor is of jasper, impressed with flowers of various colours and patterns beautifully cut out of marble, and the doors are of solid ebony. The tomb of the Saint is of pure white marble, surrounded by a lattice work of the same material and covered with a precious piece of brocade. Over this is a sort of canopy, shaped like an oblong umbrella, supported by four slender staves, each encrusted with fine mother-o'-pearl work, carved in various geometrical designs. On the northern side are the tombs of women and children; and an enormous mausoleum beyond

The tomb of Islam Khan.

that of the Sheikh, in the same direction, is the tomb of Islam Khan, the grandson of the Sheikh, who was Governor of Bengal during the reign of Jahangir.

The entire structure has a most pleasing effect, and the mausoleum stands unrivalled among similar buildings for the elegance of its design, as well as the delicacy of its execution. It is, indeed, one of the finest and most perfect specimens of Indian architecture. As originally built by Akbar, the tomb was of red sandstone, and the marble trellis-work, the chief ornament of the tomb, was erected subsequently by the Emperor Jahangir. The tomb, although above three hundred years old, is in a state of excellent preservation, which shows the extreme care bestowed on it by those who have held charge of it.

Knots, or bits of string or ribbon, are bound by barren Hindu and Mohamadan women to the marble trellis surrounding the tomb of the Saint, as a vow to offer money, sweetmeats or bread if blessed with a son, which it is supposed the mediation of the Saint with God will procure for them. Similar votive offerings are placed on Akbar's tomb in Sekandrah.

Inscription on the tomb.

The following inscription on the gateway of the Dargah gives the chronogram of the Sheikh's death.

مغیث ملت و پیر طریق شیخ سلیم

که در کرامت و قربت جنید و ثانی اوست

منور است از و شمع خانواده چشت

فرید گنج شکر را خلف ترین پور است

در بین مباش زخود فانی و بحق باقی

که سال رحلتش اندر زمانه مشهور است

The Tomb of Nawáb Islám Khan.

Page 144.

The asylum of faith, the Saint of the pious sect, Sheikh Salem,
Who in excellence and nearness to God is like unto Juned and Tyfur.
To him is due the brilliancy of the lamp of the house of Chisht,
For he is chosen descendant of Farid, surnamed Ganj Shakar.
'Abstain from polytheism, forget yourself and join the essence of the Everlasting.'
The above is the well known phrase giving the date of his death.

If the figure 2 is taken out of the numerical value of the phrase زخود فاني وبحق باقي, the balance will be 979 (1571 A.D.), which gives the era of death.

A beautiful archway on the west of the mausoleum leads to a walled enclosure, in which is the tomb of Bibi Zenab, the grand daughter of Sheikh Salem. The sarcophagus, which is of marble, has the following chronogram on it:

Tomb of Bibi Zenab.

چو رحلت کرد این عصمت پناهي   فلک جيب شکيبائي دريده
بسال انتقالش گفت هاتف   بفردوس برين بيشک رسيده

When this chaste lady departed to the other world,
The heavens through grief tore the collar of patience,
An invisible voice said for the year of her death,
'She has, without doubt, gone to the sublime paradise.'

Close to the above is the tomb of Haji Hosain, the *Khalifa* and successor of Sheikh Salem. The following chronogram is inscribed over the gateway of the tomb:

of Haji Hosain.

شيخ امير قافله حاجي حسين آنکه   بردش تمتع ز حج و عمر جاودان
چون در صفا و مروه عمرش نماند سعي   رحمت کشيد جانب مقصود راعنان
سال وصال اهل مناسک رقم زدند   بهر طواف کعبه مقصود شد بجان
سنه ۱۰۰۰ هجري

The Sheikh, the chief of the assembly of the pious, Haji Hosain,
Who had the benefit of Haj * and was endowed with eternal life,
When his worldly life drew to a close in Safa and Marwa,
The mercy of God attracted him towards the object of his heart,
The pious wrote for the year of his death:
'He has gone on a pilgrimage to the Temple of God.'

The above gives 1000 A. H. (1594 A.D.) as the year of death.

* Namely, had the benefit of pilgrimage to Mecca.

The Boland Darwaza.

But the grandest object of attraction in the entire group, indeed the marvel of the place, is the *Boland Darwaza*, or "lofty gateway," which, according to one authority, is 'one of the loftiest and most majestic in the world.' Fergusson calls it 'the finest in India.' It is raised on a lofty flight of steps, and towers 130 feet above the breast of the ridge on the south of the *Khangah*. It is an exceedingly imposing and handsome edifice, surmounted with cones and minarets; and although gigantic in form, such is the symmetry of its proportions and the sublimity and grace of its general appearance that it cannot fail to impress the observer with its massive dignity and stately beauty. The borders of the gateway are carved in granite of a buff colour, and flowers of diverse forms, cut out of stone, are arranged in it with great elegance.

A flight of 120 steps leads to the summit, which affords a splendid view of the adjacent country, with a distant glimpse of the Taj, 25 miles away, and the fort of Bharatpur. The colossal grandeur of this huge gateway dwarfs the buildings to which it is at present attached, but it must be borne in mind that the edifice formed no part of the original design. The *Boland Darwaza* was intended to serve as a triumphant arch to commemorate the victory of the royal troops under Akbar in Khandes, and was built several years after the Khangah and the mosque. The following is the inscription in bold relief on a sandstone wall to the right of the sacred quadrangle as you enter the mausoleum.

Inscription on the Eastern wall.

حضرت شهنشاه فلک بارگاه ظل الله جلال الدين محمد اکبر بادشاه بعد
فتح ملک دکن ودانديس که سابقا مسمي به خانديس بود در سنه ۴۶
الهي مطابق سنه ۱۰۱۰ بفتحپور رسيده عزيمت آگره فرمودند

تا نام زمين و آسمان ست   تا نقش وجود در جهان ست
نامش به سپهر هم نشين باد   ذاتش بجهان ابدقرين باد

وقال عيسى عليه السلام — الدنيا قنطرة فاعبروها ولاتعمروها ومن تامل
عيش غدا تعدل عيش ابدا وقيلت الدنيا ساعة فجعلها طاعة بقية
العمر لا قيمت لها

The Boland Darwaza or High Gateway.

Page 146.

His Majesty, King of kings, of heavenly palace, the shadow of God, Jalaluddin Mohammad Akbar *Badshah,* having conquered the country of the Deccan and Dandes, formerly known as Khan Des, in the 46th Divine year, corresponding to 1010, reached Fattehpur and then proceeded to Agra.

So long as earth and sky endure,
So long as the impression of existence lasts on the surface of the earth,
May His Majesty's name rank with that of heaven,
And his life last so long as there is duration to the world.

So said Jesus, on whom be peace ! The world is a bridge ; pass over it, but build no house on it. He who reflected on the distresses of the Day of Judgment, gained pleasure everlasting.

Worldly pleasures are but momentary ; spend, then, thy life in devotion and remember that what remains of it is valueless.

Inscription on the Western wall.

من قام الي الصلوٰة وليس معه قلبه فانه لايزيده من الله الا بعدا—
خير المال ما أنفق في سبيل الله—
بع الدنيا بالاخرة تربح الفقر ملك ليس فيها محاسبة
نامي چه شد ارتو تخت گاهي كردي وزقصر زراند وده پناهي كردي
خوبي جهان بصورت آئينه دان خود گير تو هم درونگاهی كردي
قايله وكاتبه محمد معصوم نامي بن سيد صفا الترمذي اصلاو البكري
مسكناو النسبت الي سيد شيرين بابا حسن ابدال السبزواري مولودا
والقندهاري موطنا—

He that standeth up to prayer and his heart is not in it, verily he does not obtain nearness to God, but draws himself to a distance from Him. Thy best possession is what thou givest in the name of God ; thy best traffic is selling this world for the next, and this will benefit thee ; piety is a world in which there is no account for anything.

What name hast thou acquired if thou hast constructed a throne.
And taken shelter in a palace wrought with gold ?
The loveliness of the world is like a looking glass ;
Take it not as thine, more than what thou lookest upon it.

Said and written by Mohammed Masum,* poetically styled Nami, son of Syed Safa, of Turmuz, born at Bhakkar, descendant from Syed She son of Baba Husan Abdul of Subzwar, resident of Kandahar.

Eccentric as Akbar was in religious matters, and unsettled as was his belief as to the true religion, the pious tone of the inscriptions above written confirms the statement made in contemporary histories, that, a few years before his death, he showed a decided inclination to the faith of his ancestors, and that he died a good Mussalman. He died only four years after the above inscriptions were written.

The Grand Mosque. West of the Dargah is Akbar's 'grandest mosque,' as Fergusson calls it. It has lofty square pillars richly carved, the wings being of red sandstone and the inner court paved with white marble. The walls and surroundings are painted with rich and delicate tints, disposed in a variety of geometrical designs, the centre being an immense vaulted chamber which provides accommodation for the congregation.

The following chronogram is inscribed on the main arch :—

در زمان شه جهان اکبر که از وملک را نظام آمد
شیخ الاسلام مسجدي آراست کز صفا کعبه احترام آمد
سال اتمام این بناي رفیع ثاني المسجد الحرام آمد

سنه ۹۸۹ هجري

---

* Mir Mohamad Masum of Bhakkar belonged to a family of the Syeds of Turmuz in Bokhara. His ancestors, two or three generations before him, came to Kandahar, and his father, Mir Safa, settled in Bhakkar. Through the influence of Mirza Nizamudin Ahmad, author of the Tabbakat, he was introduced to Akbar, who made him a Commander of 250. Akbar, recognising his merit, became his patron, and, in 1012 (1603 A. D.), sent him as ambassador to Teheran, where he was received with distinction by Shah Abbas.

Mohamad Masum enjoyed a great reputation as a poet and historian. He composed under the poetical name Nami and was the author of the Tarikh-i-Sindh and many other books. He was skilled as a composer and tracer of inscriptions, and was always accompanied on his travels by sculptors. His metrical inscriptions adorn numerous mosques and public buildings from India to Isphahan and Tabriz. Besides the cathedral mosque at Fattehpur, his inscriptions are found over the gate of the fort of Agra, the fort of Mandu and various other places. He embellished Sukkar with many edifices, and, in the midst of a branch of the Indus which flows round Bhakkar, he built a dome (the date of which was found in the words گنبد دریای (water dome) giving 1007 A. H. (1598 A. D.) He was pious and very liberal and left 30 or 40 lacs of rupees, which were inherited by his son, Mir Buzurg.

The Mosque of Fattehpúr Sikri.

Page 148.

In the time of the King of the world Akbar
To whom is due the discipline of State,
The Sheik of the age laid out a mosque
Which on account of its chasteness deserves reverence like the Kaba.
The year of the completion of this lofty edifice
Is found in the words, 'duplicate of the Holy Place.'

The above gives 979 A. H., or 1571 A. D., as the year of construction. The mosque was built by Sheikh Salem himself during his lifetime. He had said his prayers in it for only six months when he died.

Religious meetings.

Allami Abul Fazl, in his Akbarnama, has given a full account of the religious meetings that were held by Akbar in the *Jama Masjid*, or Cathedral Mosque of Fattehpur Sikri. In the 24th year of the reign, or 987 A. H. (1579 A. D.), it was publicly declared that His Majesty united in his person the powers of the State and those of the Church. The *Mullahs* signed the famous document which settled the superiority of the *Imami Adil* (just leader) over the *Mujtahid* (head of the Church). It declared that the king of Islam, the Amir of the Faithful, *Abul Fath Jalaluddin Mohammad Akbar Badshah-i-Ghazi*, was a most just, most wise, and most God-fearing king, and that on all religious questions regarding which the opinions of the *mujtahids* should be at variance, the decree of His Majesty was to be binding on the whole nation. The document was signed and sealed by *Mukhdumul Mulk* Maulana Abdullah Sultanpuri, *Sheikhul Islam*, Sheikh Abdul Nabi, the *Sadrul Sadur*, *Hakimul Mulk*, Ghazi Khan Badakhshi, *Kaziul Kuzzat* Kazi Jalaluddin of Multan, the Sadar Jahan, the Mufti of the Empire, Sheikh Mubarik, the deepest writer of the age, and others.

Akbar declares himself to be the Imam of the age.

The famous document.

The document stands unique in the whole Church History of the Islamitic faith. Al Badaoni has happily preserved a complete copy of it. The following is a copy taken verbatim from his work.

محضر

مقصود از تشئید این مبانی وتمهید این معانی آنکه چون هندوستان
جنیت عن الحدثان بیمن معدلت سلطانی وتربیت جهانبانی
مرکز امن و امان ودایره عدل واحسان شده طوایف انام از خواص وعوام

خصوصاً علماي عرفان شعار وفضلاي دقايق آثار كه هاديان باديه
نجات وسالكان مسالك اوتوا العلم درجات اند از عرب وعجم رو بدين
ديار نهاده توطن اختيار نمودند جمهور علماي فحول كه جامع فروع
واصول وحاوي معقول ومنقول اند وبدين وديانت و صيانت انصاف
دارند بعد ازتدبر وافي وتامل كافي در غوامض معاني آيه
كريمه اطيعو الله واطيعو الرسول و اولي الامر منكم و احاديث
صحيح أن آحب الناس الي الله يوم القيامة امام عادل يطيع
الامير فقد اطاعني ومن يعص الامير فقد عصاني وغير ذالك من الشواهد
العقليه والدلايل النقليه قرارداده حكم نمودند كه مرتبه سلطان
عادل عند الله زياده از مرتبه مجتهد است وحضرت سلطان الاسلام
كهف الانام امير المومنين ظل الله علي العالمين ابو الفتح جلال الدين
محمد اكبر بادشاه غازي خلد الله ملكه ابدا اعقل واعلم بالله اند
بنا بر ان اگر در مسايل دين كه بين المجتهدين مختلف فيها ست
بذهن ثاقب وفكر صايب خود يك جانب را از اختلاف بجهة تسهيل
بني آدم و مصلحت انتظام عالم اختيار نموده بان جانب حكم فرمايند
متفق عليه ميشود و اتباع آن برعموم برايا وكافه رعايا لازم ومتحتم
است وايضا اگر بموجب راي صواب نماي خود حكمي را از احكام قرار
دهند كه مخالف نصي نباشد وسبب ترفيه عالميان بوده باشد عمل
بران نمودن بر همه كس لازم و متحتم است ومخالفت آن موجب
سخط اخروي وخسران ديني ودنيوي است واين مسطور صدق وفور
حسبة الله واظهار الاجراء حقوق الاسلام بمحضر علماي دين وفقهاي
مجتهدين تحرير يافت وكان ذالك في شهر رجب سنه سبع وثمانين
تسعمايه (٩٨٧) ✝

The object of writing this document is this:—Whereas Hindustan, protected from all calamities, has through the blessings of the justice of His Majesty and the disciplines introduced by him now become the centre of security and peace and the land of justice and beneficence; and multitudes of people, dignitaries and plebeians, especially learned men of sanctity and scholars of high wisdom, who lead the way to salvation and are the guides in the path of righteousness, having immigrated to this country from Arabia and non-Arabia, have adopted this as their home. Therefore, the principal learned men well versed in the several branches of law and in the principles of jurisprudence, and accomplished in edicts which rest on reason and testimony, and who are known for their piety, honesty and sanctity, have, after fully considering the deep meanings, *first* of the verse of the Quran (Sura iv 62), "Obey God and obey the Prophet and those among you who may be in authority," and, *secondly*, of the genuine traditions, (1) "Surely the man who is dearest to God on the Day of Judgment is Imami Adil (just leader) ;" (2) Whosoever obeys the Amir, obeys me ; and whosoever rebels against him, rebels against me," and, *thirdly*, of several other proofs based on reason and testimony, agreed that the rank of *Sultan-i-Adil* (just ruler) is, in the eyes of God, higher than the rank of a *mujtahid* (head of the Church). Wherefore, the King of Islam, the asylum of the Nations, the Amir of the Faithful, the Shadow of God over the people of the world, Abul Fath Jallaluddin Mohammed Akbar Badshah Ghazi, may God perpetuate his kingdom, being the most just, the most wise, the most learned and the most God fearing, it is declared that, should, in future, a religious question come up, regarding which the opinions of the *mujtahids* are at variance and His Majesty in his penetrating wisdom and right judgment is inclined to adopt, for the benefit of the nation and as a political expedient, any of the conflicting opinions which exist on that point, and issue a decree to the effect, we do hereby agree that such a decree shall be binding on us all and on the whole nation.

Further, we declare that, should His Majesty, in his vast wisdom, be inclined to issue a new order, not contrary to the Quran, which may be conducive to the public benefit, obedience to it shall be binding on the whole nation, and opposition to it shall involve damnation in the world to come and loss of religion and property in this life.

This document has been written with honest intentions, for the glory of God and the propagation of Islam, and is signed by us the principal learned men of Religion and the pious devotees of the Faith in the month of Rajab 987 Hijri (1579 A. D.).

The draft of the above document was in the handwriting of Sheikh Mobarak. The others signed it against their will ; but the Sheikh added at the bottom the following passage :—

واین امر یست که من بجان ودل خوا هان اواز سالها باز منتظرآن بودم

This is a matter which I had desired from all my heart and which for several years I had been anxiously looking forward to.

From the moment His Majesty obtained this legal instrument, the superiority of intellect of the *Imam*, or King, became the sole law. His Majesty, having heard that the *Imams* of the age and the *Khalifs* of Islam had themselves read the *Khutbas* (public litany) at Friday prayers, and that their example had, in later times, been followed by Amir Tymur the Sahib Kiran, and Mirza Ulegh Beg of Gorgon, resolved to do the same, with the object, according to Abul Fazl, of 'taking upon his own shoulders a pious duty for the benefit of the Mohammadan community,' but, according to the malcontent Badaoni, 'of appearing in public as the *Mujtahid* of the age.'

Appears as the Imam of the age at the grand mosque.

Accordingly, on Friday, the 1st *Jamadiul awal,* 987, mounting the pulpit of the grand mosque at Fattehpur Sikri, he read the following Khutba, which, at his instance, had been composed by Sheikh Abul Fyz Fyzi :—

بنام آنکه مارا خسروي داد   دل دانا وبا زوي قوي داد
بعدل وداد مارا رهنمون کرد   بجز عدل از ضمیر ما برون کرد
بود وصفش زحد فهم برتر   تعالی شانه الله اکبر

The Lord to me the kingdom gave,
He made me prudent, strong and brave,
He guided me in faith and truth,
He filled my heart with right and truth ;
No wit of man can sum His state,
Alla ho Akbar ! God is great !

He cited passages from the Koran and offered thanks to God for his benevolence and mercies ; then, repeating the *Fatiha*, he came down from the pulpit and read his prayers with the congregation, standing behind Hafiz Mohammad Amin, the Imam of the mosque, who conducted the service.

Believes the so-called predictions as to his being the Lord of the period.

About this time, Haji Ibrahim, of Sirhind, produced before the Emperor an old worm-eaten manuscript in queer characters, said to be in the handwriting of Sheikh Sher-i-Arabi, in which it was predicted that the Sahib-i-Zaman (Lord of the period) would have many wives and have his beard shaved. The characteristics mentioned in the book were found to agree with the usages of Akbar. Other proofs were brought to show that in 990, a man would rise up who would remove all differences of opinion among the seventy-two sects of Islam. Khawaja Maulana of Shiraz produced an old pamphlet quoting the tradition that the promised appearance of Imam Mahdi would immediately take place.

Abul Fazl, in the Akbarnama,* has given an interesting account of a religious meeting in the *Jama Musjid* of Fattehpur Sikri, when he was himself introduced to the Emperor (1574 A. D.). He writes :—

Abul Fazl's introduction to Akbar.

" During these days the writer of these pages (Abul Fazl) gained the fresh honour of an interview with His Majesty. I had the good fortune of paying my respects to the Emperor at the capital of Agra in the beginning of the year.

Owing, however, partly to vanity and pride and partly because my father was unwilling to give me leave to depart, I refrained from a journey to the eastern countries. Matters continued in this fashion until I received a letter from my brothers, informing me that the King wanted to see me. Not having sufficient means, I was at a loss to understand how to go to the presence of the King empty handed. At last, I resolved on presenting a literary production, as the best offering suited for a man in my condition of life, and, with that object in view, wrote a commentary on the *Surah Fatiha* of Al Koran. As the Royal camp reached Ajmere, I received another letter from my elder brother repeating the desire of His Majesty to see me. My literary compilation being complete, I resolved to join the Royal camp ; and, as it reached Fattehpur Sikri, I repaired to that place, after obtaining my father's permission. When I reached that chief town (Misr-i-Jama), I found that there was no friend through whom I could be introduced to the Royal presence. Assumption of self-importance again prevented my asking the mediation of anybody to introduce me to the King, until my elder brother, older in wisdom and age, asked me to attend the religious meeting which was to be convened under the direction of His Majesty.

Accordingly, the following day, I attended the grand mosque, which is one of the grandest edifices built by His Imperial Majesty. Suddenly, His Majesty made his appearance. He saw me from a long distance. I made my obeisance. His Majesty made a sign to me to come. I instantly walked to the Royal presence and paid my homage. His Majesty addressed

* Akbarnama, page 52, vol. III.

me kind words and spoke of me in most flattering terms to the people assembled, and gave particulars of myself which were even unknown to me.

وحال مرا چنانچه من هم نميدا نستم بخا صان بزم اقدس و امي نمودند

'He began to relate my circumstances to the people present in the assembly in such a way that even I was not aware of them.'

The kindness and consideration paid me by His Majesty won my heart. From that moment royal favours increased, and from day to day I was raised in the estimation of my august master and sovereign."

At about this time, a section of the *ulema* charged the Emperor with apostacy. Abul Fazl, in the Akbarnama (Vol. III.), devotes a whole chapter to refuting the charge, and shows that Akbar never laid claim to become God, or the apostle of God, though he received His Light from the Supreme Being above and was directly guided in all his affairs by Him.

Infant's tomb.

At the back of the mosque is an enclosure, containing a small tomb of an infant. This, the legend goes, is the tomb of an infant son of Sheikh Salem, aged six months, who, having talked to his revered father in a marvellous fashion, sacrificed his own life for that of a son to the Emperor, whose children were fated to die in infancy unless some one gave a child of his own to die instead. Nine months after the generous infant died, prince Salem came into the world. In the *debris* about here will be found a door leading to a cave which was the original abode of the Saint before the spot attracted the attention of royalty. The place is also pointed out where he used to teach his pupils, as also the place where the holy man persuaded the royal couple to take up their abode, in the neighbourhood of his own hut, and where the prince who bore his name was born.

The Saint's cave.

Palaces of Abul Fazl and Fyzi.

North of the Dargah are the houses of Abul Fazl and his brother Fyzi, both almost united. The drawing-rooms and the *Zanana* of the Royal courtiers have been now utilized as English class rooms; the other buildings were used by the erudite brothers as audience chambers and public rooms.

Bir Bar's Palace.

Page 155.

North of Abul Fazl's house is the palace of Bir Bal,* one of Akbar's favourite companions, whose wit and wisdom delighted His Majesty. It is a two-storeyed building of great beauty, ornamented with a profusion of carvings of minute finish, still in an almost perfect state of preservation. The lower storey contains four rooms, each 15 feet square, with a ceiling of slabs, 15 feet long by one broad. The roofs rest upon projecting cornices, supported by high arches. The chambers in the upper storey are of the same size as the lower ones and are surrounded by massive domes. Mr. Keene, who is never profuse in his praise, writes of this building:—"Nothing can exceed the massiveness of the materials excepting the minuteness of the finish. It seems as if a Chinese ivory-worker had been employed upon a cyclopean monument." The whole structure is of stone, not a stick of timber has been used in any part. Its chief beauty lies in the fact that, although small in size, it is exceedingly delicate and handsome. Indeed, nothing could be done better with the same materials within the same space and dimensions. Victor Hugo writes of this house:—"Everywhere was magnificence at once refined and stupendous: if it was not the most diminutive of palaces, it was the most gigantic of jewel cases."

Bir Bal's Palace.

Bir Bal's palace was finished in the 27th year of Akbar's reign. When the building was completed, His Majesty, at Bir Bal's request, honoured it with a visit. Abul Fazl, in the Akbarnama, thus notices the event:—"In these days the house of Raja Bir Bal was illuminated with the lustre of the Emperor's feet. The Raja enjoyed the distinction of being a personal favourite of His Majesty, who ordered a spacious palace of sandstone to be constructed for him. When this edifice was completed, he solicited the honour of a royal visit, that his dignity might be exalted. On 7th of Bahman the Emperor honored the palace with his presence, and the Raja became the recipient of Royal favours."

Palace of the Hindu Empress.

South-east of the above is the palace wrongly attributed by the guides to Jodh Bai, who, as already noted, was the consort of Jahangir, and not his mother, and whose palace has been mentioned

* Keene erroneously calls it Bir Bal's daughter's house. According to the Akbarnama the Emperor made it for Bir Bal himself, and no mention is made in it or the 'Ain' of Bir Bal's daughter.

in the description of the Fort. From its being the central *corps de logis*, Keene conjectures that it was the palace occupied by *Żan-i-Kalan*, or Akbar's chief wife, Ruquina Sultana Begam, the daughter of Mirza Hindal, the Emperor's uncle. But, from the Hindu nature of the building, it is most probable that it was the dwelling of Akbar's Hindu consort, the daughter of Raja Bihari Mal, known as Mariam-uz-Zamani. There are on the walls the carved images of Hindu gods and goddesses—Mahadeva the great grandfather of gods, Lakshmi the goddess of fortune and prosperity, and elephant-headed Ganesh, who has power over civil matters. Some of the fragments found in this palace eem to have belonged to a Hindu temple. The quarters are the most extensive and spacious of the buildings which stand here, almost in a line from west to east, and were intended as special apartments for the Emperor's chosen consort, or the Emperor himself. Entering from a lofty and exquisitely carved gateway, one comes on a platform, or open gallery, 177 feet by 57 feet, paved with sandstone flags and surrounded on all sides by a colonnade with two-storeyed and three-storeyed rooms on the north and south, the roofs being of sloping slabs, covered with blue enamel. In another court close by, is an elegant

The reservoir. reservoir of water crossed by four raised passages which meet in the middle. This was, no doubt, a place of recreation for the Emperor and the ladies of the royal household.

The palace of the Hindu princess, with those of Istamboli Begum and the Sonehri Manzil already described, are the most superb of the whole series of buildings in this quarter. Fergusson thus describes them :—"The richest, the most beautiful, as well as the most characteristic of all his (Akbar's) buildings here are three small pavilions said to have been erected to please and accommodate his three favourite Sultanas. They are small, but it is impossible to conceive anything so picturesque in outline or any building carved and ornamented to such an extent without the smallest approach to being overdone or in bad taste."

The Royal Stables. Surrounding a quadrangular courtyard, north-west of the Hindu Princess's palace, are the stables for the accommodation of horses, elephants and camels. Like the other structures, they are made of red sandstone and are of massive construction. The

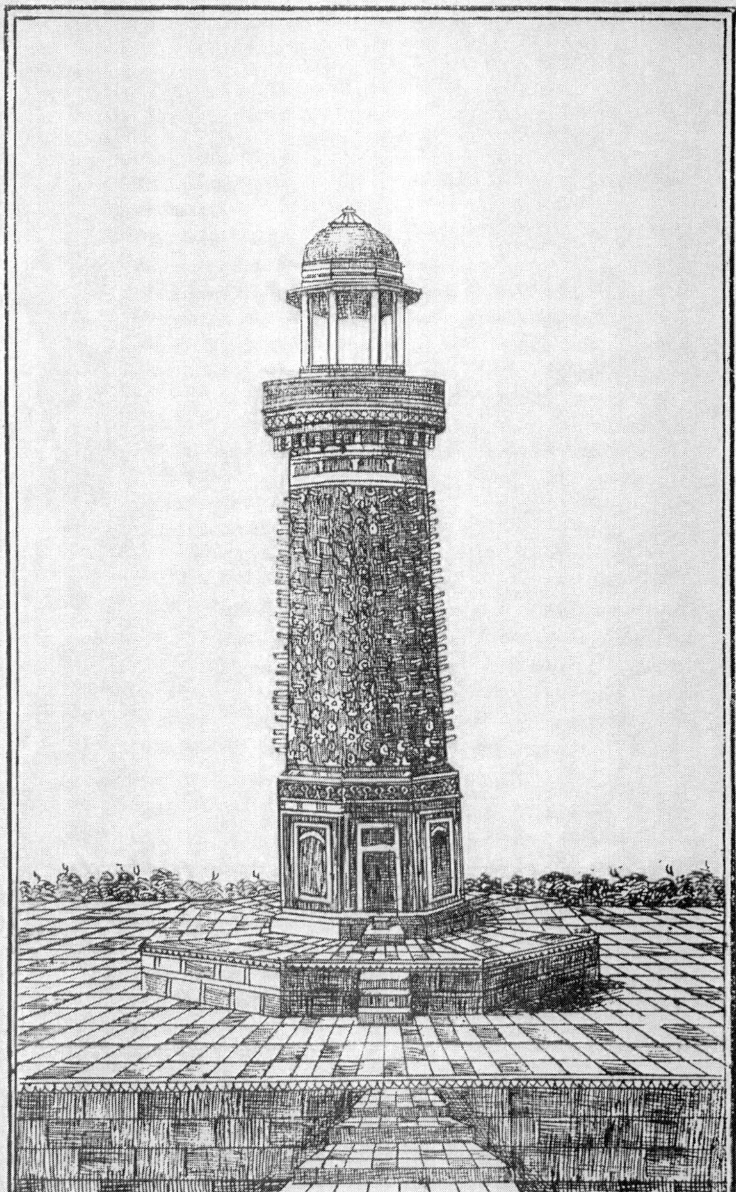

The Hiran Minara.

Page 157.

stone mangers and the huge stone rings to which the horses were fastened still remain on the spot, and are objects of attraction to the curious observer. A little further removed from the stabling is a stall of substantial masonry set apart exclusively for the Emperor's favourite elephant, which, in size and sagacity, was unrivalled among the rest.

The Elephant's Tower (called the *Hiran Minara*).

In this group of singular structures there is a minaret quite unique in shape and design. It is of circular form and 90 feet high, being studded (excepting the top, which is surrounded by a cupola) from the summit to the base with stone imitations of elephant's tusks of full size, which project from the sides of the massive column like brackets, giving it an odd and fantastic appearance. It is supposed to have been erected by Akbar over the grave of the favourite elephant alluded to above. It is also called the *Hiran Minara*, or Antelope Tower, from the circumstance that Akbar enjoyed sport from its summit, shooting the game which were brought from all parts of the country, in an enclosure here. His Majesty's love of sport has been fully noticed in the works of Abul Fazl and Nizamuddin Ahmad, his biographers. He was a skilful marksman, and his personal dexterity in hunting the lion and the bear has been the subject of praise. At Fattehpur Sikri, owing to press of State business, we see the Emperor, to use Mr. Keene's expression, 'in his dressing-gown and slippers'.

The popular name, *Hiran Minara*, is also justified from the fact that antelopes abound in its neighbourhood to the present day. Herds of them may be seen trotting on the fallow ground, or reclining in the ravines, or grazing in green meadows. They are, of course, the descendants of those which were the objects of Akbar's sport.

The Hathipol.

A little further down the hill is the famous Hathipol, or Elephant Gate. It is a massive and noble structure, flanked by two octagonal bastions. The arch is 20 feet high from the ground, and on either side of it, over a lofty pedestal, is the figure of a colossal elephant, life-size, with their trunks entwining each other, as in the act of fighting, and thrown over the entrance. The iconoclastic zeal of the fanatical Aurangzeb has destroyed the heads of the effigies, or otherwise mutilated the ornamentations of the gate, than which no more superb ornament for the gateway of a royal Eastern palace can be imagined.

The Sangin Burj. In the vicinity of the Elephant Gateway is a splendid bastion called the *Sangin Burj*, the remnant of fortifications commenced on a grand scale by Akbar, but discontinued subsequently, owing to the disapproval of the holy man, Salem Chishti. of the design to make Fattehpur a royal residence.

The *Caravan Serae*. Between the Hathi Pol and Sangin Burj is an extensive *Caravan Serae* where resorted merchants from distant parts of the Empire and from Afghanistan and the countries of Asia, with their goods for sale. Here is a closed gallery with a beautiful pierced network of stone, used by the ladies of the *harem* as a passage for communication with the different apartments of the palaces. Here were displayed for sale to the fair residents mercantile stores consisting of embroidered silk fabrics, muslins, shawls and other textures, and here are also pointed out jewellers' shops, where were exhibited piles of gold and silver ornaments and of the jewels which embellished the royal dresses and robes. These, however, are all buried in their own debris, and only vestiges of them can be seen here and there to show where they stood and with what object they were built.

Nothing is more depressing than the solitude of the deserted dwellings and palaces once full of vitality and the seat of a literary and luxurious court.

Water works. Under the higher parts of the rock to the westward, and below the gateway of the great mosque is an elaborate system of water works, by which water was raised by means of a system of Persian wheels, and brought and collected in a series of reservoirs, and then distributed by means of conduit pipes to different parts of the residences on the hills.

The Hauz. Amongst these is a wide oblong masonry *hauz*, or reservoir, from which cool water was drawn up through a trap door in the hot weather.

The height from the summit of the wall is about 100 feet, and men and boys are always found ready to amuse the visitor by a leap from the top for a small gratuity, which is much valued by them.

Badaoni makes mention of *Anup Taláo*, or Anup's Tank in Fattehpur Sikri, where the Emperor invited learned men and the lawyers of the realm to hold meetings on religious questions. One night he invited Qazi Yakub, Sheikh Abdul Fazl, Haji Ibrahim and a few others, when a lively discussion took place on the legality, or otherwise, of a *muta* marriage (a temporary agreement of matrimonial alliance). It was urged that, according to the traditions of Imam Malik and the Shias, the *muta* marriage was legal, but that, according to the doctrines of Imam Shafai and Hanfiah, it was illegal. Mulla Abdul Kadir Badaoni gave it as his opinion that, should a Quazi of the Malki sect decide that *muta* is legal, it is legal, according to the common belief, even for Shias and Hanfis. His Majesty was much pleased with this opinion.

Meetings here held.

In the midst of a series of arcaded buildings, not far from the Dargah of Salem Chisti, is a *Baoli*, a large pond, constructed of masonry. The water of the pool is now stagnant, and the cloisters or galleries all round open towards it. A long flight of steps leads to the cistern, and the place is so constructed as to secure perfect privacy on the door leading to the steps being properly closed. This was the bathing place for the ladies of the royal household.

The *Baoli*.

North of the hills there was, in the time of the Moghul Emperors, a large lake closed by a huge embankment on one side, and a range of hills on the other. This formed a large sheet of water, six miles in length, by two in breadth, which, in Akbar's time, supplied water to the inhabitants of the place and irrigated the neighbouring fields and gardens.

The ancient *Jhil* or lake.

Abul Fazl informs us, in the Akbarnama (Vol. III.), that on the banks of this lake the princes and grandees of the Empire had their palaces and summer houses, which served as retreats during the hot weather, where various sorts of public amusements were held. The Emperor joined in these festive entertainments, and the Amirs played chess and *Ganjifa*, a game of cards. In the 27th year of the reign (1582 A.D.) the embankment broke up, the water of the lake overflowed, the houses on the bank were swept away and great damage to property was done, though no lives were lost. The Emperor had a narrow escape, and offerings were made as a thanksgiving to the Almighty for

Abul Fazl's description.

the safety of the King. The nobility followed the example of His Majesty in this respect. The water was drained off during the administration of the Hon'ble James Thomason, Lieutenant-Governor, N. W. Provinces. The soil has turned out most productive, and the cultivation of cereals is carried on very successfully on it. Chili is very extensively sown in the neighbourhood of Fattehpur, the soil being particularly favourable for its growth.

Traffic in stone. The quarries of Fattehpur supply stone pillars, columns and slabs for roofs of edifices in Agra and elsewhere in the North-Western Provinces, while an extensive trade is carried on in *chakkis*, or handmills for grinding grain, which are articles of household use and for which the demand is universal.

Manufacture in Akbar's time. During the time of Akbar there was an Imperial workshop in Fattehpur on the same scale as in Agra and Lahore, and according to the *Ain*, carpets of wonderful varieties and charming textures were manufactured here. All kinds of carpet-weavers settled here and they produced masterpieces. In this workshop skilful masters and workmen were employed to teach people an improved system of manufacture, and not only were hair-weaving and silk-spinning brought to perfection, but a taste for fine materials became general.

Speaking of the trade in red sandstone, Abul Fazl writes in chapter 86 of the *Ain*: "It is obtainable in the hills of Fattehpur Sikri, His Majesty's residence, and may be broken from the rocks of any length or breadth. Clever workmen chisel it more skilfully than any turner could do with wood; and their works vie with the picture book of Mani (the great painter of the Sassanides)."

Game. Not far from the embankment of the dry lake previously mentioned, and on the bank and in the neighbourhood of the *Utangem Naddi*, or rivulet, wild hogs in large numbers are found. The *Naddi* produces large fish of fine flavour which are brought into the streets of Agra for sale. Pea fowls, aquatic birds and blue pigeons are also plentiful. They are entrapped by a race of degenerated Indian gipsies called *Kanjars*, who subsist on the flesh of the fox, jackal and beasts of prey, and eat lizards and other reptiles.

In 1583 His Majesty built alms-houses outside the city, that for the Mahomedans being called Khorpura and that for the Hindus Dharmpura. The places were put in charge of Abul Fazl's men. A third was also built, to which was given the name Jogipura. A large number of *jogis* flocked to this institution from different parts of India. His Majesty gave them private interviews at night, 'enquiring into abstruse truths; their articles of faith; their occupations; the influence of meditation; their several practices and usages; the power of being absent from the body; or into alchemy and physiognomy, and the power of omnipresence of the soul.' **Kherpura.** **Dharmpura.** **Jogipura.**

His Majesty learned alchemy and exhibited a quantity of gold made by himself. Being informed of the longevity of the Lamas of Thibet, Mongolian devotees and other recluses and hermits, who, by acts of abstinence and retaining the breath, lived to two hundred years or more, he, in imitation of these religious men, limited the time spent by him in the Harem, curtailed his food and drink, and, as a religious penance, abstained from meat. The killing of animals on certain days was forbidden, and an order was passed to worship the sun four times a day, in the morning and evening and at noon and midnight. **Retention of breath.** **Worship of the sun.**

His Majesty repeated daily the one thousand and one Sanscrit names of the sun, devoutly turning his face towards the luminary, and applied the Hindu mark to his forehead. He gave his religious system the name *Touhid-i-Ilahi*, or 'Divine monotheism,' and made chelas, or disciples, from among both Hindus and Mahomedans. He prayed to the sun every morning, and, after he had repeated its 1001 names, stepped out into the balcony and there showed himself to thousands of people assembled opposite the window, who prostrated themselves before him. They professed to have vowed that, until they had seen His Majesty's blessed countenance, they would not rinse their mouths, nor eat and drink.* **Divine monotheism.**

The glory of Fattehpur Sikri as a royal residence, and as the seat of the Empire of India, commenced with Akbar, its founder, and terminated with him. It was shortlived, being built and **The glory of Fattehpur shortlived.**

* On the religious innovations of Akbar, see Chapter III.

reduced to ruins in fifty years. Akbar was the first to occupy it and the last to build there, not a single building having been erected after him. Indeed, when Finch visited it, in the early part of the reign of Jahangir, the son and successor of Akbar, he found it almost deserted. He thus describes the place:—"Ruin all; lying like a waste desert and very dangerous to pass through in the night." When Fattehpur had reached the height of its magnificence, the saint Salem Chishti found it most inconvenient to live there. He had been attracted to the spot by its loneliness, and now, having attracted the attention of royalty, it had become one of the most populous cities of India. The bustle of the busy city, the gaieties and pageants of the court, interfered with the saint's devotions. At last the Emperor, unaware of the feelings of his spiritual guide, commenced to surround the hills with a chain of massive fortifications. The holy man could then no longer restrain himself. He told his royal disciple that he had travelled twenty times on pilgrimages to Mecca, but his peace had never been so much disturbed; accordingly he expressed his wish that either the Emperor or he should depart. "If it be your Majesty's will," replied the Emperor, "that one should go, let it be your slave, I pray." Akbar removed to Agra, which city he rebuilt. The court and the townspeople were transplanted to the latter place, at that time a desolated spot; and Fattehpur Sikri, with its stupendous and picturesque palaces, its elegant mosques, described as the goodliest in the east, its unrivalled mausoleum, its sumptuous residences and its deserted streets, remains to this day a monument of the splendour and wealth of its founder and a testimony to the despotic power which a reputation for sanctity has in all ages conferred! In the eloquent words of the practical Fergusson: "Taking it altogether, this palace of Fattehpur Sikri is a romance in stone such as few, very few, are to be found anywhere; and it is a reflex of the mind of the great man who built it more distinct than can easily be obtained from any other source."

It is deserted.

SHEIKH SALEM CHISHTI.

The circumstances under which Sheikh Salem *Chishti* settled in Fattehpur Sikri, and the incidents which caused that place, from being once an insignificant hamlet, to become one of the most flourishing cities of India and the capital of the Empire, have been already mentioned. A brief account of the family of the saint who held so high a place for sanctity in India during one of the best periods of its history will, no doubt, be read with interest. Sheikh Salem, son of Sheikh Bahauddin, and called *Chishti* after the name of the village in Persia whence his father came, was a lineal descendant of Sheikh Farid-ud-din, surnamed Shakargunj, son of Jamal-ud-din Salman. According to the *Akbarnama* of Abul Fazl, Sheikh Farid traced his descent from Farukh Shah, King of Cabul. In the time of the great Tartar conqueror, Chengez Khan, one of his ancestors, Quazi Shoeb, came to the District of Lahore and settled in the town of Kasur. He was much respected by Sultan Balham and subsequently went to Multan. Sheikh Farid-ud din was born in Khotowal, in Multan. Having heard of the religious sanctity of Khawja Kutb-ud-din usi, the *Khalifa*, or successor, of Khwaja Moin-ud-din, he went to Delhi and became his disciple. On his death the Sheikhs of the time unanimously robed him with the asintly cloak of the deceased saint, and Farid-ud-din settled in Pak Pattan, then known as Ajuddhn, where he died, on 5th Mohurram 668 H (1269 A. D.)

According to the *Tabakati Akbari*, Sheikh Salem Sikriwál was one of the most revered Sheikhs of India and surpassed all the devotees of his time in sanctity and austerity. He possessed the power of miracles (so the author says) and had performed pilgrimage to Mecca twenty four times in his life. He then travelled to Hijaz. Once he remained in Mecca for fifteen years. "His Majesty the shadow of God (Akbar) made Fattehpur his capital for his sake." He died in 979 H. (1571 A. D.).

Abul Fazl, in the *Akbarnama* mentions Sheikh Ahmad, the second *(mianí)* son of Sheikh Salem. 'He was possessed of high virtues, never spoke ill of any body and was never seen in anger. He was of reserved habits and dignified demeanour.' He was created an *Amir* (noble of the Empire) and was honoured with the distinction of becoming the Atka * *to* the heir-apparent. He caught cold in the campaign of Malwa, and, arriving at Fatehpur Sikri, had an attack of paralysis. As the Royal camp

* A Turki word meaning husband of wet nurse.

was about to move to Ajmere, he came to pay his last respects to his Majesty, and immediately on his return to his house, breathed his last.

The event occurred in the 22nd year of Akbar's reign (985 A. H. or 1577 A. D.). He served in the court with Sheikh Ibrahim.

Sheikh Ibrahim was son of Sheikh Musa, elder brother of Sheikh Salem, who lived a retired life in Sikri. Ibrahim lived chiefly at court, in the service of the Princes, and in the 23rd year of the reign was appointed Governor of Fattehpur Sikri. In the 28th year, he served with distinction under Khan-i-Azim Mirza Aziz Kokah, in Behar and Bengal, and when, in the 30th year, Akbar went to Cabul, he was made Governor of Agra, which post he held until his death, in 999 (1590 A. D). He was also son-in-law of Sheikh Salem.

Sheikh Bayazid (Moazzam Khan) was grand-son of Sheikh Salem. Bayazid's mother nursed Prince Salem (Jahangir) on the day of his birth. In Akbar's time he rose to the command of 2,000, but after Jahangir's accession, he received the rank of 3,000, with the title of Moazzam Khan. Soon after, he was made Governor of Delhi, and in the 3rd year of Jahangir's reign he rose to the command of 4,000 and 200 horse. He died at Fattehpur where he was buried.

Islam Khan Sheikh (Alauddin) another grand-son of Sheikh Salem, married the sister of Abul Fazl. He was Governor of Bengal, where he died in 1022 (1613 A. D.).

Mukarram Khan, son of Sheikh Bayazid, married the daughter of Islam Khan, whom he served in Bengal. He was made Governor of Orissa, and in the 21st year of Jahangir's reign was made Governor of Bengal, *vice* Hasan Ali Turkoman.

Other men of note in Fattehpur Sikri.

It will be interesting to know what men renowned in the political history of Akbar's time lie buried in the once metropolitan city of Fattehpur.

Sultan Khwaja.

1. Sultan Khwaja (Azam Khan), son of Khwaja Khawind Dost, is described in the Tabakat as a saintly philosopher. He enjoyed in a high degree the confidence and friendship of the

Emperor Akbar. In 984 (1576 A. D.) he was created Mir Hajj, or chief of the party proceeding on Hajj, and, as such, had charge of a numerous body of courtiers who went to Mecca on a pilgrimage in that year. Never had such an influential body of the Court nobles before started for Arabia. He was also put in charge of six lakhs of Rupees and 12,000 suits of clothes for distribution to the people of Mecca.

On his return, in the 23rd year, or 1577, he was made a Commander of one thousand and was created Sadr of the Empire, which office he held till his death, in 992 (1583 A. D.). He was buried outside the Fort of Fattehpur, to the north. He became a member of the Divine Faith after his return from Mecca.

According to Baddoni, Sultan Khwaja did not meet with a good reception at Mecca at the hands of the Sheriff, or hereditary Custodian, of the place, and returned to India much discontented. No sooner had he returned to this country than, freeing himself from the restrictions of Islam, he shaved his beard and joined the Divine Faith of Akbar, under the guidance of the Reverend Master, Abul Fazl. In social meetings he was ever in the front, and he took a warm part in religious discourses. Akbar, pleased with his new disciple, conferred on him the Jagir of Ghazipur and Hajipur.

When the last moments of Sultan Khwaja arrived, he said to his Majesty: "I hope I shall not be buried like a mad man." He was buried in a grave with a peculiar lamp: a grate was laid over the grave in such a posture that the light of the rising sun, the great luminary which cleanses from all sins, might shine on the face of the corpse.

Qutbuddin Khan.

2. Sheikh Khubi, of Fattehpur, better known by his title of Qutbuddin Khan, was daughter's son of Sheikh Salem. He was son of a Sheikh Zada of Badaon and was foster brother of Jahangir, who used to say that Khubi's mother was dearer to him than his own. Jahangir, when in Allahabad in rebellion against Akbar, conferred on Khubi the title of Kutbuddin Khan and made him governor of Behar. On ascending the throne, he raised him to the viceroyalty of Bengal, *vice* Man Singh. His death is connected with one of the most romantic

incidents known to Eastern history. Jahangir, when a prince, became enamoured of Mehr-ul-nissa, the beautiful daughter of Mirza Ghias Beg Tehrani, Lord High Treasurer of Akbar. She had been previously affianced to Ali Kuli Beg Istalju (Sher Afghan Khan), a Turkoman nobleman who was *Safarchi* or table attendant of Shah Ismail II, King of Persia. After the King's death, Ali Kuli came to India, and at Multan met Mirza Abdul Rahim, Khan-i-Khanan, son of Behram Khan, the general and tutor of Akbar. During the war at Thatta, he rendered distinguished service under the Khan-i-Khanan, and, on his recommendation, was created a noble of the Empire. The treasurer's wife had access to the Queen Mariam Zamani, Akbar's wife, and at her palace the eyes of Salim and Mehrulnissa met. The passion was mutual. Akbar, having heard of the amour, honourably resolved that his son's passion should not interfere with the completion of the union. She was married to her betrothed and sent with him to Burdwan, his Jagir.

The young nobleman accompanied the prince on his expedition against the Rana of Mewar and for his gallantry in the field received from him the title of Sher Afgan, or the lion killer. Jahangir, on ascending the throne, sent Ali Kuli to his Jagir. His passion for Nur Jahan revived, and he charged his foster-brother, Kutbuddin Khan, to rid him of his hated rival. Kutb ordered Sher Afgan to Court, but the latter refused to go. Kutb then sent Ghiasa, his sister's son, to Burdwan, to persuade Sher Afgan that no harm would be done to him. He himself followed Ghiasa to Burdwan. On his approach, Sher, expecting no treachery, went to receive him, accompanied by two men. Kutb, seeing him, lifted up his horse whip as a signal to his followers to cut down Sher. "What is all this?" exclaimed Sher. Kutb, advancing towards Sher, upbraided him for his disobedience. The royalists now attacked Sher, who killed six men with his own hand. Rushing then with his sword against Kutb, he gave him a deep wound in the abdomen. Kutb, who was a corpulent man, seizing his protruding bowels with his hands, called on his men to despatch the scoundrel. Ambah Khan, a Kashmerian noble of royal blood, thereupon advancing against Sher, inflicted a sword cut over the head, but Sher cut him through with his sword at the same time. Seeing that he must fall a victim to the number of his assailants, he challenged them to single combat; but this was an invitation which they were ill-prepared to accede to.

Sher dismounted from his horse, and turning his face towards Mecca and taking up earth, threw it on his head by way of ablution, for want of water, and stood his ground firmly. His body was pierced by bullets discharged by the crowds of assailants who surrounded him, and he fell like a lion, as his name was. Not a single man of his numerous assailants dared to approach the corpse of the fallen hero, such was the terror inspired by his bravery, until they had actually seen him in his last agonies. Kutbuddin was still on horseback when he heard that Sher had been killed. He sent Ghiasa to bring the effects and family of Sher from Burdwan. He was then removed in a palanquin, but died on the way. His corpse was taken to Fattehpur Sikri, where it was buried.

A handsome domed mausoleum still stands in the neighbourhood of Burdwan, and marks the last resting place of the hero, Sher Afgan.

3. Quadri of Shiraz. He was an excellent poet and came **Quadri.** from Mecca to India, where he was well received by Akbar. He subsequently fell into disgrace and died at Fattehpur Sikri.

SIKANDRA.

At some little distance from the right bank of the Jamna is the old military road used by the Mughals in travelling north-west to Lahore and Kashmir, now converted into an excellent highway by British enterprise. It has been aptly called the 'Appian way' of Agra, being traversed by cultivated fields, strewn for miles with the remains of old monuments which recall to mind ancient ages. There is the old Delhi gate of the imperial walls, a massive structure of red sandstone, still in a good state of preservation, and some of the ancient mile-stones. On one side is the District Jail and on the other the Lunatic Asylum, both on sites of ancient buildings of which nobody knows anything now. Amidst these mutilated remains of ancient might and greatness is the village Sikandra,* in the vicinity of which, in the garden of Bahisht Abad, stands the singular and solid tomb of Akbar, a monument of surpassing beauty. It was designed and commenced by the great Emperor himself and is the most characteristic of Akbar's buildings. Though apparently after a Hindu, or more correctly Buddhist, model, it is quite singular in shape, and, according to the best judges, unlike any other monument erected to the memory of man in the oriental world. A recent German writer has justly observed, 'as Akbar was unique amongst his contemporaries, so was his place of burial amongst other Indian tombs—indeed one may say, with confidence, amongst the sepulchres of all Asia.' Like the countless memorials of his beneficent rule, like the numberless good works of his long and happy reign, the stone symbol of his creative genius which enshrines his mortal remains will ever stand the admiration of the whole world. Lofty as was Akbar in soul, great as was his might and magnificence, he has left a monument to himself equally great, rich in variety of detail, copious in its amazing beauties; charming in the juxtaposition of its various parts. It is due to the fertile imagination and broad mind possessed by this great-souled man that, centuries after his death, travellers from the remotest regions of earth are moved to enthusiasm by the mere sight of his mausoleum, the monument of his own genius. What power of conquering men's minds must not this great dead have possessed in life?

The design of the mausoleum.

The tomb stands in the midst of an extensive square garden (forming an area of about a mile or more in circuit), girt by a battlemented wall, each side of which has in its centre a lofty gateway of deep-toned red sandstone. The red colour of these structures is delightfully broken by delicate minarets of white marble at the angles, as well as by decorations of glazed blue tiles and other inlay work of exquisite beauty. The stately height and magnificence of the gates is such that each in itself might be mistaken for a palace.

* According to common accounts, it is named after Sikandar Lodi, the second Emperor of the Lodi dynasty.

43

The Gateway, Sakandra.

Page 169.

Long before the mausoleum is reached, its tall, slender minarets and white domes greet the traveller's eye from afar. Reaching it, you pass the western or principal portal, upwards of seventy feet high, with mutilated turrets and double arches, one facing the entrance and the other one of the four grand causeways of hewn stone, that converge to the central platform on which the monument stands. The chief portal.

Above the grand portal is the *Nakkàr Khana*, or music gallery, a spacious arcaded chamber, with a balcony, from which, at one watch after sunrise and at dawn, kettle-drums were beaten in honour of the dead, together with their accompaniments, the *Karna*,* *Nafiri*,† *Sarná*‡ and other instruments. The room whence once issued royal music is now occupied by a British sergeant. There are also quarters for the custodians of the tomb, and the *nullas*, who perpetually repeated the *Korán* at the grave. The interior spaces of the four wide sections are laid out as gardens and filled with fruit trees of all sorts (among which the tamarind and some other trees are almost as old as the monument itself); but the gardens are entirely neglected now, and the immense tanks and elegant fountain basins, in the centre of the causeways, and the water-courses which transect the beds of fragrant flowers and odorous forest creepers that were once the charms of this 'abode of paradise,' are dry. The platform of white marble which terminates these magnificent approaches forms a base of above 400 feet in length and breadth, and on it rises the curious structure of red sandstone in fine terraces in a pyramidal form. The lower storey, 30 feet in height, measures 320 feet on each side, exclusive of angle towers, and is composed entirely of wide and open arches, ten on each side surrounded by rows of cupolas, the three to the east, west and north being large and lofty, and the fourth to the south, facing the sarcophagus, loftier still. A sloping passage leads from the main entrance to the mortuary hall, a vaulted chamber in the pavement, 38 feet square, and here, under a plain unpretending tombstone, almost sublime in its simplicity, repose the mortal remains of the great Emperor. The Nakkar Khana. The Mortuary Hall.

* A kind of Citrone.

† Clarionet.

‡ A kind of pipe.

The hall is covered with dark blue plaster and gold. In opposition to the prevailing Mahomedan custom, which requires the dead man's face to be turned in the direction of Mecca, the tomb of Akbar is so situated that his head is to the west. Consequently his face is to the east and the rising sun, thereby giving indication of the Emperor's Hindu proclivity. On the tomb are always lying wreaths of flowers, and Lord Northbrooke, the late Governor-General, has given proof of his sense of admiration for the great-souled dead by providing it with a gorgeous covering at his own expense. Well does the memory of Akbar deserve such recognition by all lovers of true merit in the departed great. The fervour of a noble German mind was excited as he laid his roses on the grave of this high-minded king; as the following passage from the pen of Prince Fredrick Augustine of Schleswig Holstein, Count von Noer, will show: "Then there came vividly to my mind some words of the amiable and open-minded Sleeman, 'considering all the circumstances of the time and place, Akbar has always appeared to me among sovereigns as Shakespear was among poets, and, feeling as a citizen of the world, I revered the marble slate that covers his bones, more perhaps than I should that one of any other sovereign with whose history I am acquainted.' I too could say that no other burial place had so moved me as this of Akbar."

The Emperor's relics.

By the side of the tomb lay the books, raiments and armour of the Emperor, ready to his hand if he were to rise; but these were, during the last century, carried away by the Játs of Bharatpur, and it is conjectured that some of these relics might still be traced somewhere in that State if a search for them were made.

The various terraces rising one above the other.

Above the first terrace rises another, 14 feet 9 inches high, and measuring 186 feet on each side. The third is 15 feet 2 inches, and the fourth 14 feet 6 inches high, all composed of turrets, columns, arches and pillars of red stone, each terrace gradually diminishing in size, but in open arched galleries, till they terminate on the summit in an open enclosure 157 feet on each side, which is just half the size of the lowest terrace. The whole mausoleum thus formed rises to the height of 100 feet.

The Mausoleum of Akbar.

45

The Tomb of Akbar.

Page 171

A long flight of stone steps, close to the colossal arch to the south of the mausoleum, leads to the upper or second terrace, encircled like the rest by beautiful colonnades resting on light arches, very capacious and airy and affording perambulation all round. The storeys higher up are approaced by similar stairs, though of smaller dimensions. The task of ascending these long flights of steps is tiresome; but the trouble is more than recompensed by the pleasure derived at each stage from the spacious and delightful chambers visited, the free current of air obtained, and the sight of verdant fields and ruins of ancient buildings scattered around this abode of paradise, as its name has it.

The highest storey.

The highest storey, which is open to the sky, is surrounded by an outer wall, of marble filigree or trellis work, of the most beautiful patterns, elaborately carved out of solid slates of the same material, and representing a variety of geometrical designs of the most chaste and intricate workmanship. The panels and perforated marble work are of marvellous richness and variety, and, from the occasional apertures left in them for the purpose, an extensive view is obtained of the country, with the serpentine course of the Jamna to the north-east and 'the white domes of the Taj resting on the eastern horizon like the rising moon'. Inside, the storey is surrounded by a colonnade of the purest marble. Mr. Taylor is quite enthusiastic in describing the beautiful scene here. He observes:—" I thought the Alcazar of Seville and the Alhambra of Grenada had already presented me with the purest type of saracenic, but I was mistaken. What I had seen of the splendour of the Moghals, and what I then saw, overpowered me like a magnificent dream."

The second tomb in the uppermost storey.

On a raised platform in the centre of the white marble enclosure above described, is the second tombstone, exactly in the same position as the one in the lowest terrace, which represents the true tomb. The platform is enclosed by fretted marble screens of great beauty. The cenotaph is cut out of one solid block of the purest white marble and is exquisitely carved with arabesque tracery of such delicate and lovely design as to represent live blossoms and flowers scattered over a snowy sheet.

At the head of the tombstone are inscribed in bold relief in the Persian characters the words:—

الله اکبر

"God is Great."*

and these two simple words are enough to tell who lies below.

At the foot of the tombstone appear the words

جل جلا له

"Magnificent is His Glory."

On either sides of the sarcophagus are inscribed the ninety-nine attributes of the Deity, in raised Arabic characters of elaborate scroll-work. At the four angles are turrets of white marble, the domes of which are covered with gilded and enamelled Chinese tiles. The block at its base is surrounded by a Mosaic pavement of white and black marble, while at its head is a sort of half pillar, with a circular cavity of a few inches in diameter at the top, where formerly was kept a golden censer.

The Minarets.

The two minarets on either side of the main entrance to the garden of Bahishtabad had their tops blown away by the Játs when they sacked Agra in 1764, and a mark is thus left on these elegant structures of their wantonness. The minarets were formerly covered with domes and open pavilions which have long since been destroyed. Fergusson thinks the highest storey was never finished, and, from the traces of foundations on this terrace, conjectures that it was intended to have a splendid ceiling and a dome of considerable size over the present marble enclosure. However that may be, there is nothing to detract

* The words serve the double purpose of praising God as great and pointing to the person (Akbar, meaning great) enshrined in the mausoleum. In an other sense, by omitting the adjunct, they mean that "God is Akbar," namely "Akbar is God" which was the essence of the new Divine faith created by Akbar. This is, however, susceptible of an explanation that, according to the *Sufi* doctrines followed by Akbar, God's light or spirit is in every object, animate or inanimate, and thus Akbar's followers argued he was the spirit of God, or God himself, for, as king, he was shadow of God and received light from on high. The ambiguity of the expression, nevertheless, is quite obvious, though an attempt has been ingeniously made to explain it by the words inscribed at the foot, which praise the magnificence of His glory, which could only be the attribute of God. The Emperor caused the same words (Allah-o-Akbar), الله اکبر to be engraved on his seal and had them inserted on the heading of all public correspondence. At one time he ordered them to be substituted for the ordinary salutation *Salam-alekum* (peace be with you) to which answer was given *Jalli Jalalo hu* جل جلا له (magnificent is His Glory).

from the intrinsic value of the reality as it now exists. Peculiar in style of architecture, unique in plan and execution, it is a perfect work of art. As remarked by the German Prince already alluded to, 'it is only in the closest neighbourhood to the building that one receives a just impression of it as a whole, with its magnificent height and with its amazing wealth and gracious variety of detail. Such is the enhancement of this reality that one seems face to face with some fairy castle of ancient legend.' The noble Prince thus concludes his eloquent notice of this monument: "To me it was all like a dream, but on my return to Agra, I formed the resolution to hold in remembrance Akbar and the age of Akbar."

The building completed by Jahangir.

Although the mausoleum was designed by Akbar himself, who had great part of it constructed in his own life-time, there is no doubt that it reached completion in the time of his son and successor, Jahangir, who modified the buildings. That emperor has given the following notice of the mausoleum in the *Tuzuk*, his autobiography, in connection with the events of the 3rd year of the reign:

Jahangir's account of the building.

"On Monday, the 17th of *Jamadi-ul-sani*, I started on foot (from Agra) to pay my homage and respects to the illuminated resting-place of my father, the dweller of the 9th heaven (*Arsh-ashyani*).* Had it been possible for me, I should have traversed this distance walking by my eye-lids and by my head. My revered father, to fulfil a vow which he had made for my birth, travelled on foot from Fattehpur to Ajmir, a distance of 120 kos, to pay his respects to the mausoleum of His Holiness Khawaja Moin-ud-din Sanjri Chishti. Were I to traverse the distance on my head and on my eyes, what act wonderous should I have performed? Having acquired the honour of a visit to the illuminated tomb, I examined carefully the buildings which had been constructed on it. It struck me that these were not such as I should have wished, for my desire was that the edifice should be such that travellers from the remotest corners of the world should confess that the equal of it they had never seen anywhere on the earth's surface. While the building was in progress, the unfortunate Khusrow rebelled, and I was under the necessity of

* This was the title given to Akbar after death.

proceeding to Lahore. The architects, according to their own understanding, progressed with the work in a fashion which seemed to them best. They made certain innovations, until the whole of the money sanctioned for the building was spent in a space of three or four years. By my orders other artizans, well-versed in the art of architecture, in consultation with skilful engineers, rebuilt certain parts, according to models that were approved of. By degrees a magnificent building was constructed. Around the illuminated mausoleum extensive gardens were laid out, and a lofty and stupendous gateway, comprising minarets of white marble, was constructed.

Cost of building. It was reported to me that, in all, fifteen lacs of Rupees equal to fifty thousand Tomans of Iran, and forty-five lacs of Khani, the current coin of Turan, had been spent on the building."

Account of Thomas Herbert. Thomas Herbert, who visited Agra during the reign of Jahangir, has given the following notice of the Sikandra Mausoleum in his *Travels*.

"At Sikandra, five miles from Agra as we go to Lahore, is the mausoleum or burial-place of the great Mughal, the foundation of which was begun by Akbar, the superstructure continued by Jahangir, his son, and yet scarce finished, albeit they have already consumed fourteen millions of rupees in that wonder of India. * * * Of this noble fabric I may say

such a monument

The sun through all the world sees none more great." *

The following is the inscription on the grand southern portal leading to the mausoleum :—

بسم الله الرحمن الرحيم

مرحبا خورم فضاي خوشتر از باغ بهشت

مرحبا عالي بناے برتر از عرش برين

جنے اورا هزاران روضۂ رضوان غلام

روضۂ اورا هزاران جنت الماوے زمين

کلک معمار قضا بنوشت بر درگاه او

هذه جنات عدن فادخلوها خالدين

كتبه عبد الحق شيرازي في ۱۰۲۲

---

* Herbert's Travels in India, Africa, &c., page 64, edition of 1677, London.

In the name of God the merciful and compassionate.

Hail happy grounds, more pleasant than the garden of paradise !
Hail lofty edifices which rise above the highest heaven !
A paradise where slaves like Razwan abound in thousands,
A garden with numberless heavens for its pleasure ground.
The pen of the architect of destiny has on the top of its threshold inscribed :
'This is the garden of Eden, enter thou into it like those who dwell in paradise.'

Written by Abdul Haq of Shiraz in 1022 A.H. (1613 A.D.)*

The following verses are inscribed on the arches of the gateway in the interior :—

بسم الله الرحمن الرحيم

بفرمان شاهنشه ذوالجلال — که با شد شهنشا هیش بے زوال
شد آراسته آنچنان روزگار — که حیران شد اندیشه هوشیار
گیتے ز فیض ازل باد شاه — بود سایه نور ذات اله
چو از هر آن سایه گردد نهان — فتد سایه دیگر اندر جهان
بدنیا بود تا سر انجام کار — بنزد خرد گردش روزگار
زمانه دگرگون شود هر نفس — نگردد بیک گونه با هیچکس
فلک رتبه شاه اکبر عرش گاه — که از هیبتش کوه گشتی چو کاه
نشستی چو بر تخت شاهنشي — گرفتے جهان فر ظل اللهي—
فروزنده افسر و تخت بود — کریم و رحیم و جوان بخت بود
دل روشن وجان اگاه داشت — جهان خورد و داد و گرفت و گذاشت
بباغ جهان تخم نیکي بکشت — بر آن گرفت و ریاض بهشت
روانش چو انوار خورشید وماه — فروزنده باد از نور اله

In the name of God the merciful and compassionate.

By the command of God the glorious King,
Whose sway over the universe is everlasting,
The world has been provided in such profusion
That, in an attempt to comprehend it, the wisdom of the wise is baffled.

---

* As appears from the date inscribed on the building, the gateway was built by Jahangir in 1613 A. D., or three years after his marriage with Nur Jahan, when that Emperor was procecuting war in Mewar.

In the world, through eternal grace, a King
Is the shadow of the splendour of God.
When that shadow is concealed from earth,
Another is sent over the world in its place.
In this way worldly affairs have been arranged,
And the wheel of time rolls on, as the wise know.
Time changes with every breath we pass.
With none it remains in one condition.
King Akbar, dignified as the firmament, exalted as the highest
heaven,
Through whose awe a mountain would be reduced to a grass blade.
When he took seat on the Imperial throne
The world felt dignified by God's grace.
The embellisher of diadem and state,
Generous, merciful and of fortunate fate,
Possessed of pious soul and enlightened heart,
He ruled over the world, won it, gave it, and left it at last.
In the world's garden, he sowed the seed of virtue,
Partook of its fruit and then departed to paradise.
May his soul, like the rays of the sun and moon,
Ever receive brilliancy from God's light.

بسم الله الرحمن الرحيم

شاه اکبر ز روے دانائي گر بظاهر زين هر فاني رفت
دولتش بيزوال بود ازان دل بدنياے با زوال نه بست
مرغ روحش چو بود طاير عرش رفت و بر آشيان خويش نشست
دوام ملک بقاے قديم کس را نيست
خدا گير است بقاے قديم و ملک دوام

In the name of God the merciful and compassionate.
Although King Akbar, out of motives of wisdom,
Has to all appearance left this earthly kingdom,
Imperishable as his state was,
He did not fix his mind on this perishable world.
His soul being a bird of the highest heaven,
It flew and took its seat in its own nest.
State durable and life imperishable to man was never known.
Eternity of existence and monarchy everlasting is due to God alone.

The following quatrain and date of the Emperor's death are inscribed over the arch of the gateway :—

طاقيکه از رواق نهم چرخ بر تر است
روشن ز ماه اش رخ تا بنده اختر است

این طاق زیب نه فلک و هفت کشور است
از روضهٔ منور شاه اکبر است
تاریخ دوازدهم جمادی الآخر سنه هزار و چهارده هجری

This is a niche higher in loftiness than the highest heaven,
Its shade has given lustre to the shining stars.
To the nine heavens and seven climes this niche has given their grace,
For it belongs to the King Akbar's illuminated resting place.

12th Jumadi-ul-Akhir.
1014 A.H. (1605 A.D.)

The following poems are inscribed on the arches of uppermost storey around the sarcophagus of the tomb. There are 36 arched doors, nine on each side, one couplet being inscribed on each arch :—

بنام شهنشاه عالی قدم
که ذاتش مبرا بود از عدم

همه پادشاهان روی زمین
ازو صاحب تاج و تخت و نگین

کند از عدم آشکارا وجود
بود ذات او مظهر عدل وجود

ز لطفش که وهم طلبگار کام
بود درگهش قبله خاص و عام

نگارنده جوهر آب و خاک
طرازنده گوهر جان پاک

دو عالم ز فیض ازل آفرید
یکی کرد پنهان و دیگر پدید

ببخشید زانکه سرای سپنج
به شاهان با افسر و تاج و گنج

که از عدل ایشان شود روزگار
شگفته تر از باغ در نو بهار

ره داوری را چو گیرند پیش
شناسند بیگانه را همچو خویش

شهی کو چنین زیست در روزگار
بود سایهٔ ذات پروردگار

زنهصد فزون بود شصت و دو سال
که شاه اکبر آن سایه ذو الجلال

ببالای زرینه مسند نشست
بر تخت او گشت افلاک پست

جهان را بیاراست از عدل و داد
دل اهل عالم ازو گشت شاد

بر پایه تختش از هر گروه
شده جمع مردان صاحب شکوه

بمهر ار فگندی نظر سوی خاک
بگوهر شدی بهتر از جان پاک

گرفتی بیک حمله ملکی بزرم
بایمای ابرو بدادی ببزم

چو لطف خدا لطف او عام بود
بهر کار چشمش بانجام بود

بدرگاه او هر که بردی پناه
چو اندیشه رفتی زماهی بماه

چنان پر شد آوازه اش در جهان
که در دل نگنجید راز نهان

بپرداخت آنگونه روی زمین
که کرد آفرینش جهان آفرین

بگیتی دو افزون ز پنجاه سال
چنین کرد شاهی ز روی جلال

چو از عدل آباد کرد این جهان
سوی آن جهان رفت روشن روان

شه هفت کشور ازین پیش بود   کنون هفت جنت مسخر نمود
بنزد خرد مند هشیار دل   سرا ئیست این عالم آب و گل
مجو مهر از جوهر نه سپهر   که با کس بپایان نبرد است مهر
سپهر است پر کینه مهرش مدار   که با کینه ور مهر ناید بکار
جهان است مانند موج بر آب   ازان تشنه دل کے شود کامیاب
نه بست است پیمان به کس روزگار   که نشکست آنرا بهنگام کار
نماند بگیتي کسے جاودان   ز دست اجل کس نبرد است جان
چه خوش گفت آن کامل نکته سنج   که از گوهر دانش اندوخت گنج
جهان اے برادر نماند بکس   دل اندر جهان آفرین بند و بس
شد از عدل شاه اکبر کامگار   بسان بهشت برین روزگار
جهان گشت خورم بدوران او   زمین و زمان شد بفرمان او
ولي دهر بے مهر پیمان گسل   زکین مهر او کرد بیرون ز دل
زتاثیر بیمهر ئي این جهان   روان شد سوے عالم جاودان
روانش همیشه زحق شاد باد   از و عالم قدس آباد باد

In the name of the monarch of eternal sway,
Whose monarchy is imperishable.
All the monarchs of the surface of the earth
Owe their crown, diadem and seal to Him.
From non-existence, He creates existence,
His being is the source of justice and munificence.
Of His bounty the great and small stand in need;
Before His threshold pray the noble and ignoble.
The creator of the gem of vitality from water and clime;
The embellisher of the pearl of life so pure.
He created both worlds from His eternal grace;
The one He kept concealed; the other He displayed.
Then He bestowed this temporary abode
On kings with diadem, state and treasure.
That by their justice the world
Might look more fresh and green than a garden in a blooming spring.
When they sit to administer justice,
They deal a stranger on the same level as they would their own man.—
A king who so passed his life in this world
Is truly the shadow of God.
It was in the year nine hundred and sixty-two
That King Akbar, that shadow of God the Great,
Took his seat on a cushion * embroidered with gold,
The heavens bending before his throne,

He embellished the world with justice and equity,
Thus gladdening the people's heart.
Before his throne from every tribe and race
Assembled men of dignity and grace.
If with kindness he happened to look on dust,
Its worth increased compared to precious life.
In a single assault he would conquer a country in the field of battle ;
But in the cabinet he would bestow on people by the sign of his eye-brow.
Like the bounty of God, his bounty was general ;
In every business, he looked to the result.
Whoever sought an asylum in his court,
His dignity rose from the earth to the moon.
The world was so overfilled with his good fame
That no room was left in heart to conceal a secret.
He so embellished the earth's surface
That the Creator of the world showered praises on him.
He ruled over the world for fifty-two years with splendour,
Having rendered the world prosperous with his just sway,
He departed to the other world with an enlightened soul.
Ere this he was king of the seven climes,
Now he conquered the seven heavens.
To the wise and enlightened mind,
This abode of water and clay is like an inn.
Never seek friendship with this world,
For that friendship has lasted with none.
The world is bent on revenge, attach not your mind to it ;
For with a revengeful spirit friendship can be of no avail.
The world is like a wave in water,
From which the thirsty cannot quench his thirst.
The world with nobody entered into a contract,
That it did not break it when the time came to fulfil it.
Nobody is to remain for ever in this world,
None has saved life from death's hands.
How beautifully has sung that accomplished scholar *
Who from learning's treasure hoarded up vast wealth.
'The world, O brother ! shall last with none.
Attach thy heart to the world's Creator alone !'
With the justice of the king Akbar, of fortunate fame,
Like a sublime paradise the world became.
All people became glad in his time,
The earth and the world were under his sway.
Alas ! merciless time, which with no one has kept faith,
Out of spite lost affection for him from its heart.

---

* Namely, Saádi.

On account of the faithlessness of this world,
He proceeded to the world of eternity.
May God ever keep his soul happy,
And may heaven's domain ever flourish through him!

Tomb of Aram Bano.

In a room to the east of Akbar's tomb is the tomb of his daughter, Aram Bano Begam. The marble sarcophagus is of exquisite beauty and adorned with carved ornamentation of the most chaste workmanship. At the head of the sarcophagus is the inscription :—

اللہم اغفر لي ذنوبي

O God, forgive my sins.

And at the foot the inscription :

هذ القبر آرام با نو

This is the tomb of Aram Bano.

On either side of the sarcophagus is inscribed in the Persian characters the passage from the Koran known as the *Ayatul Kursi* :—

The tomb of Shakurulnissa Begam.

In another room, to the west of Akbar's tomb, is the tomb of Shakurulnissa Begam, another of Akbar's daughters.* In elegance of style and excellence and purity of construction it resembles exactly the tomb of Aram Bano. At the head of the grave is inscribed the prayer :

اللہم اغفر ذنوبي

O God, forgive my sins.

And at the foot is the inscription :

هذ البقر شکر النسا بیگم

This is the tomb of Shakurulnissa Begam.

The tomb of Mirza Suleman Shikoh.

Close to the tombs above mentioned is the tomb of Mirza Suleman Shikoh son of the Emperor Shah Alam, and own brother of Akbar Shah II, who died in Agra in 1253 A. H.

* She was married to Shah Rukh Mirza, son of Mirza Ibrahim, son of Mirza Suleman, generally called *Wali* of Badakhshan. See Chapter III.

(1837 A. D.) and was buried here. The sarcophagus, which is of marble, bears the following inscription:

الله و محمد وعلي فا طمه- حسن وحسين—

چوفرمودرحلت سليما ن شكوه　　ز دار الفنا سوے ملک بقا

بسا ل دو صد الف و پنجاه وسه　　به ذيقعد بست ونهم زين سرا

دران دم زها تف ندا اين رسيد　　بگو كرد بر شاه رحمت خدا

لوح منور مرشد زاده آفاق مرزا سليما ن شكوه ابن محمد شاه

عا لم باد شاه غا زي—

God, Mohamed, Ali, Fatima, Hussan and Hussain.
When Mirza Suleman Shikoh departed
From this transitory world to the world of eternity,
It was then the year twelve hundred and fifty-three,
And the date twenty-ninth of Zikaad.
At that time the invisible voice was heard saying,
'Say, God has had mercy on the king.'
The illuminated sepulchre of Prince Mirza Suleman Shikoh, the son of Mohamed Shah Alam, the king valiant.

To the west of this tomb is another tomb, highly interesting for the chastity of its design and the richness of its ornamentations. It is not known to whom this tomb belongs. Mr. Beal, in his *Mifta-ul-Tawarikh*, conjectures that it is the tomb of Rukia Sultan Begum, the daughter of Mirza Handial, the senior wife of Akbar, who died at Agra in 1030 A. H. The Arabic incription on the sarcophagus is as follows:— Another Tomb.

بسم الله الرحمن الرحيم

لا اله الا لله الملک الحق المبين - لا اله الاالله الخالق العليم -

لا اله الاالله رب الجلال المعين - اشهد ان لا اله الاالله وحده لا شريک له -

و اشهد ان محمدا عبده و رسوله - اشهد ان وحده حق و الموت

في الميت حق - و النار حق و التوريه و الا نجيل حق و الزبور حق -

و الفرقان حق - و الميزان حق و الصراط حق و ان الساعت آتيته

لاريب فيها - و ان الله يبعث من القبور برحمتک يا ارحم الراحمين *

In the name of God the merciful and compassionate.

There is no God but God, the Lord true and manifest ; there is no God but God, the Creator and possessor of knowledge ; there is no God but God, the God Almighty and helper. Hereby I witness that there is no God but He : He is the one with no compeer ; hereby I witness that Mohammed is the servant and messenger of God ; hereby I witness that the unity of God is true ; that the death of the dead is true ; that the fire of hell is trurc ; that the Old and New Testaments are true ; that the Psalms of David are true ; that the Alkoran is true ; that the scales of the Day of Judgement are true ; and the bridge of the Day of Judgement is true. Verily the Day of Judgment is to come ; there is no doubt regarding it. And verily God shall make to rise those in the tombs. In Thy mercy alone I rely, O Most Merciful God !

THE TOMB OF ITIMAD-UD-DAULA.

Across the pontoon bridge, on the left bank of the river, is the garden tomb of Itimad-ud-Daula. It stands within a quadrangular enclosure, in the centre of a garden, upon a sandstone terrace 149 feet square and 3-4 feet high from the ground, The garden is well kept and stocked with flowers, plants, shrubs, and tall cypress trees. The lower, or central, hall standing on this terrace is a parallelogram, measuring 22 feet 3 inches on each side. The floor consists of marble, richly decorated with mosaic work. The real tombs of the Wazir and his wife are in this hall. They are of a yellow variety of porphyry, of high polish and surpassing beauty and elegance. On the walls are inscriptions in the *Toghra* characters from the *Koran, Suras, Inna Fatehna, Mozamble* and *Tubárakal Lazi,* boldly carved out of beautiful stone. The hall is surrounded by small chambers in which are the tombs of other members of the same family. In the centre of the structure, on the first floor, is an elegant pavilion, reached by a sandstone staircase and covered by an oblong dome, topped with two pinnacles of gold. The cenotaphs in this upper room are of plain marble, but contain no inscriptions. At the four corners of the second storey are four round towers, about 40 feet high surmounted by marble

The Mausoleum of Itimad-ud-Doula.
Page 182.

kiosques. The whole structure is of white marble, inlaid with coloured stones and representing in arabesque beautiful patterns of flowers, cypress trees, vases and other decorations formed of gems, as in the Taj, but of less delicacy, though producing a most agreeable general effect. These ornaments are displayed to the best advantage by the light thrown from marble lattice work on the walls, which are of exquisite beauty and elegance, admitting free passage of air and light and, by their delicacy of design and combination of artistic merits, contributing materially to the beauty of the building.

The walls of Itimad-ud-Daula to the west are washed by the waters of the river Jamna, and a fine view of the river-front of Agra City is obtained from the summit of the minars on the four corners.

History of Itimad-ud-Daula.

Itimad-ud-Daula, after whom the garden-tomb is known, is the surname of Mirza Ghias Beg, a Persian adventurer from Tehran, father of the celebrated Nur Jahan and of her brother Asaf Khan, whose daughter, Mumtaz Mahal, the lady of the Taj, was the Queen of the Emperor Shah Jahan. From the post of Lord Treasurer to the empire, he was raised to the dignity of Wazir, which he held until his death, which occurred at Kangra, on his way to Kashmir, in 1621-22. His body was embalmed and brought to Agra by his imperial daughter, who raised over it the present mausoleum. His son was, on his death, appointed to the vacant office, under the title of Asif Khán. Jahangir, in his autobiography, has given an interesting account of his father-in-law. He was a poet, and imitated the old classics. He was genial and jovial, of a lively and humorous temperament, punctual in his habits and anxious to do good to the people. He was liked by every body and had no enemies. He was never idle, and his official accounts were always in the greatest order. The dutiful son-in-law also places it among the revered old man's merits that he "liked bribes and freely and without reserve asked for them." When the old minister was on the point of death, the Emperor and his wife, Nur Mahal, happened to be by his bedside. The daughter asked her father if he recognized His Majesty. Instantly,

His last moments.

the dying Minister repeated the following verse from a Persian poet :—

آنکه نا بینا ي ما در زاد اگر حا ضر شود
در جبین عا لم آرا به بیند مہتر ے

Even if a born-blind man should happen to be present,
He will at once recognize the chief by the splendour of his brow.

Date of building.

A short time afterwards, the old man died. The tomb was completed by the Wazir's imperial daughter in 1628. The Empress at first proposed to build over his remains a mausoleum of solid silver; but she was dissuaded by her architect from carrying out her resolution, on the plea that silver was likely to excite the cupidity of thieves and of beholders, and that marble would be more beautiful and lasting, while less portable and less costly.

OLD MONUMENTS IN THE CITY AND THE SUBURBS.

The Jámă Masjid.

Opposite the principal gateway of the Fort, on the north-west, stands the *Jama Masjid*, or the Cathedral Mosque. It was built by Jahan Ará Begam, the elder daughter of Shah Jahan, called the Begam Saheb, whose modest epitaph in Delhi has been often noticed by travellers. Her influence over her father, whose captivity she subsequently shared, was known and felt to the extremities of the Empire. She drew enormous allowances from the Imperial Treasury, and the nobles of the empire gave her costly presents. The mosque is built of red sand-stone and is situated on a raised platform, surrounded by a colonnade of the same material. It is reached by a broad flight of steps, eleven feet high. The main building, 130 feet long by 100 feet broad, is to the west. It is divided into three compartments panelled with white marble, with red stone borders, and supported by rows of arches, there being five archways in the front, and one large and two smaller ones on each side, all opening on a spacious courtyard. The central archway is over 40

The Jámá Masjid or Cathedral Mosque.

Page 184

feet in width. At each corner of the roof stands an octagonal domed cupola, and the front is adorned with a row of smaller square cupolas, of great beauty. From the four corners of the roof of the central apartment rise four slender minarets, and from its rear three large domes, inlaid with wide bands alternately of sand-stone and white marble.

The mosque is a fine structure of bold design, excellent finish and magnificent proportions.

The cloisters on the east side, together with the eastern gateway, which were very imposing, were destroyed during the mutiny for strategical reasons.

As the inscription shows, the mosque was built in 1058 A. H. (1648 A.D.) at a cost of five lacs of rupees, and it took five years to complete. Cost of building.

On the top of the central arch is inscribed the following passage in Arabic: *

بسم الله الرحمن الرحيم

وَالشَّمْسِ وَضُحٰهَا - وَالْقَمَرِ اِذَا تَلٰهَا - وَالنَّهَارِ اِذَا جَلّٰهَا -

وَالَّيْلِ اِذَا يَغْشٰهَا - وَالسَّمَاءِ وَمَا بَنٰهَا - وَالْاَرْضِ وَمَا طَحٰهَا -

وَنَفْسٍ وَّمَا سَوّٰهَا - فَاَلْهَمَهَا فُجُوْرَهَا - وَتَقْوٰهَا - قَدْ اَفْلَحَ مَنْ

زَكّٰهَا - وَقَدْ خَابَ مَنْ دَسّٰهَا - كَذَّبَتْ ثَمُوْدُ بِطَغْوٰهَا - اِذِ انْبَعَثَ

اَشْقٰهَا - فَقَالَ لَهُمْ رَسُوْلُ اللّٰهِ نَاقَةَ اللّٰهِ - وَسُقْيٰهَا - فَكَذَّبُوْهُ فَعَقَرُوْهَا -

فَدَمْدَمَ عَلَيْهِمْ رَبُّهُمْ بِذَنْبِهِمْ فَسَوّٰهَا - وَلَا يَخَافُ عُقْبٰهَا .

In the name of God the merciful and compassionate.

By the sun, and its rising brightness; by the moon, when it followeth him; by the day, when it showeth his splendour; by the night, when it covereth him with darkness; by the heaven and Him who built it; by the earth and Him who spread it forth; by the soul, and Him who completely

* This is the *Surâh* Shamms (the sun) of the Alkoran, Chapter XCI, revealed at Meccâ. According to Zamakhshari, the Mohamedan who shall devoutly read this *Surâh* shall be rewarded as if he had bestowed in alms all that the sun and the moon enlighten in their course.

formed it and inspired it with its faculty of distinguising and power of choosing between wickedness and piety : now is he who hath purified the same, happy ; but he who hath corrupted the same, is miserable. Thamuel accused their prophet Saleh of imposture, through the excess of their wickedness : when the wretch among them was sent to slay the camel ; and the apostle of God said unto them, "Let alone the camel of God ; and hinder not her drinking." But they charged him with imposture ; and they slew her. Wherefore their Lord destroyed them for their crime, and made their punishment equal unto them all : and he feareth not the issue thereof.

In the middle of the arch is inscribed the *Ayat-ul-kursi*, a passage from the Koran. The passage is as follows :

اَللّٰهُ لَا اِلٰهَ اِلَّا هُوَ اَلْحَيُّ الْقَيُّومُ ط لَا تَاْخُذُهُ سِنَةٌ وَّلَا نَوْمٌ ط

لَهُ مَا فِي السَّمٰوٰتِ وَمَا فِي الْاَرْضِ ط مَنْ ذَا الَّذِيْ يَشْفَعُ عِنْدَهُ اِلَّا

بِاِذْنِهِ ط يَعْلَمُ مَا بَيْنَ اَيْدِيْهِمْ وَمَا خَلْفَهُمْ وَلَا يُحِيْطُوْنَ بِشَيْءٍ مِّنْ

عِلْمِهِ اِلَّا بِمَا شَاءَ وَسِعَ كُرْسِيُّهُ السَّمٰوٰتِ وَالْاَرْضَ وَلَا يَؤُدُهُ حِفْظُهُمَا

وَهُوَ الْعَلِيُّ الْعَظِيْمُ ۝

God, there is no God but He ; the ever-living and the self-subsisting, neither slumber nor sleep seizeth Him ; to him belongeth whatsoever is in heaven and on earth. Who is he that can intercede with Him, but through His good pleasure ? He knoweth that which is past and that which is to come unto them, and they shall not comprehend anything of His knowledge, but so far as He pleaseth. His throne is extended over heaven and earth ; and the preservation of both is no burden unto Him. He is the high and mighty.

Around the arch is inscribed the following Persian passage :—

این مسجدیست شریف خدائی مکان روئی زمین را و معبدیست

منیف للهٔ و الفرمان عبادت گزین را و منظریست نور افزای

دیده وران عبرت آئین را و مسکینست دلکشا عارفان حقیقت

بین را — که با مر رفیع القدر نواب فلک جناب خورشید احتجاب

همت قباب عفت نقاب سده نساء زمان صاحب نسوان دوران

ملکه جهان مالکه گیهان ناموس العالمین اعز اولاد امیر المومنین

جهان آرا بیگم در عهد سعادت مهد صاحب عصر والی دهر

ظل ظلیل حضرت سبحان خلیفه نبیل ایزد منان باعث امن وامان

بادشاه هفت اقلیم فرازنده تخت ودیهیم حارس ملک وملت

قامع جور و بدعت بادشاه دین پناه شهنشاه حق آگاه مظهر کرم
وجود برگزیده حضرت معبود فرمان فرمائی بحر و بر داد ده عدل
گستر رافع لوائے بر و احسان جهان آباد ملک ستان مقنن قوانین رعیت
پروری و پرورده نوازی - ابو المظفر شهاب الدین محمد صاحب
قران ثانی شاهجهان بادشاه غازی بمبلغ پنج لک روپیه که قریب
هفتده هزار تومان رایج ایران و بست و پنج لک خانی نافق
توران باشد در عرض پنج سال صورت انجام پزیرفت ایزد بی نیاز
بے انباز این بنائی رفیع را چون بیت المعمور پایدار و این اساس
منیع را چون کاخ فلک برقرار داراد پروردگار این بنائی اسنیت
آثار بانیه مبانی خیرات عام را مراسم مبرات عاید گرداناد
تم فی سنه ۱۰۵۸ هجری

This is a mosque dedicated to God, the Lord of the earth, and a place of worship of the Creator Who rules the universe and to Whom alone worship is due ; it is a spot that increases brightness in the sight of those who survey the world with eyes of warning ; it is a munificent abode for the pious who have insight into the mysteries of the universe.

It was built by order of the high in dignity, elevated as the firmanent, screened with curtains bright as the sun, possessing a glorious palace, veiled with chastity, the most revered of the ladies of the age, the pride of dames, the princess of the realm, the possessor of diadem, the chosen of the people of the world, the most honoured of the issue of the head of the Faithful, Jahan Ara Begam.

Built during the auspicious reign of the lord of the age, king of the world, shadow of God, the glorious, the august representative on earth of the Divinity, the restorer of peace and contentment, the sovereign of seven climes, the honour of throne and diadem, the protector of the country, the defender of the faith, the extinguisher of tyranny and crime, the king the asylum of religion, the Emperor having a knowledge of God, the fountain of, generosity, and good, the chosen of God, the ruler of land and sea, the dispenser of justice, the exalter of the standard of goodness and benevolence, possessing power of populating countries and of conquering countries, the author of laws for the protection of the subjects and the well-being of the suppliants, the father of victory, Shahab-ud-din Mohammed, the lord of the second constellation, Shah Jahan, the king valiant.

Built at a cost of five lacs of rupees, equivalent to nearly 17,0CO Tumans of the coin of Iran, and 25,000 khani, the current coin of Turan, and completed in a period of five years.

May God, the ever existing and without compeer, maintain this high edifice and this noble temple for ever, like unto the temple for angels

(*Bytal mamur* *) and the palace of the firmament, and may God ever render this holy place, founded for public worship, an object of blessing. Completed in 1058 A. H. (1648 A. D.)

The mosque was closed to the Mohamedans after the mutiny of 1857, on the ground that it was too close to the fort and might be used for the purposes of a popular rising.

The mosque restored to the Mohamedans.

Lord John Lawrence, as Governor-General, acting in the same honourable spirit of toleration which characterised his whole career, finding, in 1858, that it was still shut up, gave orders that it should at once be thrown open and restored to its rightful owners. Great credit is also due for this benevolent and just measure to Mr. John Batten, who, as Commissioner of Agra, brought the facts to the notice of the Viceroy ; "and for many years afterwards," writes Bosworth Smith, the Biographer of John Lawrence, "the names of 'Jan Battan' and 'Jan Larens' might have been heard in the prayers of the faithful in the mosque, and they thus afforded one proof more that it is toleration and not intolerance which strengthens our hold on the country."

The Rám Bágh.

From the Railway Station, a few minutes' drive along a metalled road to the north-east of the city will lead the visitor to another place of recreation, the Rani Bagh, called by some the Aram Bagh (the garden of repose), but better known as the Rám Bágh. This is one of the oldest garden enclosures in Agra in which was the garden palace of Nur Afshan, noticed in Baber's memoirs. It was the scene of many imperial pic-nics in the time of Baber and his successors, and served, as it does now, as an orchard and pleasure ground. The jovial emperor, with his gay courtiers and jolly companions of both sexes, spent his leisure hours in revels, sitting in the moon-light and open air, on the banks of a fountain, filled with grape wine, and giving a personal example of merry-making in the fashion described in the well-known Persian couplet of his own composition :

ابر مست ونو بهار و مي ودلبرنا خوش ست
با بر بعيش كوش كه عالم دو با ره نيست

* The *Bytal Mamur*, believed to be the temple of angels, is, according to the belief of the Mohamedans, above the seven heavens.

How delightful are the clouds, the new spring, the wine and the company of a sweet-heart!

Try, O Baber! to be merry, for we cannot again come to this world when from it we once depart! *

It was the temporary resting-place of the body of the Emperor Baber before it was removed to Kabul. The name Ram Bagh was given to it by the Mahrattas.

The gardens are extensive and comprise different terraces which rise one above another and are divided into square beds, with stone and marble pavilions. The garden is well stocked with fruit trees and bordered with flowering shrubs and plants. It is well looked after and serves as a pleasant place of retreat for European residents during the scorching heat of summer.

Of the old buildings, some subterranean vaulted chambers looking out on the river, still exist. Two well furnished suites of apartments, with glazed doors and commodious furniture, and having two storeys, will be found at one extremity of the garden as one enters it to the left. These serve as a favorite resort for holiday makers, or those who visit the place for temporary change.

Though there is little attractive in the buildings, the place nevertheless possesses an antique interest, for, where many a newly married couple now pass their honeymoon and where resort many worn-out men, to gain renewed breath and vigour, over the same spot walked, three centuries back, the tall thin figure of the adventurous Baber, that knight errant of Asia who, with his hosts of beautiful Tartar damsels and jolly companions, forgetting for a time the concerns of State, drowned in the favourite cup all the anxious cares of a vast and turbulent empire.

Chini-ka Rouza or the tomb of Afzal Khan.

About half a mile from the north-eastern end of the pontoon bridge, on the left bank of the river, is the *Chíni-ka Rouza*, so called from the beautiful porcelain or glazed tiles which decorate the exterior of the building. The mausoleum is sacred

* This was the Persian couplet inscribed by Baber on the banks of the marble fountain in his palace garden in Kabul, which he was accustomed to fill with wine at times of festive entertainments.

to the memory of Afzal Khan, originally named Shukrulla, a native of Shiraz, who came to India in the 17th century. As a literary adventurer coming by way of Surat, he entered the service of Jahangir about the year 1617. He won high favours at the Imperial court and succeeded in obtaining the appointment of Diwan, or accountant, under Shah Jahan. He died at Lahore in 1639 and was buried at Agra, in the tomb built by himself during his own life-time. This was the time when the Emperor Shah Jahan was busy in founding new Delhi and the palace there.

The building is quadrangular, nearly eighty feet square, surmounted, by a bulbous dome, with a spacious central octagonal domed chamber, having in the centre two brick cenotaphs, with four-side chambers one on each side. The dome is in the old Pathan style. On the top of the inner chambers are inscribed passages from the Koran, but these are now rapidly peeling off.

Of the ancient buildings across the Jumna, the following also deserve mention :—

Garden of Buland Khan.

1. The garden of Buland Khan, a eunuch of the court of Jahangir. It has an extensive tower, supported by thirty-two pillars, and seven large wells are attached to the garden.

Zohra garden.

2. The Zohrá garden, between the Rám Bagh and Chini-kà-Rouzá, thought to have been a garden of Baber's daughter, with its dependent wells and pleasure houses. The building is in transition style between the Pathan and the early Moghal period.

Moti Bagh.

3. Moti Bagh, opposite the tomb of Itimad-ud-daulá, believed to have been founded by Shah Jahan, but now quite modernized.

Nawab Ganj.

4. Nawab Ganj, an enclosure with high walls and towers, said to have been built by Nawab Salàbat Khàn, the paymaster of Shah Jahan, now used as a residence.

Mosque of Humayun.

5. In the small village of Kachpurá, nearly opposite the garden palace of Baber, on the south-east side of the Jumna, is a ruined mosque, built by the Emperor Humayun. The building is 93

feet in length by 35 feet in depth. The domes are low and are not perceptible from outside. The arch opens on a great central recess, or compartment, on either side of which are four smaller chambers. On the west wall, over the *kibla* apsis is the following inscription :—

محمد همایون شه عرصهٔ دین   که بنیاد قدرش بود فوق گردون
بفرمان عالی وحکم رفیعش   مرتب شد این فرش واین سقف میمون
بتاریخ اتمام این بیت مشعر   شه عرصهٔ دین محمد همیون
قایله وراقمه شتاب المعالی غفر ذنبه

Mahomed Humayun, the king of faith's domain,
The basis of whose glory is in heaven's height.
By his exalted order and command sublime
These conspicuous floor and roof were constructed.

The date of the completion of this temple is found in the words :
'The sovereign of the Region of the Faith Mohamed Humayun.'
The writer and composer of this is Shitab-ul Moali ; may his sins be forgiven.

On the left hand is the inscription :—

این بقعه بود چون دل صوفی صافی   انکار صفائی ویست بی انصافی
چون یافت بسعی زین خوافی اتمام   تاریخ شدش بسعی زین الخوافی
مرید باید انکه بانی را بتکبیری یاد کند ناظمه وراقمه شتاب

This place is pure like unto a holy man's heart,
To deny its purity is from justice to depart.
Having been completed by the labours of Zen Khawafi,
The date of its foundation is found in the words, 'By the labours of Zen Khawafi.'
The disciple is enjoined to offer prayers for the benefit of the soul of the founder.

Composed and written by Shitab.

The building was founded in 937 A. H., corresponding to 1520 A. D.

6. The Char Bagh, or garden palace of Baber, is situated to the east of the Kachpura village. It is now entirely in ruins. *Char Bagh.*

7. The Mahtab Bagh, opposite the Taj. This is the site of the garden on which Shah Jahan intended to build his own **MahtabBagh.**

monument, a counterpart of the Taj, on the opposite bank, and to connect the two monuments by a marble bridge. The foundations of the western tower are still to be traced, while the eastern tower, with its decorations, is almost perfect.

Achanak Bagh.

8. Achanak Bagh, one mile east of Kachpura, said to have been founded in the time of Baber by a princess whose name it bears. Nothing is now left of this garden except some chambers opening on the river.

Chatri of Raja Jaswant Singh.

9. Chatri Raja Jaswant Singh. The walls are beautifully carved and decorated with figures of vases and flowers. A good view of this handsome building is obtained from Ram Bagh on the opposite side of the Jumna.

Other old buildings.

Of the old interesting places near the Taj may be mentioned the Haveli of Nawab Khan-i-Dauran Khan, the mausoleum of Shah Ahmad Bukhari, the bastion tower known as Lat Diwar, the small mosque near the south-east enclosure of the Taj, and the remnants of some ancient palaces in the quarters known as Tilyar-ka-Baghicha.

Garden of Mahabat Khan. Rouza. Diwan Ji.

Between the Taj and the cantonments, in a large walled enclosure, is the garden of Mahabat Khan. Close to it, in the village of Basai, is the tomb known as Rouza Dewan Ji.

Idgah.

On the Khair Garh road is the Idgah of the time of Shah Jahan, said to have been built in forty days. It is built of red sandstone and is 159 feet in length by 40 feet in breadth. It consists of six high arches, of which the central one is very lofty, and is enclosed by a wall of great height, surmounted by a cupola at each of the four corners, the enclosure being 570 feet by 530 feet.

Mausoleum of Jodh Bai.

This mausoleum is situated close to a village called *Khawája-ki-Serae*, between the Malpurá and Fattehpur Sikri road, near the Artillery practice-ground, Agra. It was originally a square building of 78 feet each side; but a great portion of it was blown up by the Government, about 1832 A. D., for the purpose of building barracks in the cantonment. The gates, the walls and the towers of the outer enclosure were all pulled down. "The mausoleum itself," says Mr. Beglar, " was too tough, too hard a nut to crack, for that purpose, and it was therefore left as it is, after being blown up,—a huge shapeless heap of massive fragments of masonry, which neither the hammer of man nor of time can dissolve or destroy!"

Jodh Bai, or the princess of Jodhpur, was Akbar's Rajput Queen, the mother of Jahangir and the daughter of Rajá Maldeo Rao of Jodhpur. As Akbar's mother had the title of Maryam Makani, so was Jodh Bai called Maryam Uzzamani. The real marble tomb, or cenotaph, of Jodh Bai is below the floor of the building, in a large vaulted underground chamber, descent to which is obtained by four passages like the passages into Egyptian pyramids. Three of these passages are closed with debris; the fourth may be entered by crawling.

Tombs of Ladli Begam, Shekh Fyzi and Shekh Mobarik.

About a mile to the north of the Sikandrá road and Alam Ganj, and immediately behind the Candahari Bagh, there is a great walled enclosure, of red Fattehpur sandstone, each side measuring 335 feet, with a grand and lofty gateway. The walls have crenelated battlements, and there are towers at the four corners. The old building was completed in 1004 (1595 A. D.) The enclosure contains a garden, with a raised platform in the middle. This is the tomb of Ladli Begam, sister of Abul Fazl, Akbar's famous friend and councillor. She was the wife of Islam Khan, the grandson of Shekh Salem Chishti, of Fattehpur, who was viceroy of Bengal under Jahangir. She died in 1017 A. H. (1608 A. D.), or five years before the death of her husband. Where the platform now stands in the middle, there was formerly a grand mausoleum, built entirely of marble; but it was destroyed by Lakhmi Chand Seth, of Mathra, who purchased the ground from Government, and, having dug up the marble stones, sold them. The new owner has built, instead, an ornamental pavilion on light arches.

The enclosure also contained the tombs of Sheikh Mubarak and his eldest son, Fyzi, the brother of Abul Fazl, but these have been destroyed by the Mathrá Seths.

Outside the grand gateway there is a large well, the grandest anywhere in Agra or its neighbourhood. This has a splendid

Baori, or underground room, round the shaft of the well, which is reached by deep and broad galleries, affording a pleasant retreat in the hot weather.

Over the entrance of the high walled enclosure, the following inscription in the Tughra characters may still be seen :—

بسم الله الرحمن الرحيم

و به ثقلتي ۔ هذة الروضته للعالم الرباني و العارف الصمداني

جامع العلوم شيخ مبارک الله قدس سره قد وقف ببنايته بحرالعلوم

شيخ ابوالفضل سلمه الله تعالي في ظل دولت الملک العادل يطلبه

المجد و الاقبال و الكرم جلال الدنيا و الدين اكبر بادشاه غازي خلد الله

تعالي ظلال سلطنته با هتمام حضرت ابى البركات في سنه اربع و الف

In the name of God the Merciful and the Compassionate, in Whom alone I trust! This mausoleum was constructed for the divine scholar, the holy sage, the most learned Shekh Mubarak ; may his last resting-place be sanctified! It was founded by the ocean of knowledge, Shekh Abul Fazl (may God the Most High preserve him !) under the Royal shadow of the just king, whom honour, prosperity and graces follow, the splendour of the world and religion, Akbar, the king valiant, may God the Most High ever perpetuate his kingdom! Built under the superintendence of Abul Barakát in 1004 A. H. (1595 A. D.)

The Rauzah was completed in the same year in which Fyzi died.

According to the account furnished by Abul Fazl in the Ain, his father and elder brother were originally buried close to the mausoleum of Sheikh Ala-uddin *Majzub,* in the Chár Bagh of Baber, opposite Agra, on the left bank of the Jumna. The bodies were removed to this side of the river by Abul Fazl himself, who built the Rouza. But when that occurred, does not appear.

Tomb of Mariam Zamani. To the south-west of Akbar's tomb, between the road used by the old Moghals to go northward to Lahore and the river, and after passing the old Delhi gate of the imperial walls, is the tomb of Mariam Zamani, a Portuguese lady, one of the Queens of Akbar, who doubtless exercised great influence over that emperor in inducing him to tolerate the Christians, as he is acknowledged to have done. This was originally the Baradari, or summer-house of the Emperor Sikandar Lodi, and was built by him in 1495. It is an extensive two-storeyed building of red sandstone, surmounted by a carved octagonal tower at each corner, and containing about forty chambers on the ground floor. It is reckoned among the most ancient buildings in the neighbourhood. The tomb was used as a printing office by the Church Mission, who have established an orphanage and industrial school here, which are worth visit.

Tomb of Kandahari Begam.

The tomb of Kandahari Begam, queen of Shah Jahan and daughter of Muzaffar Hussain, grandson of Shah Ismail Safwi, king of Persia, is situated in the Kandahari Bagh, now the town residence of the Maharaja of Bharatpur.

Palace of Raja Bhoj.

Close to the temple of Mahadeo Walkeshwar are the remains of some old palaces, reported to be the Mahal of Raja Bhoj, of ancient fame.

Tomb of Bakshi Salabat Khan.

About half-way between Sikandra and Agra, in the fields to the left of the road, is a tomb with an adjoining hall of sixty-four pillars. This is a monument built in honour of Bakshi Salabat Khán, pay master of Shah Jahán, killed by Amar Singh Rohtas, after whom the present Amar Singh gate of the fort of Agra is named.

Of Sadiq Khan.

Adjoining the above is a domed building, with a crypt, but without a monument, or inscription. This marks the last resting place of Sadiq Khán, one of Akbar's *Pirs*, or spiritual guides, who was *Mansabdar* of 4,000 and was one of Akbar's best officers. He was a nephew of our old friend, Itimád-uddaulá, father of Nur Jahán, and died in 1579.*

Gunbaz Pahalwan.

Three miles from Agrá on the left of the Gwalior road, is the Pahalwan's Mausoleum, so called from its being the last resting-place of a celebrated wrestler of the time of Shah Jahán. A large village has grown round the tomb of this notable man. The tomb stands in the centre of a large square platform, and is surmounted by a arge dome, with a cupola at each corner. The four corners of the square platform have each a beautiful four-pillared cupola of red sandstone.

*It is supposed by some that he is buried in Dholpur. See Keene's Agra, page 39.

Tomb of Firoz Khan.

On the right of the Gwalior road, at about the same distance as the Rouzá Pahalwan, is another mausoleum of an early style, and the most beautiful in the neighbourhood. This is the tomb of Firoz Khán, the chief of eunuchs in the Court of Akbar. It is an octagonal edifice, of red sandstone, and is raised on a high platform of the same shape. The entrance to the enclosure of this elegant mausoleum is by a fine gateway on the east side. The front of this portal is elaborately carved and ornamented. The dome is decorated with abundance of glazed tiles of various colours, and many other parts of the buildings are similarly embellished. The walls are covered with sculptures of the richest and most elaborate style in relief. Firoz Khán, who lies buried beneath the dome, is the noble who founded Firozábád, and who gave his name also to Tal Firoz Khán, an extensive masonry tank which lies in the immediate vicinity of the tomb.

Serai of Itbar Khan Khawja.

Four miles from Agra, on the Sikandra road, is the Serai of Itibar Khán Khawja. It was once an open summer house, but the doors have now been closed with masonry.

The stone statue of a horse.

Near the garden of Suraj Bhán on the way to Sikandra, and about two miles from Agrá, on the left hand side of the road, is a full size statue of a horse, made of red stone. Opposite this is a tomb of pucca masonry. No authentic accounts of this statue have been preserved. The story told by the people is that a certain horse-rider was coming to Agrá from Delhi. When he reached this spot, he asked an old woman how far the city of Agrá was. She replied:—"As far as you have travelled from Delhi." The horse-rider was struck with dismay and forthwith died. A statue of a horse was constructed in memory of this event by a certain sympathizing rich man, and the tomb quite opposite is pointed out as the disappointed man's last resting-place.

The following architectural monuments in the city deserve mention.

Akbari Masjid.

1. The Akbari Masjid, near the Kinari Bazar, originally built by Akbar. It has recently been entirely remodelled. The length of the building is 84 feet 6 inches and its breadth 25 feet.

2. The masjid of Mohtamid Khán, Treasurer of Jahangir, in the Kashmiri Bazar. It is of red sandstone, with some exquisite carvings. The dimensions are 53 feet by 20 feet. **Masjid or Mohtamid Khan.**

3. The *Kali Masjid*, or black mosque, otherwise known as *Kalan Masjid*, or the grand mosque, near the Government Dispensary. The domes look black through age, hence the name given to it, *Kali Masjid*. The mosque is believed to be the oldest in Agra. It is built of large and flat bricks and mortar but was originally faced with sandstone. There are fine archways, of equal width in the front, surmounted by five domes, of which the central one is the largest. It measures 128 feet in length and 33 feet 9 inches in depth. The mosque is a specimen of the early Hindustani style approaching the Pathan period, and is a fine specimen of architecture.—The mosque was founded by Mazaffar Hussain, grandson of Shah Ismail Safvi, King of Persia, so often mentioned by Abul Fazl in the 'Akbarnama', and father of the wife of Shah Jahan, buried in the Kandahari Bagh, the town residence of the Maharaja of Bharatpur. Mazaffar Hussain held the rank of 5,000 and died a disappointed man in 1600, or about five years before Akbar. His character is described as 'tricky and wavering'. **Kali or Kalan Masjid.**

4. The *Masjid Mukhan nisan*, or mosque for eunuchs, is situated in *Loha ki Mundi*, or the iron market, in the western, part of the city. It is built of pale red stone and is a very handsome building. It has three domes, that in the middle being the largest, with an octagonal tower at each end of the front wall. High up in the wall, to the west, are two large windows, of stone lattice work, of great beauty and elegance. The mosque is said to have been built by Akbar in honour of a favourite eunuch, named Yatím, whose prayers, in a season of drought of unusual severity, brought down rain from the heaven when all other means to alleviate the distress had failed and who was so indifferent to worldly riches that he refused to receive a reward when one was offered to him. **Masjid of Eunuchs.**

5. The Dargah and mosque of Shah Ala-ud-din *Majzub*, commonly called Alawal Bilawal, or Shah Wilayat, son of Syed Suleman of Medina, in mohalla *Nai-ki-Mundi*. The dimensions are **Dargah of Shah Ala-ud-din.**

46 feet by 19 feet. These are the oldest buildings of the Pathan period in the city. The saint flourished in the time of Sher Shah *Sur*, Afghan, and came to India *viâ* Khorasan. He established a school of Mohamedan law at Agra and built the mosque. He also founded a monastery, which is supported by an endowment and is still kept up. The mosque is sunk into the ground up to the middle of the walls, and a curious story is told about it. A camel-driver in the Imperial service wished to use it as a stable and even tied his beasts in the sacred edifice. The holy man expostulated, upon which the building began to sink, thus crushing the unfortunate beasts to death and did not cease descending till the saint bade it stop.—The holy man died in the reign of Salem Shah, in 1546. The mosque has three plain domes and is a fine specimen of Pathan architecture of a later period.

Hammam of Allah Warp Khan.

The *Hammam*, or bath house, of Allah Wardi Khan is situated on the left hand side of the Chipi Tola street. A handsome red sandstone arched doorway, with elaborate carvings, leads into the great quadrangle of the *Hammam*, surmounted by a dome, the diameter of which at its base is 30 feet. The gateway has on it the following inscription in Persian verses :—

در ایام شهنشاه جهان گیر   که مي زيبد با و عالم پناهي
بشهر آگره دا رالخلا فتة   كه با شد پا ي تخت با د شاهي
بخير الله ورد ي خا ن بنا كرد   چنين پا كيزه حما مي كه خوا هي
صفا يش روبرو باروے خورشيد   فضا يش تا فلک در با ر گا هي
ز موج آب وعكس قرص كلجام   هميشه حوض او پرما ه و ما هي
پئي تا ريخ بنيا دش د لم را   بعسل فكر شستم از سيا هي
گرفتم دا من پا كان و گفتم   بنا ئي خير حمام صبا هي

During the reign of the Emperor Jahangir,
Who is fittingly called the Asylum of the World ;
In the city of Agra, the Dar ul Khilafat,
Which is the seat of the Kingdom's throne ;
By command of Verdi Khan, Kherullah founded,
A Bath as chaste as one could wish.
Its cleanliness equals the shining face of the moon,
Its appearance is as spacious as the sanctuary of heaven.
On account of its rippling waters and the reflection of the orb of the moon in them,

Its fountain is ever, as it were, filled up with the fishes and the moon.

In order to find the date of its foundation,
I washed away anxiety from my mind with the honey of reflection.
Taking hold, then, of the skirts of pure men, I said :
'This glorious Bath has its foundation in good!'—1030 A.H. (1620 A.D.)

Its length from east to west is 122 feet and breadth from north to south 72 feet.

There are two sets of chambers, formerly used as Caravan Sarais. The bathrooms were so skilfully constructed and arranged as to maintain any temperature required.

The Masjid of Ajmere gate.

To the south of the spot where the Ajmere gate of Agra lately stood, there is a small masjid. A stone let into the wall in front of the masjid bears the following inscription. The first three lines, being a quotation from the Koran, are in Arabic, and the fourth or last line is in Persian :—

اَللّٰهُ لاَ اِلٰهَ اِلاَّ هُوَ اَلْحَيُّ الْقَيُّومُ ـ لاَ تَاخُذُهُ سِنَةٌ وَّلاَ نَوْمٌ ط لَهُ

مَا فِي السَّمٰوَاتِ وَ مَا فِي الْاَرْضِ ط مَنْ ذَالَّذِيْ يَشْفَعُ عِنْدَهُ اِلاَّ بِاِذْنِهِ ط

يَعْلَمُ مَا بَيْنَ اَيْدِيْهِمْ وَ مَا خَلْفَهُمْ وَلاَ يُحِيْطُوْنَ بِشَيْءٍ مِنْ عِلْمِهِ اِلاَّ بِمَا شَاءَ

وَسِعَ كُرْسِيُّهُ السَّمٰوَاتِ وَ الْاَرْضَ وَلاَ يَؤُدُهُ حِفْظُهُمَا وَ هُوَ الْعَلِيُّ الْعَظِيْمُ ۝

بنا کرد در عصر نورالدین محمد جهانگیر بادشاه این مسجد و گنبد

بنده احقر حاجي سلطان در سنه ١٠٣١ يكهزار سي و يک *

God; there is no God but He; the Ever-living, the Self-subsisting; neither slumber nor sleep seizeth Him; to Him belongeth whatsoever is in heaven, or on earth. Who is he that can intercede with Him, but through His good pleasure? He knoweth that which is past, and that which is to come unto them, and they shall not comprehend anything of His knowledge, but so far as He pleaseth. His throne is extended over heaven and earth, and the preservation of both is no burden unto Him. He is the High and Mighty.

In the time of the king, Nur-ud-din Mohammed Jahangir, this contemptible slave, Haji Suleman, built this mosque and dome, in the year 1031 (A D. 1621-22.)

There is no dome at this spot, however. The stone originally belonged to an old mosque in the Mohammedan burial ground south-west of the Ajmere gate, which having fallen into ruin, the stone was removed and fixed in the wall of a small mosque near the gate previously named.

The Mosque of Alamgir. In the quarter of the town known as Alamganj is the mosque of Aurangzeb, surnamed Alamgir; but it has now been completely remodelled and is utilized as the Collector's office. Mr. Blunt, the late Collector, built around it a number of shops, which have been rented to traders.

The following passage is inscribed on this mosque.

لله الحمد این چه مکانست - که پاک تر از جان مست - تعالي شانه
ازسویدا دا غدار - بفیض گلزمینش سینه ها ازشوق تجلي بهار - اجابت
معتکف محرابش - طهارت وقف خاک رآبش - وسعت صحنش زیر مد نظر
نگنجد - وبر فعت کنگره اش مده مبالغه نر مد - فضا یش عالمي امت
که دریاے جون چون نهرے ازو درگزشته - بلکه همچو رشته در گو هرش
جاکرده - از ینجا صفارا دریاب - که گوهر را دریاآبست - و اینجا دریا از رشک
صفایش چون رشته در پیچ وتاب - از انجا که خانه حق جل وعلے است - اگر فرش
را عرش گویند روا مت پهشطا قش از کوهي تا سقف فلک خمیده - یا همچو
راکعان پشت بتواضع خم کرده - هر که را بدین مکان گزر افتاد - چون سایه
سر بسجده نهاد - اگر زمینش درین سرزمین امر مي شنید - هر گز از سجده
سر نمي پیچید - حضور با آنکه توام نجات در صلواة - برغم باین قرار که
گابانگ شهر تش اقطار امطار گرفته مسجد عالمگیر گفتنش بجا مت - وباین
اعتبار که از خاک بر داشته بجا ده تاب رساند رواست - بادشاه زمان ملك
الملوک دوران - المتخلق با خلاق الله - البالغ کل بالغ - المحي سنت
رسول الله - چنان بر تبه فنا في الله پرداخت که خانه خود سر خانه خدا
ساخت - هما یون دلي که ارخصا یل سلطاني بصفات سبحاني گرآید -
مبارک منزلي که از دار الخلا فه به بیت الهي پنجنوبت زن آید - ذات
اشرفش زیب افروز اورنگ - کمترین چاکرش باجگیر چین وفرنگ -
تعمیرش مسجد کن کلیساے اهل شرک ونفاق - تحریمش آتش زن
آتش کده وسراے فارس وعراق - امام باستحقاق بهترین امر

گزیده عرب وعجم - ابوالمظفر محي الدين محمد اورنگ زیب عالم گیر
است اگر بناے عالم گیر گویند بسیار خوشنما ست - بنائش بناے اثبات دین
کامل - لالیس لاي لقي - آئین باطل - بناي اسلام تاریخ بنایش یعني
کلمه — اشهد ان لااله الله وحده وان محمد عبده ورسوله ——
بعد از سال ایجادش

God be praised! What a temple more sacred than life! The outlines of its construction exhibit the Creator's great might; by the blessings of its soil the breast of the faithful are with the lustre of piety illuminated; acceptance of prayer has seat under its archway; purity is subservient to its water and clay; the extent of its court is beyond the power of perception of the eye; the loftiness of its parapets is out of all conception; its enclosure is as extensive as the world, from which the river *Jun* (Jumna) flows like a canal; nay, it (the river) is like a thread to its rosary of pearls. Here imagine its chastity: a pearl owes its excellence to the ocean, but in this place the ocean itself, from envy of its purity and splendour, is entangled in a twisting and winding course like a thread. Inasmuch as it is the house of God, the Mighty and the Most High, should its ground-floor be styled the highest heaven, it is right. Its front arch has curved at the level of the roof of the sky, or has bent its back out of compliment, like those who bow in prayers. Whoever resorted to this temple touched the ground with his forehead, like a shadow, in adoration to God. Had the site of this place heard the command, it would never have refused to bow before the Creator.*

Although His Majesty's name is inseparable from salutation in prayers, still the mosque is known as *Masjid-i-Alamgir*, on account of its fame throughout the world; and it is right that it should have been so named, for, from its terrestrial position, its fame has reached the regions of heaven.

The King of the world; the Lord of lords of the time; possessing in his nature God-like virtues; the most perfect of all the perfect, the embellisher of the institutes of the Prophet of God; so much absorbed is he in the essence of divinity that he made the house of God his own abode; happy the mind which from royalty is bent to Divine qualities; fortunate the king who from his Capital comes out five times to the House of God; his august person increases the splendour of the throne; his meanest servant levies tribute from China and the Frank; his religious edifice has broken through the temple of polytheism and paganism; his place of prayer has extinguished the flames of the fire-worshippers of Persia and Iraq; he is the Leader of the Faith, by virtue of the best command of the choicest of the countries of Arabia and Non Arabia;† the Father of Victory, Mohyuddin,

* This passage has reference to the command of God given to Azazil, or the fallen angel, who, when commanded by God to bow before the from of man created by God, refused to comply, and, according to Mohamedan belief, became a devil.

† Erroneously, Mohammad, the Prophet.

Mohammad Aurangzeb Alamgir. Should we style this foundation as of world-wide fame (Alamgir), it is most befitting; its foundations are the foundations of the perfect Faith; furthermore, he who beheld it never went in the wrong path. Its date is to be found in a passage that is the mainstay of Islam, namely, in the words, 'I witness that there is no God but God: He is one, and Mohammad is the servant and messenger of God.' This is the date of its foundation.

The date found is 1082 A.H. (1671 A.D.), when Aurangzeb was engaged in war with Sivaji, the Mahratta.

The tomb of Nazír the poet.

Nazír was a great Urdu poet of modern time. He was contemporary with the celebrated Urdu poets Zaffar, Zouk, Momin Khan and Ghálhib of Delhi. His diction was graceful and simple, and he had a particular genius for describing nature and its beauties. His descriptions of youth and old age, life and death, seasons, fairs, wealth and poverty, *Fakirs* and *Calandars*, are particularly striking, and his poems are on the tongue of old and young, rich and poor, in the country. His tomb in Agra is the resort of people of all sects, and a fair is also held at it.

The tomb of Samru.

The tomb of Samru is in Padri Tola, at Agra. His original name was Walter Reinhardt, and he held command at Agra in the time of Najaff Khan* and was the founder of the now defunct principality of Sirdhana. He died at Agra on the 4th May, 1778, and was succeeded in his vast estates by his widow, known as the Begum Samru, who also succeeded to the command of his forces. The Begum figured prominently during the accession of Ghulam Kadir the Rohilla, son of Zabita Khan, and, when that chief entered Delhi in 1787, she hastened from Panipat with her forces and appeared before the palace. Overawed by this loyal lady and her European Officers, the Rohilla chief retired across the river. For her service to the Imperial cause, she was publicly thanked by Shah Alam and proclaimed the Emperor's daughter under the title of Zeb-ul-Nissa (ornament of women).

The quarter known as Padri Tola is situated in the rear of the courts of justice and forms part of the original area attached to the neighbouring township of Lashkarpur. It is one of the most ancient Christian cemeteries in Asia. Proprietary rights

---

* For an account of Samru, see page 59 *ante*.

in this estate were conferred on the Roman Catholic Mission by the Emperor Akbar. There are a number of Christian tombs here, with Armenian and Portuguese inscriptions, more than two hundred years old.

The mausoleum of Samru is an elegant octagonal building, surmounted by a dome, with a deep drip-stone, so as to resemble a Constantinople fountain. The inscription is in Portuguese, a proof that there were no English or French in Agra about the time of its construction. The inscription is as follows :—

Aqvi iazo Walter Roinhardt morreo Aos 4 Demayo, no anno de 1778.

"Here lies Walter Reinhardt, died on 4th May, in the year 1778."

The tomb of John Hessing.

Close to the tomb of Samru is the edifice containing the remains of John Hessing, the Dutch General in the Mahratta service, who commanded the Agra fort down to the time of his death, shortly before its siege by Lord Lake. * It is a more imposing and splendid edifice than that dedicated to the memory of Samru, being a counterpart of the matchless Taj Mahal in its design and general outline, though on a much smaller scale.

* *Vide* Chapter I, page 64 *ante*.

CHAPTER III.

AKBAR AND HIS COURT

THE EMPEROR AKBAR.

Humayun's flight to Sindh, 1541.

AFTER his defeat near Kanouj by Sher Shah, in 1541, Humayun proceeded to Sindh, with a view to establish himself there, and staid in that country for about two and a half years. At Pátar, about twenty miles west of the Indus, he met his brother, Handal, who was accompanied by his nobles and his seraglio. Humayun received his brother with great ceremony. During the course of the festivities, Handal's mother, who, it may be observed, was not the mother of Humayun, gave a grand feast to the Emperor and the ladies of the court. At this entertainment Humayun happened to see a girl of exquisite beauty, called Hamida Bano. So fascinated was he with her person that he enquired on the spot who she was, and, being informed that she was a daughter of a nobleman who had been Handal's preceptor, he asked whether she had not already been affianced. He was informed, in reply, that she had been promised, but that no betrothal ceremonies had yet been regularly gone through. Humayun asked her in marriage for himself. The idea was disliked by Handal, and the brothers quarrelled and even came to a rupture; but, Handal's mother being in favor of the match, Humayun was married to Hamida Bano, who had just then completed her fourteenth year, and, a short time afterwards, the couple repaired to the camp at Bhakkar. Handal, irritated at the marriage, deserted Humayun and repaired to Kandahar.

Marries Hamida Bano.

Birth of Akbar, 1542.

The result of the union was the birth of Akbar, on 15th October, 1542, at Amarkot, on the edge of the deserts of Marwar, whither Humayun had been compelled to fly, driven by the inhospitality of Mal Deo, Raja of Jodhpur. He was hospitably received by Raja Rana Parshad, the ruler of Amarkot. Four days previous to Akbar's birth, Humayun had left Amarkot to invade the District of Jun. The Emperor, on hearing the joyful tidings, prostrated himself on the ground to thank God for the birth of a son and heir. The nobles and commanders assembled round him and offered their congratulations. In default of the customary largesses, the Emperor ordered his ewer-bearer and secretary

Rejoicings in the Imperial Camp.

Jauhar (the historian, author of Tazkarat ul Waqiat) to bring him a pound of musk. This he broke on a China plate and divided among his nobles, saying: "This is the only present I can now afford to make to you on the birth of my son, whose fame will, I trust, one day expand throughout the world, as the perfume of the musk now fills this apartment." Kettle-drums were then beaten and trumpets sounded to celebrate the auspicious event. The Emperor named the child Jalaluddin Muhammad Akbar.

When the Emperor Humayun, with the auxiliary army of Shah Tahmasp, of Persia, was about to invade Kandhar, Askari, Humayun's brother, who was then holding that city, at Kamran's request, sent the little Akbar and his half-sister, Bakshi Bano Begam, from Kandhar to Cabul. After the fall of Kandhar, in March, 1545, Humayun marched to Cabul, which he occupied in November, 1546, amidst the rejoicings of its inhabitants. Here in addition to his success in the field, Humayun had the gratification of being, after three years' separation, reunited with his beloved son, Akbar. As the Empress had also, by this time, arrived from Kandhar, the circumcision ceremony of Akbar, which had been deferred by circumstances, was performed, in accordance with the injunctions of the law, amidst great rejoicings and with great splendour.*

The circumcision ceremony of Akbar.

* Moulvi (now Sir) Syad Ahmad at the instance of Sir John Kay, the eminent historian of the Sepoy War, wrote a note on the subject of the circumcision ceremony of the Moghal Emperors. In it the writer maintained that all the Moghal Emperors up to the time of Humayun had been actually circumcised. Akbar owing to the adverse circumstances of his father, when he was born, could not be circumcised. When Humayun regained the throne of Hindustan, Akbar was fully thirteen years of age and far advanced for the circumcision ceremony. The Hindu connections of the Emperor Akbar and his descendants made them look upon the circumcision ceremony with disfavour, and it was made a condition of all Hindu marriages that the offspring should not be circumcised. The minute was written by Sir Syad when Bahadur Shah, the last nominal king of Delhi, shortly before the mutiny of 1857, raised the question of succession to the privileges enjoyed by him and was anxious for the succession of the younger son, Jawán Bakht, by his favourite Queen Ziuat Mahal, to the exclusion of Mirza Fakhr-ud-din, *alias* Mirza Fakhru, his son by another wife. The old king maintained that the younger son was intended for the succession, not having been circumcised, while Fakhr-ud-din had been subjected to the ceremony and was therefore unfit for the honour. It was ascertained that Fakhr-ud-din had been circumcised for physical reasons. Sir Syad's statement, so far as it concerns Akbar, is wrong. Both Abul Fazl and Mirza Nizam-ud-din Ahmad, the author of the Tabakat, notice the circumcision of Akbar. The Mirza writes :--

مرزا یادگار ناصر در ملازمت مریم مکانی به کابل آمده وطویهائے عظیم
درین ایام ترتیب یافته وسنت حضرت شاهزاده درین ایام بوقوع آمد

"Mirza Yadgar Násir came to Cabul in attendance on the Empress Mariam Makani (Hamida Bano). Great rejoicings were made in these days, and the cremony of circumcising the young prince was performed." Elliott V. 223. Akbar was then four years two months and five days old.

His early training.

After the circumcision ceremony and when Akbar was in his fifth year, he was, according to Abul Fazl, "first brought to the school of human knowledge,' and Moulana Azam-ud-din was selected to be his tutor. Akbar learnt nothing from his first preceptor, and Moulana Bayazid was, after some time, appointed to replace him. Later on, Moim Khan was appointed to prepare the prince for his sovereign office and he was trained in the use of arms, in riding, in the management of the bow and lance, the sword and the matchlock, but he never learnt to read and write. On Byram Khan becoming the regent of Akbar, the young sovereign was put under the tutelage of Mir Abdul Latif, of Kazwin. Akbar studied the mystic *ghazals* from his erudite master and committed the odes of Hafiz to memory. The motto of the Mir was "Peace with all," and there is no doubt that Akbar owed much of the enlightenment and toleration which characterised his career to the early teachings of his generous minded tutor.

Akbar's policy towards the Hindus.

It was Akbar's highest aim to treat the two opposed creeds of India on terms of perfect equality and to make no distinction between Hindu and Mohammedan. He wished to convert India into a garden in which the Hindu banyan, that tree of vitality ever fresh and vivid, might flourish and stand side by side with the slender and aspiring palm of the Moslem, which had journeyed with him from the deserts of Arabia to the sources of the Nile and from the highlands of Iran to the shores of China and the Pacific. He had been born under the sheltering roof of a Hindu and from the time he ascended the throne he showed a decided inclination to form intimacy with the Hindus.

His marriage with a Hindu princess of the house of Amber.

This was, indeed, hereditary with him. When his grand father, Baber, was forming plans to conquer India, he entered into negotiations with Rana Sanka, a Rajpoot chief, to dethrone Sultan Ibrahim Lodi. His father, Humayun, elected to become the *Rachi band bhai* (bracelet-bound brother) of Karnavati, the noble mother of Ude Singh, Rana of Chittor, whom he assisted against Bahadur Shah. Akbar allied himself with the Rajpoots, and it was from this martial race that he drew not only his bosom friends, but some of his most trusted councillors and brave generals. He was also the first Chaughattai who formed a matrimonial connection with a Hindu Rajpoot princess. The circumstance happened thus:—Raja Behari Mal, chief of Ambar, and a much esteemed prince of the house of Kachwaha, had rendered important military service to Humayun when that king had been compelled to fly to Persia. He mediated with Haji Khan, a general of Sher Shah Sur, to allow Majnun Khan Qashál, Humayun's governor of Nárnoul, an unmolested retreat. On the accession of Akbar, Behari Mal paid his first visit to the royal camp, two days after Hemu's defeat, near Delhi. Here, instead of the usual repose and order of a royal court, he witnessed a tumultuous scene; soldiers, servants and dignitaries were seen hustling one another in their efforts to avoid tent pegs and ropes which were flying in all directions, while a young man sat calmly on the neck of a *mast* elephant and endeavoured to reduce him to obedience by the blows of an iron goad which he held in his hand, a task requiring no less intrepidity than calm judgment. At last the young man forced the wearied animal to kneel; he sprang from his seat and welcomed the old Hindu chief, who was accompanied by his son, Bhagwan Das, and grandson, Man Singh, who applauded the young fellow for his courage and dexterity. Indifferent to their commendations, the young man made a sign to the old chief to follow him into the royal crimson tent, and it was here that Behari Mal discovered who the young fellow was. He was no other than his own sovereign. It was here that the Rajput chief was, for the first time, impressed with the indomitable bravery and cool-headed skill of the Chaughattai king. Five years after, Behari Mal and his whole family attended on the king at Sankanír and were most honourably received. The Raja expressed his desire to enter the royal service and to strengthen the ties of friendship by giving his daughter in marriage to Akbar. Both requests were granted without hesitation, and, the proposed alliance having been formed, the result of the union was the birth of Salem, afterwards the Emperor Jahangir. From that time the marriage of the Rajput princesses with the members of the Moghal Royal family became a matter of form, and it was conducive to the best results for

How the marriage was brought about.

the amelioration of the two chief sects of the population of India. On arrival at the capital, Raja Behari Mal was made a Commander of Five Thousand, and his son and grandson received high military commands.

His inventive genius.

Akbar possessed an inventive genius and a mechanical mind. He was skilled in various mechanical arts and had a knowledge of casting cannon and making heavy weapons of war and ordnance.

His workshops.

He had his workshops in the immediate vicinity of the palace and looked with great scrutiny into the working of his arsenal. He introduced new methods, which he reduced to practical form.

Invents guns.

He devoted special attention to the manufacture of guns and matchlocks and regarded the efficiency of this branch 'as one of the higher objects of a king.' He invented a gun which, on marches, could be easily taken to pieces and put in order again when wanted. By another invention, seventeen guns could be fired simultaneously with one match. There was a kind of gun which could be easily carried by a single elephant, and another of such enormous size and proportions that the ball weighed twelve maunds, and several elephants and a thousand cattle were required to transport it.

Matchlocks.

A matchlock was invented by His Majesty which could be fired by a slight movement of the cock. He also invented a wheel which could clean sixteen gun-barrels in a very short time.*

Tents.

He invented several tents and made great improvements on fashions then existing. The tent called *Gulabdar*, covered with red cloth and tied with tape, was his invention. It was never less than one hundred yards square and had strong doors, secured with locks and keys. His camp was a moving city, and he had pavilions of enormous size, which, in journeys, served as private and public halls, as *jharoka*, as places of worship, and for various other purposes.

Candlesticks.

In the department of illumination, he invented several candlesticks of the choicest patterns. He worshipped fire

* The wheel is illustrated by a plate in the Ain-i-Akbari.

as an emblem of the deity, and at sun-set twelve candlesticks of gold and silver were brought before him, when a singer of sweet melodies, with a candle in his hand, sang a variety of songs in praise of God, beginning and concluding his tunes with a prayer for His Majesty.

He made many inventions for reducing unruly elephants to obedience. He invented a *charkhi*, or a piece of hollowed *bamboo*, covered with sinews and filled with gunpowder, an earthen partition dividing the powder into two halves. On fire being put to both ends it turned round and made a fearful noise, which frightened an elephant and thus quieted him. Previously fire on a large scale was lighted to separate two elephants that were fighting, but that caused much trouble and seldom had the desired effect. The method devised by Akbar to quiet the animal was of great utility.

Method for reducing unruly elephants to obedience.

His Majesty invented extraordinary carriages, among them being a cart drawn by an elephant, and so large that it contained several bath rooms. It was a travelling bath and could also be easily drawn by cattle. Water-wheels and carts of different fashions were constructed, and a machine was invented which drew water from a well and at the same time moved a millstone.

Invention of carriages.

Akbar invented the game of *chandal mandal* and could play it in several ways, which are all detailed in the *Ain*. He made several alterations in the game of cards and was a good player at chess; "his chief object in amusing himself with these games," according to his historian, "being to test the value of men and to establish harmony and good fellowship at court."

And of games.

Akbar, though born a Mohammadan, was gifted with an inquiring mind. He was a seeker after truth, and his idea was to unite all his subjects, whatever their origin and creed, into one common nationality. He did not favour the Mohamadans because they belonged to the ruling race. He collected the opinions of the professors of various religions and sectarian beliefs, weighed them carefully, retained what he approved and rejected what he considered unacceptable. "From his earliest childhood," writes Badaoni, "to his manhood, and from his manhood to old age, His majesty passed through the most various phases and through

Akbar a seeker after truth.

all sorts of religious practices and sectarian beliefs," and he collected everything in a spirit of enquiry. These enquiries created a strong conviction in his mind that there were men of mental and moral accomplishments and abtruse thinkers in all religions, and he believed that there were men in all nations who possessed miraculous powers. He abolished the *Jazia*, or tax on infidals.

Abolishes the *Jazia*.

Believes in the doctrine of transmigration of souls.

He rejected the tenet of resurrection, and believed in the doctrine of the transmigration of souls. He heartily approved of the saying: "There is no religion in which the dogma of transmigration of souls has not taken firm root." Brahmans composed treatises in order to find evidence for this doctrine. He imbibed his Hindu notions at the religious meetings of *Jogipura*, the *Ibadat khana*, and other places for such assemblies. His desire to gather knowledge regarding religions was not confined to public meetings. Even in his sleeping apartments, when he retired from all public functions, he was not without the company of the learned. He ordered a Brahman, named Vasu Khotam, to compile a vocabulary in Sanskrit of all things in existence. Another Brahman, named Debi, used to go to the Emperor in his sleeping apartments in quite a novel way. Admittance of men being strictly prohibited to the Harem, he was, according to Badaoni, pulled up the wall of the palace on a *charpoy* (cot) till he reached the balcony where the Emperor slept. While thus suspended between heaven and earth, he instructed His Majesty in the secrets and legends of Hinduism, in the manner of worshipping idols, the fire, the sun and the stars, and the chief Hindu gods, Brahma, Mahadeo, Bishen, Kishen, Ram and Mahama. His Majesty worshipped the sun as the greatest light, of which all lights were subjects, and he adopted costumes of seven different colours, which were worn by him on particular days of the week according to the seven colours of the seven planets. He interdicted the use of beef, believed it was wrong to kill the cow and regarded cowdung as pure. The doctors produced passages in their books, showing that the use of beef was injurious to health and productive of various diseases.

His Brahman teachers.

Worship the sun.

And fire.

Akbar believed in Zoroaster's doctrines, and regarded fire as one of the manifestations of God and 'a ray of His rays.' From his youth, he celebrated *Hom*, a kind of worship. Following the custom of the ancient kings, he ordered that the sacred fire be kept burning at court by day and by night and appointed Sheikh Abul Fazl superintendent of the fire temple. He prostrated himself before the sun and fire in worship, and when candles and lamps were lighted in the palace, he ordered the courtiers to rise. On the 8th day of the Vigaro, he appeared in the Audience-hall with a mark of saffron on his forehead like a Hindu, when the Brahmans, by way of auspiciousness, tied *rakhi* or a piece of cloth, with pearls and jewels, as an armlet round his hands. **Establishes fire temple.**

Akbar's mother, Hamida Bano, having died in Agra on 20th August, 1604, Akbar clad himself in the deepest mourning and shaved his head, beard and mustache. The body of the deceased Empress was conveyed to Delhi, His Majesty carrying the bier on his shoulders for several paces, and his example being followed by the Chief *Umras* of state. All the nobles of the Court shaved themselves and clad themselves in mourning costume. **Shaves beard and moustache on his mother's death.**

Akbar set aside the Islamitic revelations regarding the resurrection, the Day of Judgment and the ordinances founded on the traditions of the Prophet. Nothing would satisfy his inquisitive mind, but proofs based on reason and testimony and dogmas having their origin in self-evident truth. By frequent private interviews with the learned men of all creeds and by studying various treatises on religions, moral and physical sciences, he had judged fully of both the perfections and frailties of human nature. He denied future rewards and punishments in as far as they differed from metempsychosis; denied the existence of the soul after the dissolution of the body; denied the miracles of the Prophets and saints; denied the existence of genii, of angels and of all other beings of the invisible world. **Rejects Islamatic principles.**

He founded a new religion of his own, which he called *Dini Ilahi*, or the "Divine Faith." It consisted in the acknowledgment of one God and of Akbar as his vicegerent on earth. The Mohammedan confession of faith, "There is no God but God and Mohammed is His Prophet," was abolished, and for it was substituted the formula: **Founds a new religion.** **The New formula.**

لَا اِلٰهَ اَللّٰهُ - اَکْبَرُ خَلِیْفَةُ اللّٰهِ -

There is no God but God and Akbar is His vicegerent.

For the fear that the new formula might excite discontent among the masses of the Mussalman population, its use was restricted to the palace.

At this time (990 A. H., 1582 A. D.) Mulla Sheri composed a poem of ten verses of which the following are some :—

شورش مغزست اگر در خاطر آرد جاهلے
کز خلایق مهر پیغمبر جدا خواهد شدن
خنده مے آید مرا زین بیت بس کز طرفگی
نقل بزم منعم و ورد گدا خواهد شدن
پادشاه امسال دعوی نبوت کرده است
گر خدا خواهد پس از سالے خدا خواهد شدن

It is utter confusion of the brain if a fool should think in his mind,
That love of the Prophet can ever be banished from mankind.

I cannot suppress laughter at the couplet which on account of a novel plan,
Will be recited at the feast of the rich and become a watch-word with starving man.

The King has laid claim to be a prophet this year.
After the lapse of a year, please God, his own divinity he will declare.

The Din-i Ilahi a political fraternity.

The Din-i-Ilahi, founded by Akbar, had an important political significance. It was a religious community, uniting in a political fraternity a body of men the members whereof bound themselves by oath to stand by the Emperor in good and evil fortune, in happiness and in woe. During the year 988 (1580 A.D.) the four degrees of faith in His Majesty were defined. These were (1) readiness to sacrifice to the Emperor property, (2) life, (3) honour, and (4) religion. Whoever sacrificed all four things possessed four degrees and whoever sacrificed one possessed one degree. All the members of the court had their names enrolled as faithful disciples.

All public correspondence and other writings commenced with the words *Allah-o-Akbar* (God is great), associating Akbar's name with God and the use of the time-honoured *Bismilla* (in the name of God) was discontinued. The Islamitic prayers were rejected as illiberal and inaccurate, and the fasts put down as *Taqlidi*, or religious blindness. Prayers partaking of the nature of those of the fire-worshippers of Iran and the followers of the Bráhma were introduced as more comprehensive and efficacious. Man's reason alone was acknowledged as the fundamental basis of all religions. A new era, according to the new faith, was introduced in all Government records, and the mode of salutation was changed. A member of the Divine Faith, when he saw another, said :—*Allah-o-Akbar* (God is great) to which the other responded, *Jalli-Jalalo-hu* (magnificent is His glory). "The motive of His Majesty," writes Abul Fazl, "in laying down this mode of salutation, is to remind men to think of the origin of their existence, and to keep the Deity in fresh, lively, and grateful remembrance" The members abstained from eating flesh; they were not even to approach it during the month of their birth. Instead of a dinner given in remembrance of a man after death, each member was to give a dinner during his lifetime. He was also to arrange for a sumptuous feast on the anniversary of his birth-day. It was absurd, it was argued, to offer food, which was material, to the spirit of a dead person, since he could not be benefited by it; it was more reasonable to have a grand feast on the day of one's birth. Every member was to fast during the month of his birth.

Ordinances of the new faith.

An interesting essay by Mr. E. D. Maclagan, I. C. S., on "the Jesuit Mission to the Emperor Akbar" and based on notes recorded by the late General R. Maclagan, was read in a monthly meeting of the Asiatic Society of Bengal, held on 1st April, 1896. It describes fully the proceedings of these Missions furnished by the Jesuits.—

The Jesuit Mission to the Emperor Akbar.

A letter from Father Aquaviva, written on the 27th of September 1582, furnishes an interesting account of the final stage of the first mission. It says :—"The Emperor brings confusion into the Court by the many novelties daily introduced, among other things, the giving praise to creatures as the Sun and

Account furnished by the Mission.

Moon, and abstaining from meat from Saturday night and all Sunday. I have certain information that many of the heathen, out of superstition, because it is the day of the Sun and Moon, eat absolutely nothing. In general, it is forbidden to kill any meat in the market, and we are generally unable to get any to eat on Sundays. Two or three days after their Lent has commenced a new Easter has been introduced called "Merjan," on which it is commanded that all the chiefs be dressed out in State, and listen to music and dances. I enquired of the Emperor's astrologers, and they told me that it was a feast observed by the ancient fire-worshipping Kings of Persia. The Mahammadans were very scandalised and would not imitate the observers of the feast,—they cannot understand whether they do these things becanse they like them or whether they do them by way of experiment. In truth, I also cannot understand the matter, for the Emperor converses with me familiarly, as he has done this rainy season, always enquiring into the faith, and yet he seems confused with other things, and confessed to me one day that he would be much surprised if one could really discern the truth. On Tuesday, the 24th of September, the Emperor came in the afternoon to see the marriage of Domingo Pires in our Chapel. We decorated the chapel very well and painted two trophies in his honour, and Domingo Pires ordered a Portuguese banquet to be prepared for him at our house. The Emperor was delighted with everything, and showed me much affection for entertaining him to the best of my power. At the marriage, I preached a sermon to the couple; the woman did not understand me, and the Emperor interpreted to her in her own language what I was saying in Persian. The Emperor remained in our house till nearly 8 o'clock at night. With great pleasure he brought to the house all the principal chiefs of the Mahammadans and the heathen. One of the heathens, a ruler in these lands, was much amazed, and made a jest of the chapel. Others, children of the Emperor, were present and dined at the house, as well as two of the principal Mahammadan chiefs whom the Emperor sent for."

Akbar as spiritual guide.

Akbar, as a spiritual guide of the nation, took people to discipleship. The offering of a vow to His Majesty was looked upon as the means of solving difficulties. Streams of sick and indigent women with infants at their breasts, beggars and cripples, were seen at Sikri to snatch one look from the Emperor; or to secure some object which he had touched—the possession of such articles being considered propitious. Those at a distance offered their names in secret. When His Majesty left the court on tour, crowds of men and women from hamlets and towns waited on him with offerings in their hands, and, touching the ground with their foreheads, asked for lasting bliss, for an upright conscience, for the birth of a son, the reunion of friends, a long-life, increase of wealth, promotion of rank and many other things. His Majesty gave answers to everyone and endeavoured to relieve their religious perplexities. Instead of the usual tree of discipleship, the Emperor gave his disciples his own likeness. They looked upon it as a symbol of faith and a safeguard of righteousness and happiness, and placed it, enclosed in a jewelled case, in their turbans.

Is worshipped as the deity.

Akbar adored the sun and made long prayers to it four times a day; but he also allowed himself to be worshipped as a deity. Each morning, as he appeared at the window of the palace, multitudes of people prostrated themselves before him. Women brought their sick infants to receive his benedictions and, on their recovery, offered him presents. People brought cups of water that he might breathe upon it. The Emperor took the water, exposed it to the rays of the Sun, and, after muttering some sacred words, or, in the eloquent words of Abul Fazl, "after reading the divine orders in the book of fate," breathed upon it.

Adopts Hindu customs.

Everything Mohammadan was disdained, or discarded, and everything contrary to the faith of Islam encouraged and introduced. Thus, it was ruled that the *Sijda*, or prostration, was due to kings, but, instead of *Sijda*, the word *Zamin bos* (kissing the ground) was used. The coins, instead of the Hijra year, were to bear the era of Millennium. Wine was allowed if used to promote the strength, or prescribed by the doctor. Influenced by the numerous Hindu princesses of the Harem, His Majesty foreswore not only beef, but also garlic, onions and the wearing of a beard. On the day of the Dewali festival, when the Hindus worship the cow, several cows, adorned and

The Dewali.

Form of ordeal.

beautified, were brought before His Majesty.* Cases between Hindus were to be decided by learned Brahmans, and not by Mussalman Quazis and Muftis. Instead of the usual oath, ordeals were prescribed, to determine the guilt or innocence of accused persons; heated iron was put into their hands, or they were made to put their hands into hot, liquid butter. If they were unhurt, they were declared innocent; if hurt, they were considered guilty. Another form of trial was to make the accused jump into deep running water; if he came to the surface before an arrow had returned to the ground, which had been discharged when the man jumped into water, he was considered guilty.

Shaving of the beard.

The shaving of the beard was looked upon as the highest sign of friendship and affection for the Emperor; and the custom thus became general. Everything repugnant to Hindu taste was given up. The ringing of bells was introduced.

Dogs and swine not abhorred.

In opposition to the tenets of Islam, swine and dogs were no longer looked upon as unclean, but kept in the Harem and in the vaults of the castle. The saying of some sages that 'a dog has ten virtues, and that, if a man were possessed of but one of them, he would be a saint,' was cited as an argument for considering the dog clean.

Flesh of wild beasts.

The flesh of the wild boar and tiger was permitted, on the ground that it would impart the courage possessed by these animals to the person feeding on it. In favour of allowing the use of forbidden animals and insects, the following two verses from the *Shahnama* of Firdousi were constantly quoted at Court:—

زشیر شتر خوردن وسوسمار　　عرب را بجاے رسیدست کار

که ملک عجم را کنند آرزو　　تفو باد بر چرخ گردان تفو

Anti-Islamitic orders.

By taking the milk of she camel and eating lizards,
The Arabs such progress have made,
That they now aspire to the throne of Persia,
Fie upon fate! Fie upon fate!!

The wearing of gold and silk dresses at the time of prayer was made compulsory; the Islamitic prayers, the fast and the

---

* Chapter 81, on the Muster of Cattle, *Ain-i-Akbari*.

pilgrimage were forbidden; circumcision before the age of twelve was held to be unlawful, and was then left to the will of the persons who were to be operated upon; the Hijra year was abolished and the year commencing with the Emperor's accession introduced; it was called the *Tarikh-i-Ilahi*; the reading and learning of Arabic by the common people was prohibited, because such people were the cause of much mischief; the study of the Mohammedan Law was disapproved; astronomy, philosophy, medicine, mathematics, poetry, history and novels were studied and considered necessary.

Feasts. His Majesty, having been informed of the feasts of the Jamsheds and the festivals of the Parsis, adopted them and made them occasions for conferring benefits on the people. The people hailed these occasions with rejoicing, and there was a display of splendour at the court, which became a scene of gaiety and merry-making. The most important feast was new year's day, which lasted from the beginning to the 19th of the month of Farwardin. On the first days of this feast coloured lamps were lighted in the palace for three nights, and on the second for one night, and the joy was general. The last day of *Jáshn-i-Nouroz*, on which the sun entered the nineteenth degree of Aries, was considered particularly holy by His Majesty. On this day the grandees were promoted, or received Jagirs or horses and dresses of honour, according to their respective ranks.

Jashan-i-Nouroz.

Banquets. Again, His Majesty, following the custom of the ancient Parsis, held splendid banquets on those days the names of which coincided with the name of a month. Thus, banquets were held on the 19th Farwardin, 3rd Urdibahisht; 6th Khurdad; 13th Tir; 7th Amurdad; 4th Shahriwar; 16th Mahir; 10th Aban; 9th Azar; 8th, 15th, 23rd Dai; 2nd Bahman; 5th Isfandarmuz. Feasts were held on each of these days. Playing with dice, and the taking of interest on money loans advanced were held to be lawful. The Emperor encouraged usury by building a gaming house at the court and advancing money from the exchequer on interest to the players.

Usury held wful.

Fancy Bazars. On new year's day fancy bazars were, under the orders of His Majesty, opened for a stated period, for the amusement of the Begams and ladies of the Royal Harem and also of other married ladies. The Emperor was profuse in spending money on such occasions. Important affairs of the Harem people were decided, marriage contracts made and betrothals of boys and girls arranged at such meetings.

Social meetings.

With a view to establishing harmony among people of different classes, Akbar held social meetings, called 'feasts of friendship and union,' to which large numbers of people were invited. They all partook of His Majesty's hospitality, and he cheered them all with his affable disposition. 'Through the discipline and careful arrangements of His Majesty' observes Abul Fazl in the Ain, 'the court was changed from a field of ambitious strife into a temple of a higher world, and the egotism and conceit of men directed to the worship of God. Even frivolous and worldly people learnt zeal in their private life and attachment and loyalty to the throne.' *

The Khush Roz, or the joyful days.

On the first feast day of every month, the Emperor held a large fair for the purpose, according to Abul Fazl, 'of enquiring into the many wonderful things in this world'. Merchants exhibited their articles for sale. The members of the Royal Harem graced the fair with their presence and the ladies of the nobility were also invited. Buying and selling was the order of the day. His Majesty selected articles for purchase at fixed prices, thus adding greatly to his knowledge. 'The secrets of the Empire, the character of the people, the conduct of the officials and the state of each office and workshop were fully known.' After the Fancy bazars for ladies, bazars for men were held, and in them merchants from all countries produced their wares for sale. All sorts of people were freely admitted to these fairs and men having grievances against any official had free access to the Emperor to lay their complaints before him, without hindrance from the mace-bearers.

Conversion to other faith.

Hindus who had been compelled to become converts to Mohamadanism, while still too young to understand the nature of their act, were left at liberty, on reaching the age of discretion, to return to the faith of their ancestors. No man was to be molested or interfered with in any way on account of his religion; everyone was allowed to renounce his own religion and embrace another, as suited his taste and convenience. If a Hindu woman fell in love with a Mohamadan and changed her religion, she was

* Chapter 84, Ain-i-Akbari.

taken from his custody by force and given back to her own family. In the same way, if a Mussalman woman fell in love with a Hindu, she was prevented from joining Hindus. No one was allowed to meddle with the religious belief and liberty of another; everyone was at liberty to build churches, prayer rooms, idol temples or fire temples as he pleased. Perfect liberty of action was given, and no encouragement shown to any particular sect or preference given to people of one sect over those of another. **Religious liberty and toleration.**

Akbar was a great patron of horticulture. Skilful gardeners were brought from Iran and Turan to Agra and Fattehpur Sikri, and were specially patronised by him. The work of planting new trees and flowers of various kinds was carried on with much vigour. Ripe fruits were imported from Kabul, Kandhar and Kashmere, and melons, pears and apples from Samarkand. **Taste for horticulture.**

Akbar abhorred cruelty to animals, and towards the end of his life even gave up hunting and animal fighting. He was often heard to say: 'O that my body were larger than all bodies together, so that the people of the world could feed on it without destroying other living animals'. Out of benevolence to mankind he never liked to call a *bandah* (slave) as such, for he believed mastership to be the domain of the One invisible God. He therefore called this class of men, *chelas*, which in Hindí signifies a 'faithful disciple.' All His Majesty's disciples were also called *chelas*. He raised these people, according to their desert, to high offices, from the position of a common soldier to higher dignities in the State. **His humanity.**

As an example of Akbar's humanity, it is stated that, when Hemú, after his defeat in 1526, in the battle of Panipat—that desert which from the days of Mahabharata had served as the battlefield of nations—was brought before Akbar, then a boy, struck by an arrow in the eye, and Akbar was asked by Bahram Khan to strike off the prisoner's head, and thus, by slaying an infidel, win for himself the title of *Ghazi*, or a hero in the cause of Islam, the generous boy shrunk from the idea of killing a fallen and helpless foe. On this, Bahram, to avoid delay, and 'to accustom his young sovereign to the sight of blood,' himself cut off Hemu's head. **Its example.**

His tenderness of mind.

An instance of the Emperor's tenderness of disposition is given by Badaoni. When His Majesty reached Fatehpur Sikri from Ahmedabad, in June 1573, Husain Kuli Khan, governor of the Panjab, brought to him three hundred prisoners from the army of the rebel, Ibrahim Mirza, whom he had defeated near Multan. Among these prisoners was Masud Husain Mirza, a general of Ibrahim. Masud's eyes were sewed up, but Akbar ordered them to be opened. The other captives were all covered with the skins of hogs, asses and dogs, but the Emperor gave a free pardon to them all, including Masud, and liberated them.

The Jesuit Father who visisted Akbar in Fattehpur Sikri in 1582, has recorded a story of the Emperor's gentle temper. Once, when His Majesty was on the Jhelum, twelve absentees were produced before him for punishment. Having heard the case personally and given it his mature consideration, he ordered some of them to be beheaded and others to be kept in confinement. Amongst the first, a convict begged His Majesty to be allowed to speak. On being permitted, he begged the king that he might not be killed, as he possessed an art in which no body in the world excelled him. On the king's asking to what art he referred, he replied : "Lord of the universe, I sing better than any one." "Then sing," said the Emperor. The poor devil began his performance so wretchedly that the Emperor could not suppress his laughter. On this the prisoner remarked: "Asylum of the world, pardon me ; I am very hoarse to-day, and cannot sing." This remark pleased His Majesty so well that he not only forgave the man, but also modified his order condemning the deserters to death, and they were kept in confinement until he should order further enquiry into their offence. *

Marriage ties.

Akbar disliked the custom of Hindustan whereby a man is married to a woman whom he has never seen, and with whom he has not associated. He maintained that the consent of the bride and the bridegroom, and the permission of the parents, if the couple to be bound by marriage tie were minors, was necessary to render a marriage contract lawful. He disapproved of marriage between a man and woman before they had reached years of discretion, maintaining that such a union caused serious

* *Akbar* by Count of Noer, Vol. II, p. 57.

want of love when the couple ripened into manhood and made their house either desolate or unhappy in after life. Marriage was necessary for the stability of the human race, the durability and progress of the world. It acted as a preventive against the outbreak of evil passions, as a check against wicked and sinful human propensities; it led to the establishment of homes and promoted happiness and comfort. But people, in contracting marriages, must be actuated by higher motives than mere sensual gratification; they must be imbued with notions of spiritual union, and this could only be attained by equality of essence in marriages. He passed an edict prohibiting marriage between first cousins and near relations, because it was destructive of sexual appetite. Boys were not to marry before the age of 16, or girls before fourteen, because the offspring of early marriage was weakly. He appointed officers called *Tavi Begi*, or masters of marriages, to regulate and arrange marriages. They made enquiries into the circumstances of the bridegroom and bride, and they were paid by a tax levied from both the contracting parties. According to Abul Fazl, the payment of this tax was looked upon as 'auspicious', and it was levied to enable people 'to show their gratitude.' Mansabdars commanding from five to one thousand paid ten gold mohurs; Mansabdars of one thousand to five hundred paid four mohurs; Commanders of one hundred, two mohurs; Commanders of forty, one mohur; Commanders of ten, four rupees. The latter fee was also paid by rich people. The middle classes paid one rupee and the common people one *dam*. The common people were also to cause their marriages to be registered in the Kotwal's office.

Regulations for marriage.

His Majesty disapproved of high dowries, fixed extravagantly without regard to the means of the contracting parties, the affair being a mere sham; but he admitted that high dowries acted as a preventive against rash divorces.

Dowers.

He did not approve of a man marrying more than one wife, for polygamy ruined a man's health and disturbed the peace of the house. Intercourse with a pregnant woman, or with one old and barren, or with girls under the age of puberty, was prohibited.

Polygamy.

He censured old women who took young husbands, because this was against all modesty. Similarly, women whose period of fertility had ceased were not to marry; but widows, if they liked, might, subject to the above provision, marry. No one was to marry more than one wife, except in the case of barrenness; in all other cases the rule observed was 'one God and one wife.'

Widow marriage.

Burning of Hindu widows on the pyre of their husbands.

A Hindu girl who lost her husband before consummation of marriage was not to be burnt. But a Hindu woman who wished to burn herself on the funeral pyre of her husband was at liberty to do so; but she was not to be forced to commit the act.

Administration of justice.

Akbar was strict in the administration of justice. He heard all causes and investigated everything which required his orders, himself personally. The Jesuit priest from Goa who visited the Court at Fattehpur in 1582, says: "He can neither read nor write, but is extremely eager after knowledge and has always learned men about him whom he invites to discuss or narrate one thing or another. While he halts in any place, no person may be put to death without his permission. He also has all the facts of important civil suits communicated to him." He patiently heard matters of all kinds and he found time for it. It was a pleasure to him to work in order to dispense justice between man and man.

Akbar sparing in diet.

Akbar was abstemious and sparing in his diet. He abstained from flesh, and whole months passed without his touching it. He lived mostly on rice, milk and sweetmeats and never made more than one meal in the course of the twenty-four hours.

His meals.

The food was first tasted by the Mir Bakhawul, or master of the kitchen, served up in dishes of gold and silver, stone and earthenware, and tied up in red or white cloths and sealed and then carried to the apartments of the Emperor, guarded by mace-bearers. Bags duly sealed, containing various kinds of bread sauces of curds, plates of pickles and various greens, were forwarded in the same manner. The servants of the palace again tasted the food, and, the dishes having been arranged on a table cloth spread on the ground, His Majesty partook of them. After he had dined, he prostrated himself in prayer. It happened in 1580 that, while Akbar was sitting at his table, an idea occurred to him that, while he was enjoying his meals, there might be hungry persons who had looked upon his victuals with longing eyes. "How, therefore," asks the historian Mirza Nizamuddin Ahmad, "could he eat while the hungry were debarred from it?" He therefore, ordered that a part of the food prepared for himself be first given out to hungry persons, and that afterwards it should be served. It will appear that his tenderness extended to all, without distinction of race or creed.

Care of drinking water.

As His Majesty regulated his food, so he was strict about his drink. He did not drink well water, and was very careful as to its wholesomeness and purity. His *Abdarkhana*, or place for keeping water for drinking, forms the subject of a separate chapter in the *Ain*. His Majesty called water 'the source of life,' 'the water of immortality' *(Ab-i-Hayat)*. Whether at home or on travel, he used Ganges water, which came sealed in jars from Sarun, the nearest station on the Ganges to Agra when the court was at the place last mentioned, or at Fattehpur, and trustworthy persons were employed to despatch water from the river bank. Food for His Majesty was cooked with rain water, or water brought from the Jamna, or the Chenab (when the Emperor was in the Punjab), but a little Ganges water was invariably mixed with it. He shunned the pleasures of the world. "In Multan," writes the author of the Dabistan, "I saw Shah Salimullah, who has renounced the world and is a unitarian. He is very rigid in discipline and avoids the society of man. He said he had often been with Jalaluddin Akbar and had heard him frequently say: 'Had I previously the knowledge which I possess now, I would have never chosen a wife for myself; for on old women I look as mothers, on women of my own age as sisters and on girls as daughters.' A friend of mine said he had heard the same reported of Akbar by Nawab Lashkar Khan of Mashhed."

He shuns pleasure.

Division of his time.

Akbar spent nights in the private audience hall in the company of philosophers and in discourses with learned men. At these meetings old institutions were described and new ideas were hailed with delight. He took a little sleep in the evening and again in the morning. At the nightly meetings, His Majesty started fitting subjects for conversation, while on other occasions affairs of State were brought forward and orders passed. Four watches before sunrise, he retired to his private apartments for the purpose of contemplation and prayer, and, about a watch before day-break, he was entertained by musicians who sang songs and religious strains. Soon after daybreak, he appeared at the balcony and received the salutations of the multitude who stood below. This, in the language of the country, was called *Darshan* (view). He then received the members of the Harem and transacted some business. Then he retired to his private apartments for a little repose. Towards evening, he appeared at a window which opened into the State Hall and here he transacted business and dispensed justice.

His Dress.

Following the practice of the *Sufis* (from *suf*, wool), Akbar preferred to wear woollen stuffs, especially shawls. He changed the names of many garments and invented his own terms and names for them.

Akbar's fondness for sports.

To an indomitable courage and invincible bravery, Akbar added prodigious bodily strength, which, with his great presence of mind and extraordinary tact and personal dexterity, never failed him in the severest trials. He was fond of sport and of witnessing animal fights and took great delight in the combats of elephants, which he at times conducted personally, himself acting in the place of the *Mahawat*, or elephant driver, and making the rival animals fight. An incident of the 6th year of the reign, which took place at Agra, is described by Abul Fazl in the Akbarnama; it strikingly illustrates the chivalrous spirit and prowess possessed by this remarkable man. In the *chaugan** grounds outside the Fort of Agra, which had been laid out for His Majesty's pleasure, two State elephants of the most fierce type, named *Hawai* and *Ran Bakh*, which could not be managed by the most skilful tamers, were made to fight with each other. The entire court assembled to witness the scene. While the elephant *Hawai* was in the height of ferocity and excitement, Akbar mounted it and made it charge the rival elephant, which was equally frantic and impetuous. The princes and nobles assembled, considering that the life of their King was

Combats of elephants.

Remarkable feats of valour performed by Akbar.

* A game resembling cricket or tennis, but played on horseback.

endangered, became alarmed, and the greatest consternation prevailed. None of the men present, even the greatest Lords however, had the courage to represent to the King the fears they entertained for his life. At length they communicated their apprehensions to Shamsuddin Mahomed Atgah Khan,* who was in high favour with the Emperor. This noble, approaching the Emperor's elephant, represented to His Majesty with folded hands the anxiety and dismay the nobility were feeling at the sight, and begged of him to dismount. Akbar threatened to throw himself off the elephant if Atgah persisted in his request, and bade him depart. Then, with a turn and twist of the driving instrument, and with a skill which astonished all the by-standers, he made *Hawai* strike the rival elephant with his head, and, the attacks being continued amid uproar of the populace, *Ran Bakh* gave way and fled in the direction of the river. The Emperor with his elephant followed him. The worsted elephant made his way to the bridge of boats. *Hawai* was close on his heels. The enormous weight of the huge animals caused the boats of which the bridge was formed to shake violently, which created fresh alarm for fear the bridge should give way. The bye-standers threw themselves into the river on both sides of the bridge, and, swimming in the water, followed the running elephants with the object of assisting the Emperor, who was still on the back of *Hawai*. Both elephants crossed the bridge in safety, and, the defeat of *Ran Bakh* being completed, all cause for anxiety was removed. The Emperor came down and was hailed with feelings of intense joy by his Amirs, who congratulated him on his success. Shekh Abul Fazl here writes, His Majesty had repeatedly told him in private audiences : " When I mount a furious elephant which has thrown its driver, I do so with an unshaken belief and trust in God who has given me life and made me prosperous and strong, for without His grace I could not do anything." The Shekh, in his zeal to flatter the King, assigns the Emperor's feats of valour displayed on such occasions, to His Majesty's 'illuminated and enlightened mind, which enabled him to see future events and to judge with his extraordinary wisdom about them'.

---

* His wife became wet nurse (*Angah*) to Akbar when the latter was born at Amerkot. Humayun conferred on him the title of *Ji Ji Angah*. He was appointed Governor of the Punjab by Akbar. He defeated Byram Khan near Jallandhar before Akbar could come up, for which service Akbar honoured him with the title of Azam Khan.

Akbar rode every kind of elephant and made it obedient to his command. He put his foot on the trunk and mounted it quickly, even when the animal was in the rutting season, to the astonishment of all the spectators. One swift-paced elephant, with a comfortable turret on its back, was always ready at the palace for His Majesty's use. Courier horses were similarly kept in readiness at the palace.

Is fond of variety of games.

Akbar took great delight in a variety of games and fights between animals, from elephants to deer and rams, and from cocks to nightingales. He was fond of witnessing the performances of wrestlers and kept in his court noted wrestlers and boxers from Iran and Turan. Every day two well matched men fought with each other. We find among the wrestlers the names of Mirza Khan of Gilan; Mohammad Kuli of Tabrez, to whom His Majesty gave the title *Sher Hamla*, or lion attacker; Sadiq of Bokhara; Murad of Turkistan; Mohammad Ali of Turan; Shah Kuli of Kurdistan; Hilal of Abyssinia; Sri Ram, Mangal, Kanhia, Ganesh, Anba, Nanak, Ballabhader, &c., of Hindustan.

Spider fights.

Out of curiosity, Akbar liked to see even spiders fight. He had an enquiring mind and his object was to acquire a knowledge of nature and to see the wonders of creation.

Hunting.

He was fond of hunting. He kept hunting dogs,* and tamed antelopes and panthers to hunt other wild beasts. Nets were fastened to the horns of tamed antelopes to entangle wild animals. He remembered the names of all his elephants, gave names to his horses, wild beasts, antelopes and pigeons and knew each of them by its name. The *Ain* contains regulations for the management of the numerous departments of domesticated animals and birds and the establishment attached to each. Akbar closely supervised each department and took a keen interest in it. In the midst of these diversions he despatched important State business and passed orders on serious State questions of an urgent character, which were brought before him.

Akbar's business-like habits.

Abul Fazl has given several instances of Akbar's physical activity, courage and expertness of mind. Once information was

* Akbar's hunting dogs came mostly from Kabul, especially from the Hazara District, north of Rawal Pindi. Dogs were ornamented and names were given to them.—*Ain*.

given of a man-eating tiger having made its appearance in the District of Bárí. His Majesty mounted the elephant Náhar Khan and repaired to the jungle. The tiger, being enraged, fixed its claws in the forehead of the elephant and dragged its head to the ground, but was killed by the attendants. On another occasion during the *Qamraqah* hunt (or chase for which drivers are employed) a tiger which had been started attacked the Emperor, who shot it through the head and killed it. Once, in a hunting party, a tiger struck one of the men to the ground. His Majesty aimed at the brute, killed it and saved the man's life. In the Mathra forest a follower became suddenly terrified at the sight of a tiger. But Akbar kept his ground and looked furiously at the brute, which crouched down and was killed. In 1561, when Akbar was a youth of nineteen, he set out on his return march from Malwa to Agra. While riding ahead alone, in the neighbourhood of Narwar, he suddenly came across a tiger with five cubs which came out of the jungle on his path. Without the slightest hesitation, he drew his sword and at one blow sent the beast's head rolling on the ground. When his retinue, which had been left behind, came up, the boy Emperor was seen standing quietly near his dead foe. His chiefs recognised in him a youth of great personal bravery and endowed with cool resolution and determined action.

Dexterity in sport and personal bravery.

Various examples are given of Akbar's valour in the field of battle. The calm devotion, tact and gallantry he displayed in the siege of Chittor (1567-68) deserve mention. The reigning Rana was Ude Singh, son of Rana Sanga, Baber's competitor, and the place was regarded by the Rajpúts of Mewar as a sanctuary of their power, and the stronghold of Hindu independence. Akbar prosecuted the siege with great caution and regularity, and laid his trenches after the fashion of modern European warfare.* He examined the minutest details of his approaches and was indefatigable in his superintendence of an undertaking which was to serve as a landmark on his path of glory. So concerned was he about this war that he made a solemn vow to travel on foot to the grave of the most revered saint Moin-ud-din *Chishti* of Ajmere, to pay his respects to it, as

His prowess in the field of battle.

* Elphinstone, Vol. II, page 234.

soon as the place should fall. He constructed two *sabats* or zig-zag approaches, formed by gabions and trenches thrown up to reach the walls of the fort, to be breached by mining. Akbar cheered his soldiers to deeds of valour, and his presence exercised a magic influence over them. Akbar's own intrepidity and contempt for danger set a living example to his followers and spurred them on to deeds of bravery. On one occasion as he was directing the siege operations at a place where a lively fire of matchlocks and artillery was maintained by the enemy, cannon ball from the fort fell near him, but left him untouched, although it stretched twenty of his followers on the ground. On another occasion his general, Khan-i-Alam, was standing by his side when a bullet hit him and passed through his coat-of-mail and tunic, but it was checked in the inner garment and caused no injury, and it was considered that he owed his life to the good fortune attendant on the Emperor's presence. Akbar was so unremitting in his zeal and activity that he would often take up a gun and fire at one of the enemy on the ramparts of the citadel with effect. One night, as he was visiting the trenches, he perceived, by the fitful light, among the host of Rajpoots, a person of commanding aspect armed in mail directing the repairs of the trenches by torch-light. Forthwith the Emperor snatched Sangram, his favorite gun, from his attendant and shot him in the forehead. At this time Akbar was not aware who his victim was. Presently, he turned to Raja Bhagwan Das and remarked that "he felt afraid from his steadines of hand that he must have hit his mark." In truth, he had brought down his formidable foe, for the fallen hero was no other than the lion of Chittor, Jay Mal, governor of the place, a chief of great courage and ability. The garrison, on seeing that their gallant leader was no more, lost all heart, and abandoning the trenches, withdrew to the interior of the fort. The body of Jay Mal was carried to the tomb, where the women committed themselves to the flames with their leader's body. Nine queens, five princesses, with two infant sons, and many wives of commanders immolated themselves on the burning pyre. The men ran out to meet death, and, the Mohammedans mounting the ramparts unopposed, a desperate fight took place, in which eight thousand Rajpoots fell. By day-break Chittor was reduced and Akbar,

Siege of Chittor.

mounting his elephant, *Asman Shikoh*, entered it in triumph. From the ramparts of the fort there waved now in the place of the sun banner of the Rana, the green standard of Islam.

On 8th February 1658, Akbar, in pursuance of his vow travelled barefooted and in homely garb, with a small retinue, towards Ajmere, to pay his homage to the shrine of the saint. He had travelled as far as Mandelgarh when one of the disciples at the shrine heard the Saint in his dream saying that His Holiness had been strongly impressed with the sense of piety and devotion which the Emperor entertained for him, and that consequently he was pleased to direct that his Majesty should, dispense with continuing further a journey so inconvenient to himself. Accordingly, the Emperor performed the remainder of his journey on horse-back until within one stage of Ajmere when he alighted and resumed his journey on foot, reaching the mausoleum safely on Sunday, the 6th March, 1658.

In commemoration of his victory at Chittore, Akbar caused a pyramidal column of white stone, 35 feet high, to be erected on the spot where his tent had stood. The summit was crowned with a huge lamp, access to which was obtained by a spiral inner staircase. It is called Akbar's *dya*, or Akbar's lamp. Another measure which Akbar adopted to commemorate the event was the construction of two gigantic stone elephants with the figures of Jey Mal and Patta, the Rajput generals of Chittor, sitting on each. The Mahrattas when they captured Delhi, towards the end of last century, wreaked their vengeance by breaking them to pieces and burying the pieces underground. After the Mutiny the English found them uninjured, but riderless, buried 12 feet underground. They were disinterred, and one of them now stands in the public garden at Delhi.

Statues of Jay Mal and Patta.

Akbar generally hunted leopards thirty or forty kos from Agra. He had the faculty of taming a newly caught leopard for the chase in the short space of eighteen days. The royal leopard-keepers (of whom there were some two hundred) with difficulty trained it in a space of two or three months.

Hunting leopards.

Two remarkable stories of leopard-taming are mentioned by Abul Fazl, and are credited as miracles of Akbar. Once a leopard which had been caught, at a mere hint from His Majesty,

Remarkable stories of leopard-taming.

and without any previous training, brought a prey for Akbar. 'Those who were present had their eyes opened to truth.' At another time, 'attracted by the wonderful influence of the loving heart of His Majesty,' a leopard followed the Imperial suite without collar or chain, and obeyed every command like a sensible man. Once a tame deer made friendship with a tame leopard. They lived together and enjoyed each other's company. The leopard, when let loose against other deer, would not molest them. Previously leopards were never allowed to remain at liberty towards the close of the day; but, in consequence of the practical rules of training framed by Akbar, they were, in his time, let loose in the evening and yet remained obedient. The practice of blindfolding them was discontinued, and they were kept without covers for their heads without becoming unmanageable or molesting by-standers.

Deer hunting.

Deer were hunted by tamed leopards, They got the scent of the prey and indicated its position. They were taught, after having been shown a deer from a distance, to lie in ambush until the time came for them to spring and catch the animal. The feats performed by this animal show what artifices he resorts to in capturing his prey. In order to conceal himself, he would raise up dust with his fore feet and hind legs, or lie down so flat that it would be impossible to distinguish him from the surface of the ground. Akbar was greatly skilled in deer hunting. He could tell, by merely seeing the hide, to what hunting ground the deer had belonged.

Deer were also hunted with deer. A tamed and trained deer was let off, with a net put over his horns, which in the course of the struggle with the wild deer caused the latter's horn, or foot, or ear, to be entangled in it, whereupon the hunters, who lay in ambush, came and caught it.

Its sagacity.

Many stories are related of the sagacity and fidelity of deer. Abul Fazl gives an account of one trained deer which caused much sensation at Court. It had run away from Allahabad, where it had been taken from the Punjab, and, after crossing rivers and plains, returned to its home in the Punjab and rejoined its former keeper. The sound of musical instruments fascinates deer, as also does singing. Akbar, however, disapproved of these methods of hunting deer.

Akbar kept deer studs; and the animals born in captivity were employed for hunting purposes. His Majesty devised new methods of hunting deer. The skins were often given away to poor people as presents.

Hunting Siah-gosh.

In fulfilment of a vow made by Akbar on the birth-day of the heir-apparent, Salem, he never hunted on Fridays. He used the Siah-gosh, a plucky little animal, for hunting the hare and the fox. It also killed black deer.

Elephant hunts.

Previously, wild elephants were hunted with the aid of the beating of drums and blowing of pipes; the noise thus created confusing the unwieldy animal and frightening it, they ran in all directions in their terror, when the hunters threw ropes round their necks or feet and caught them. Tame female elephants were also employed in catching wild elephants. The driver stretched himself on the back of the female elephant and became motionless, so as not to betray his presence. The male elephant approached the female and was caught by means of ropes. Another method was to cause wild elephants to fall into a pit covered with grass, where they were then starved and kept without water until tamed. Another was to catch elephants by kindling fires and making much noise round their retreat, where an artificial door was put on one side of an artificial ditch. The animal was driven to it and caught with a rope. His Majesty invented a new method of catching herds of wild elephants. They were surrounded on three sides by drivers, one side being left open, at which several female elephants were stationed. The male elephants approaching from all sides to cover the females, the latter were gradually conducted to an enclosure, whither the males followed and were caught.

Hunting with hawks.

Akbar was very fond of hunting with hawks and trained falcons, *shahin* (royal white falcons), and *shanqar* (a black eyed species of falcon), and made them perform curious feats. He gave his *bashas* (sparrow hawks) several names. He also trained *báshás, bahris, shikruhs, lagars, jhagars, charghs, reckis, tarmatis, nusrelus, dhotis, molchins,* sparrows and quails for game and took great delight in sport of this kind. There were *Mir Shikars* (or superintendents of the chase) who taught these birds to chase and attack others. Under the *Mir Shikars* were *Ahdis* and other soldiers and footmen, mostly Kashmiris and Hindustanis. Birds were also received in the Imperial aviary as *pesh-kash* (or tribute), the aviary being in the charge of an officer called *Qush Begi* (superintendent of the aviary).

And with partridge. Hunting with partridge afforded much amusement. A trained partridge being put in a cage, hair-nets were placed round it. On a signal from the fowler the bird began to sing; and its voice attracted wild birds, which, coming to pay it a friendly visit, were entangled in the snares.

Hunting water-fowls. The hunting of water-fowl also afforded much entertainment. They were caught by hawks, or *baz* falcons, while swimming about, and were kept down till the hunters, with their boat, came and seized them. A rather curious way of catching them is mentioned by Abul Fazl. An artificial water-fowl of skin, with wings, beak and tail, was made. The body was hollow, and two holes were left in the skin to look through. The hunter put his head into it and stood in the water up to his neck, so that the figure of the bird only could be seen. He then went slowly towards the birds, who took the figure for one of their own species, whereupon the fowler pulled them, one after another, below the water. Other devices were also employed in the catching of birds.

Frogs. Frogs were also trained to seize sparrows, which afforded much amusement.

The game of *chaugan*. Akbar was fond of all manly sports and exercises. He was an excellent player of *chaugan* (hockey) and encouraged his Amirs to play it. According to his historian, he 'saw in it the means of acquiring promptitude and decision.' 'It tested the value of a man and strengthened the bonds of friendship.' It revealed concealed talents. It taught men the art of riding; it prompted courage; it accustomed animals to perform feats of agility and obey the reins. His Majesty astonished the spectators by the quickness of his motions and the ease and promptitude with which he hit the ball. He hit it in various ways and struck it while it was still in the air. He could play *chaugan* in the dark of the night, which caused no less astonishment to those with pretensions to being well versed in this art.

Akbar called pigeon-flying *Ishqbazi* (love-play). He occupied himself in this amusement with a sense of appreciation of the mysteries of nature which gifted a little creature like the pigeon with a sagacity peculiar to it, and with a view of setting an example to men of obedience to the commands of authority. It was, so his biographer maintains, from high motives that His Majesty paid so much attention to this amusement. Pigeon flying.

Presents of pigeons for the Emperor were sent by the kings of Iran and Turan, while merchants also brought many varieties from different countries. Akbar was fond of pigeons while very young; he discontinued pigeon-flying on growing to manhood, but on mature consideration again took to it.

A beautiful and well trained pigeon of bluish colour belonging to Khan-i-Azam Gokal Tash Khan, Akbar's foster brother, fell into His Majesty's hands. It was named Mohna, and the Emperor was so much pleased with its beauty and colour that he made it the chief of the Imperial pigeons. Several excellent pigeons descended from it and got the names *Ashki* (weeper), *Parizad* (the fairy), *Almas* (the diamond) and *Shah ludi* (Alo Royal). These, again, produced the choicest pigeons, and the species are mentioned in detail in the *Ain*. Akbar was an excellent judge of pigeons and carefully distinguished their several classes, for each of which seperate aviaries were constructed.

Pigeons were taught various feats, besides flying in the air in large numbers together, such as ascending and descending, now moving in one direction and now in another, at one time sitting on the umbrella and at another flying and beating the adversary's flock of pigeons, also in the act of flying, all at the whistle of the players, or on signs made by moving backward and forwards a flag attached to a long bamboo. They were made to perform the *bazi*, or lying on the back with the feet upwards and quickly turning round, and *charkh* (a rapid movement ending with the pigeon throwing itself over in a full circle) and many other interesting feats. Pigeons were kept for the sake of such sports as much as for the beauty of their plumage. The excellence of the form and the diversified hue of the birds were always objects of gratification to the Emperor.

According to the *Ain*, there were more than twenty thousand pigeons at the court, five hundred of which were of the finest breed called *khach*. These were held in great repute for their skill and for their many colours, which were very pleasing. Tumblers were much admired. The Emperor was so fond of pigeons that he would take them to his camp on cots carried by bearers. When the camp broke up, the pigeons followed. He improved the species of pigeons by cross-breeding, a thing never practised before. His intimate knowledge of the breeding of these birds caused no small amount of astonishment and admiration to his courtiers.

Akbar severe in punishing foes but generous towards friends.

Akbar was prompt in punishing enemies and showed them no mercy; but he was excessively kind to friends for whom he entertained feelings of affection. This feeling was mutual. Abul Fazl gives several instances of this. An incident is related in the description of the 7th year of the reign, 1562 A.D., the scene of the tragedy connected with it being the citadel of Agra.

A tragedy.

Adham Khan, son of Maham Angah, was a noble of Akbar's Court with a rank of 5,000. He and Monim Khan, *Khan-i-Khanan*, both envied and hated Mohammed Shamsuddin Atgah Khan, the foster father of Akbar. On the night of 12th Ramzan, when Monim Khan, Atgah Khan, Shahabuddin Ahmad Khan and other grandees, were holding a State council in the Dewan-i-Khas of the fort, Adham Khan suddenly entered the hall with a number of followers. All rose to greet him, when Adham Khan struck Atgah Khan with a dagger and made a sign to Khusham, one of his armed retainers, to despatch him. Khusham, having drawn his dagger, struck Atgah a blow with it on the breast. Atgah fled in the direction of the door-way, but fell down in the court-yard of the Dowlat Khana and instantly expired. Adham, with drawn dagger in his hand, then repaired to the sleeping apartment of the Emperor, who had been awakened by the noise in the State Hall. His Majesty came out, sword in hand, and cried, "Why have you killed my foster father, you son of a bitch *(bacha-i-lava)* Adham, seizing both the arms of Akbar with his hands, answered him: 'Stop a moment, your Majesty, and first enquire.' Akbar drew away his hands and struck Adham a blow in the face.

Adham was a powerful man, but the blow inflicted was so severe that he fell to the ground. 'What are you looking at'? said Akbar to two of the bye-standers, Farhat Khan and Sankram ? 'bind the man.' This was obeyed, and, by order of Akbar, Adham Khan was thrown down from the dais *(safu)* of the Dewan Khana to the ground, with his head downwards. Life not being quite extinct, he was dragged by the hair of the head to the terrace and again thrown down, which completed his death. The corpses of Adham Khan and Atgah Khan were sent to Delhi to be interred there.

Maham Angah, * the mother of Adham Khan, was ill at Delhi when the events above-mentioned took place. Believing that her son had only been imprisoned, she repaired to Agra. Akbar, on seeing her, said: He had killed my foster father, and I have taken his life.' He consoled the old lady, who left the hall saying: 'Your Majesty has done well.' Her malady increased and she died of a broken heart within forty days of the death of her son. Her corpse was sent to Delhi; Akbar, with the entire court, following it personally for a few paces, with tears in his eyes. He also sat in mourning. At Delhi a monument† of great beauty was built over the remains of Adham Khan and Maham Angah, by the orders of the Emperor. Maham Angah.

In the same way, Akbar consoled Mirza Aziz *koka*, son of Atgah Khan,‡ on the death of his father. The body of Atgah

* Maham Angah was one of Akbar's nurses and attended on Akbar from the cradle till after his accession. Her influence in the Haram and over Akbar himself was unbounded. She played a conspicuous part in bringing about the fall of Bahram Khan.

† The tomb of Adham Khan, otherwise known as *Bhul Bhulian*. or the Labyrinth, stands on the right of the road leading from the Qutub Minar, Delhi, to the village Mahrouli, within five minutes walk of the Minar. It is an octagon, with a diameter of 200 feet.

‡ The tomb of Mohammed Shamsuddin Atgah Khan, surnamed Azim Khan, is situated in the village of Nizamuddin *Aulia*, Delhi, within 20 yards of the tomb of the Saint. It was built by his second son Mirza Aziz Gokal Tash Khan.

Khan was removed to Delhi and burried in the village of Nizam-ud-din *Aulia.**

Akbar's walks in disguise.

With a view to keeping himself informed of the real condition of his people, and as a safeguard against the mal-practices of his officials, that the weak might not suffer at the hands of the strong, His Majesty used to visit the different quarters of the city and suburbs in disguise. In connection with the events of the 6th year of the reign, Abul Fazl notices an interesting incident relating to the Emperor's appearance in disguise in the suburbs of Agra, related to him by His Majesty himself. In the town of Bharaich, in Oudh, a grand fair is held annually at the tomb of Sálár Masud, a general of the armies of Mahmúd, who fell a martyr in one of the battles fought in India by that conqueror, and spears are displayed on the occasion in honour of the saint's memory. Large multitudes of people joined the fair from Agra. In the suburbs of the city itself a large fair was held in memory of the saint;† Akbar joined one of the Agra fairs in disguise, and was walking at random, when he was recognised by one of the roughs. This individual informed his associates of what he had seen, and the men began to look at the king with marked attention. Akbar, noticing this, instantly changed his face with such a skill that the fellows who had observed him fell into doubt regarding his identity, were puzzled and confessed that they had been mistaken and the person seen by them was not Akbar. The Emperor's own account as given by him to Abul Fazl and quoted by the latter in his book, is highly interesting. "Having noticed what the men said, I instantly moved one of my eyes, so as to appear squint eyed and changed my face in such a manner as not to be recognised by any body who had ever seen me. Having thus changed my features, I continued my rambles through the fair quite unconcerned and with the utmost composure of mind, looking at the objects in the fair. The men, having scrutinised me carefully, said to each other: 'Certainly, the king has not such eyes or features.

* The tomb of Mirza Aziz Gokal Tash, the foster brother of Akbar, is situated about 20 yards from the tomb of Azim Khan, his father, in Delhi. It is a 69 feet square hall, of sixty four pillers, and is hence called Chousath Khamba. It was built by the Mirza himself during his life-time. The pillars, screens, floor and ceiling of the tomb are all of marble.

† This fair called *Charion ka mela* is still held in Agra. It is also held in many other large towns of India.

He is not the king.' I then silently retired from the scene and entered the place."—Abul Fazl writes that, as His Majesty narrated the story to him, he, by way of illustration, moved one of his eyes and changed his face just as he had done at the fair, thus affording amusement as well as instruction to his learned friend and prudent minister.

He is witty.

Akbar possessed a witty genius, and his familiar conversation was full of humour. Once Shah Fání, a poet and a Chaughattai Turk of noble descent, said in Akbar's presence that no one surpassed him in three C's—chess, combat, composition—, whereupon the Emperor replied that he had forgotten a fourth, *viz.*, conceit. Fání was distinguished for personal courage in war and was proud of it.

And a good physiognomist.

He was a good physiognomist and had the power of seeing through men at a glance. He was a believer in lucky and unlucky days. This was due, of course, to his friendship with the Pandits and Brahmans.

Akbar's Library.

Akbar could neither read nor write, but he was gifted with a marvellous memory, penetrating judgment, quickness of fancy, and wise forecast. He had an extensive library, both in the Assembly Hall and the Harem, which was divided into several parts. The books consisted of Hindi, Persian, Arabic, Greek and Kashmerian works. His Majesty had every book read to him from beginning to end. At whatever page the reader stopped daily, His Majesty made a mark with his own pen, and the reading was renewed the following day from the place so marked. His Majesty rewarded the reader with gold or silver coin, according to the number of pages read to him. He was never tired of having a book read to him over again, but took renewed delight in rehearing it.

State offices.

Akbar observed no class or race distinction in bestowing State offices. From the lowest to the highest appointment in the gift of the Crown, every post was open to all his subjects, whatever their creed or nationality. Hindus were promoted side by side with Mohammedans and enjoyed equally his confidence and regard. He paid no regard to hereditary influence or genealogy, or ancestral fame, but favoured those who excelled in manners and attainments. He employed in his military service people of all classes, Jews, Persians, Turanis, Georgians, Pathans, Afghans, Kashmeris, &c., 'because,' maintained he, 'one class of people, if employed to the exclusion of others, would cause rebellions, as in the case of the Uzbecks and Quazilbashes, who dethroned their kings and raised the standard of revolt.'

System of advancing loans to officers.

Higher Officers of State who held grants of land and enjoyed high monthly salaries, might require money to meet their wants, or fall into pecuniary embarrassment. Under such circumstances, it would be contrary to Government rules to ask for a present. To provide for this contingency, His Majesty appointed a treasurer and a separate Mir Arz, who were to advance money to officers on loan, without prejudice to their dignity and honour, and without the annoyance of delay. Nothing was charged for the first year; in the second year the debt was increased by a sixteenth; in the third year by one-eighth. In the tenth year the sum was doubled, and after that there was no further increase. His Majesty also made donations and gave away elephants, horses and valuable articles as presents to officials and others. A treasurer was always in waiting at court, and alms were freely given to needy people, who also had daily, monthly, or yearly, stipends assigned to them.

Donations and presents.

Alms.

Ceremony of weighing His Majesty.

His Majesty was weighed twice a year against each of the following articles, namely, gold, quicksilver, perfumes, copper drugs, ghee, iron, rice, milk, seven kinds of grain and salt, which were all given away in alms. Sheep, goats, and fowls, to the number of years His Majesty had lived, were also given away as charity. On the lunar birthday he was weighed against eight articles, silver, tin, cloth, lead, fruits, mustard, oil and vegetables. On both occasions the birthday ceremony was celebrated with great eclat, and donations and grants of pardon were bestowed on people of all ranks.

Birth-day ceremony.

The real religion of Akbar.

Much has been said about the religious views of Akbar, but the question nevertheless remains unanswered, what religion he really professed. There is no doubt that his tolerant notions and independent ideas displayed themselves in his early years. They did not proceed from contempt for the religion of the Quran, or want of faith in the texts of Islam, but were rather the outcome of a contemplative mind, naturally given to research and investigation. In the early part of his reign, he was a Musalman of orthodox type, visiting the mausoleums of saints and paying obeisance and reverance to religious men. Even up to the 21st year of his reign, he spoke seriously of a pilgrimage to Mecca. It was not until the twenty-fourth year of his reign (A. D. 1579) that his religious ideas seem to have undergone a change. Notwithstanding his singular eccentricities, which at one time made him appear in the public hall of audience with the Hindu saffron mark on his forehead and at another prostrating himself before fire; now worshipping the sun, again causing himself to be worshipped; now placing the Christian Cross on his forehead, and again disputing the revelation claimed for the Quran, it seems that, whatever he may have been persuaded to do or adopt, by the persuasive eloquence of his councillors, Abul Fazl and Fyzi, known apostates from Islam, he never, in his heart, lost respect for the religion of his ancestors. This is manifest from the fact that the same Badaoni who has laboriously detailed the king's innovations in religion, has, in connection with the events of 990 A. H. (1582 A. D.), noted a circumstance which shows that the King never, at heart, gave up his respect for Islam. The author writes :—

"At this time Shah Abu Turab and Itimad Khan Gujrati, who had been together on a journey to Hijaz, returned and brought with them a stone of great weight, which required a strong man to lift it. A footprint was clearly to be seen on it, and Shah Abu Turab declared it to be the impression of the foot of the Prophet (God bless him and his family and give them peace).

برلوح سر تربت خود نقش تو کنند یم   تا روز قیامت سر ما وقدم تست

We have engraved thy foot's impression on the tablet of our grave,
In order that until the day of resurrection our head may be under thy foot.

His Majesty went a distance of four koss* to receive it and commanded his *Amirs* to carry it by turns a few steps, and in this way they brought it to the city."†

* The Emperor at this time (1582) resided in Futtehpur.

† Badaoni II, 310.

The whole conduct of Akbar through life shows that he really professed no religion. The whole aim of his life seems to have been to be at peace with all and respect so much of each religion as seemed to him to be based on just principles. His disgust with the Mullahs was caused chiefly by the machinations of Sheikh Mobarak and his two sons, who had suffered personal wrongs at their hands before they became the chief favourites of Akbar. His love for the Hindus was real. It was based on policy, and he was greatly influenced by his Hindu wives,* whom he desired to please. He believed in the existence of God and respected men of piety and sanctity in all religions. He was susceptible of flattery and thought there was no harm if he gave himself out as a viceregent of God upon earth, a position which, as a king, he actually held. He believed in the omnipotence of God, and thought that, as the one favoured by Him, his actions, which he understood really proceeded from Him, might affect the welfare of the community in matters yet in the womb of futurity. Hence his declarations as the leader of nations and his taking people into discipleship.

Divisions of Empire.

The Empire under Akbar was divided into fifteen Subas or Provinces,† which were subdivided into 105 Sirkars, which, again, were split into Parganas, or Mahals, regrouped into *dasturs*, or administrative jurisdictions. Agra was a *Suba*, as well as a *Sirkar*. The *Sirkar* of Agra, a tract of 1,864 square miles, comprised 31 Parganas, which were grouped into five *Dasturs, viz.*, Hawali, Agra, Etawa, Biana and Mandawa.

The *Suba* of Agra.

Mansabdars.

The royal princes held Mansabs, or military ranks, from 10,000 to 7,000 horse. After them came 30 Mansabdars, varying from 5,000 to 10. The soldiers under the Mansabdars were recruited from the clans of which they were the head. The monthly pay of a commander of 5,000 varied from Rs. 10,637 to Rs. 30,000; of 1,000 from Rs. 3,015½ to Rs. 8,000; of a captain of 100 from Rs. 313 to Rs. 760. The rank-holders had to provide horses, elephants, camels, arms, &c., out of their salaries. Each Mansabdar was to provide horses in proportion to his command,

Salaries.

* Akbar married two Hindu Rajput princesses.

† These were: Allahabad, Agra, Oudh, Ajmere, Ahmedabad, Behar, Bengal, Delhi, Kabul, Lahore, Multan, Malwa, Berar, Khandes and Ahmednagar.

so that a *Hazari*, or commendor of 1,000, was required to bring 1,800.

According to Abul Fazl, the local Militia of the provinces under Akbar amounted to 4,400,000; but this is probably an exaggeration. According to Badaoni, the standing army, *viz.*, troops under the Emperor's pay, numbered 25,000, of whom 12,000 were troopers and 13,000 artillery and matchlock-men. These troopers were paid from the royal treasury and formed the Emperor's bodyguard. The Army.

The revenue system of Akbar was essentially the same as that introduced by Sher Shah Sur, Afghan. He only carried that system into effect which Sher Shah was unable to extend to all parts of India during his short reign. The objects of this system were three-fold:— Revenue system.

1. To obtain a correct measurement of all lands.

2. To ascertain the produce of each *bigha* of land, and to fix the Government revenue on it.

3. To settle in money the Government share of the produce.

He worked out this system under Todar Mal and Mozaffar Khan, both eminent financiers. His estimated annual gross income, according to Edward Thomas, was £32,000,000. Annual gross income.

Akbar's Harem, according to the *Ain*, comprised more than five thousand women, for each of whom a separate apartment was allowed. They were divided into several sections, and there were female Daroghas to superintend each section. The women of the highest rank each received from Rs. 1,610 to 1,028 rupees *per mensem*. Under Shah Jahan and Aurangzeb, the Queens and Princesses drew much larger salaries. Mumtaz Mahal, wife of Shah Jahan, was allowed ten lakhs, and the Begam Saheb, sister of Aurangzeb, twelve lakhs per annum. The inside of the Harem, in Akbar's time, was guarded by chaste and sober women, the most trustworthy of them being placed about the Emperor's apartments. Outside the enclosure were placed eunuchs, and Imperial household.

beyond them Rajput guards, the watchmen at the gates being the last of the guards.*

The Imperial household did not differ materially from that of the later sovereigns; the expenditure in 1595 was Rs. 7,729,669, although the salaries of several officers of the court figured in the military budget.

Akbar had eight wives:—

Akbar's wives and children.

1. Sultana Raqia Begam, daughter of Mirza Handal, uncle of Akbar. She was Akbar's first wife. She tended Shah Jahan; and Nurjahan, after the murder of Sher Afgan, staid with her. Akbar had no children by her. She died in her 84th year, in 1035 (1625 A. D.), or the 20th year of Jahangir's reign.

2. Sultana Salema Begam, daughter of Mirza Nuruddin, Mohammad and Gul Rukh Begam (a daughter of Baber). Behram Khan married her in the beginning of Akbar's reign. After the death of Behram Khan, Akbar married her, in 968 (1560 A. D.). Her poetical name was Mukhfi (concealed).

3. The daughter of Raja Behari Mal and sister of Raja Bhagwan Das, married to Akbar in Sambhar, in 968 (1560).

4. The beautiful wife of Abdulwasi, married in 970 (1662.),

5. Jodh Bái, or princess of Jodhpur, the mother of Jahangir, called Mariam ul Zamani.† She died in the month of Rajab, 1032 (1622 A. D.), or the 17th year of Jahángir's reign.

6. Bibi Doulat Shád.

7. A daughter of Abdullah Khan Moghal.

8. A daughter of Miran Mobarak Shah, of Khandes.

Akbar had three sons, Sultan Salem (the Emperor Jahangir); Sultan Morad and Sultan Danial; and three daughters, Shahzada Khanam, born three months after Salem; Shukrunnissa Begam, who, in 1001 (1592), was married to Mirza Shah Rukh; and Aram Bano Begam, both born after Sultan Danial.‡

* The Moghal Emperors lived in the same style as the old Hindu Rajas. They kept extensive seraglios, went out in camp with their armies, took their wives with them to camp and were guarded by armed women. They also took their trained beasts with their camp.

† Akbar's mother had the title Marian Makani.

‡ For an account of their tombs see Chapter II. "Sekandra."

His personal appearance and character.

Akbar was a strongly built man, with a handsome face, and charming manners. The Portuguese Jesuits who went from Goa, describe him as "a man of about fifty, white like a European, and of sagacious intellect." He was of middle height, but rather inclined to be tall, and, like his father, having a tendency to be corpulent, which, however, was well kept in check by the physical activity for which he was so much noted. Like Taimur, he had long arms and hands. His complexion was nut-coloured; his forehead open; his eyes black, and his eyebrows joined each other from opposite directions; under these bushy brows his eyes sparkled with stately dignity. The lion's strength which he possessed was probably due to the extraordinary breadth of his chest and to his long sinewy arms and hands. A fleshy wart on the left side of his nose gave his countenance additional grace, and physiognomists considered it very auspicious. He possessed a loud, commanding voice, and his speech was elegant and pleasing. He possessed prodigious strength, and was proud of it and of his sporting feats, his hunting exploits, his riding excursions and his mastery over elephants. His iron constitution enabled him to undergo toil and fatigue. On one occasion he rode from Agra to Ajmere (220 miles) in two successive days. He was both affable and majestic, forbearing and severe. Although he had to fight many battles and effected reforms in the civil administration of his country such as had never been introduced before, yet he so judiciously arranged his time that he found ample leisure for increasing his knowledge and for prosecuting sportive pursuits. He was never fond of war, but was always ready to take the field and was firm and decided in action He was generous towards a conquered foe and respected the law of Manu in regard to kingcraft which provides, that "when a Raja has conquered a country, he should respect the laws of the country; or he may form an alliance with the Raja whom he has conquered and act in union with him, for, by securing a firm ally a Raja obtains greater srength than by gaining wealth and territory." Following these noble principles, Akbar not only forgave his vanquished opponents, but raised them to the highest rank of local nobility. He protected his Hindu subjects by the abolition of slavery and the poll-tax, and sheltered their priests and temples. He tolerated all religions. Jahangir, who held different notions from those of his father on religion, thus describes Akbar's views on the subject in his autobiography.

His advice to Jahangir his son.

"Having on one occasion", writes he, "asked my father why he had forbidden any one to prevent or interfere with the building of these haunts of idolatry (*i. e.* Hindu temples) his reply was in the following terms:—'My dear child, I find myself a puissant monarch, the shadow of God upon earth. I have seen that He bestows the blessings of His gracious Providence upon all his creatures without distinction. Ill should I discharge the duties of my exalted station, were I to withhold compassion and indulgence from any of those entrusted to my charge. With all of the human race, with all of God's creatures, I am at peace; why, then, should I permit myself, for any consideration, to be the cause of molestation or aggression to any one? Besides, are not five parts in six of mankind either Hindus or aliens to the faith; and were I to be governed by motives of the kind suggested in your enquiry, what alternative could I have but to put them all to death? I have, therefore, thought it my wisest plan to let these men alone. Neither is it to be forgotten, that the class of whom we are speaking, in common with the other inhabitants of Agra, are usefully engaged, either in the pursuits of science or of improvements for the benefit of mankind, and have in numerous instances arrived at the highest distinctions in the State, there being, indeed, to be found in this city men of every description and of every religion on the face of the earth.'"

His idea of the Hindus.

What he thought of the Hindus of Agra.

The Emperor's illness.

The causes of the Emperor's illness have been explained in the chapter on the history of Agra.* It was chiefly brought about by depression of spirits and vexation. One immediate cause was the worry and excitement caused by the conduct of Khusrow, the eldest son of Salem (Jahangir), at an elephant fight. Salem had an elephant known by the name of *Giran bar* which was supposed to be a match for any elephant belonging to Akbar's stables, but whose strength was believed to be only equal to that *Abrup*, one of Khusrow's elephants. Akbar, therefore ordered a fight, to see which of them would prove the champion. A fight was arranged. The custom in such combats

* See pages 21 and 22 *ante*.

between two elephants was to keep a third in readiness, as *Tabancha, i.e.*, to assist any animal when it was severely handled by its adversary. At the show, Akbar and Khuram (Shah Jahan) sat in one window. Salem and Khusrow were on horse back in the *maidan*. *Giranbar* completely defeated *Abrup*; and, as he was being worsted, the *Tabancha* elephant was sent forward to assist *Abrup*. Salem's men, anxious to see the final victory won by *Giranbar*, pelted the *Tabancha* with stones and wounded the driver. Akbar was annoyed at this, and sent Khurram to Salem to ask him not to break the rules, as all the elephants would be eventually his. Salem said that the attack with stones had not received his sanction, and Khurram, satisfied with this answer, returned to his grandfather. An attempt was then made to separate the elephants by means of fireworks, but in vain. It so happened that *Giranbar* beat the *Tabancha* elephant also, and the defeated elephants, running away worsted, threw themselves into the river Jumna. Akbar was more annoyed at this; but his anger was intensified when Khusrow openly abused his father in unmeasured terms in the hearing of the Emperor Akbar rose and withdrew, in great disgust, and, next morning, he sent for his physician, Ali, and told him that the bad behaviour of Khusrow had caused him much vexation and made him ill. He was attacked by dysentery, or acute diarrhœa. His physician refrained for eight days from administering any medicine, hoping that the Emperor's strength of constitution would overcome the disease. But, the hope not being realized, recourse was had to a most powerful astringent. This had the effect of putting a stop to the dysentery; but fever and strangury supervened. **His death 1605.** Purgatives were administered, but these renewed the first ailment, to which the Emperor succumbed. The event occurred on 13th October 1605. As stated elsewhere "he died in all the forms of a good Mossalman."*

---

* See page 22 *ante*.—Our account receives further corroboration from the narrative of the 3rd mission despatched to Abkar's Court by the Jesuit authori- ties at Goa which succeeded in establishing Churches in Lahore and Agra, and which persevered its labours from 1595 to a time considerably later than the Em- peror's death. The head of the mission was Father Jerome Xavier, a nephew of St. Francis. The mission failed, in converting the Emperor. The nature of Akbar's end is clearly shown in a manuscript report written by Father Antony Botelho, who was Provincial some years after Akbar's death. In this report the Father narrates a conversation, which he held with the Adal Shahi Prince of Bijapur and in which the prince had said to him, "Sachehe quibara Batxa Hacabar Khristan muha qul nan?" (Such hai ki bara badshah Akbar Khristan mua ki nahin ?) Is it true or not that the great Emperor Akbar died a Christian? To which the Father replied, "Sire, I would it were so, but the Emperor while living failed to be converted, and at the last died, as he was born, a Muham- madan." "Jasuit mission to the Emperor Akbar," by E. D. Maclagan, Esq.

THE COURT OF AKBAR.

The chief friend and minister of the Emperor Akbar was

SHEIK ABUL FAZL.

He was born at Agra on 6th Moharram, 958 (14th January, 1551), during the reign of Islam Shah *Sur Pathan*.

Abul Fazl has devoted a chapter in the third volume of the Ain-i-Akbari to an account of his family.

Family home, Yaman in Arabia Felix.

"I had intended," he says, "to write a book on the history of my family; but the demands on my time have been so great that this intention could not be fulfilled. I therefore take this opportunity of giving a brief account of my family at the conclusion of this work and trust it will be read with interest." The Sheikh then informs us that his ancestors were originally residents of Yaman or Arabia Felix. Sheikh Musa, his fifth ancestor having emigrated from the country in the 9th century, settled in a place called *Riè* in Siwistan (Sindh). Although he had come from a desert to the city, he did not give up his habit of seclusion and devoted his time to contemplation and prayer. His children followed his good example in piety and devotion, and the whole family lived in happiness and peace in their adopted home.

Sheikh Musa, Abul Fazl's 5th ancestor, settles in Sindh, 9th century A. H.

Towards the beginning of the 10th century, Sheik Khizr, the then head of the family, after a sojourn in Hijaz in Arabia and renewal of his acquaintance with the people of his tribe, emigrated to India, with a number of relations and friends, and settled at Nagor, north-west of Ajmere. He was a pious devotee, and his mind was imbued with mystic lore. He lived in the society of pious and holy men and enjoyed the confidence and esteem of personages renowned for piety, like Syad Yahya Bokhari of Uch, the successor of Makhdum Jahanian, Sheik Abdul Razzak Quadri of Baghdad, the descendant of the great saint, Syad Abdul Quadar of Jilan, and Sheik Eusuf of Sindh, all men of great accomplishments and erudition.

Sheikh Khizr, head of the family, emigrates to India, 10th century A. H.

Settles in Nagor.

Sheikh Mobarak, father of Abul Fazl, born 1505 A. D.

Sheik Mobarak, the father of Abul Fazl, was born at Nagor in 911 (1505). At the early age of four, signs of wisdom were apparent from his forehead and he gave abundant proof of extraordinary mental capacity. At nine, he amassed vast treasures from the store-house of knowledge, and at fourteen he became an accomplished scholar. He moulded his character in the company of Sheik Atta, a learned man of Turkish origin who having received his early education in Turan and Iran, settled in Nagor in the time of Sekandar Lodi, became a disciple of Sheik Sálár Nagouri and died at the advanced age of hundred and twenty. Sheik Khizr had now resolved to make Nagor his permanent abode, and, with that object in view, he again proceeded to Sindh to bring more members of the family to Hindustan; but he died on the way. At this juncture Nagor was visited with a severe famine and pestilence, and the family was reduced to such misery that, of the whole of its members, only Sheikh Mobarak and his old mother survived.

His early youth.

Death of Sheikh Khizr.

Sheikh Mobarak was very fond of travel and intercourse with the great teachers of the country, his object being to benefit by their society and to gain varied experience; but he could not carry out this desire, owing to respect for his aged mother, who, out of maternal affection, was unwilling to part with her son. He formed the acquaintance of Sheikh Fyazi, of Bokhara, and was, through him, introduced to the great saint Obedullah, surnamed Khawja Ihrar, and was greatly benefited by his teachings and companionship. About this time his mother died, and, the Maldeo disturbances having commenced, Mobarak carried out his old plan of journeying through the country. He proceeded to Ahmadabad, in Gujrat, and, by association with the renowned masters such as Sheikh Ibn-i-Arabi, Sheikh Ibn-i-Farz and Sheikh Sadrud-din, increased and embellished his encyclopædic attainments. His knowledge extended to every branch of learning, and he became thoroughly versed in the laws of *Málik, Sháfai, Abu Hanfia, Hambal* and *Imamia*, the great sections of the sect of Islam. At the outset he was himself a follower of *Abu Hanfia* doctrines. In Ahmadabad he took to the discipleship of Abul Fazl, the celebrated orator from Khawarazm in Persia, and was greatly benefited by the society of several men of great sanctity and learning, such as Sheikh Omar of Thatta and Sheikh Eusuf.

Sheikh Mobarak's reverence for his mother.

Her death.

Journey to Ahmadabad, Gujrat.

His great teachers.

After a stay of several years in Ahmadabad, Sheikh Mobarak, acting on the advice of his religious teachers, proceeded

Proceeds to Agra, 1543 A. D.

to Agra, the capital of the Indian Empire. The advice of his Sheikhs was that, if success should not attend his undertakings in Agra, he should then make his way to Turan and Iran. Mobarak arrived at Agra on Wednesday, the 6th of Moharram, 950 (1543), and had an interview with Sheikh Ala-ud-din *Majzub*, a holy man who, says Abul Fazl, " knew the secrets of the heart and the mysteries of the grave." The saint predicted a great and brilliant future for Mobarak on the soil of Hind. Gladdened by the happy prophecy of the holy man, Mobarak settled on the left bank of the Jumna, opposite the city of Agra, close to the Charbagh villa of Babar, then called Nur Afshan, but now styled Ram Bagh, and in the neighbourhood of Mir Rafi-ud-din Safvi, a saintly man, who received him with great kindness. The Mohalla was inhabited by a Kuresh tribe, among whom Mobarak made many personal friends. The Mir was a native of Injú, in Shiraz, and lived in Agra on a magnificent scale. He had travelled in Hijaz, Arabia and Egypt and was a disciple of Moulana Jalaludin *Dawámi*. In Egypt he took to the discipleship of Sheikh Sakháwí, of Cairo, the follower of Sheikh Ibni Hajar Asqalani. Mobarak secured a conspicuous place among the Mir's disciples, and when the Mir died, in 954 (1547), he embarked on his career of diffusing knowledge by becoming a teacher of sciences. He had a large number of pupils, while hundreds were benefited by his oratory and preachings on different subjects. This was the time when the Pathan Emperors held sway over India, and, as the fame of Mobarak spread, his friends made a proposal to have an allowance fixed for him from the Imperial court; but, possessed as the Sheikh was of a lofty spirit, he declined the idea. It was about this time that Mobarak's two eldest sons, Abul Faiz and, four years later, Abul Fazl, were born. Abul Fazl says in his description of Agra in the *Ain* 'On the other side of the Jamna is the Char Bagh villa, founded by *Firdous Makani* (the Emperor Baber). There the writer of these pages was born, and there are the resting places of his father and his elder brother.* Sheikh Alaudin *Majzúb* and Mir Rafiuddin *Safwi* also lie buried there.'

Settles in Charbagh on the left bank of the Jumna.

His acquaintance with Mir Rafi-uddin Safvi.

Becomes a teacher of sciences.

Period of Pathan Emperors.

Birth of Abul Faiz(1547) and Fyzi (1551).

---

* The bodies were subsequently removed to the other side of the Jamna ; but when that was, does not appear. See Chapter II.

Mubarak's instruction of his sons.

The encyclopædic knowledge possessed by Sheikh Mubarak and the universality of his erudition are apparent from the instruction he gave to his sons, Fyzi and Abul Fazl. It was this early instruction that implanted in the minds of the brothers the anti-Islamitic views which so much influenced Akbar's life. There are numerous passages in Abul Fazl's works in which he speaks of his father in terms of filial piety and devotion. He possessed a comprehensive genius and a wonderful memory which served him as a repository of his vast learning.

Their anti-Islamitic views.

The teachings of Sheikh Mobarak.

Hitherto Sheikh Mubarak had devoted his time to teaching science; but, on Humayun's reconquering India, he also made theology and a discourse on the mysteries of nature the theme of his teachings. Public peace was disturbed in 1556, when Hemu occupied Agra. Sheikh Mubarak withdrew from public life temporarily; but his influence at the court of the usurper of the throne of India was still so great, that, on the Sheikh's recommendation, a number of Ulemas and notables of the city who had been captured by his men were released and Hemu offered his apologies to the venerable Sheikh through a deputation of his officers sent to him.

First year of Akbar's reign. A severe drought.

The first year of Akbar's reign was marked by a severe drought, which caused great ravages throughout the country. The population dispersed, and in Agra only a few families of any importance remained. This was followed by a plague, which desolated the country, and many cities were depopulated. None of these calamities led Sheikh Mubarak to desert his adopted home. Abul Fazl writes that he was at this time in his fifth year. He had a perfect recollection of this great calamity, in which family after family perished. In the once flourishing village in which Sheikh Mubarak had settled, only seventy persons of both sexes were left. These dragged on their existence on a few *sirs* of boiled grain obtained with much difficulty, and to some only its juice could be served to keep flesh and soul together. When order and prosperity were restored in the country, people as usual flocked round Sheikh Mubarak to receive from him lessons in science and theology. With the fame of his learning, the number of his disciples increased and the importance and influence he gained created jealousy among

And plague.

Jealousy of the Ulemas.

rival Ulemas. He was charged with being a follower of the *Mahdawia* sect which had found a zealous supporter in Sheikh Alai.

Ascendancy of the Mahdawia sect in later Pathan period

There is a tradition among the Mohamadans of a prophecy by Mohammad of the appearance of the Imam Mahdi, or the 'Lord of the period,' towards the end of the world's existence. This Mahdi is to be of the family of the Prophet, a descendant of Fatima, daughter of the Prophet and wife of Ali. He is to appear in the latter days of Islam, when there shall be 'a general decadence in political power and in morals' in the Moslem world. Towards the beginning of the 10th century, of the Mohamadan or the beginning of the 15th century after Christ, several Mahdis of great pretensions arose in India. Foremost among them was Mir Mohammad, son of Mir Syad Khan of Jaunpur. He announced to the world his mission that he had been sent to this earth to deter men from sin and wickedness and lead them to the path of virtue and righteousness, and that a voice from heaven had whispered in his ears the divine errand, *Anta Mahdi*, 'thou art Mahdi.' Thus declaring himself commissioned, he embarked on his career as a public preacher and teacher of religion. His great oratorical powers gained for him many followers who believed in his miracles. He found a zealous follower in Sultan Mohammad I, King of Gujrat, but was subsequently compelled by his enemies to leave for Mecca, whence he proceeded to Baluchistan, where he died in 911 A. H. (1505 A. D.). His tomb became a place of great pilgrimage, and after his death the sect founded by him continued to flourish.

Mir Mohammad of Jaunpur declares himself the Mahdi of the age.

His death, 1505 A.D.

Sheikh Alái another Mahdi, 1528.

Another Mahdi who appeared about this time was Sheikh Alai, a Bengali Musulman, who settled in Biáná in 935 A. H. (1528 A. D.). His fame reached Islam Shah, who summoned him to Agra, and although the King was resolved at first to put him to death as a dangerous demagogue, he was so charmed by the eloquence of an address which Alai delivered, in the presence of His Majesty, on the vanity of the world and the instability of earthly riches, that he not only pardoned the Sheikh, but sent cooked provisions for him from the royal kitchen.

Mubarak becomes attached to Mahdawia sect.

It was about this time that Sheikh Mubarak became attached to the Mahdawia sect; and an influential body at court, namely the learned men of the Empire, became bitterly hostile to his interests. This body of learned men was headed by Moulana Abdulla, of Sultanpur, surnamed *Makhdum ul Mulk;* and for more than twenty years Mubarak was persecuted; his lands were confiscated, and he was compelled to flee for his life, until his sons grew up and turned the tables on his persecutors. **He is persecuted.**

The persecution of the Mahdawia leaders went on rigorously during the latter part of Islam Shah's reign. Thus, Mian Abdullah, a Niazi Afghan and a disciple of Syad Mohammad of Jaunpur, who, being summoned to His Majesty's presence at Bianah, had failed to observe the usual etiquette, was so severely beaten in the King's presence that he was left for dead on the ground. While the royal camp was in the Panjab, Sheikh Alai was, under the King's orders, whipped by a menial so severely that some bad wounds he had on his neck broke open and the Sheikh fainted and died. His body was trampled under the feet of an elephant, and orders were passed that it should not be buried, when, to the terror of all, a most destructive cyclone suddenly arose, and, when it abated, Alai's body, so the story goes, was found literally buried under roses and flowers. This happened in 957 A.H. (1550 A.D.). The end of Islam Shah and the downfall of his Empire soon followed. **So are other leaders of Mahdawia sect.** **Death of Sheikh Alái, 1550 A.D.**

The death of Sheikh Alai was a severe blow to the Mahdawis and a great triumph to the learned at court. The persecution of the Mahdawis continued with vigour until after Akbar established his court at Agra. The party of *Ulemas*, conspicuous among whom were Sheikh Abdul Nabi and Makhdum-ul Mulk, poisoned Akbar's ears against Sheikh Mubarak, representing that he belonged to the class of innovators, and was not only himself beguiled, but led others astray. Having in some sort obtained the king's permission, they sent police officers to seize the person of Mubarak and to produce him before the Emperor. Not finding the Sheikh and his two sons in his house, they pulled down the pulpit of his prayer room. The Sheikh fled to Fattehpur Sikri and employed Sheikh Salem Chishti, who was then in the height of his glory, to mediate in his behalf with the Emperor; but the venerable Sheikh sent some money through his disciples to Mubarak, and advised him **Persecution of Mahdawis continues till the beginning of Akbar's reign.** **Flight of Mubarak Fattehpur Sikri.**

The troubles of Mubarak and his sons.

to proceed to Gujrat. Mubarak, seeing that Sheikh Salem took no interest in his well-being, returned secretly to Agra, where he went to the house of a friend to seek protection. 'That friend,' writes Abul Fazl, 'stood up in dismay and fear', and pointed out to Mubarak a dark and small inner room of the house, in which he lived for two days with his sons Fyzi and Abul Fazl, suffering much trouble and inconvenience. The friend ultimately showed the cold shoulder to his uninvited guests, who now went successively to the house of a second and third friend, who each of them harboured them for a day or two and then turned them out. They then fled from Agra and went to a village where they were hospitably received by a friendly Zamindar. The king was at this time at Agra; and Fyzi went to Fattehpur Sikri, and induced some of his father's friends there to make representation on his behalf to His Majesty. Mubarak and Abul Fazl, after remaining for a month in the village, returned to Agra and concealed themselves in the house of a friend.

Akbar's wrath against him.

The representations at Court made in behalf of Sheikh Mubarak by his friends had the contrary effect. The King's wrath against the Sheikh was renewed. He severely censured the men who had mediated, and, addressing them, said: "Do you think I am ignorant of his whereabouts? I know where he is. But don't you know the *Ulemas* have passed *fatwas* (or religious sentences) against him, and I am unable to pass any orders contrary to their decree."

Akbar's first attachment to the Ulemas.

The above incident shows how strongly Akbar was attached to the party of the learned, before Mubarak and his sons, having gained the ascendancy, turned the scale in their favour, a complete change was effected in Akbar's mind and so severe a blow was inflicted on the *Ulemas* that it resulted in their final downfall.

Mubarak again flies from Agra.

When the news from court reached Mubarak, he was again compelled to fly from Agra to save his life. This time he sought protection with an Amir in the king's service who was just then in camp, a few miles from the metropolis, and in whose friendship he reposed some reliance. The fugitives (father and sons) reached the Amir's camp at night. Not knowing the state of affairs at Court, he accorded them a warm reception; but when, after three days, he learnt how matters stood, he assumed a dubious attitude. One morning, without giving his now unwelcome hosts any notice, he left his camp, and his servants began to take down the tents. The tent in which Mubarak and his sons had been accommodated, was also taken down, packed up on the backs of mules and taken away, while Mubarak and his two sons remained sitting on the bare ground. The fugitives walked to a village on foot, but, on reaching it, found, to their dismay, that there was an enemy of theirs in it who would seize them instantly if he knew of their visit. Tired of life, they fled to another village, but found themselves unwelcome there also. They therefore retraced their steps to Agra at night and took refuge with a friend by whom they were well treated. They remained in his house for two months, during which time their friends at Court seized favorable opportunities of speaking to the king in their behalf. They were much assisted by Akbar's foster brother, Khan-i-Azim Mirza Kokah, who allayed all doubts in the Emperor's mind. His Majesty's displeasure abated by degrees, and he was so far conciliated that he ordered Sheikh Mubarak to attend the Court. The Sheikh repaired to the Court, accompanied by his son, Fyzi, and had the honour of an audience with the Emperor. Abul Fazl was still too young to be introduced to His Majesty. Akbar received Sheikh Mubarak honourably and spoke to him with kindness. From this time Mubarak embraced the *Sufi* creed and professed to be of Chishti's persuasion. When the Court was at Delhi, he paid regular visits to the Mausoleums of Khawaja Kutabuddin, Bukhtiar Kaki and Khawaja Nizamuddin *Aulia*, the celebrated saints of Delhi, this may have been due to policy, for Mubarak had no religion. He regularly attended Court and in one of his visits introduced Abul Fazl to the Emperor, who was much struck by the youthful scholar's address and the great intelligence he showed in his conversation. From this time Akbar began to look on Mubarak and his sons with much favour, and his regard for them increased. Abul Fazl, having been brought up in the school of adversity, learnt to be polite and forbearing. He writes: "I made a vow to the Creator not to be revengeful to my enemies, but to forbear and be forgetful of their vicious acts." And be it said to his honour that he kept his word to the last. He rose to

His and his sons' misfortunes and troubles.

Khan-i-Azim Mirza Kokah intercedes in his behalf to the Emperor.

Is introduced to His Majesty.

Youthful Abul Fazl's first interview with Akbar.

How Abul Fazl's character was formed.

the highest offices in the realm and enjoyed the most valued privilege of the king's confidence, yet he behaved mildly towards his enemies; when hot words occurred at religious gatherings, his speeches were characterized by moderation, and he never lost his self-control. There are several passages in the *Ain*, the *Akbarnama* and his famous *Munashiat*, or letters, in which he has dealt with the question of religious controversy; but even towards the worst enemies of his family, like Sheikh Abdul Nabi and Makhmdum-ul-Mulk, who had persecuted them, brought ruin on them, and all but killed his father, he has used temperate language, and, in commenting on their actions, never exceeded the bounds of fair criticism. How magnanimous Abul Fazl was, may be judged from the circumstance that when noticing, in his great work, the *Akbarnama*, the banishment of these men, he has used not a word indicative, even indirectly, of his personal grievance.

His early education.

At the early age of fifteen he showed signs of development of mental powers and had completed the course of study in the branches of knowledge known as *maqul* and *manqul*, namely, those based on reason and testimony. Like his father, he commenced his career by taking to the profession of teaching at the age of twenty. As an instance of his extraordinary mental powers, it is related that a manuscript of rare value, composed by Isphahani, a celebrated poet, was handed to him in a damaged condition, one half of each page vertically from top to bottom being effaced in most parts, or burnt, and the passages in them being either wholly wanting or unintelligible. Abul Fazl, with a sagacity and skill peculiar to himself, restored the passages wanting in each of the half lines so precisely and accurately that when, several months after, a complete copy of the work turned up, so remarkable an agreement was found, on comparison, that it appeared as if the author himself had been restored to life and rewritten the manuscript from memory. His friends were not a little struck by the wonderful acuteness, quickness and soundness of perception possessed by the youthful scholar.

His extraordinary mental powers.

His indifference for politics.

Abul Fazl was so completely given up to study that he thought little of the outside world and was indifferent to the affairs of court, where his father had numerous enemies. It was not until Akbar had invited Fyzi to attend court, and the latter had persistently admonished him to look after the interests of the family at the Imperial Court, that Abul Fazl was persuaded to give up the idea of leading the life of a recluse. It was in the seventeenth year of his age that a change was wrought in his mind and he adopted a different mode of living from that which he had until then pursued.

Of his first introduction at Court, Abul Fazl thus writes in the *Akbarnama :* "In these days (19th year of the reign, or 1574 (A. D.), assisted by good fortune, I was invited to the king's presence and had the honour of an interview with him. The particulars are briefly these. From the age of five to fifteen, I was under the tutelage of my father end acquired proficiency in the branches of science known as *Hikami* (philosophy) and *Naqli* (tradition). Although the gate of wisdom opened on me and I was familiar with the laws of thought, yet, owing to bad luck, I became conceited and arrogant, and preferred a retired life. The number of pupils that gathered around me only served to increase my pedantry. Imprudence and injudiciousness had so gained the mastery over me, that I became intoxicated with the ideas of seclusion and solitude. Although my days were spent in teaching science to students, yet I went to the wilderness at night and there enjoyed the company of the seekers after truth and was profited by men who, though empty-handed, were rich in mind and heart. The controversies among the so-called learned and the dissensions among the false pretenders excited my wonder and disgust. I had neither the power to keep silence nor the will to speak out. Although the wholesome advice of my father prevented me from outbreaks of frenzy, yet judicious treatment failed to be of any avail to my disturbed mind. Sometimes my heart was drawn to the philosophers of Khata (Northern China), at others to the works of Lebanon; sometimes I felt inclined to try arguments with the *Lamas* of Tibet; at others I thought of venturing on an interview with the Christian Fathers of Portugal; sometimes I longed to associate with the Sun-worshippers of Fárs; at others I felt anxious to have recourse to the doctors of the Zendavesta. I had become tired of the company of the learned of my own land. I was advised by my father, brothers and friends, to go to Agra and attend

His account of his first introduction into the Court.

the Imperial Court, as an interview with the Emperor was calculated to relieve me of much of my anxiety. I was indifferent at first to their admonitions, but at last yielded, proceeded to Agra, the capital, and there had the honour of an audience with the Emperor. Having no riches to present, I laid before His Majesty the commentary on the *Ayat ul Kursi* of the Koran, as a present. The offering was graciously accepted and a favorable reception accorded me. Thus, I was, for the first time, introduced to Court. I need hardly add, the affable and courteous manner in which I was received, and the frank and kind conversation His Majesty had with me, acted on me like magic, and produced in my mind a deep impression of affection which I have ever since cherished for him."

Fyzi accompanies the Royal camp to eastern Bengal and Behar.

Soon after this (1575 A. D.), the Emperor embarked on his great enterprise, the subjugation of eastern Bengal and Behar. Fyzi accompanied the royal camp, while Abul Fazl staid in Agra. The Emperor asked Fyzi after Abul Fazl in camp, and so the latter presented himself before His Majesty as soon as the Emperor returned to Fattehpur Sikri. How the Emperor noticed him in the grand mosque of Fattehpur Sikri and was presented with a commentary on the opening chapter of the Koran, entitled *Surah Fath*, or the chapter of victory, has been related in the account of Fattehpur Sikri.*

Abul Fazl's interview with Akbar in the grand mosque of Fattehpur Sikri.

The Thursday evening meetings.

It was soon after the Emperor's return from Bengal that the memorable Thursday evening religious controversies, in which His Majesty himself took a prominent part, were instituted. The leader of the Emperor's party was Abul Fazl, who succeeded in breaking the union of the *Ulemas*, who now were divided among themselves. Abul Fazl so skilfully shifted the disputes from one point to another that the dissensions among them reached the highest pitch. It was at this time that Akbar was persuaded to assume the spiritual, in addition to the temporal, power, and the famous document, drafted by Sheikh Mubarak, was promulgated in which the rank of *Mujtahid*, or infalliable authority on all matters relating to Islam, was assigned to the Emperor, and the power of the Church concentrated in the person of the "Just King," who alone

Akbar assumes the spiritual leadership of the people.

* See Chapter II., page 153 *ante*.

had power to legislate, the learned and the lawyers of the faith being bound by his decision. "The document," says Abul Fazl, "was productive of excellent results.—(1) The court became the resort of the learned men and sages of all creeds and nationaalities; (2) peace was given to all, and perfect toleration prevailed; (3) the disinterested motives of the Emperor, whose labours were directed to a search after truth, were rendered clear, and the pretenders to learning and scholarship were put to shame."

The brothers Fyzi and Abul Fazl become the personal friends of the Emperor.

The brothers now enjoyed the personal friendship of the Emperor, who placed implicit confidence in them. In those days tutorship to the royal princes was considered an office of great trust and distinction. The degree of confidence enjoyed by Fyzi may be judged from the circumstance that, when, in the 24th year of the reign (1579 A. D.), Kutb-ud-din Khan Bahari was appointed to the tutorship of the heir apparent, Prince Salem, Fyzi was appointed to the same office, to educate Prince Murad, who had then reached his eighth year and had just recovered from a long illness. Kutb-ud-din Khan was an old and confidential servant of the royal family, and the appointment of Fyzi to the office of tutor to Prince Murad showed that he was taken into the Emperor's personal confidence like an old family dependent. If Kutb-ud-din Khan for his services received the distinguished title of Beglar Begi,† Fyzi was, two years after, exalted to the office of Sadar to Agra, Kalpi and Kalinjar. In the beginning of the year 1585, Abul Fazl was promoted to the rank of *Hazari*, or Commander of one thousand horse, and he was, the following year, appointed Dewan of the province of Delhi.

Fyzi appointed Sadar to Agra, &c.

Abul Fazl appointed Dewan of Delhi province.

Towards the end of 1589, Abul Fazl lost his mother. He has recorded the following simple poems in the Akbarnama expressive of the intense grief felt by him on this occasion :—

چون مادر من بزیر خاک است   گر خاک بسر کنم چه باک است

دانم که بدین شعب فزائی   زانجا که تو رفتهٔ نیائی

لیکن چه کنم که نا شکیبم   خود را به بهانهٔ فریبم

Death of Abul Fazl's mother, 1589.

† A Turkish title, tantamount to the Indian Amir-ul-Umera, or the Premier Noble.

Because my mother is buried in the earth,
Should I (out of grief) throw dust on my head, what is the harm ?
By thus raising tumult and noise I know,
She cannot return from the place whereunto she has gone.
But what can I do ? my mind has no rest,
Having an excuse to make I allow myself to be deceived.

Sympathy expressed by Akbar.

To console his friend, the Emperor paid him a visit of condolence and thus spoke to him.

اگر جہانیان طراز پایندگی داشتے وجز یکے پای نیستی نسپردے
دوستان شناسا دل را از رضا وتسلیم گزیر نبود-هرگاه درین کاروان
سرا هیچکس دیر نماند نکوهش ناشکیبائی را کجا اندازه بر توان
گرفت—

If the people of this world had been endowed with immortality and they had not been subjected to death sooner or later, friends with the knowledge of God would not have learnt resignation to His will and trust in Him. Whereas, in the *Caravan Serae* of this world, permanent life has been given to none, nothing is left for the afflicted but to accept consolation.

"This prudent advice," writes Abul Fazl, "took a deep hold on my mind which was relieved of its distress."

Literary undertakings.

It was about this period that literary undertakings were commenced under the auspices of the Emperor himself. Thus, Lilavati, a Hindi work on Arithmetic, was translated into Persian by Sheikh Fyzi, who was also appointed to translate some chapters of the *Mahabharat.* He also translated, in metrical form, the Hindi story of the love of Nal and Daman after the Masnawi metre of Laila-o-Majnun. It was composed in 1003 A. H. (1594 A. D.), and comprises about 4,200 verses, and, according to Badaoni, it took Fyzi only the short space of five months to compose this admirable work. It was presented to the Emperor by the author with a few Ashrafis, or Gold Mohurs, and His Majesty was so much pleased with it that he appointed Naqib Khan to read it to him. Abul Fazl translated the Kalelah Damna under the title of *Ayari Danish.*

Abul Fazl created an Amir of the Empire.

In the beginning of 1592, Abul Fazl was promoted to the rank of two thousand horse. He now belonged to the circle of the great Amirs of the Empire. During the same year Sheikh

Fyzi was deputed to the courts of Burhan-ul-Mulk, in the Deccan and Raja Ali Khan, of Khandes, as a plenipotentiary of the paramount Power; but his younger brother, Abul Fazl, remained in immediate attendance at court.

Death of Sheikh Mubarak, in Lahore, 1593.

After the publication of his famous document, Sheikh Mubarak lived a retired life; but, when the Royal camp was in Lahore, the Emperor sent for him. The Sheikh was now in his extreme old age. He joined the Royal camp, but his health broke down soon after, and he suffered from illness for seven days. Abul Fazl was present at his father's last moments. The aged Mubarak gave his son some admonitions, and in a state of perfect consciousness closed his eyes and was no more. He died on Sunday, the 17th Ziquadah, 1001 A. H. (or 4th September, 1593 A. D.), at the age of ninety. Towards the end of his life, he lived in seclusion. His last years had been occupied in writing a commentary on the Quran, which he styled *Manbau Nafayas-ul Ayun*. He completed it, in spite of failing health and defective eye-sight, before his death. He had committed to memory the *Farizi* ode, consisting of seven hundred verses, the *Kasidah Barda*, the ode of *Ka-ab Bin Zuber* and other sacred odes in praise of the Creator, and recited them as daily homilies.* This shows that he died as a good Mohamedan.

His last literary works.

Death of Fyzi, 1595.

Two years afterwards Abul Fazl also lost his elder brother, Fyzi. He was taken ill at Lahore in the autumn of 1595, and his complaint developed into pulmonary apoplexy. His illness lasted for two months, and for two days before his death he remained in a state of unconsciousness. Al Badaoni writes that, up to his last moments, Fyzi rejected Islam. "It is related of him," writes the historian, "that, when in his last agonies, he was heard barking like a dog. Extremely bigoted as he was, from apostacy and disbelief in Islam, he talked heresy and nonsense with the leaders of the true faith, even in a state of semi-consciousness until he became speechless and went to his original abode." The date of his death was found in the words,

وے فلسفي وشيعي وطبعي ودهري

He was a philosopher, sectarian, rationalist and atheist.

---

* Badaoni.—Abdul Quader says that, when he was young, he studied at Agra for several years in company of Sheikh Mubarak.

Another date was found in the words :—

قاعده الحاد شکست

" The institute of atheism is broken.

The grief of the Emperor on his death.

When he was in the agonies of death, the Emperor went to him at midnight, and, raising his head gently with his own hands, cried out many times, " Sheikh, Jio ! Sheikh, Jio ! I have brought Hakim Ali with me ; why don't you speak to me ? " As he was unconscious, no reply or sound came. Again did the Emperor put the same question, but no reply was returned. Upon this His Majesty, overpowered with grief, tore off his turban and threw it on the ground. He then spoke some words of consolation to Sheikh Abul Fazl and withdrew. Soon after this, the death of Fyzi was announced. The event occurred on 5th October, 1595. Abul Fazl's account of his brother's death, given in the *Akbarnama*, is naturally more favourable than that of the historian Badaoni. According to Abul Fazl, when the Emperor cried out, Fyzi, in his last moments, " he opened his eyes and looked on the Emperor with despair, but could not speak."†

Unpopularity of Abul Fazl in Court.

Abul Fazl was now promoted to the rank of two thousand five hundred horse. But he had many enemies at Court, and they were anxious to see him deputed on some military expedition in a distant region like the Deccan, where he might mismanage the campaign, or show want of skill in administration, and thus incur the royal displeasure. But the real reason, in Abul Fazl's own words, was that he never deceived Akbar, and what he 'knew about others he represented faithfully to him whenever His Majesty had occasion to ask him.' This was what made him unpopular at Court, and the heir-apparent, Salem, belonged to the party of the disaffected. Towards the close of the forty-third year of the reign (1597 A. D.), Abul Fazl was, for the first time, sent on active duty. He was sent

He is sent out on active service to Deccan.

† There is a section of the Mohamedan writers who have tried to save Fyzi from the charge of apostacy, and assert that he praised the Prophet before his death. In the same way, it is related of Abul Fazl that, when Shah Abul Moali Quadri, of Lahore, once denounced Abul Fazl as an unbeliever, he saw the Prophet in his dream holding a meeting in Paradise. Abul Fazl, so the story goes, came to the meeting, when the Prophet made him to sit down, and said : " This man did for some time during his life evil deeds, but one of his books commences with the words, ' O God, reward the good, for the sake of their righteousness and help the wicked for the sake of Thy love,' and these words have saved him."—*Blochmann*.

to the Deccan, where Prince Murad, the Emperor's second son, had, with the assistance of Mirza Abdul Rahim, *Khan-i-Khana*, assembled an army. His instructions were that, should the *Amirs* of the Deccan undertake the protection of that country, Abul Fazl was to bring the Prince to Court. If not, he was to send the prince to Court and himself remain in the Deccan in command of the troops under Shah Rukh Mirza, the Emperor's son-in-law.‡ The Prince, however, died of *delirium tremens*, in 1066 (1597 A. D.), on the banks of the Purna, twenty kos from Dowlatabad. Abul Fazl arrived at Burhanpur, where Bahadur Khan, king of Khandes, whose brother had married Abul Fazl's sister, and who was unwilling to aid the Imperialists in their war on the Deccan, tried to bribe the minister by sending him a rich present, which, however, Abul Fazl refused, saying that the favors showered on him by the Emperor had extinguished in him all desire of receiving presents from others. When Prince Danial, third son of the Emperor, was appointed to the command of Ahmadnagar, Abul Fazl, at Akbar's request, left Mirza Shah Rukh, and, the Emperor having now himself proceeded to the seat of war, Abul Fazl met His Majesty at Khargon, near Bijagarh. Akbar received him with the following verse : **Akbar proceeds to the seat of war.**

فرخندہ شبے باید وخوش مہتابے تا با تو حکایت کنم از ہر بابے

Fortunate is the night and welcome the moonlight
When I should talk with thee on different topics with delight.

Abul Fazl's rank was raised to the command of four thousand horse. He distinguished himself in war and received the commendation of his royal master. **Meeting between Akbar and Abul Fazl.**

Meanwhile Prince Salem, who had been sent against the Rana of Udepur, with Raja Man Singh as Lieutenant, rebelled against his father. He assumed regal functions at Allahabad, seized on the treasury there, which contained £300,000, and coined silver and gold money in his own name. Akbar, who had returned from Burhanpur to Agra, irritated at the conduct of **Rebellion Salem.** **Akbar's return to Agra.**

‡ He was married to Shakrunnisa Begum in 1001 A. H. (1592 A. D.). He was made governor of Malwa and distinguished himself in the conquest of the Deccan. His grandfather, Mirza Suleman, generally called Wali Badakhshan as grandson of Abu Saied Mirza, was 6th in descent from Tymur. Shah Rukh held a rank of seven thousand, which was continued in Jahangir's reign.—*Blochmann.*

his son, sent for Abul Fazl, his only trustworthy servant. The minister, putting his son Abdul Rahman in charge of his corps, and taking leave of Prince Danial, set out for Agra, accompanied by two or three hundred horsemen. Shah Salem, who knew how hostile Abul Fazl was to his interests, apprehending, not without grounds, that his presence at the Imperial Court at this juncture would be productive of harm to him and exasperate his father still more against him, determined to devise means to despatch the minister on his way to the capital. He accordingly induced Raja Bir Singh, a Bundela chief of Archa, whose territory Abul Fazl was to pass, to intercept and kill him, promising him a large reward, with a command of some thousand cavalry for the service. The Raja posted one thousand cavalry and three thousand infantry at a distance of three or four kos from Gwalior and lay in ambuscade. Abul Fazl continued his journey unawares through Bir Singh's territory. He was warned at Ujjen of Salem's intentions, but said that nothing could stop him on his way to the capital. He came in sight of the Raja's troops near Serae Bar, six kos from Narwar. At this last moment one of his old faithful servants, Gadai Khan, a Pathan, advised him to cut his way to Antri, where three thousand of the royal troops were stationed under Rai Rayan and Suraj Singh; but the high spirited minister thought it beneath his valour to retreat. He was soon surrounded by Bir Singh's troops. The handful of horsemen who formed his escort defended him bravely to the last, but were gradually worn out by superior numbers. Abul Fazl, standing under a neighbouring tree, fought like a hero against tremendous odds, and his body was pierced by the lances of the troopers. Thus, covered with wounds, he fell to the ground and expired. His head was severed from his body and sent as a trophy to the Prince, who was delighted to see it and ordered it to be thrown on a dirty spot where it lay exposed for a long time. The event happened on Friday, the 4th Rabi-ul-awal, 1011 A.H. (12th August, 1602 A.D.)

He sends for Abul Fazl from Deccan.

Salem plots to cause the minister's murder.

The plot succeeds.

Murder of Abul Fazl, 1602.

Jahangir's notice of the event in his memoirs.

Jahangir frankly admits his guilt in his memoirs and pleads the mischief done by the Sheikh to his interests at court as the reason of his avenging himself on him. "Although my father," writes Jahangir in his memoirs, "was much vexed at first, I could now go to him without annoyance, and he was gradually reconciled with me."

When the intelligence of Abul Fazl's death reached the court, no one had the courage to inform the Emperor of it. The greatest of the nobles, the foremost among the grandees, trembled to approach His Majesty with such bad news as the death of his most beloved friend and valued councillor, or felt reluctant to do so. There was an old Tartar custom, still prevailing among the descendants of the house of Tymur, of announcing the death of a prince of royal blood by the introduction of his *vakil* to the royal presence with a blue handkerchief tied round his wrist. Following this custom, Abul Fazl's *Vakil* presented himself before the throne with a blue handkerchief tied over his wrist. Akbar perceived what had happened. Intense was the grief felt by him at the death of his friend and minister. He felt it more keenly than that of his own beloved son. He refused to see people for several days, and when the particulars of the murder were narrated to him, he exclaimed: "If it was Salem's desire to become Emperor, he might have killed his father, but spared Abul Fazl," and then recited the following verse:

Intense grief of the Emperor.

شیخ ما از شوق بیحد چون سوے ما آمده
زاشتیاق پائے بو سي بے سرو پا آمده

When our Sheikh, with boundless sincerity, came to us to meet.
Out of a keen desire to kiss our feet, he came without head and feet.

The Emperor sent Patr Das and Raja Raj Singh with detachments of troops to punish Bir Singh, but, after some slight encounter, he fled to the jungles. Other detachments were subsequently sent, and on one occasion Bir Singh was wounded and had a narrow escape; but the Emperor's own end was near. By His Majesty's death all fears were allayed. Bir Singh boldly presented himself before the new Emperor, who, as a reward for his services, granted him the jagir of Undecha and created him a Commander of three thousand horse.

Jahangir rewards Bir Singh, the murderer of Abul Fazl.

Abul Fazl possessed a lofty character and a noble heart. He displayed no taste for poetry, but his style of composition is

The character of Abul Fazl.

very characteristic and can be easily recognised. Its chief peculiarities are purity of ideas, perfect freedom from bias, exalted moral aspirations and refined taste. Not a passage is to be found in his voluminous works in which immorality is passed over with indifference. The style is unique and dignified, and, though difficult and perplexing for beginners, has a beauty of its own. The arguments are weighty and the subjects dealt with so admirably treated that they cannot fail to impress the reader's mind and inspire him with a sense of admiration for the accomplished writer. His style was much admired in the court of Tehran, and His Majesty, king Abdullah, of Bokhara, said, "He was more afraid of Abul Fazl's pen, than of Akbar's sword."

His literary genius.

His private life.

Of the private life of Abul Fazl the author of *Ma-a-sir ul Umera,* quoted by Professor Blochmann, writes: "He desired to live at peace with all men. He never said anything improper. Abuse, stoppages of wages, fines, absence on the part of his servants, did not exist in his household. If he appointed a man, whom he afterwards found to be useless, he did not remove him, but kept him on as long as he could, for he used to say that, if he dismissed him, people would accuse him of want of penetration in having appointed an unsuitable agent. On the day when the sun entered Aries, he inspected his whole household, and took stock, keeping the inventory with himself, and burning last year's books. He also gave his whole wardrobe to his servants, with the exception of his trousers, which were burnt in his presence.

Extraordinary appetite.

"He had an extraordinary appetite. It is said that, exclusive of water and fuel, he consumed daily twenty-two seers of food. His son, Abdul Rahman, used to sit at table as *sufarchi* (head butler); the superintendent of the kitchen, who was a Mohamedan, was also in attendance, and both watched to see whether Abul Fazl would eat twice of one and the same dish. If he did, the dish was sent up again the next day. If anything appeared tasteless, Abul Fazl gave it to his son to taste, and he to the superintendent, but no word was said about it. When Abul Fazl was in the Deccan, his table luxury exceeded all belief. In an immense tent (*Chihil Rawati*) one thousand rich dishes were

His munificence.

daily served up and distributed among the Amirs; and near it another large tent was pitched for all comers to dine, whether rich or poor, and *khichri* (rice and *dal*) was cooked all day and was served out to any one that applied for it."*

Notwithstanding the high rank held by him in the realm and the confidence reposed in him by the Emperor, Abul Fazl never accepted a title. It is true that he is charged by all Mohammadan writers with being an unbeliever, and Akbar's apostacy from Islam is ascribed to him and his brother, Fyzi, yet the credit is greatly due to the brothers of enunciating, under the guiding spirit of their great master, those principles of toleration and freedom which had the happy result of reconciling people of all creeds and nationalities to the Moghul rule in India and attached them strongly to the throne, thus making the period of Akbar's rule one of the brightest and most prosperous in the history of native rule in the East.

Akbar's conduct in life greatly influenced by the brothers Fyzi and Abul Fazl.

KHAN-I-AZIM Mirza Koka found the date of Abul Fazl's death in the hemistich:

يفعل الله ما يشاء و يحكم الله ما يريد   تيغ اعجاز نبي الله سر باغي بريد

God doeth what He chooses and commandeth what He may.
The miraculous sword of God's Prophet has the rebel's head cut away.

The numerical value of باغي (rebel) is 1013. The head, or first letter, of the word Baghi is ب with two for its value. Thus, cutting off 2 from 1013, the balance is 1011, the Hijra year of Abul Fazl's death. The hemistich shows the contempt in which Abul Fazl was held by the orthodox class of Mohammadans. It is said that Abul Fazl appeared to Khan-i-Azim in a dream and said: "The date of my death lies in the words, Bandah Abul Fazl" بندہ ابوالفضل, which likewise give 1011 A. H.

Abul Fazl's well known works are (1) the *Ain-i-Akbari*, or the institutes of Akbar, which he completed in the 42nd year of Akbar's reign; (2) the *Akbarnama*, in three volumes, containing an account of Akbar up to the 46th year of his reign; (3) the *Inshai Abul Fazl*, containing letters written by Abul

The literary works of Abul Fazl.

* Blochmann, page XXVIII.

Fazl to kings and chiefs. The book includes interesting letters written to Portuguese Fathers and the kings of Bokhara and Persia. It was compiled, after Abul Fazl's death, by Abdul Samad, son of Afzal Mohammad, son of Abul Fazl's sister, and also his son-in-law ; (4) The *Ayar-i-Danish,* a Persian translation of *Kalelah Damnah*; (5) the *Risalah Munajat* or 'treatise on prayers'; (6) *Jami-ul Lughat,* a lexicographical work; (7) *Kashkol,* or Beggar's Bowl, a collection of anecdotes and short stories; (8) Commentaries on some chapters of the Koran. The part he took in translations from Sanskrit works has already been referred to.

His acknowledgment of God's gifts. In his biographical notes, given at the end of the Ain, Abul Fazl enumerates the blessings of God happily enjoyed by him, for which he expresses his gratitude to the Almighty. He mentions the gifts as an acknowledgment proceeding from a grateful heart. They are as follows:—

1. High birth and parentage.

2. A period of blessings and peace. 'The ancients have prided themselves on the justice of the kings of previous ages. If I am proud of the age of harmony brought about by the justice of the King, it is no wonder'.

3. Good fortune.

4. Nobility of descent on the father's side.

5. A healthy and well-proportioned body.

6. Long service to the king, which is a source of protection from internal and external dangers.

7. Unfailing health.

8. Splendid house to live in.

9. Perfect freedom from anxiety about means of livelihood.

10. 'Daily increasing desire to serve my parents and to please them.'

11. 'Ever increasing kindness of my father.'

12. Suppliance to the threshold of God.

13. Respect for those who are the beloved of God.

14. Unfailing perseverance.

15. An extensive library, containing works on every branch of useful and entertaining knowledge.

16. 'My Father's hearty desire that I should not waste my time, but spend it in the pursuit of knowledge.'

17. Enlightened and genial companions.

18. A desire to search after truth.

19. Service of the 'King of the World' (*Gehan Khadeo*).

20. The shunning of habits of pride and arrogance.

21. Peace with all.

22. Loyalty to 'my Royal master, having the knowledge of God.'

23. Securing of the king's confidence and patronage without being indebted to anybody for it, and without personal exertion.

24. Dutiful and learned brothers.

25. Marriage into a good family.

26. A dutiful son.

27. A grandson.

28. Fondness for reading books on morals.

29. A correct estimate of man.

30. A habit of speaking the truth and hatred of speaking ill of any man.

31. Lack of trust in worldly affairs.

32. 'Ability to write this important work' (the *Ain*).

Abul Fazl has eloquently dwelt on each subject; but it has been thought sufficient to note his 'acknowledgment of God's gifts' to him briefly here. In connection with the last gift, he records his pleasure at completing the work in the following poem :—

یکے نامه ساختم پر شگفت   که هر دانشے زو توان بر گرفت
چنان گفتم این نامه نغز را   که روشن کند خواندنش مغز را

I have composed such wonderful a book,
That through its pages any wisdom may be gathered.
I have so compiled this work of wisdom,
That its study imparts light unto the mind.

Relative merits of Abul Fazl and Fyzi.

As regards the relative talents and accomplishments of Abul Fazl and Fyzi, it is difficult to venture a verdict as to which of the two was the greater scholar. Both were gifted men and possessed extraordinary genius. Fyzi had a poetical mind, while Abul Fazl excelled him in prose. If Fyzi's poems command the admiration of the learned for their beauty and excellence, Abul Fazl's prose is famous for the originality, purity and nobility of its sentiments, its statesmanship and the perfection of its style. Both possessed political genius. The school of adversity in which Abul Fazl was brought up taught him to be polite and forbearing even beyond the expectations of the time.

It is to the greatest credit of his father that he gave such sound instruction to his sons, and there is no doubt that the sons owed much of their learning to the great personal accomplishments of their father. The love which the brothers Fyzi and Abul Fazl had for each other, and the esteem with which they regarded one another, is apparent from their respective writings.

Abul Fazl has given proof of his devotion to his brother by introducing numerous passages from his works. In a long ode composed by Fyzi, he thus compares himself with his brother Abul Fazl :—

The odes of Fyzi in praise of Abul Fazl.

جا ئیکه از بلندي وپستي سخن رود
از آسمان عمر آمد واز خاک کمترم
بااینچنین پدر که نو شتم مکارمش
در فضل مفتخر ز گرامي برادرم
بر هان علم وعقل ابوالفضل کز دمش
دارد زما نه مغز معاني معطرم
صد ساله ره میان من و اوست در کمال
در عمر گر ازو دو سه ساله فزون ترم
در چشم با غبان نشود قدر او بلند
گر از درخت گل گذرد شاخ عرعرم

Wherever a talk from loftiness and lowness is found
I count my station above the skies and again humbler than the ground.
With a father whose kindness I have portrayed
In learning my pride from my esteemed brother is made.

Ornament of learning and wisdom Abul Fuzl from whom
The brain of knowledge is filled up with sweet perfume.
In accomplishments there is a journey of hundred years between him and me,
Although in age I am older to him by years two or three.
In the eyes of the gardener its estimation cannot rise high,
If the lean branch of a barren tree towers higher up a rose standing by.

Abul Fazl, in the Ain, gives the following list of Sheikh Mubarak's sons :— The sons of Sheikh Mobarak.

1. Sheikh Abul Faiz, known by his poetical name Fyzi, born 954 A. H. (1547 A. D.); died childless 1595.

2. Sheikh Abul Fazl, born 14th January 1551, murdered 12th August, 1602.

3. Sheikh Abul Barkat, born, 17th Shawal, 960 (1552 A. D.). "Though his attainments are not very high, yet he is well informed, is a good-man of business and well versed in fencing. He is good natured, fond of Darweshes and anxious to be of use." Served in Khandes under Abul Fazl.

4. Sheikh Abul Kher, born 967 A. H. (1559 A. D.) A student of Amir Fathullah Shirazi. Served in the Dekkan.

5. Sheikh Abul Makarm, born 976 A. H. (1568 A. D.)

All the above were born of the same mother.

6. Sheikh Abu Turab, born 988 (1580 A. D.)

Of Mubarak's daughters, Professor Blochmann mentions four : His daughters.

1. One married to Khudawand Khan, of the Dakhan, a Commander of one thousand. He was a man of imposing stature and well known for his personal courage. His temper was hot. Once Abul, Fazl invited four grandees to a dinner party in his house. Among them was Khudawand Khan. Dishes of fowl were placed before him, but before others roasted meat was laid. Khudawand became excited and left the party. The good natured Akbar tried to assure him that no insult was intended, but he was never reconciled to Abul Fazl.

2. One married to a son of Raja Ali Khan of Khandes.

3. One married to Hisamuddin, son of Ghazi Khan Badakhshi and a Commander of one thousand. He served in the Deccan under Khan-i-khanan. Once he expressed his wish to renounce

the world and turn a Fakir at the tomb of Nizam-ud-din Oulia, in Delhi. Khan-i-khanan in vain tried to persuade him to abandon the idea, but Hisam, the next day, tore his clothes, covered his body with mud and clay and went into the jungle. Akbar permitted him to resign. Hisam lived as an ascetic at the tomb of Nizam-ud-din for thirty years. The Saint Khawaja Baqi Billah "empowered him to guide travellers to the path of piety." He died in 1034 (1624 A. D.). His wife (Abul Fazl's sister), by the desire of her husband, gave away all her jewels to the Darveshes. She fixed an annual allowance of 12,000 Rupees for the maintenance of her husband's cell.

4. Ladli Begam, married to Islam Khan, a grandson of Sheikh Salem *Chishti*. She died in 1017 (1608 A. D.), or five years before her husband's death.*

Abdul Rahman, the son of Abul Fazl.

Abul Fazl's only son was the well known Abdul Rahman, born in 979 A. H. (1571 A. D.). The *Sunni* name was given to him by his grandfather. He distinguished himself in the war in Talangana. Jahangir did not transfer to him the dislike which he had for his father, for he raised him to the dignity of Commander of four thousand horse and conferred on him the title of Afzal Khan. In the third year of Jahangir's reign, he was installed in the office of the Governor of Behar, *vice* Islam Khan, the husband of Abul Fazl's sister, and Gorakhpur was conferred on him as a Jagir. As Governor of Behar, his headquarters were at Patna. He died in 1022 (1613 A. D.), in the eighth year of Jahangir's reign, or eleven years after his father's death. Abdul Rahman had a son, Bishotan, born 999 (1590 A. D.) He was Commander of seven hundred, with three hundred horse, in the time of Jahangir, and Commander of five hundred horse in the time of Sháh Jahán. He died in the 15th year of Sháh Jahán's reign.

Ministers State.

The man next in importance to Abul Fazl in Akbar's Court was his elder brother, Sheikh Fyzi. The events of the lives of both brothers are intermixed with each other, and so much has been said about the latter in the present sketch that it is only necessary to record here a brief note of his life.

---

* For an account of her tomb, See Chapter III. p. 193 *ante*.

Sheikh Fyzi.

Sheikh Fyzi, the eldest son of Sheikh Mubarak of Nagore, was born at Agra in 954 (1547 A. D.). His original name was Abul Faiz, and his poetical surname Fyzi; but towards the end of his life, he styled himself Fayazi, in imitation of the title of Allámi, assumed by his younger brother, Abul Fazl. He was a profound scholar and a great poet. He obtained great distinction in Arabic literature and in the art of poetry. He was also well-versed in the art of Medicine and treated the poor gratis. Before he was introduced to Akbar, he applied for a grant of 100 *bighas* to Sheikh Abdul Nabi, the Sadar at Agra; but he was turned out of the hall with indignity, being suspected of a tendency to Shiaism. Akbar heard of his literary fame, and he was introduced to His Majesty in the 12th year of the reign. By the force of his genius, he became the Emperor's chief favourite and constant companion. He was made Commander of four hundred, and, in 1588, His Majesty, in recognition of his great poetical genius, conferred on him the high appointment and title of Poet Laureate. Akbar was never known to pay much attention to poetry: yet his appreciation of Fyzi's talents showed that he was not slow to recognise true merit. He was appointed tutor to the Royal Princes and acted also as ambassador to kings. He composed 101 books, among them being *Sawati-ul-Ilham*, a commentary on the Koran in Arabic, and *Mawarid-ul-Kalám*, both being *be nuqát*, or without the use of dotted letters, in which Fyzi has displayed his great lexicographical accomplishments. Abul Fazl estimates his verses at 50,000. The *Akbarnama* contains numerous extracts from Fyzi's works. He was a member of the Divine Faith. He died at Lahore in 1595.†

Literary attainments of Sheikh Fyzi. **Introduced to Akbar.** **His literary works.** **His death 1595.**

After the brothers, Abul Fazl and Fyzi, Akbar's personal friend and favorite was Bir Bar.

Raja Bir Bar.

Raja Bir Bar. From an early age the Emperor Akbar was fond of discourse with people of different tribes, nationalities and religions. According to Abdul Quadar Badaoni, he showed early Hindu propensities and delighted in the company of Brahmans, *Bad Farosh*

† For particulars of his death, see page 259 *ante*.

(dealers in encomiums) and jesters. Accordingly, a Brahman from Kalpi, named Braham Das, who was by profession a *Bhat*, or minstrel, came to the Court in the beginning of the reign. He was very poor, but was smart and ready-witted. His profession was to please people by facetious and humorous conversation, and his bon-mots and witty repartees soon made him a general favorite at Court. In a short time he gained so much influence over the Emperor that he became his personal favourite and was constantly near him. A high *Mansab* was conferred on him, and he became one of the trusted councillors. He was at first honoured with the title of *Kab Rae*, or *Poet Laureate*, and soon after received that of Bir Bar, or the valiant, with the rank of Raja. When Raja Jey Chand of Nagarkot (Kangra) fell into disgrace and was imprisoned, the fort of that place was bestowed on Bir Bar as a jagir, and orders were issued to Husain Kuli Khan, governor of Lahore, to take possession of the fort and put it under the charge of Bir Bar. The Khan marched to Nagarkot with the *Umeras* of the Panjab, such as Mirza Yusuf Khan, Jaffar Khan, son of Quazzaq Khan, and Fattu, with a large number of cavalry, elephants, camels, ordnance, big cauldrons and camp followers, and laid siege to the fort. The fort was gallantly defended by Bidhi Chand, son of the Raja. Nagarkot was a great place of Hindu pilgrimage. Lakhs of people assembled there periodically to pay their devotions to the Hindu goddess and made large offerings in gold, coin and other valuables. The invading troops slaughtered the hill men and pierced with arrows the gold canopy spread on the dome of the temple. They also slaughtered the cows, so sacred to the Hindus, which had been offered at the temple by the votaries of the Brahma, and coloured the walls of the temple with their blood. According to Badaoni, who has described these details, so many Brahmins and attendants at the temple were slaughtered that they are beyond description. On account of these proceedings, the name of Raja Bir Bar was execrated by the Hindus, who considered all this bloodshed to have been caused for his sake. The city of Nagarkot was occupied and a huge cannon was pointed at the palace of Bidhi Chand, a single discharge from which killed eighty men on the spot. The invaders were on the point of capturing the fort when Bidhi Chand sued for peace. In the meanwhile intel-

His original name.

Is honored with the dignity of Poet Laureate.

Nagarkot (Kangra) is given to Bir Bar as Jagir.

Battle of Nagarkot.

ligence arrived from Lahore of the advance of Mirza Ibrahim Husein and Masud Husein Mirza on the Panjab. The royal troops began to suffer for want of supplies, and it was therefore resolved to conclude peace. Bidhi Chand made a present of five maunds of gold, which was equal to one year's income of the temple, and brought a large number of valuable articles as) ransom. On Friday in the month of Shawal, 980 (1572 A. D. the *Khutba* was read and coin struck in the name of the Emperor. On the gateway of Raja Jey Chand's palace a high arch of a mosque was constructed, and the Mohamadan victory having been thus signalised, Husein Kuli Khan marched back to Lahore to expel the Mirzas. Bir Bar thus never got possession of the Nagarkot jagir which had been granted to him.

Terms of peace.

Money compensation given to Bir Bar.

According to the *Akbarnama* (account of 18th year of the reign), the peace with Raja Bidhi Chand, who was a minor, was concluded on the following terms, which were accepted by Raja Gobind Chand, uncle and guardian of the minor chief. First, that a daughter of Raja Jey Chand be sent to Akbar's harem; 2nd, that a suitable present in cash be sent for the Emperor; 3rd, that one of the Raja's sons be sent to Agra as a hostage; and 4th, that, as the Imperial order was to give the Raja's territory to Bir Bar, a large sum of money be paid to the latter as compensation. All these conditions were fulfilled by the defeated Raja. After the conclusion of this treaty, Raja Gobind Chand accompanied the Imperial troops under Husein Kuli Khan to Dipalpoor, near Multan, where a battle being fought between the Imperialists and the invading army, the army under Mirza Ibrahim Husein was routed. Husein Kuli Khan was, for his gallant conduct, honoured with the title of *Khan-i-Jahan*. Raja Bir Bar distinguished himself in this battle and received the title of *Musahib-i-Danishwar*, or 'the wise councillor.' Ibrahim Husein Mirza, who had taken refuge with the Beloches, died, a short time after, of grief; but Masud Husein Mirza and other men of his party were sewn in the hides of cows, with horns, and in this position exhibited before Akbar in the Court at Fattehpur. His Majesty, who always showed toleration on such occasions, had the unfortunate men taken out of the cow skin, had them bathed and dressed, and, on their being presented to him on a subsequent occasion at Court, gave them a free pardon thus giving proof of his high sense of honour and generous disposition.

He accompanies Akbar to Deccan.

The following year (1573 A. D.), when Mirza Ibrahim Husein again raised the standard of insurrection in Gujrat and Akbar made his famous march to that place, accompanied by his nobles, Raja Bir Bar was in his royal master's train. His Majesty performed a journey of more than 450 miles with such celerity, during the rainy season, with 300 of his officers of rank on camels, that he reached Pattan on the 9th day after leaving Agra, and, though his forces were very unequal to those of the enemy, he defeated the latter, and, tranquillity having been completely restored, returned to Agra.

Is deputed on foreign duties.

Raja Bir Bar was often employed on foreign duties. Thus we find him, in the 21st year of the reign (1576 A. D.) accompanying Raja Loun Kiran to Dungarpur to conduct the Rae's daughter to Agra, as the Rae, through sincerity and out of respect for the Emperor, had offered her for His Majesty's Harem, and as "a special honour to the chief," the Emperor had granted his request. When, in the year 977 (1569), Raja Ram Chand, of Bhath, surrendered the fort of Kalinjar to Majnun Khan, Akbar's Commander, he sent his son, Bir Bahadur, to Court as a hostage, but from want of confidence would not pay his respects personally to His Majesty. Annoyed at the high tone assumed by the Raja, Akbar ordered a force to march to Bhath, but, on representations being made to him, he changed his mind and resolved to send a deputation of his most trusted Umeras to Bhath to bring the Raja to the Court. Raja Bir Bar and Zen Khan Koka were selected for the duty, and the chief came at last to the Court, where he was honourably received by the Emperor. This happened in the 28th year of the reign (1582 A. D.)

The Raja of Bhath was among the three great Rajas of Hindustan mentioned by Baber in his memoirs. He was a great patron of music, and the celebrated Mian Tan Sen was taken by Akbar from his service. The Raja possessed a high spirit and had acquired a reputation throughout India for his generosity. Thus, on one occasion, it is said, being pleased with his musical skill, he made a present of a karor of rupees to Tan Sen; he had also served the Emperor Sultan Ibrahim Lodi with distinction. The fact of his coming to pay his respects to the Moghal Emperor in the capital of his dominions was regarded as an event which marked the culmination of the Mahomedan conquest in India.

Bir Bar became the Emperor's trusted adviser, and their mutual intimacy was such that His Majesty placed the most implicit confidence in him. A palace was erected for Bir Bar at Fattehpur Sikri, near that of the Emperor; and, when it was completed, in the 27th year of the reign (1582 A. D.), the Raja entertained the Emperor with great pomp and magnificence.

Becomes the Emperor's trusted adviser.

Palace built for him in Fattehpur Sikri.

Akbar mixed with his courtiers and ministers freely and had a strong hold on the minds of the people. Thus, we find in the *Akbarnama*, when the Emperor was on his journey in the *Suba* of Allahabad called *Diari Sharqui*, or the Eastern country, he was entertained at Etawa by Zen Khan *Koka*, at Kalpi by Mathab Khan *Tiul*, and at Akbarpur, near Allahabad, by Raja Bir Bar.

Entertains the Emperor at a banquet.

It was principally due to Bir Bar's influence over Akbar that the latter became so much attached to Hinduism and went even so far as to adopt the Hindu form of worship and perform Hindu religious ceremonies. Thus, according to Badaoni, Bir Bar styled "the accursed," impressed on His Majesty that the Sun was the primary origin of every thing. Its heat ripened the grain in the field, the fruits in the garden, and the vegetation in the fields, and the illumination of the world, and the lives of its inhabitants depended on it. For these reasons it should be worshipped and revered by all mankind, and people, when praying, should do so with their faces turned towards the quarter where the great luminary rises, not towards that where it sets. On similar grounds, urged Bir Bar, should reverence be paid to fire, water, stone, trees, and all other forms of existence, down even to cows and their dung.

Akbar's attachment to Hinduism due chiefly to Bir Bar's influence.

When Akbar established his Divine Faith, Bir Bar became one of its members, along with Abul Fazl, Fyzi, Sheikh Mubarak, the Sadr Jahan, or Crown Lawyer, Sultan Khawja,

Becomes member of Akbar's Divine Faith.

Azim Khan *Koka* and others. One day, writes Badaoni, there was a conversation about religion in the presence of the king. His Majesty tried hard to convert Qutbuddin Mohammad Khawja and Shah Baz Khan, but in vain. Qutbuddin said: "What will the kings of Vilayat, such as the sovereign of Constantinople, &c., say, when they hear all this. They all profess the same religion as we do, be their views broad or limited." The Emperor thereupon said: "You are secretly defending the cause of the Sultan of Constantinople, to secure his confidence, so that, when you leave this country, you may obtain employment under him without difficulty. Go away now from India and become a respectable man there." Shah Baz Khan thereupon got excited, and, when a derisive remark was made at religion by Bir Bar, he abused him soundly and said "Cursed infidel, darest thou speak in such profane language in this assembly? It can not take me long to settle with thee." The situation became awkward. The Emperor, addressing Shah Baz Khan in particular and others in general, said: "It would serve you right that shoes filled with excrement should be thrown into your faces," and, so saying, withdrew. *

Bir Bar's attitude at religious assemblies.

His professions of sincerity to Akbar.

Bir Bar professed to be a ready believer in all that Akbar propounded as regards the doctrines of his new religion, and His Majesty's faith in the sincerity of his friend's professions was never shaken. Thus, when religious men at Court, like Mir Fattehullah of the Deccan, who was a staunch *Shia* and who could not be persuaded to embrace the new faith, were assailed with arguments to convince them of the truth of the Divine Faith, "but did not utter a single syllable in answer, so obstinate were they," writes Badaoni, "Bir Bar ever readily bowed to His Majesty's arguments and said:—'Yea, we believe! yea, we trust'!"

Bir Bar resolves to turn a Jogi or ascetic; but is prevented by the Emperor from so doing.

In connection with the events of the year 990 (1582 A. D.), Badaoni notices an incident showing that Bir Bar had numerous enemies at Court, and that, but for the personal regard which the Emperor entertained towards him, he would, without loss of time, have been subjected to disgrace. Prostitutes from all parts

---

* Badaoni.

of the Imperial dominions collected in such large numbers in the capital as to defy all counting. The Emperor assigned to them a separate quarter outside the city, which was called *Shetanpura,* or Devil's villa. A Superintendent, a Deputy and a Secretary were appointed for this quarter, and they registered the names of such persons as went to these people or called them to their houses. No dancing girl was permitted to go to the house of any person at night without permission of the superintendent. The use of wine was prohibited except under medical advice, and severe punishments were provided for excessive drinking, carousals and disorderly behaviour. No one was to have a virgin from the devil's villa without first applying to the Deputy and obtaining permission from the Court. Libertines did what they liked under assumed names, or with the connivance of the officials in charge of the villa; several nobles of note were severely reprimanded and punished or confined for considerable periods in fortresses under command of the King for breaking the rules. The Emperor himself summoned some of the well-known prostitutes and asked them privately who had deprived them of their virginity, and, after learning their names, visited the grandees concerned with all severity. Among these one mentioned the name of Raja Bir Bar, "who," says Badaoni, "had the distinction of becoming a disciple of His Majesty by becoming a member of the Divine Faith, and who had gone beyond the four degrees* and acquired the four cardinal virtues.†" At this time Bir Bar happened to be in his jagir, in the pergana of Kera. Having been informed of this, he declared his intention of becoming a jogi or ascetic, and applied for the Emperor's permission for the purpose, but His Majesty invited him to court in reassuring terms and was as kind to, and familiar with, him as ever.

The Devil's villa.

Bir Bar spent his time for the most part at Court. Had he remained at the palace of Fattehpur Sikri as a gay courtier, all would have been well for the witty Raja. But circum-

Is sent on a military expedition against the Eusafzaes.

* The four degrees of faith in His Majesty were defined to be readiness to sacrifice to the Emperor property, life, honour and religion, any who had sacrificed all these four things possessed four degrees, and any who had sacrificed one of the four possessed one degree, and so on,—*Badaoni*, p. 288.

† The *Fazael-i-Arba*, or the four cardinal virtues, are wisdom, courage, chastity, and justice.

stances involved him in a military expedition, for which his genius was ill-suited, and he at last fell a prey to his inexperience and want of tact in a foreign war. In the year 994 (1585 A. D.) a military expedition was sent under Zen Khan Koka to punish the Afghans of Eusafzai, in Swat and Bajour. The General moved in the District of Bajour and defeated the enemy in several engagements. He had to ask for reinforcements, and Akbar resolved to decide by lot whether Abul Fazal or Bir Bar should go. The lot fell in favour of the latter, much against His Majesty's inclination, and Bir Bar was sent with Hakim Abul Fatteh to the seat of war. The Imperialists were defeated, and, in their retreat, were attacked by the Afghans in a very narrow valley. Arrows and stones were showered on them from all sides, and they reached the next station in the greatest disorder, most of them having lost their way in the darkness of night. The next day the Afghans attacked the flying columns of the Imperialists, and 8,000 men were cut off, with 500 officers. This was the most disastrous defeat ever sustained by Akbar's troops. Many grandees, besides Bir Bar, perished in this battle, among them being Hasan Khan, Khawja Arab, paymaster of Khan Jahan, and Mulla Sheri, the poet. Hakim Abul Fatteh and Zen Khan, with the remnant of their defeated troops, reached the fort of Attock.

Disastrous defeat of the Imperialists.

Death of Bir Bar, 1586.

Grief of the Emperor on his death.

His Majesty was concerned for the death of no grandee more than for that of his beloved courtier and personal favourite, Bir Bar. He said: "Alas, they could not even get hold of his body, that it might have been burned." For two days he remained in seclusion and refused to take food, but at last consoled himself with the belief that Bir Bar was now quite free and independent of all worldly troubles, and expressed the relief he felt on his account by saying: "The rays of the great luminary were sufficient to cleanse his body, and there was no need of fire." He was long mourned by his royal master, and Abul Fazl, in his *Maktubat*, has a letter addressed from the Emperor to Khan-i-Khanan, then Viceroy in the Deccan, expressing the intense grief felt by him on this occasion. Bir Bar died in February, 1586.

False reports spread of his being alive.

The grief felt by Akbar for the loss of his friend, Bir Bar, afforded an opportunity for designing men to invent stories of his being alive. One report spread was that he had been seen in the hills of Nagarkot (Kangra) walking about with the *jogis* and *sanniasis*. Akbar eagerly welcomed the report, thinking that Bir Bar might have felt ashamed to return to Court after his defeat in the Eusufzai country and turned *faquir*, which he had already expressed an intention of doing while in his jagir, and the Emperor's belief had been strong that Bir Bar never cared for the world. An *Ahdi* was accordingly sent to Nagarkot to enquire into the truth of the report, when it was found that it had no foundation.

The Emperor readily believes these.

Soon afterwards another report was received, that Bir Bar had been seen at Kalinjar, his jagir, and the Emperor readily believed it, inasmuch as it had been officially communicated to him by the Karori (Collector). It was alleged that Bir Bar had been recognised by a certain barber by some marks on his body which he had seen while rubbing it with oil. The Emperor ordered the barber to Court, but, as there was none to be sent, a report was submitted that Bir Bar, although really found, had since died. To give this report the colour of truth, an innocent traveller, who had been first disguised as the real Bir Bar, was put to death, and thus detection was rendered impossible. The Emperor actually went through a second mourning; but the *Karori* and several others who had originated the false reports were called to Court and tortured, the *Karori* having also to pay a heavy fine.

Bir Bar's issue.

Bir Bar left two sons, Lala and Hari Har Rai. Lala, the eldest son, was a Commander of two hundred; but he is mentioned by Badaoni as a spendthrift; and, after squandering his property, he turned a *faquir*. Hari Har Rai lived at Court, and, in the 48th year of the reign, was deputed to the Deccan to bring prince Danial to Court.

Anecdotes of Bir Bar.

The ancedotes that passed between Akbar and Bir Bar have obtained world-wide celebrity, and are to this day on the lips of the people from Cape Comorin to the Khyber Pass. Besides being ready-witted, Bir Bar was well versed in music, and his Hindi *cabats* and *dohas* (distichs) are characterised by sweetness and elegance of composition, as well as by the moral which they convey. As a poet, he composed his poems under the assumed named Barhma.

Before the ascendancy of Abul Fazl and Fyzi, the man in supreme power in India under Akbar was his famous general and tutor, Bahram Khan.

BAHRAM KHAN.

Bahram Khan enters Humayun's army.

Bahram Khan, the general of Akbar, was son of Saif Ali Beg, and was born in Badakhshan. After the death of his father he went to Balkh to study. He entered Humayun's army at the age of sixteen and fought many battles under him. The conquest of Hindustan is justly attributed to him. In 963 (1555) he was appointed tutor to Prince Akbar and was sent with him to the Punjab against Sikandar Khan. On Akbar's accession at Kalanour, he was appointed *Vakil,* or Premier of the Empire, with the title *Khan-i-Khanan.* Akbar called him Khan Baba, or 'father Khan'. In 966 (1558) Bahram married Sultana Salema Begam, daughter of Gulrukh Begam (a daughter of Baber) and Mirza Nuruddin Mohammed. Soon afterwards an estrangement between Akbar and Bahram sprung up. Bahram. leaving Agra, broke out into open rebellion in the Punjab. Akbar moved against him, but, before he arrived at Jullundur, tidings reached him of Bahram's defeat by Atgah Khan. Bahram asked forgiveness. Akbar sent Maulana-*Makhdum-ul-Mulk,* Abdullah, of Sultanpur, the Shekh-ul-Islam of the Empire, to persuade him to come to his camp, and promised personal safety to his old preceptor. Bahram Khan agreed to come to the Royal camp. A procession of nobles and dignitaries went to receive the Khan, who, however, appeared before his master in the guise of a suppliant, bare-footed and with his turban folded round his neck. He threw himself at the foot of the throne, and, moved by former recollections, began to sob loudly. Akbar's feelings of compassion and esteem for his general and tutor were aroused. He instantly rose from his seat, raised the old veteran with his own hands and seated him on his right. He was given a dress of honour and the option of assuming the government of Kalpi and Chanderi, or retiring to Makka. Bahram's pride and prudence prevailed on him to adopt the latter course. A liberal pension was assigned to him, and he set out for Makka with his family. He was, however, assassinated at

Rebels in the Punjab

Is defeated and pardoned.

Pattan, in Gujrat, by an Afghan named Mubarak, whose father had been killed in the battle of Machhiwara. The great man died with the words *Allah-o Akbar* (God is great) on his lips (30th June 1561). Akbar took charge of Abdul Rahim, Bahram's son, and soon after married his widow Sultáná Salema Begam.

His death, 1561.

Among the ministers of state who may be fittingly called the pillars of the Empire, the most prominent person was Raja Todar Mal, the Finance Minister of Akbar.

Raja Todar Mal.

Todar Mal's birth place.

This most remarkable man was a Khatri of Laharpur, in Oudh.* His father died when the son was quite young, and left no means of livelihood for him, so that the widow was in great distress. The young man commenced life in the humble position of a writer, but he worked his way up from that lowly status until the great Pathan, Sher Shah Sur, committed to him the important charge of constructing the new fort of Rohtas in the Panjab, with the object of effectually restraining the Ghakkars from their predatory inroads into that province, and also creating a barrier in the path of the Moghals. Through his judicious management, the wages of labourers were reduced from one rupee per stone at the commencement of the work to $\frac{1}{10}$th of a rupee. We are informed by the author of *Tarikh-i-Khan Jahan Lodi*, that, when the fort was finished, Todar Mal was highly extolled by the Pathan Emperor for the tact and ability he had displayed in its execution. It was under the able government of Sher Shah that Todar Mal's natural talents developed. When the supreme power passed from the house of the Pathans to that of the descendants of Tymur, Todar Mal still continued in State service. In 1567, he had pressed Sekandar, the rebel jagirdar of Oudh. During the same year, he distinguished himself in the memorable siege of Chittor. Neither he, nor Kasam Khan, had any repose in their quarters,

His first post under Sher Shah.

Enters the service of Akbar.

---

* See proceedings of Bengal Asiatic Society, September 1871, page 178; and Imperial Gazetteer of India VIII, 401. Raja Todar Mal must not be confounded with Rai Todar Mal, a Khatri of Chunian, District Lahore, a Mansabdar of 1,500 under Shah Jahan. See *Badshahnama*, Vol., II, page 728. The latter was Faujdar of Sarhand under Shah Jahan.

His talents for war.

"but worked in their galleries with such zeal that for a day and two nights they took neither rest nor food." The Emperor was himself most assiduous in directing the attack. Undeterred by the falling missiles, he quietly and with composure of mind supervised his ranks, and the soldiers under him fought with unswerving constancy.

Privileges conferred on him.

He fought bravely in Afghanistan, was recalled and sent on an expedition to Kashmir, and distinguished himself in the Bengal war under Khan Jahan and in the campaigns of Gujrat and Orissa. In the 19th year of the reign he received the high distinction of retaining *Alam* and *Nakkara*, or the coming out into public with standard and drums, a privilege allowed only to princes royal, or *Amirs* of the first rank, In the 27th year, he was appointed Diwan of the Empire. During the same year, he introduced his great financial reforms, which earned for him and his master an undying fame. The third book of the *Ain* gives full details of his new rent roll, which superseded the assessment of Mozaffar, the Diwan of Bahram Khan, based on the returns of kanungoes. He also framed regulations regarding the coinage, full details of which are given in the *Akbarnama*. The most important reform carried out by him was the introduction of Persian in the keeping of the State accounts. Formerly these accounts had been written in Hindi, by Hindu *moharrirs*. He compelled his co-religionists to learn the Court language of their rulers, and thus enabled them to compete for the highest appointments in the State which the generous policy of Akbar had opened to all.

Introduces financial reforms.

Introduces Persian in state accounts.

Is sent against the Eusufzais.

In the 29th year, the Emperor honoured Raja Todar Mal with a visit. In the 32nd year his life was attempted by a Khatri out of private hatred. He was wounded on a march, at night, but the culprit was at once cut down. During the same year Todar Mal was sent against the Eusufzais to avenge the death of Bir Bar. When the Emperor went to Kashmir, in the 34th year (1588 A. D.), Todar Mal with Raja Bhagwan Das and Kalij Khan, was left in charge of Lahore. In the same year old age and failing health compelled the Raja to tender his resignation, which the Emperor reluctantly accepted. The Raja was allowed to retire to the banks of the Ganges, there to pass the remaining days of his life and to die in peace. Experience, however, showed Akbar that he could not do without his loyal minister. He therefore sent him a message, impressing on him that attending to his personal duties was a far more meritorious act than sitting on the banks of the Ganges, and asked him to rejoin his appointment. In obedience to the Emperor's commands, the Raja returned to duty, but to die on the eleventh day after his arrival in Lahore, on 10th November, 1589. His friend, Raja Bhagwan Das, was present at the cremation. On his return to his house, he was seized with an attack of strangury, of which he died the same day. The Emperor was still at Kabul when the news was conveyed to him of the death of two of his most trusted ministers and friends. The Raja, at the time of his death, held the rank of *Char-hazari*, or Commander of four thousand, and the titles of *Vakil-us-Sultanat* (or counsellor of the Empire) and *Mushriff-i-Diwan.** Raja Bhagwan Das was *Amir-ul-Umra*, or the Premier Noble. It was with profound grief that the Emperor found himself in Lahore, in March, 1590, after the loss of two of his most trusted friends and counsellors.

Is permitted to retire.

But is recalled to duty.

His deaths, 1589.

His titles.

Abul Fazl never personally liked Todar Mal, but he praises his talents and his integrity. The Raja possessed an independent spirit, and was a strict Hindu. Abul Fazl calls him a bigoted Hindu, and even complained of his behaviour to Akbar, but the latter, who recognised and favoured old and loyal servants, took no notice of his complaints. Bir Bar, a short time before his death, became a convert to Akbar's Divine Faith. Todar Mal afforded a contrast to Bir Bar. Once, while accompanying Akbar in his march to the Panjab, Todar Mal, in the hurry of the moment, lost his idols. As he was accustomed not to transact any business before worshipping the idols, he passed several days without food and water, when, at last after much difficulty, he was induced by the Emperor to take them.

His character.

Among the grandees of the Emperor the most important personage, on account both of ties of relationship and of position, was Raja Bhagwan Das.

Grandees of the Empire.

---

* ***Mushrif*** **is the Chief Officer of the Treasury, who authenticates accounts.**

RAJA BHAGWAN DAS.

An account of the family.

Raja Bhagwan Das was the son of Raja Bihari Mal, son of Pirthi Raja Kachwaha, of the ancient family of Amber, in the Suba of Ajmere. Bihari Mal was the first Rajput who joined Akbar's Court. He was introduced to Akbar before the end of the first year of his reign. At this interview, Akbar was seated on a *mast* (wild) elephant. Bihari Mal, with his whole family, attended Court at Sankanir and was most honourably received.* The Raja's request to be allowed to enter Akbar's service and to strengthen the ties of friendship by a matrimonial alliance with His Majesty was granted. Akbar married the Raja's daughter at Sambhar, and at Pattan he was joined by the Raja, his son, Bhagwân Das, and grand-son, Kunwar Man Singh. The whole family accompanied Akbar to Agra, where Raja Bihari Mal was created Commander of Five Thousand. The Raja died at Agra.

Raja Bhagwan Das enters the Emperor's service.

Raja Bhagwan Das entered the Emperor's service with his father. In 980 (1572 A. D.) he saved Akbar's life near Sirnal, in the fight with Ibrahim Hussain Mirza. In the 23rd year, he was appointed Governor of the Panjab, and in the 29th year his daughter was married to Prince Salim, afterwards Jahangir. The result of the union was Prince Khusrow. In the 30th year he was made Commander of five thousand. Raja Bhagwan Das died at Lahore in the beginning of 998 (1581 A. D.), a short time after Raja Todar Mal. He held the title of *Amir-ul-Umera*, or the Premier noble.

His son Raja Man Singh.

On the death of Raja Bhagwan Das, Akbar conferred the title of Raja on his son, Man Singh, and gave him the command of five thousand. He died a natural death, in the Deccan, in the 9th year of Jahangir's reign.

Another man of note among the grandees of the realm was Mirza Abdul Rahim *Khan-i-Khanan*.

---

* For particulars of the first interview between, Akbar and Raja Behari Mal, see page 207 *ante*.

KHAN-I-KHANAN MIRZA ABDUL RAHIM.

He was son of Bahram Khan, and was born at Lahore in 964 (1556 A. D.) He was a child of five years when his father was murdered at Pattan. Akbar took charge of him, gave him the title of Mirza Khan, and subsequently married him to Mah Bano, sister of Mirza Aziz Koka. He twice defeated Mirza Muzaffar in Ahmedabad, although in one of the engagements he had only a contingent of 10,000, while his adversaries had an army of 40,000. For these victories Akbar made him Commander of Five Thousand and conferred on him the much coveted title of Khan-i-Khanan. **His services.**

In the 34th year he, at the Emperor's request, translated the *Wakiat-i-Babri*, or memoirs of the Emperor Babar, from the Chughttai language into Persian. The most remarkable events of his life were the conquest of Gujrat and Sindh and the defeat of Sohel Khan in Bijapur. On the return of Jahangir from Kabul, Nur Jahan sent Abdul Rahim in pursuit of Mohabat Khan and contributed herself twelve lacs of rupees for the expedition; but, before the necessary preparations could be made, the Mirza died at Lahore, in the 21st year of Jahangir's reign, in 1626 A. D., at the age of seventy-two. He was buried at Delhi, in a mausoleum which he had built for his wife. **Translates Babar's memoirs from Turki into Persian.** **His death, 1626.**

Mirza Abdul Rahim was a profound scholar in Arabic and Persian, and was well versed in the Turkish and Hindi languages. As a poet, he wrote under the name of *Rahim*. His liberality and love of learning were proverbial. On the final conquest of Gujrat, he gave the whole of his property to the soldiers, even his inkstand, which he gave to the soldier who came last. **His character.**

Among those to whom Akbar was strongly attached and who owed their rise in life to him, was his foster brother. Mirza Aziz *Kokah*, the Khan-i-Azim.

KHAN AZIM MIRZA AZIZ KOKAH.

Mirzá Aziz was foster brother of Akbar, being a son of Ji Ji Angah, his wet nurse, the wife of Shamsuddin Mohammed Atgah Khan, who received the title of Atgah (foster-father) from **The services of Mirza Aziz.**

Akbar. The Mirza grew up with Akbar, who was strongly attached to him. In 988 (1580 A.D.), he was promoted to the rank of Five Thousand and received the title of *Azim Khan.* He was twice deputed to Bahar to quell disturbances there, and in the 27th year of the reign moved to Bengal. In the 31st year he was appointed to the Deccan; in the 32nd year his daughter was married to Prince Murad. In the 34th year he was appointed Governor of Gujrat, in succession to the Khan-i-Khanán. He reduced Jám and Kach to obedience. In the 37th year, he conquered Somnath and sixteen other harbour towns and reduced Juná Garh. In the 39th year he went on a pilgrimage to Meccá. Akbar regretted his departure, and he had to embark for India. He rejoined Akbar in 1003 (1594 A.D.), became a member of the Divine Faith, was appointed Governor of Behár and, the following year, *Vakil* of the empire. His mother dying in 10018 (1599), Akbar himself assisted in carrying the coffin.

His death, 1623.

In the 5th year of Jahangir's reign, Mirzá Aziz was sent to the Deccan with 10,000 men, and when, in the eighth year, Sháh Jahán was sent to the command of the Deccan, Aziz was appointed adviser to the Prince. Mirzá Aziz died at Ahmadabád, in the 19th year of Jahangir's reign (1623 A.D.)

Mirzá Aziz wrote poems and was well-known for his address, wit and knowledge of history.

Musicians.

The most favoured of the Cabinet of Akbar, whose company was a source of pleasure and recreation to him, was Mian Tan Sen.

Mian Tan Sen.

Akbar a great patron of music.

Akbar was a great patron of music, that talisman of knowledge, in the eloquent words of Abul Fazl. He had such a knowledge of the science as trained musicians did not possess, and he was an excellent performer, especially on the *Naqqarah.* There were numerous musicians of both sexes at Court from India, Kashmir, Iran, Turan Tabrez and a few came from Transoxiania. The Court musicians were divided into four divisions, one for each day of the week, their head being Mian Tan Sen, of Gwalior, a renowned Rajput rhapsodist. He was in the

Tan Sen's original employer.

employ of Raja Ramchand of Bhath, a patron of renowned musicians and singers. Akbar having heard of his fame, sent Jalál Khan Qurchi, an Amir of his Court and a Commander of five hundred, with a *firmán* (or mandate), to request the Raja to allow Tan Sen to join the Court at Agra. The command was veiled in the guise of a request. The Raja felt powerless to refuse Akbar's request, and, with a sore heart, sent his favourite minstrel, with his musical instruments and a large and a valuable present, comprising jewels and a number of elephants, to Agra. This happened in the 7th year of the reign. The first time that he performed at Court he was right royally rewarded, the Emperor making him a present of two lakhs of rupees on the occasion. This prince of musicians remained at the Court, and it was greatly due to his Hindi songs and melodies that Akbar became conversant with the epic poems and amatory narratives of the Hindus, thus acquiring an insight into their habits and customs, which he himself subsequently adopted. His charming poems and compositions are to this day sung by the people of Hindustan, though many of his melodies owe their inspiration directly to his royal master.

Tan Sen joins the Court at Agra.

His poems and compositions.

Among the scholars and authors attached to the Court were Khawja Nizamuddin Ahmad and Mulla Abdul Quadar Badoni.

Scholars and authors.

KHWAJA NIZAM-UD-DIN AHMAD.

He was the son of Khwaja Mokim Harvi, a dependent of the Emperor Baber, who, in the latter period of his reign, raised him to the dignity of *Diwan* to the Imperial household. When, after Baber's death, the province of Hyderábád was entrusted to Mirza Askari, the brother of Humayun, the Khwaja was appointed the Mirzá's Wazir. When Humayun, after his defeat at Ghaunsá by Sher Shah Sur, fled to Agra, the Khwaja accompanied him to Agra. He subsequently served under the Emperor Akbar.

Khwaja Mokim Harvi, father of Nizam-ud-din.

His son, Nizam-ud-din, was appointed Diwan of the household of Akbar. According to the author of Ma-asir ul Umera, he was incomparably upright, and excelled all his contemporaries in administrative knowledge, as well as in clearness of

Nizam-ud-din appointed Bakshi of Gujrat.

intellect. In the 29th year of Akbar's reign, he was appointed Bakshi of the Province of Gujrat, which post he held for a long time. Akbar entertained the highest opinion of his literary attainments, zeal and integrity.

His great word the Tabákati Akbari.

He is the author of the Tabákat-i-Akbari, one of the most celebrated histories of India, recognized by all contemporary historians as a standard history of Akbar's time. He brings the history down to the 27th year of Akbar's reign (1592 A. D.) Both Abdul Kadir Badaoni and Farishta speak highly of this work. Badaoni was especially attached to him by the ties of religion and friendship. He died of fever at Lahore, on 23rd Saffar, 1003 (1594), and was buried in his garden in that city. He was one of the finest types of Akbar's Court. He was a man both of the sword and of the pen, and was as much at home in the saddle as at the writer's desk. He was much liked by Khán-i-Khanan Mirza Abdul Rahim, who employed him as the chief of his staff and invariably followed his advice in matters of war, as well as administration.

Mulla Abdul Quadur Badaoni.

Birth of Abdul Quadur.

Mullah Abdul Quadur, poetically styled Quadri, was born at Badaon—a town near Delhi, in 947, or 949 H. (1542 A.D.), and was thus two years older than Akbar. He was the son of Sheikh Mulúk Shah, a disciple of the Saint Bechu of Sambhal. He studied various sciences and excelled in music, history, and astronomy, and, on account of his beautiful voice, was appointed Court *Imam*, or prelate, for Wednesdays. Early in life, he was introduced to Akbar, and for forty years he was in the company of Sheikh Mubarak and his sons, Abul Fazl and Fyzi; but he entertained no personal friendship for them, as he looked upon them as heretics. He was strongly attached to the Mahommadan religion and absolutely disliked the innovations introduced by Akbar in the Islamitic faith. His historical work, the *Muntakhib ul Tawarikh*, is a most valuable contribution to the history of Akbar's reign up to the beginning of 1004 H. (1595), or eleven years before the death of that monarch, soon after which Badaoni died. The style is eloquent and can not fail to impress

His high attainments in science and learning.

His strong attachment to the Mahomadan faith.

His great historical work.

the reader with the vast learning and the great genius of the author. The sprinkling of Arabic and Persian poems composed by the author himself and of the sayings and sentiments of celebrated authors furnishes evidence of his extensive knowledge, and, although, in his zeal to support his own religion, he evinces no indulgence towards the opponents of Islam, yet the chief credit of his work is that, contrary to the tendency of the age, he never bestows false praise on the imperial actions or the doings of high functionaries in royal favor, but records every incident in a spirit of perfect independence, free from learnings to particular sections of the community or men of particular opinions and religious beliefs. His history is valuable, as furnishing a marked contrast to the hyperbolic style of the *Akbarnama* and the *Ain-i-Akbari*, and the fulsome eulogies of the *Tabakat-i-Akbari* of Mirza Nizamuddin Ahmud and the author of *Moasiri Rahimi*, and giving a narration of the events of Akbar's reign and an account of his Court in the spirit of a critic, never concealing individual failings, but still not departing from the general truth of history. According to Bakhtawar Khan, the author of the *Mirat ul alam*, his work was kept secret, and not made public till the reign of Jahangir.

Its chief merit.

At the command of Akbar, Badaoni translated the Ramayan from Sanskrit into Persian and parts of the Mahabharata.

In the end, Badaoni seems to have withdrawn from public life and ceased attending at Court, as the following passages in his history show :—

Withdraws from public life.

'I did not consider myself a fit person for favour, nor His Majesty a fit object of service, and I was quite content :—

بیا تا تکلف بیکسو کنیم   نه از تو پیام ونه ازما سلام

Come that we may, all ceremony wave now,
Neither from you a message nor from me a bow.

' And at long intervals, I used to prostrate myself in the ante-chamber of audience and stay there for a while, as a mere looker-on, according to the proverb :—

که صحبت بر نیاید تا موافق نیست مشربها

' Companionship will not arise where dispositions are not congenial.

'I acted on the saying :—

دیدم که دیدن رخت از دور خوشتر است
صحبت گزاشتم زتماشائیان شدم

'Perceiving that beholding thy countenance from afar was more
pleasant an aim,
I left thy companionship and a spectator I became.'

With such an isolated position the Mullah was quite content, as he explains in the following eloquent Arabic poem :

رضيت بما قسم الله لي وفوضت امري الي خالقي
لقد احسن الله فيما مضى كذلك يحسن فيما بقى

I am content with what God has given me as my share
And I commit to my Creator my every care.
To do good in the past has been, indeed, His Will ;
He will do good as well in what is to come still.

The passages in Badaoni's excellent work describing the religious views of the Emperor Akbar, of which we have given extracts, are of special value. The work also contains interesting biographies of the most famous men and poets of Akbar's time.

Among the poets of the Court, Urfi of Shiraz occupied the
Poets. most prominent place.

URFI OF SHIRAZ.

Original name of Urfi. His name was Khawaja Syadi Mahammed, and his poetical name, Urfi, has reference to the occupation of his father, who was deputy to the Magistrate of Shiraz, and, as such, had to look after *Urfi*, or well-known matters of law. He proceeded by sea to the Deccan, where his talents were not recognised. He therefore went to Fattehpur Sikri, where he found a patron in Hakim Abul Fath, the Physician royal, in whose eulogy he has composed *Kasidas*, or long poems, which form part of his celebrated *Qasaid*. On the death of his patron, he took employment under Mirza Abdul Rahim Khan-i-Khanan, and was introduced to Akbar. He died in Lahore in 1582, at
His death 1582. the early age of thirty-six years. Thirty years later, his body was disinterred and carried to Ispahan by the poet Sabir and there

buried in the holy land of Najif, the burial place of Ali. He was a Shiá, and the prophesy made by him long before his death in one of his *Qasidas* in the praise of Ali was realized :—

بکاوش مژه از گور تانجف بروم اگر بهند هلاکم کنی وگر بتتار

By the force of my eyelids, I shall travel from my grave to Nazijaf.
Should they kill me either in Hind or in Tartary.

The date of his death is found in the words,

عرفی جوانه مرگ شدی

Urfi, thou didst die young.

He was a poet of high talent, and his diction possesses peculiar grace. He was given to self-admiration.

He bequeathed to his patron about 14,000 verses, which, at the request of Khan-i-Khánán, were arranged by Siraja of Ispahan. Urfi was much attached to Prince Salem and has composed *Qasaid* in his praise, as well as that of Akbar.

One day Urfi, finding Fyzi surrounded by his domestic dogs, humorously asked him 'what were the names of these well-bred children of the family.' Their name is Urfi,'* or well known, replied the witty poet, to which the talented Urfi readily rejoined, 'Mubarak' (congratulations to you) referring to the poet's father whose name was Mubarak. The prompt reply given by Urfi caused no small degree of disgust to Fyzi. Anecdote.

Another scholar of renown in the Court of Akbar was Amir Fateh Ullah, of Shiraz.

AMIR FATEH ULLAH OF SHIRAZ.

Amir Fateh Ullah was a native of Shiraz. He excelled in all the branches of natural philosophy, especially mechanics, and Abul Fazl speaks of his accomplishments in very high terms. He says: "If the books of antiquity were all lost, the Amir, by the force of his learning, would restore them." Adil Shah, king of Bijapur, called him from Shiraz to the Deccan. On the death of Adil Shah, in 988 (1580 A. D.), Akbar called him to his Court and bestowed on him the dignity of Sadr to the Empire. Soon after he was honoured with the title *Azad ud daula* or the *Arm of the Empire.* He died in Kashmir in 997 (1588). He was Akbar's next favourite after Abul Fazl, Fyzi and Bir Bar.

* *Urfi* in Arabic means well known.

Royal physicians.

Among the royal physicians the following deserve mention :—

Hakim Ali of Gilan.

Hakim Ali of Gilan. He was a native of Gilan, in Persia, and came to India quite destitute, but he was afterwards introduced to Akbar and became his trusted servant and friend. In 988 (1580 A. D.) the Hakim was sent as ambassador to king Adil Shah of Bijapur. In the 30th year of the reign, he constructed a mysterious reservoir *(hauz)* which caused much wonder at Court. A stair-case was carried from a corner of the reservoir to the bottom, whence a passage led to an adjoining room, six yards square and capable of accommodating ten or twelve persons. The passage was so contrived that the water was prevented from finding its way into the room. When Akbar dived to the bottom and reached the chamber, he found that it was lighted up. It was furnished with cushions, carpets, pillows and other articles, and there were a few books for study and amusement. A breakfast was also furnished.

The mysterious reservoir.

In the 40th year of the reign, Ali was made Commander of 700, and the title of Jali-nus-ul-zaman 'the Galenus of the age,' was conferred on him. The Hakim became famous in Court especially for his astringent mixtures.

Akbar was treated, immediately before his death, by Hakim Ali. Jahangir, in 1017 (1608 A. D.), visited Ali's reservoir and made him Commander of two thousand. He did not, however, live to enjoy this honour long, but died in the Moharram, the following year. He was charitably disposed and spent Rs. 6,000 per annum in supplying medicine gratis to the poor.

Hakim Abdul Fath.

Hakim Abul Fath. He was a native of Gilan in Persia and attained a high place in Akbar's favour. He possessed much influence in State matters and over the Emperor himself. The great poet, Urfi, of *Shiraz*, was his encomiast, and the *Qasaid-i-Urfi* include several poems composed in his honour. Both Abul Fazl and Badaoni speak in high terms of his attainments. He died in 997 (1588), on his way to Zabilistan, and his body, according to the Emperor's orders, was taken by Khwaja Shamsuddin to Hasan Abdal, and buried in a vault which the Khwaja had built for himself. Akbar, on his return from Kashmir, said prayers at Abul Fath's tomb.

CHAPTER IV.

THE MODERN CITY.

Agra is the head-quarters of a Division, or Commissionership in the North-West Provinces, and includes the six districts of Agra, Mathra, Farrukhabad, Etah, Etawah and Mainpuri. It is a District of the Division of the same name, with its administrative head-quarters at the city of Agra. The District is bounded on the north by Mathra and Etah, on the east by Mainpuri and Etawah, on the south by the States of Dholpúr and Gwalior, and on the west by the State of Bhurtpur. A great alluvial plain between the Ganges and the Jumna forms part of the Doab to the north, the soil of which is rich and productive; but elsewhere the fertility of the land is much impaired by branching ravines. The *Kharif* crops consist of *Bajra*, *Joár*, *Moth* and other food grains and cotton, sown after the first rains in June, and the *Rabi* crop of wheat, barley, oats, peas and other pulses, sown in October or November, and reaped in March and April. Bajra and grain are sown in autumn, while indigo, poppy, tobacco and sugarcane are also sown in abundance. The total area under cultivation is about eight hundred thousand acres.

Agra Division. Agra District. Physical aspects. Agriculture.

In 1838, a great famine prevailed in the Agra District, when 1,13,000 paupers were relieved by the Government in the city of Agra alone, while 3,00,000 starving people immigrated into the District to find means of livelihood. Great scarcity again prevailed in the district in 1861, 1868-69 and 1877-78, when gratuitous support was afforded by the Government to women and invalids, while able-bodied men were employed on canal and other works.

Natural calamities.

Large cattle fairs are held at Sultanpur, Shamsabad, Jurra and Kandharpur, but the chief commercial fair is held at Batesar, on the right bank of the Jumna, where about two hundred thousand people assemble to bathe on the banks of the sacred stream. A large trade in horses, camels and cattle takes place on the occasion, and Batesar becomes the scene of festivity and merriment for many days.

Commerce.

Agra city.

The modern city of Agra is situated about the centre of the District, on the west bank of the Jumna, on a bend of the river, whence the stream turns sharply to the east, the fort being perched in the angle thus formed, at the very edge of the bank. The city is built on a raviny ground. Ancient Agra comprised an area of about eleven square miles, but the inhabited quarters now contain only about half that area, the remainder being ruins, ravines, piles of debris and patches of bare ground which form the environs of Agra.

To the south of the fort are the cantonments; north-west of it and the city, are the civil lines; while between the civil station and the river lies the city. The city contains long bazars with stone-paved roads in the principal thoroughfares, thriving markets and a much larger number of commodious and elegant stone houses than any other town in the North-West Provinces. It is well built and handsome, and, in size and importance is the second city in North-West Provinces.

Factories.

The city of Agra forms the chief centre of the trade of the District, and private enterprise already begun in various directions gives promise of increasing prosperity. There are manufactures of pottery and coarse cloth in the District, besides several indigo factories and cotton screws. Though no longer the seat of the Local Government, Agra has made substantial progress in commercial activity since the mutiny. Owing to its central position, it has attracted a large share of the cotton trade of the surrounding Districts, for it possesses seven steam presses and three ginning factories. A spining mill is in operation and another is in course of construction. It has also a tannery where the latest European appliances for the curing of leather are in successful operation. A large trade is carried on in stone, quarried in the south-west of the District. Stone carving received its first impulse at Agra, under Akbar, and it has been carried on since then with undiminished energy, taste and skill. The stone, after being dressed and carved in Agra, is exported by the Jumna.

Railways.

The city of Agra is the centre of a great railway system, to which various lines converge, and this forms the chief factor of the thriving trade and industry of the District. The East Indian Railway line runs throughout the Doab, and, crossing the bridge of the Rajputana State Railway at Agra, opposite the fort, joins the stations of Ferozeabad, Tundla and Burhan. The Rajputana Railway runs from Agra to Bombay, connecting Agra with Bhurtpur, Jeypur, Ajmere, Alwar, Mount Abu, Marwar, Baroda, Ahmedabad, Pulanpur, Surat and Broach, and uniting by branches Udepore, Indore, Nasirabad and Nimuch. The Scindhia State Railway, leaving the Rajputana line at Agra, connects that city with Dholpur, Gwalior, Jhansi and Bhopal, while a metre-gauge line, branching off from the Rajputana system at Achnera, in the Agra District, connects the city of Agra with Mathra. Good metalled roads connect it with all the important neighbouring towns in British territory and Rajputana. The Agra Canal possesses a navigable channel, and a large amount of heavy traffic is carried on eastward by the Jumna, though it has been superseded by railways for light goods and passengers. The canal is available for navigation in the Delhi, Gurgaon, Mathra, and Agra Districts, and the Bhurtpur State. It commands a total area of 375,800 acres.

Roads.

The Agra Canal.

Agra is a great grain and cotton mart and furnishes supplies to traders to the South and West. It is the chief market for the sugar of Rohilkhand, the cotton of Rajputana and the wheat of the neighbouring Districts, which commodities are all brought here before being finally dispersed for consumption. Agra is especially noted for its manufactures of gold lace of all descriptions, pipe-stems and shoes; for its carpets and inlaid mosaic work in marble. Up to this day the workmen in Agra turn out as minute and delicate inlay work and carving in stone as in the days of the Moghal Emperors. European visitors regard the stone-work of Agra as its chief *speciality.*

Chief manufactures and trade.

The chief imports are grain, cotton, sugar, tobacco and salt. The net import of potatoes is fairly constant, the bulk are sent from Fategarh to Agra. The enterprising *Kachis* of the former place import from Agra to Fategarh castor oil cake manufactured at the oil mills in Agra for manure. The exports comprise *durries,* or cotton carpets, wrought stone from the quarries of Fattehpur Sikri and the Bandroli hills, and gold lace.

Import and export.

Population. The population of Agra city within municipal limits, according to the census of 1891, was returned at 1,45,361 souls, of whom 95,711 were Hindus, 44,021 Mohammadans, 1,723 Christians and 3,906 others. The population of cantonments was 23,301, of whom 14,965 were Hindus, 5,348 Mohammadans, 2,292 Christians, 696 others. The total population of municipality and cantonment was 1,68,662, of whom 1,10,676 were Hindus, 49,369 Mohammadans, 4,015 Christians and 4,602 others. The houses are remarkable for the solidity of their architecture and are often three or four storeys high. In most cases the upper floors are decorated with carved balconies; the lower floors are open and airy, and are surrounded by arched verandahs of stone.

Hs.ouse

Municipal income and expenditure. The total Municipal income for the year 1894-95 amounted to Rs. 4,99,078, the greater part of which was derived from octroi taxation, the gross receipts from which amounted to Rs. 3,87,932, giving an incidence of Rs. 1-2-11 per head of population. The expenditure during the year amounted to Rs. 5,08,403, which includes Rs. 1,46,275 expended cn water-works.

Education. The schools managed or aided by the Municipality are the Agra College, supported by endowments from the native community after the Government determined to give it up; St. John's College, supported by the zeal of the Protestant Missionaries; the Victoria High School and the Mufid-i-am School, all for higher education. There are also the St. Peter's College and convent schools, besides nine lower Zenana schools, a Zenana mission school, the Vidia Dharm Vardhan-i-School, the Mohammadan Club and the Church Mission. The St. Peter's College stands on the ground surrendered by the Emperor Akbar to the cause of Christianity, and it confers inestimable benefits on the poorest classes of that persuation. A medical school is attached to the Thomason Hospital, where pupils are taught to a high standard of efficiency. The Lady Dufferin's Institution is attached to the Thomason Hospital.

The Sekandra orphanage school. The Sekandra Orphanage School, under the supervision of Jesuit Fathers and Nuns, is a very useful institution, which, in addition to general tuition, imparts technical education to students. Those who wish to prosecute their English studies to an advanced stage are drafted into St. John's College, while others are qualified in the Industrial branch as smiths and carpenters and become skilful handicrafts men and obtain ready employment in different railway workshops. The institution also supplies book-binders, pressmen, compositors, readers, gardeners and tailors. In the girls' branch instruction is given in needlework and useful domestic arts. The Sekandra Orphanage was established by the Christian Missionaries during the famine of 1838, when they took charge of numerous orphan children who had been abandoned by their parents.

The Municipality also maintains a Poor House, a Leper Asylum and two female dispensaries, one in Pipal Mandi and the other in Loha Mandi. The Leper Asylum is regularly visited by Baptist missionaries, who relieve the monotony and tedium of the existence led by the unfortunate inmates by the exhibition of magic lantern shows, &c. There is also the Lady Lyall Hospital for women. The female dispensaries are very popular and are doing much good and useful work. Charitable institutions.

The conservancy of the town is carefully looked after. The natural drainage is good and water does not lie about, except in places where water work stand-posts are put up. An efficient drainage system has resulted in a perfect transformation of the city. Numerous original works have been constructed for surface-drains to carry off the waste sullage waters from the stand-posts and houses, and several *mohallas* of the city have been drained in this way. The ravines which intersect the town have been considerably improved. Regular channels have been cut in the centre, and side-paths made to allow carts and vehicles to drive where with difficulty a foot passenger could pass before. Brushwood and jungle have been cut, and, where possible, trees planted. Conservancy. The drainage system.

Owing to its proximity to the sandy deserts of the west, Agra is exposed to greater extremes of temperature than the country further east. The heat during the summer is intense, while the cold in winter is equal to that of many European cities. The climate is not considered unhealthy. The temperature, which falls to 40° in January, rises to 115° in June. Life Climate.

in winter is pleasant and delightful, but in summer the heat is unbearable and artificial means are employed for cooling the temperature of rooms.

Water works. North of Belan Ganj are the new waterworks which supply the city with filtered water. The water is pumped from the River Jumna* by a pair of gigantic horizontal engines, each working a set of three throw pumps, capable of lifting 1,600 gallons per minute. The horizontal engines work, on an average, 9 hours per day. The water, after passing through three revolving purifiers, flows into three settling tanks, which have a capacity of 6½ million gallons. There are three filters, each with a filtering area of 20,000 square feet and a clear water reservoir, divided into two compartments, each compartment holding 630,000 gallons. The filtered water is pumped into the city by two compound condensing beam engines, so arranged as to work separately or together. The engines for the filtered and unfiltered supply are in the same building and take their steam supply from the same boilers, together with the machinery and electric light. The pumping station is now in telephonic communication with the office of the municipal engineer, the municipal hall and the principal police stations.

The following are the principal modern buildings :—

Modern buildings. 1. The Agra College, on the Drummond Road. It is a one-storeyed building on a high plinth. A wide passage in the middle has, on either side of it, sets of class rooms. There is a science laboratory and a gallery to accommodate large classes and to serve as a lecture room. Behind the two main wings of the college are the school buildings. There are also fine boarding houses attached to the College.

2. The Central Prison is a building about a mile and a-half in circumference. It is noted for its manufacture of beautiful and rich carpets, which not only decorate the rooms of the rich in this country, but are also sent to Europe, where they are much valued on account of the delicacy and softness of their texture.†

* After considering the results of the filtration experiments, it has been recently decided to change the present Jumna-sand which had proved so unsatisfactory as a filtering *medium*, and to replace it by sand from the River Chambal.

† The number of prisoners in the Agra Jail in October, 1895, when His Excellency Lord Elgin, Viceroy and Governor-General of India, paid a visit to it, was 2,290, of whom 74 were females. His Excellency was shown the design of a handsome carpet with a blue ground which had just then been finished for the Emperor of Germany and was much admired.

3. The Judges' Courts are held in the same premises which were used for High Court, Agra, before its transfer to Allahabad, in 1869. The Munsiff's Court and the Court of Small Causes are held in the building previously used for the District Courts, while the members of the Bar have their chambers in the rooms formerly occupied by the members of the Board of Revenue. Agra is the head-quarters of a Sessions Judge who has jurisdiction in Mathra.

4. The Catholic Mission and Orphanage is situated at the back of the Central Prison. The institution is of interest as having been founded as early as the time of Akbar, through the influence of the Jesuit Fathers. Attached to it are a college and schools for girls who are accommodated in spacious buildings. A fine cathedral and an episcopal are also maintained.

5. The Metcalfe Hall, erected in memory of Lord Metcalfe, is built in Greek style. It serves as a place for public meetings, balls, social reunions and amusements. Some very interesting tombs and monuments, with Armenian inscriptions, are to be found in the cemetery, the principal of which are the tombs of Walter Reinhardt and Dyce Sombre.*

The other buildings of note are St. John's College, a missionary institution; the Victoria College, which owes its existence to the liberality of the late Hon'ble Pandit Ajudhia Parshad, a Pleader of the High Court of Allahabad and a native of Agra.; the Middle English School, founded in the city by Rai Bahadur Munshi Sheo Narain, the able and energetic Secretary of the Municipal Committee; the Barracks for troops; the Telegraph Office; the Thomason Hospital and some other public buildings. The commercial activity of Agra centres in the Belan Ganj, where there are spacious shops of *seths*, bankers, merchants and traders.

The Agra Municipal Board.

It is very satisfactory to note that a feeling of cordiality and accord prevails amongst the Members of the Municipal Committee—Hindus and Mahomedans. This is evinced by the fact that at the Kalyash fair at Sikandra respectable people of either sect entertained the members of the other sect

* For an account of these tombs see, Chapter II page 202 *ante*.

in refreshment tents provided for the occasion. In this connection the President, Mr. R. W. Cruickshank, in the Municipal Report for 1894-95, pays a deserved compliment to Rai Bahadur Munshi, Jagan Parshad, Vice-President and Rai Bahadur Munshi Sheo Narain, the Secretary. With respect to the former gentleman, he observes :—

"It is greatly due to his suavity and dignified tact that the meetings of the Agra municipal Board are now marked by an entire absence of class feeling or personal acerbity." "Munshi Sheo Narain Rai Bahadur," observes the Chairman, "has shown that increasing years do not necessarily mean decreasing energy, and to his masterful direction and initiative the Municipal Board owe hearty thanks." §

The services of Rai Bahadur Balmokand, formerly a Deputy Collector and Treasury Officer, also deserve mention for his having harmonised the Municipal Accounts with the system in vogue in Government Treasuries.

Members.

The following are the members of the Municipal Committee :—

Munshi Abdullah ; Sheik Mahammud Azim ; Lala Choukay Lal ; Babu Mathra Das ; R. B. Balmokand ; R. B. Jagan Pershad ; Moulvi Mahommed Masud Husein Khan ; Rae Damodar Das ; Lala Kanhia Lal ; Kanwar Kanhai Singh ; Babu Shib Narain ; Seth Pitem Mul ; Sheik Moula Buksh ; Hafiz Mahammad Siddiq ; Lala Harnarain ; Lala Fakirchand ; Raja Lachman Singh ; W. M. Clarke, Esq. ; Pandit Sukhdeo Biswas ; Lala Uttam Chand ; Munshi Abdul Rasul Khan ; Pandit Amir Singh ; Babu Madhoban Das ; Lala Kishen Parshad ; E John, Esq. Syud Kazim Husain ; Munshi Ganga Parshad ; Hakim Syud Sakhawat Ali ; Babu Shama Charan Ghose ; Munshi Ganga Sahai ; Moulvi Mohammed Zenul Abidin Khan Bahadur.

The position of modern Agra as described by Sir Antony McDonnell, Lieutenant-Governor, N.-W.P.

Sir Antony Patrick McDonnell, K. C. S. I., Lieutenant-Governor of N.-W. Provinces and Chief Commissioner of Oudh, paid a visit to Agra in January last. The reply given by His

§ The author also takes this opportunity of tendering his thanks to Rae Bahadur Munshi Sheo Narain, the able and energetic Secretary of the Agra Municipal Board, for all the assistance he has readily rendered him in furnishing the latest reports and statistics of the Municipal Board, from which the materials relating to Municipality have been chiefly drawn up.

Honour to the addresses presented to him by the members of the Municipal and District Boards is most interesting, as it lays a true picture before the readers of modern Agra and its various institutions and the progress made by its industrious and active inhabitants in the arts of peace. In the course of his reply to the Municipality he said :—

"Although your city has lost its ancient splendour, still an artistic and historic interest attaches to it, which is the less likely to fade, the more we know of the brilliant epoch which witnessed the city's foundation. Memories of past greatness in the paths of government, art and literature abide with you, and there is temptation at Agra to live more in the past than in the present. You, however, have been proof against such temptation, and, as practical men, you are striving to make the best of the present time. Your thoughts dwell more on the school, the hospital and the factory than on the temples and palaces of a bygone age. You are doubtless right in this ; but still I trust that the advance of material improvement will not make you insensible to the ancient glories of your city, and that you will always take a pride and an interest in the many beautiful monuments of Indian genius that are to be found in and about Agra. I notice with much gratification that you are alive to the responsibilities which your position as municipal councillors imposes on you, and I am very willing to believe that the improvement in the sanitary condition of the city to which you call my attention bears witness to an efficient municipal administration. I also notice with satisfaction the references you make to the educational institutions in the city. In the management of these institutions you tell me that your aim is " to teach the young to trust to themselves rather than to others for support." No better motto than that could be inscribed over the door of any school ; and, if the lesson it enforces is laid to heart by the rising generation, there is hope that the Agra of the future will not be unworthy of the Agra of the past. There are other points in your address which will be better noticed when I have an opportunity of discussing municipal matters with you on a less formal occasion than the present. I shall content myself now with again thanking you for your address."

Replying to the address from the District Board, His Honor said :—" You tell me that in all the great departments of Education Medical Relief, Sanitation and Public Works, progress is being made under your control. I am very willing to believe that progress is being made. Still, from your own statement of results, it is evident that much yet remains to be done. In the matter of education, for example, you seem to me to have only just begun. It cannot be said that 129 schools, which is, all told, the number mentioned in your address, afford anything like a satisfactory provision for the educational wants of the district. The district contains between 1,800 and 1,900 square miles, with a population of over one million people. The existing schools give less than one school for every 14 square miles, and not quite one school for every 1,000 children of a school-going age, omitting the population of the city. You will have to multiply your schools four-fold before they can be pronounced even moderately sufficient."

THE END.

INDEX.

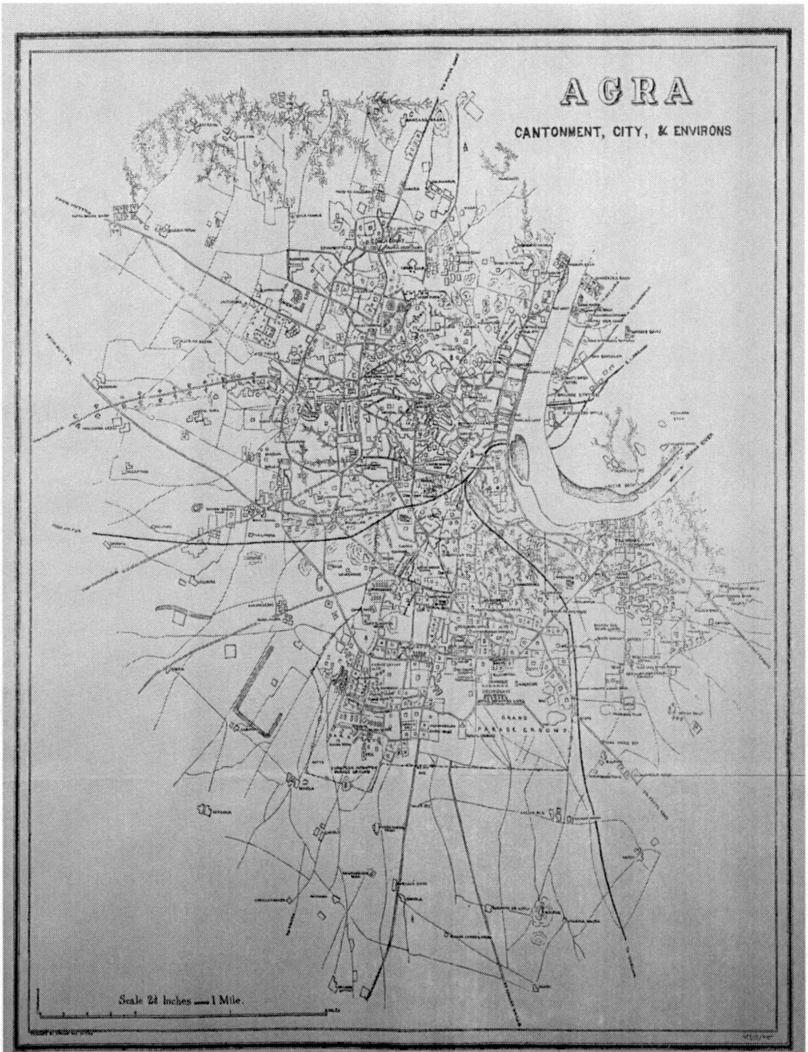
AGRA
CANTONMENT, CITY, & ENVIRONS
GRAND
PARADE GROUND
Scale 2½ Inches = 1 Mile.